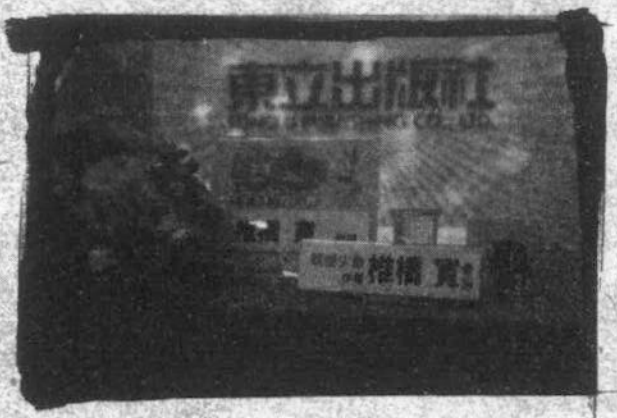
東立出版社

I started playing soccer again (mainly futsal). I was surprised at how physically weak I am! Even if you've got skills, if you can't move fast, you're useless! Listen up, everyone! In soccer, physical strength matters!

(Talking about sports in a yokai manga... That doesn't seem to fit...)

I've been making manga for more than four years, and without even realizing it, I got older... I've gained a lot, but I've also lost some things... No! I can still get them back!!

Anyway, the photo is from Taiwan.

—HIROSHI SHIIBASHI, 2012

HIROSHI SHIIBASHI debuted in BUSINESS JUMP magazine with *Aratama*. NURA: RISE OF THE YOKAI CLAN is his breakout hit. He was an assistant to manga artist Hirohiko Araki, the creator of *Jojo's Bizarre Adventure*. *Steel Ball Run* by Araki is one of his favorite manga.

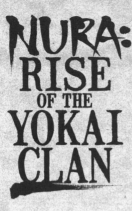

NURA: RISE OF THE YOKAI CLAN

NURA: RISE OF THE YOKAI CLAN
VOLUME 24
SHONEN JUMP Manga Edition

Story and Art by HIROSHI SHIIBASHI

Translation – John Werry
Touch-up Art and Lettering – Annaliese Christman
Graphics and Cover Design – Fawn Lau
Editors – Megan Bates, Joel Enos

...ada

...VIZ Media, LLC
...0
... CA 94107

...3 2 1
...December 2014

www.viz.com www.shonenjump.com

RATED T FOR TEEN

PARENTAL ADVISORY
NURA: RISE OF THE YOKAI CLAN is rated T for Teen and is suitable for ages 13 and up. This volume may contain fantasy and realistic violence and alcohol usage.

ratings.viz.com

NURA: RISE OF THE YOKAI CLAN

24

BATTLE OF AOI SPIRAL CASTLE

STORY AND ART BY
HIROSHI SHIIBASHI

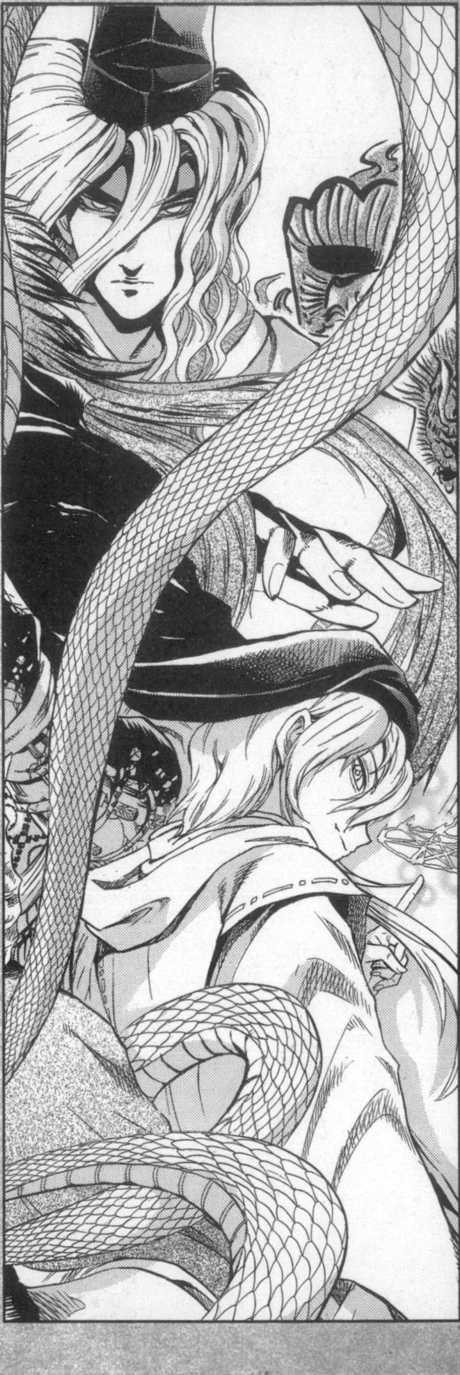

CHARACTERS

NURARIHYON

Rikuo's grandfather and the Lord of Pandemonium. To prepare for all-out war with Nue, he has passed leadership of the Nura clan—a powerful yokai consortium—to Rikuo. He's a mischevous sort.

RIKUO NURA

Though he appears to be a human boy, he's actually the grandson of Nurarihyon, a yokai. His grandfather's blood makes him one-quarter yokai, and he transforms into a yokai at times.

TAMAZUKI

Leader of the 88 Demons of Shikoku. He once opposed the Nura clan. Now he cooperates with the Nura clan to fight the Purification.

YUKI-ONNA

A yokai of the Nura clan who is in charge of looking after Rikuo. She disguises herself as a human and as Tsurara Oikawa attends the same school as Rikuo. Her mother is Setsura.

RYUJI

An onmyoji in the Keikain clan. With his magic, he can use water however he wants. He is good at confusing people with his words. Yura is his sister.

DASSAI

Young master of the Sakenomi gang. In battle, he blows sake-fueled fire so intense that the immediate area bursts into flames. He's cooperating with the Nura clan.

KIYOTSUGU

Rikuo's classmate. He adores yokai, leading him to form the Kiyojuji Paranormal Patrol. He understands Rikuo has yokai blood and encourages him.

YURA

Rikuo's classmate and an onmyoji in the Keikain clan. She is able to use Hagun, a feat only possible for those in the clan with the greatest talent.

ABE NO SEIMEI (NUE)

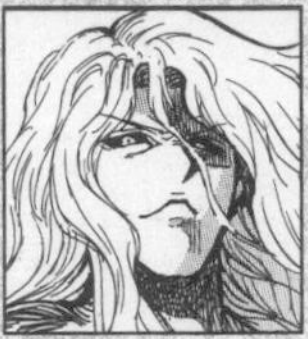

The first leader of the Gokadoin clan. He is an onmyoji, but his mother was an ayakashi (Hagoromo-Gitsune), so he is half yokai. He has reincarnated and now waits for rebirth.

HAGOROMO-GITSUNE

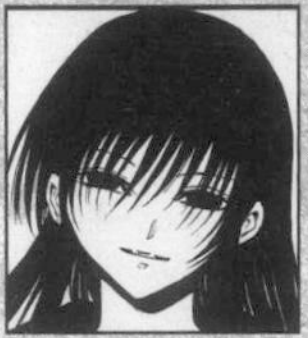

Seimei's mother and an ayakashi. Her vessel is Yamabuki-Otome, the first wife of Rikuo's father Rihan. During the battle in Kyoto, she was thrown to Hell.

TENKAI GOKADOIN

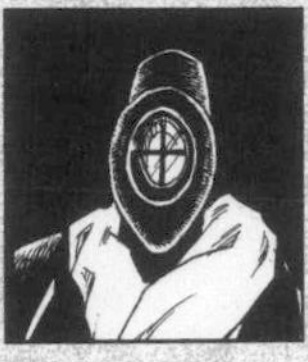

The seventh leader of the Gokadoin Clan. Black-garbed. He attacked Kyoto during the Purification. He created the barrier around Aoi Spiral Castle.

ABE NO ARIYUKI

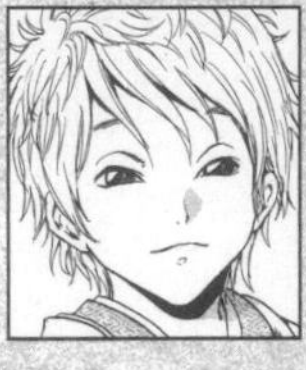

The fourth leader of the Gokadoin clan. White-garbed. During the fight against the Hundred Stories clan, he protected and helped Encho escape.

ABE NO OROCHI

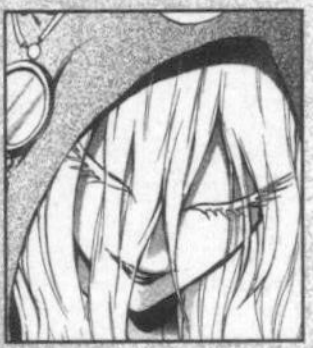

Third leader of the Gokadoin clan. White-garbed. Controls giant serpents.

YUIYUI GOKADOIN

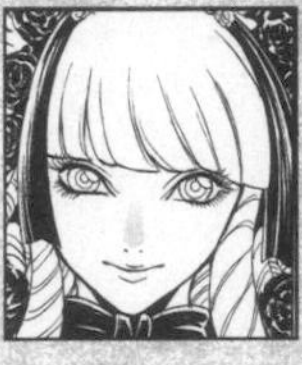

The sixth leader of the Gokadoin. Black-garbed. She attacks the ayakashi of the San'in Region during the Purification. She carries around a doll.

THE SECOND

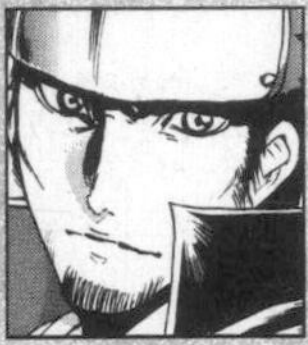

Second leader of the Gokadoin clan. White-garbed. Further details remain a mystery.

ENCHO

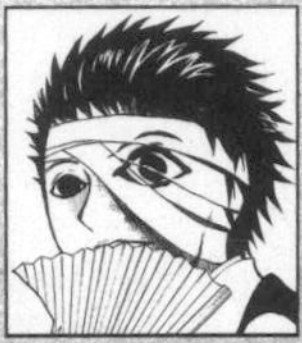

Previously one of the Hundred Stories clan's seven leaders. Now he works with the Gokadoin clan.

STORY SO FAR

Rikuo Nura is a seventh-grader at Ukiyoe Middle School. At a glance, he appears to be just another average, normal boy. But he's actually the grandson of the yokai Overlord Nurarihyon. He's also the Third Heir of the powerful Nura clan. He spends his days in hopes that he will someday become a great clan boss who leads a Night Parade of a Hundred Demons.

The enemy onmyoji of the Gokadoin clan ferociously attack Kyushu as part of their campaign of yokai Purification. Yura and Tsuchigumo are in Tsuchigumo's home territory when Hiruko, the Gokadoin's ninth leader and wielder of the five elements, attacks and the two find themselves in a pinch. But Rikuo and others arrive in the nick of time and engage the Gokadoin! Tamazuki and Dassai each win battles of their own with little trouble. With some help from Tsuchigumo and Yura—who has mastered Shikigami Fusion—Rikuo is victorious over Hiruko!!

Meanwhile, a battle between the Keikain onmyoji and Gokadoin clan unfolds in Kyoto. Tenkai, the Gokadoin's seventh leader, has used an ingenious barrier jutsu to corner Ryuji. Then who should appear but Hagoromo-Gitsune—whom someone has resurrected! Ryuji manages to escape danger, but now the Kyoto yokai have returned...

At the Nura clan Main House, Rikuo leads the Keikain clan and ayakashi from all over the country in reaffirming their determination. Together, they plan to storm Seimei's base of operations in Aoi Spiral Castle!!

TABLE OF CONTENTS

NURA: RISE OF THE YOKAI CLAN

24

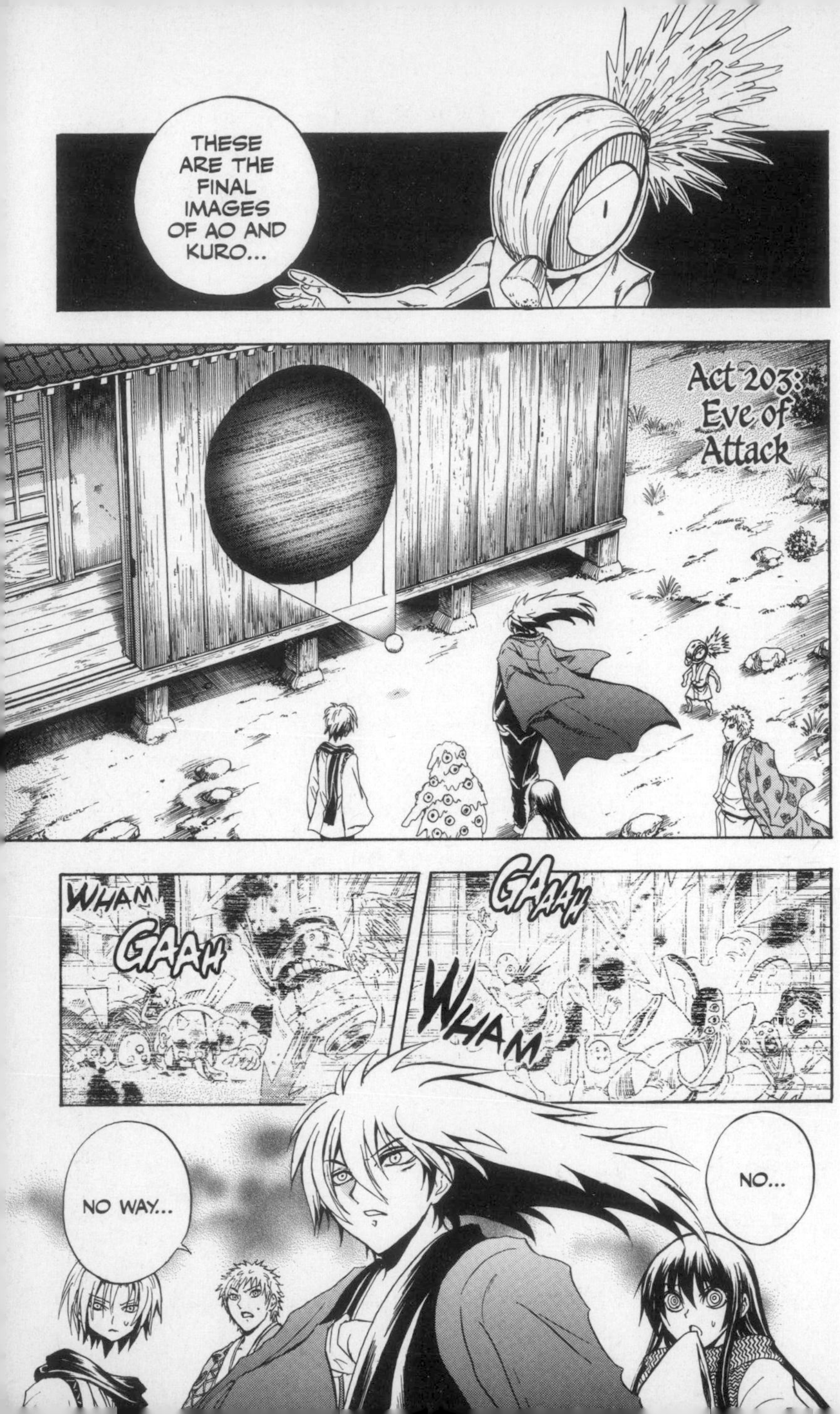
THESE ARE THE FINAL IMAGES OF AO AND KURO...
Act 203: Eve of Attack
GAAAH
WHAM
WHAM
GAAH
NO...
NO WAY...

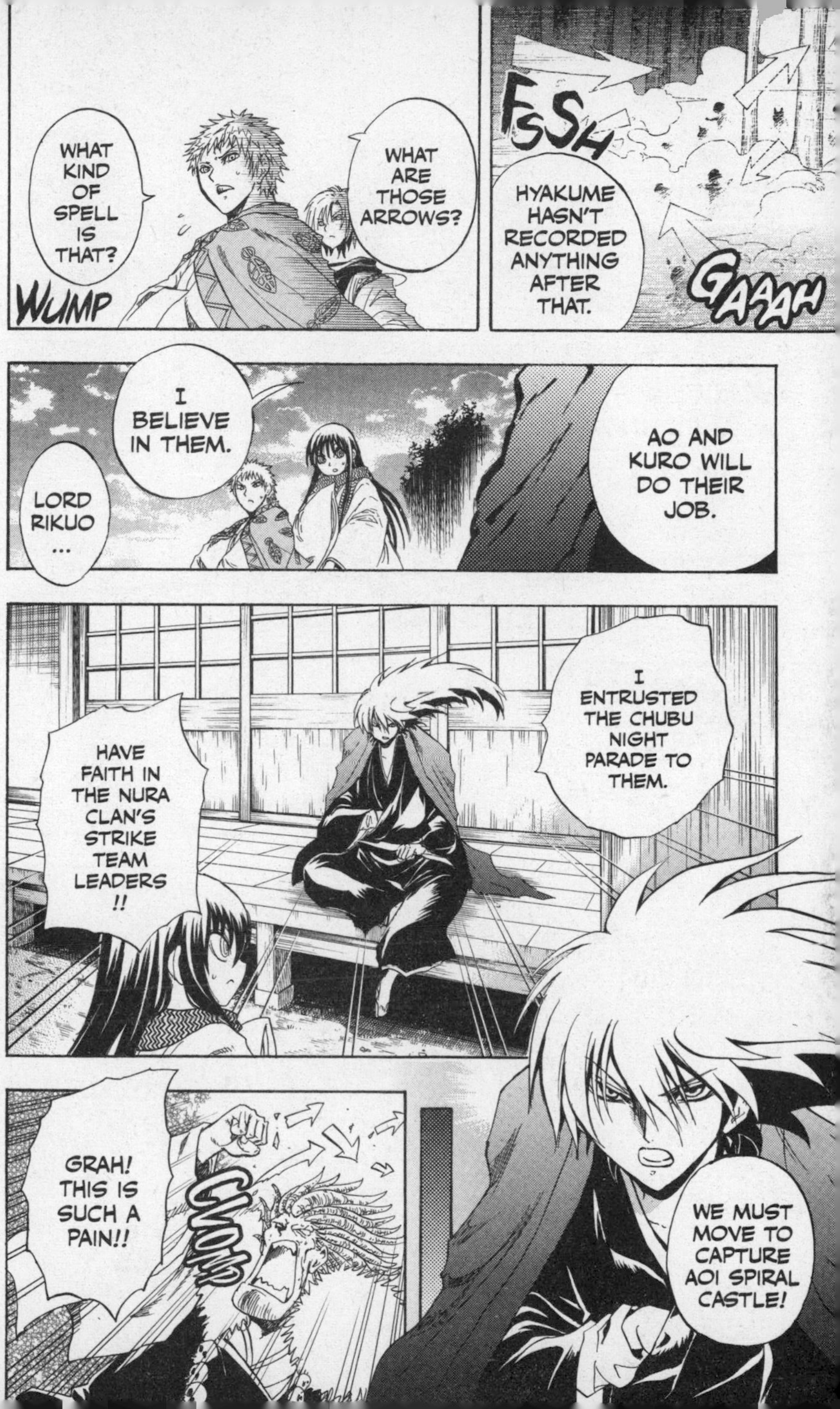
FSSH
HYAKUME HASN'T RECORDED ANYTHING AFTER THAT.
GAAAH
WHAT ARE THOSE ARROWS?
WHAT KIND OF SPELL IS THAT?
WUMP
AO AND KURO WILL DO THEIR JOB.
I BELIEVE IN THEM.
LORD RIKUO ...
I ENTRUSTED THE CHUBU NIGHT PARADE TO THEM.
HAVE FAITH IN THE NURA CLAN'S STRIKE TEAM LEADERS !!
WE MUST MOVE TO CAPTURE AOI SPIRAL CASTLE!
GRAH! THIS IS SUCH A PAIN!!

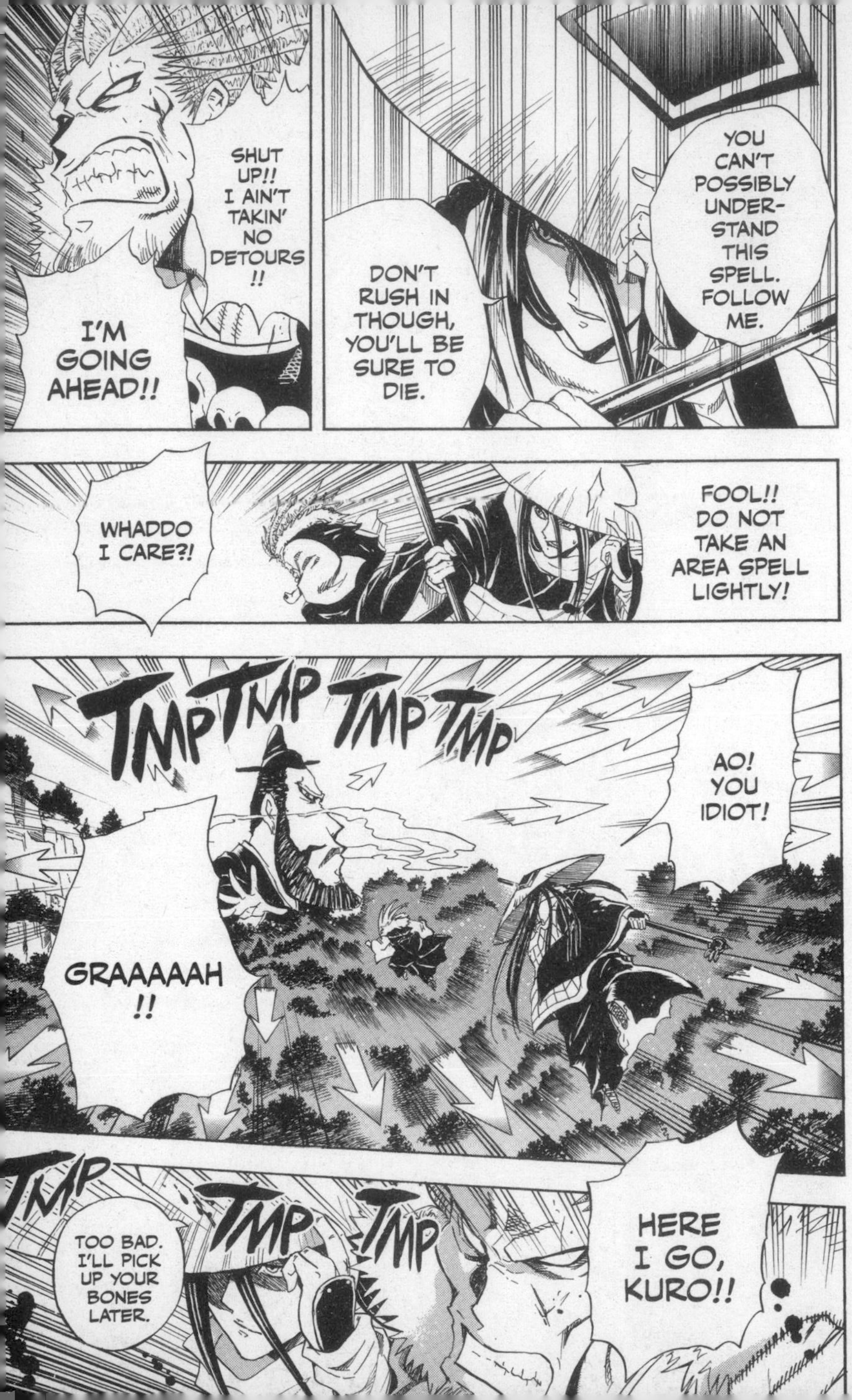
YOU CAN'T POSSIBLY UNDER-STAND THIS SPELL. FOLLOW ME.
DON'T RUSH IN THOUGH, YOU'LL BE SURE TO DIE.
SHUT UP!! I AIN'T TAKIN' NO DETOURS!!
I'M GOING AHEAD!!
FOOL!! DO NOT TAKE AN AREA SPELL LIGHTLY!
WHADDO I CARE?!
TMP TMP TMP TMP
AO! YOU IDIOT!
GRAAAAAH!!
HERE I GO, KURO!!
TMP TMP TMP
TOO BAD. I'LL PICK UP YOUR BONES LATER.

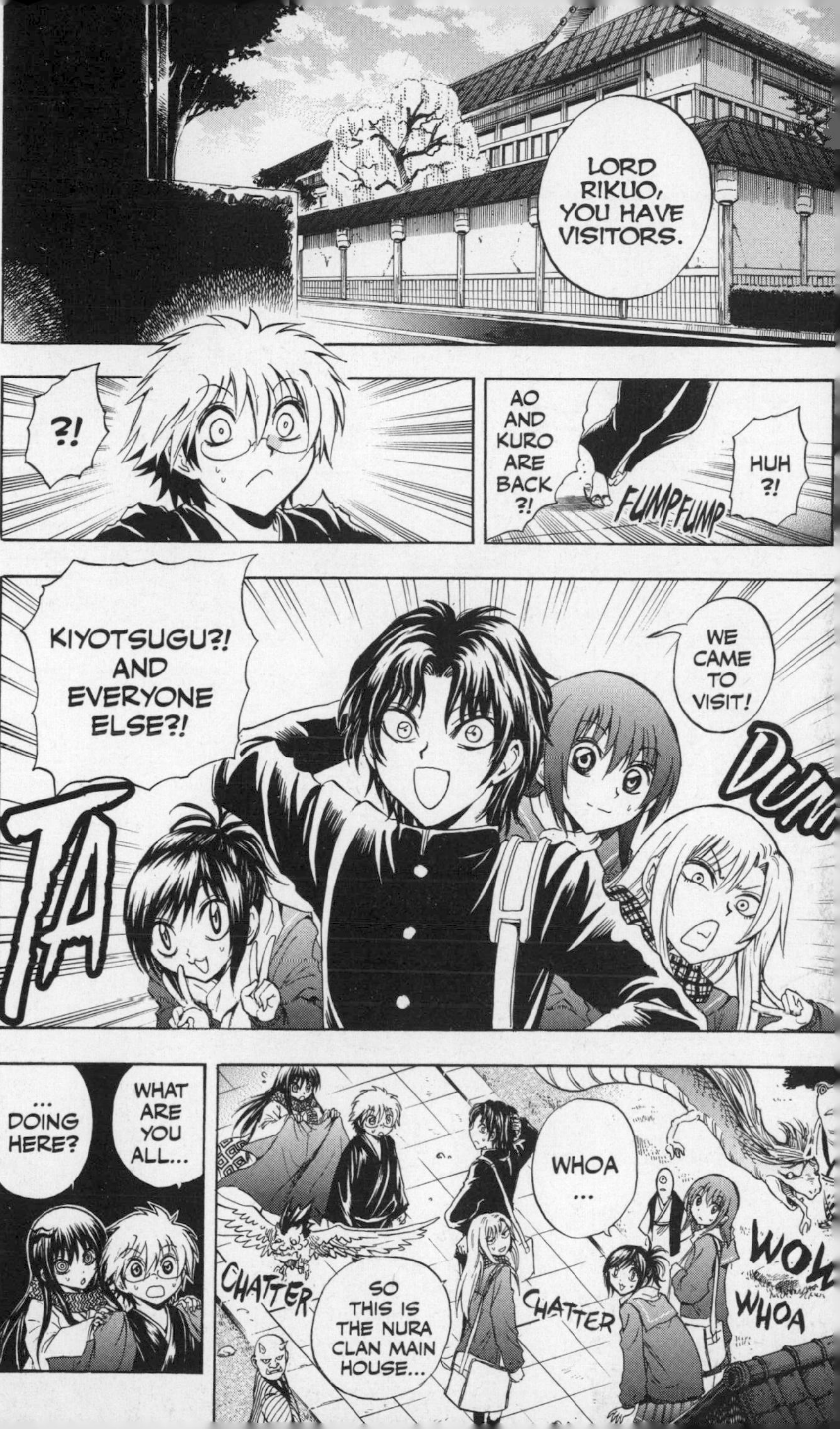
LORD RIKUO, YOU HAVE VISITORS.
HUH ?!
AO AND KURO ARE BACK ?!
FUMP FUMP
?!
WE CAME TO VISIT!
DUN
KIYOTSUGU?! AND EVERYONE ELSE?!
TA
WOW
WHOA
WHOA ...
CHATTER
SO THIS IS THE NURA CLAN MAIN HOUSE...
CHATTER
WHAT ARE YOU ALL...
... DOING HERE?

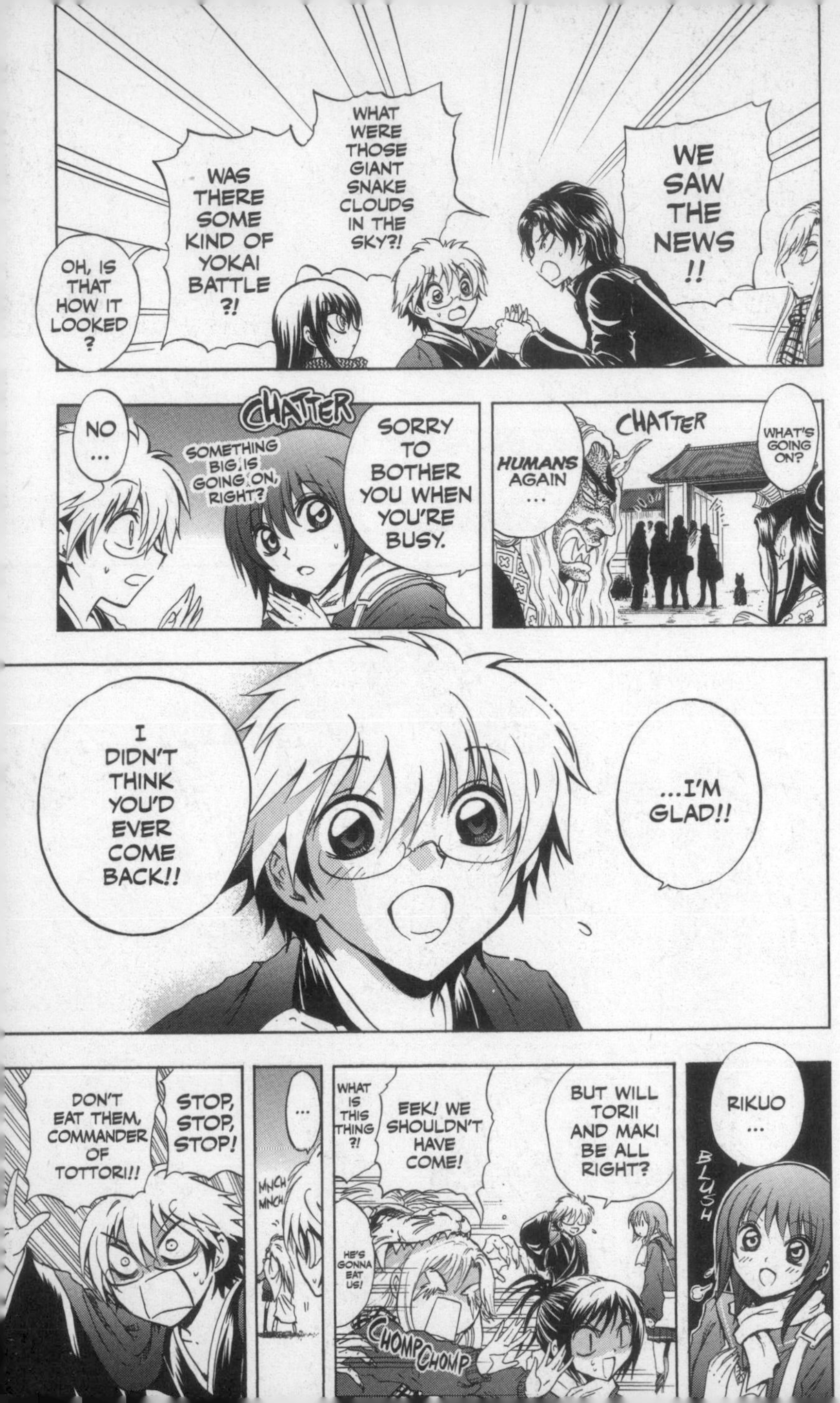
WE SAW THE NEWS!!
WHAT WERE THOSE GIANT SNAKE CLOUDS IN THE SKY?!
WAS THERE SOME KIND OF YOKAI BATTLE?!
OH, IS THAT HOW IT LOOKED?
WHAT'S GOING ON?
CHATTER
HUMANS AGAIN...
SORRY TO BOTHER YOU WHEN YOU'RE BUSY.
CHATTER
SOMETHING BIG IS GOING ON, RIGHT?
NO...
I DIDN'T THINK YOU'D EVER COME BACK!!
...I'M GLAD!!
RIKUO...
BLUSH
BUT WILL TORII AND MAKI BE ALL RIGHT?
EEK! WE SHOULDN'T HAVE COME!
WHAT IS THIS THING?!
HE'S GONNA EAT US!
CHOMP CHOMP
...
MNCH MNCH
STOP, STOP, STOP!
DON'T EAT THEM, COMMANDER OF TOTTORI!!

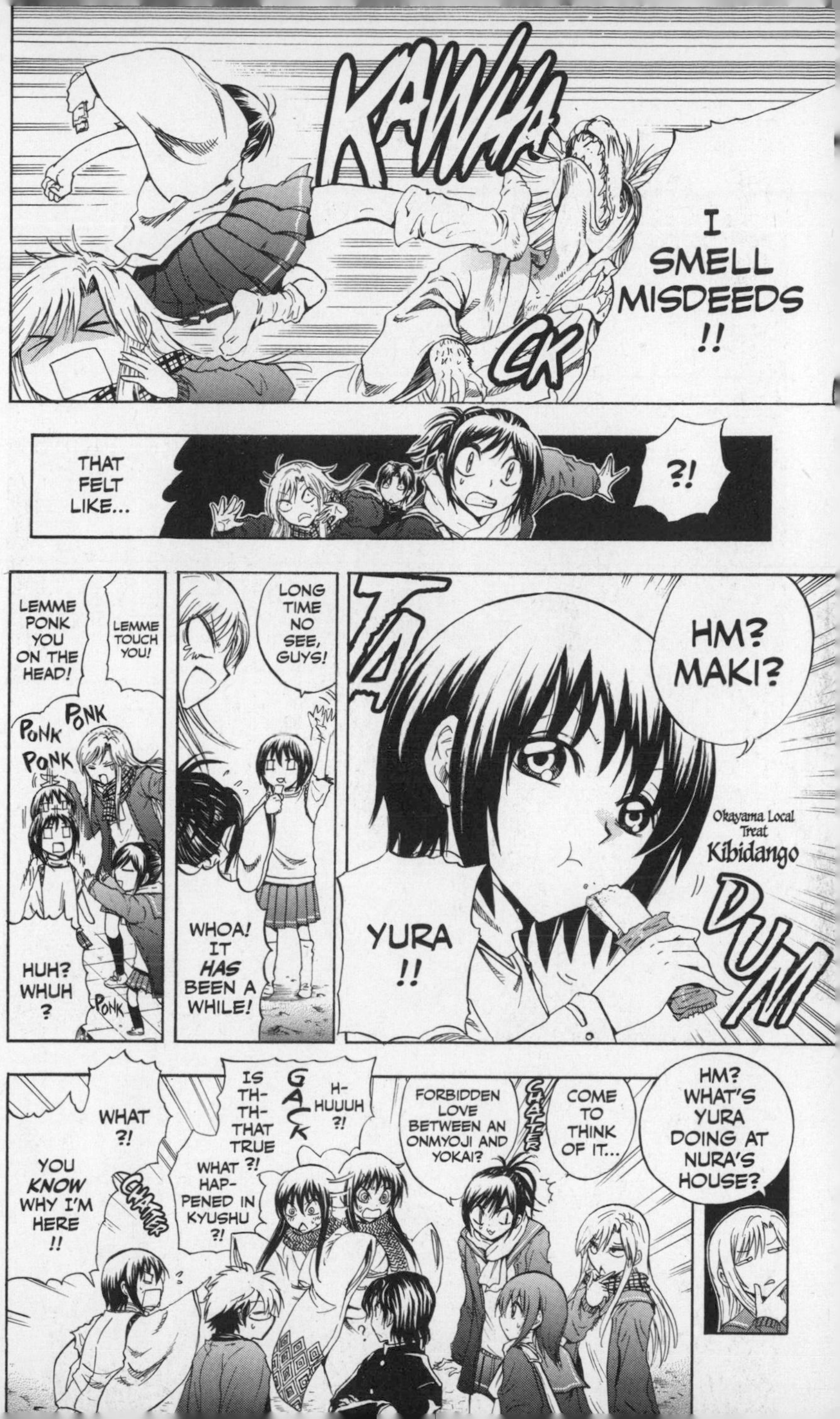
I SMELL MISDEEDS !!
KAWHA
CK
?!
THAT FELT LIKE...
HM? MAKI?
Okayama Local Treat Kibidango
DUN
TA
YURA !!
LONG TIME NO SEE, GUYS!
WHOA! IT HAS BEEN A WHILE!
LEMME TOUCH YOU!
LEMME PONK YOU ON THE HEAD!
PONK PONK PONK
HUH? WHUH ?
PONK
HM? WHAT'S YURA DOING AT NURA'S HOUSE?
COME TO THINK OF IT...
CHATTER
FORBIDDEN LOVE BETWEEN AN ONMYOJI AND YOKAI?
H-HUUUH ?!
GACK
IS TH-TH-THAT TRUE ?!
WHAT HAP-PENED IN KYUSHU ?!
WHAT ?!
YOU KNOW WHY I'M HERE !!
CHATTER

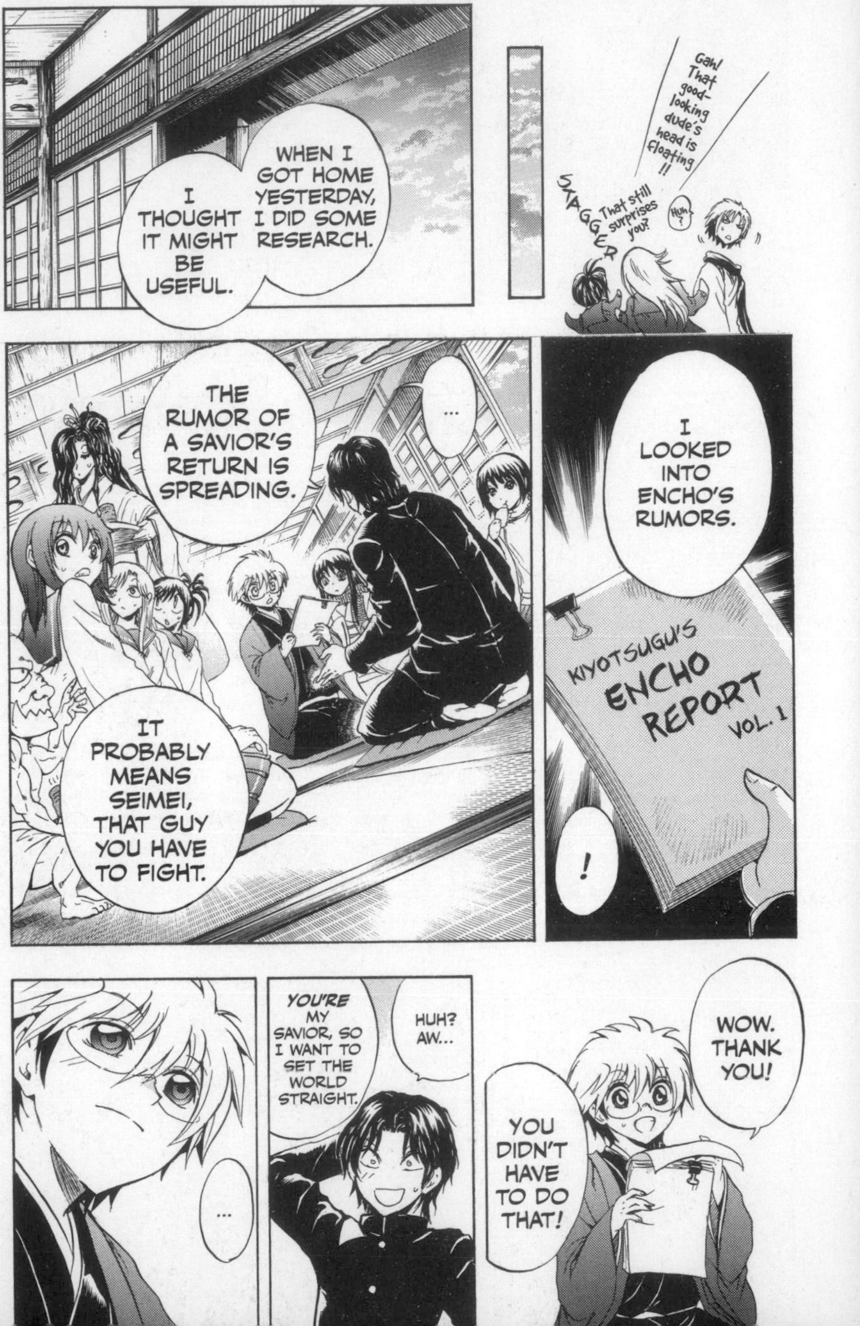
Gah! That good-looking dude's head is floating!!
HUH?
That still surprises you?
STAGGER
WHEN I GOT HOME YESTERDAY, I DID SOME RESEARCH.
I THOUGHT IT MIGHT BE USEFUL.
I LOOKED INTO ENCHO'S RUMORS.
KIYOTSUGU'S ENCHO REPORT VOL. 1
!
...
THE RUMOR OF A SAVIOR'S RETURN IS SPREADING.
IT PROBABLY MEANS SEIMEI, THAT GUY YOU HAVE TO FIGHT.
WOW. THANK YOU!
YOU DIDN'T HAVE TO DO THAT!
HUH? AW...
YOU'RE MY SAVIOR, SO I WANT TO SET THE WORLD STRAIGHT.
...

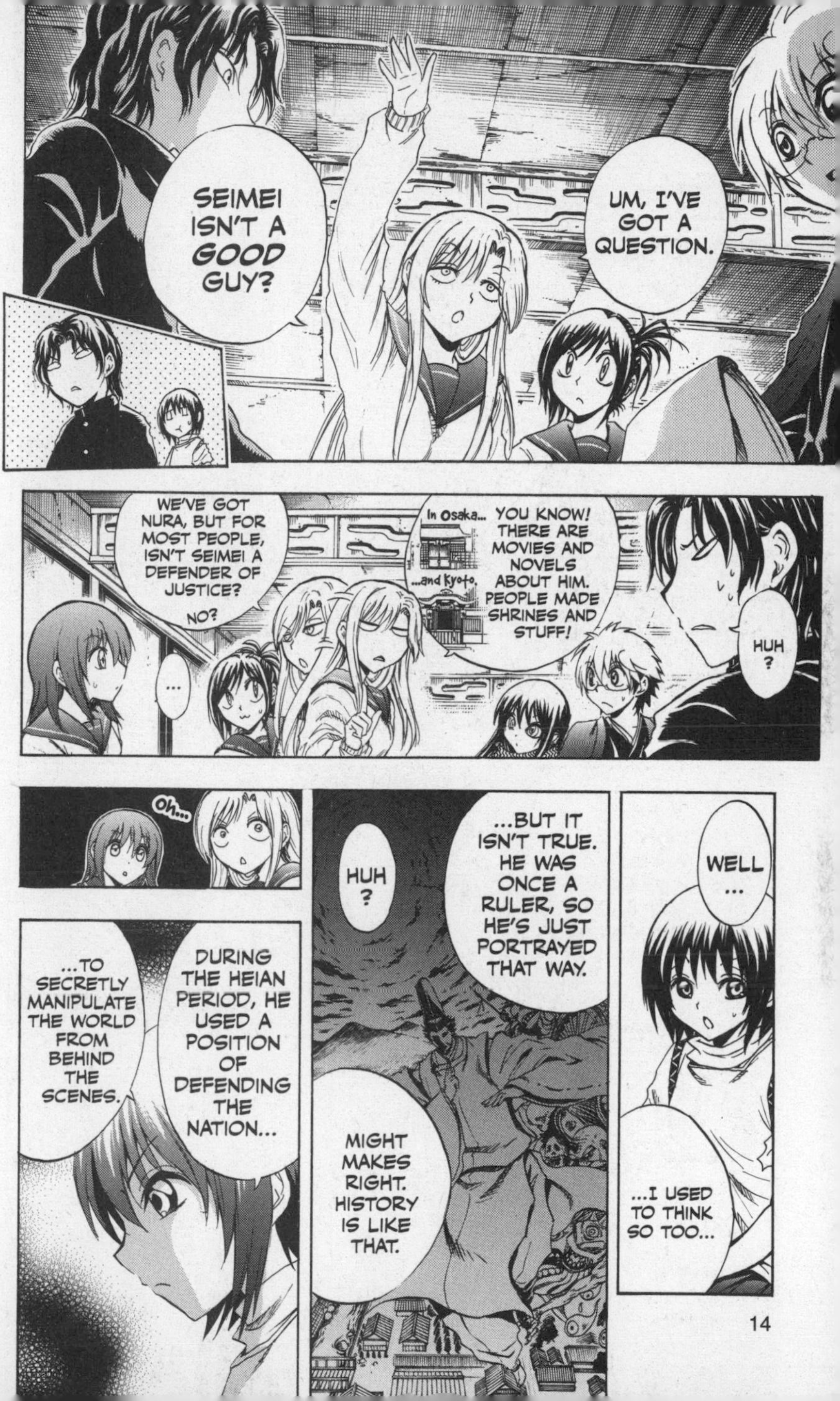
UM, I'VE GOT A QUESTION.
SEIMEI ISN'T A GOOD GUY?
HUH?
YOU KNOW! THERE ARE MOVIES AND NOVELS ABOUT HIM. PEOPLE MADE SHRINES AND STUFF!
In Osaka...
...and Kyoto.
WE'VE GOT NURA, BUT FOR MOST PEOPLE, ISN'T SEIMEI A DEFENDER OF JUSTICE?
NO?
...
WELL...
...I USED TO THINK SO TOO...
...BUT IT ISN'T TRUE. HE WAS ONCE A RULER, SO HE'S JUST PORTRAYED THAT WAY.
HUH?
MIGHT MAKES RIGHT. HISTORY IS LIKE THAT.
Oh...
DURING THE HEIAN PERIOD, HE USED A POSITION OF DEFENDING THE NATION...
...TO SECRETLY MANIPULATE THE WORLD FROM BEHIND THE SCENES.

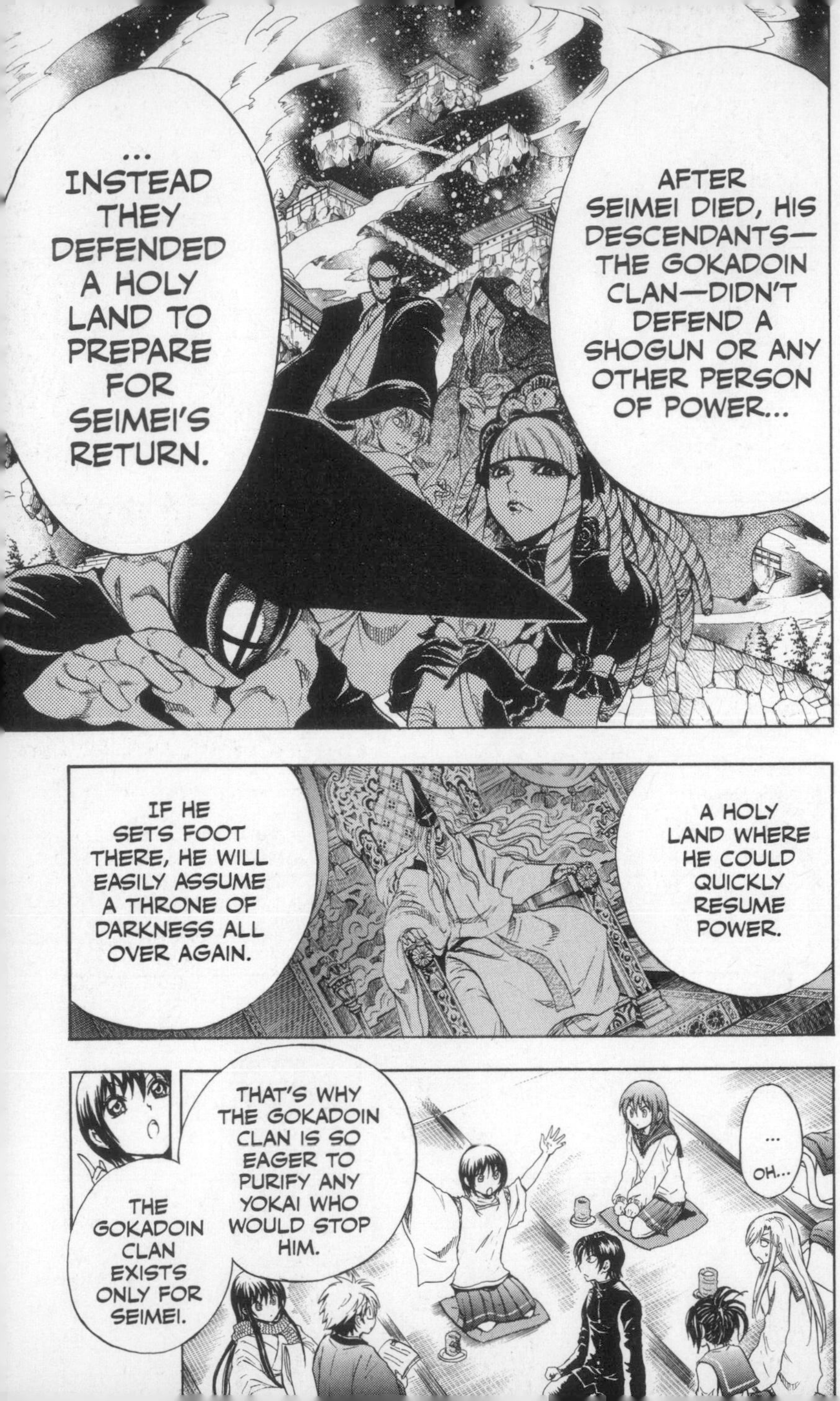
AFTER SEIMEI DIED, HIS DESCENDANTS—THE GOKADOIN CLAN—DIDN'T DEFEND A SHOGUN OR ANY OTHER PERSON OF POWER...
... INSTEAD THEY DEFENDED A HOLY LAND TO PREPARE FOR SEIMEI'S RETURN.
A HOLY LAND WHERE HE COULD QUICKLY RESUME POWER.
IF HE SETS FOOT THERE, HE WILL EASILY ASSUME A THRONE OF DARKNESS ALL OVER AGAIN.
... OH...
THAT'S WHY THE GOKADOIN CLAN IS SO EAGER TO PURIFY ANY YOKAI WHO WOULD STOP HIM.
THE GOKADOIN CLAN EXISTS ONLY FOR SEIMEI.

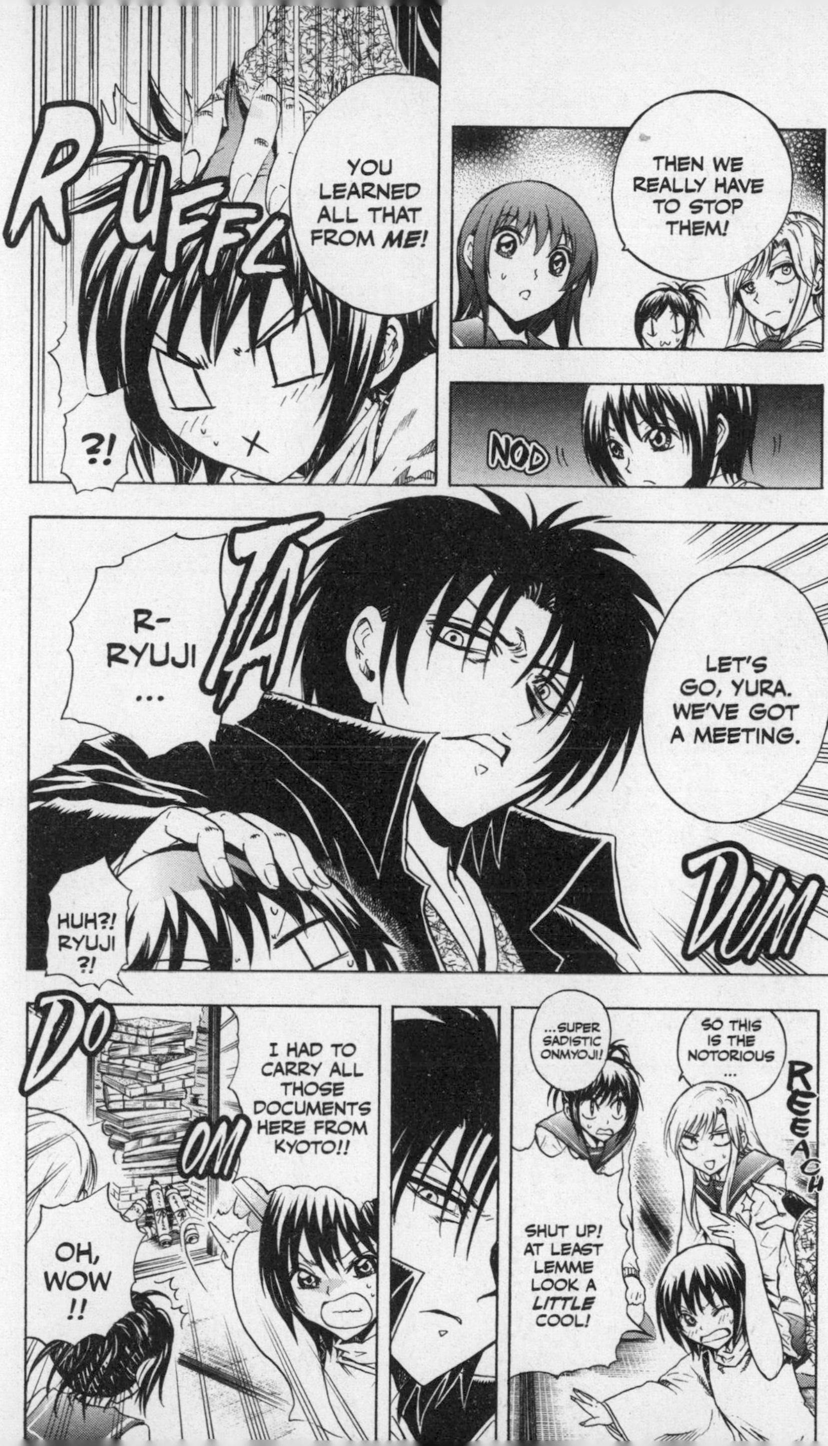
THEN WE REALLY HAVE TO STOP THEM!
NOD
YOU LEARNED ALL THAT FROM *ME*!
RUFFL
?!
LET'S GO, YURA. WE'VE GOT A MEETING.
TA
R-RYUJI ...
DUN
HUH?! RYUJI ?!
SO THIS IS THE NOTORIOUS ...
...SUPER SADISTIC ONMYOJI!
REEACH
SHUT UP! AT LEAST LEMME LOOK A *LITTLE* COOL!
DOOM
I HAD TO CARRY ALL THOSE DOCUMENTS HERE FROM KYOTO!!
OH, WOW !!

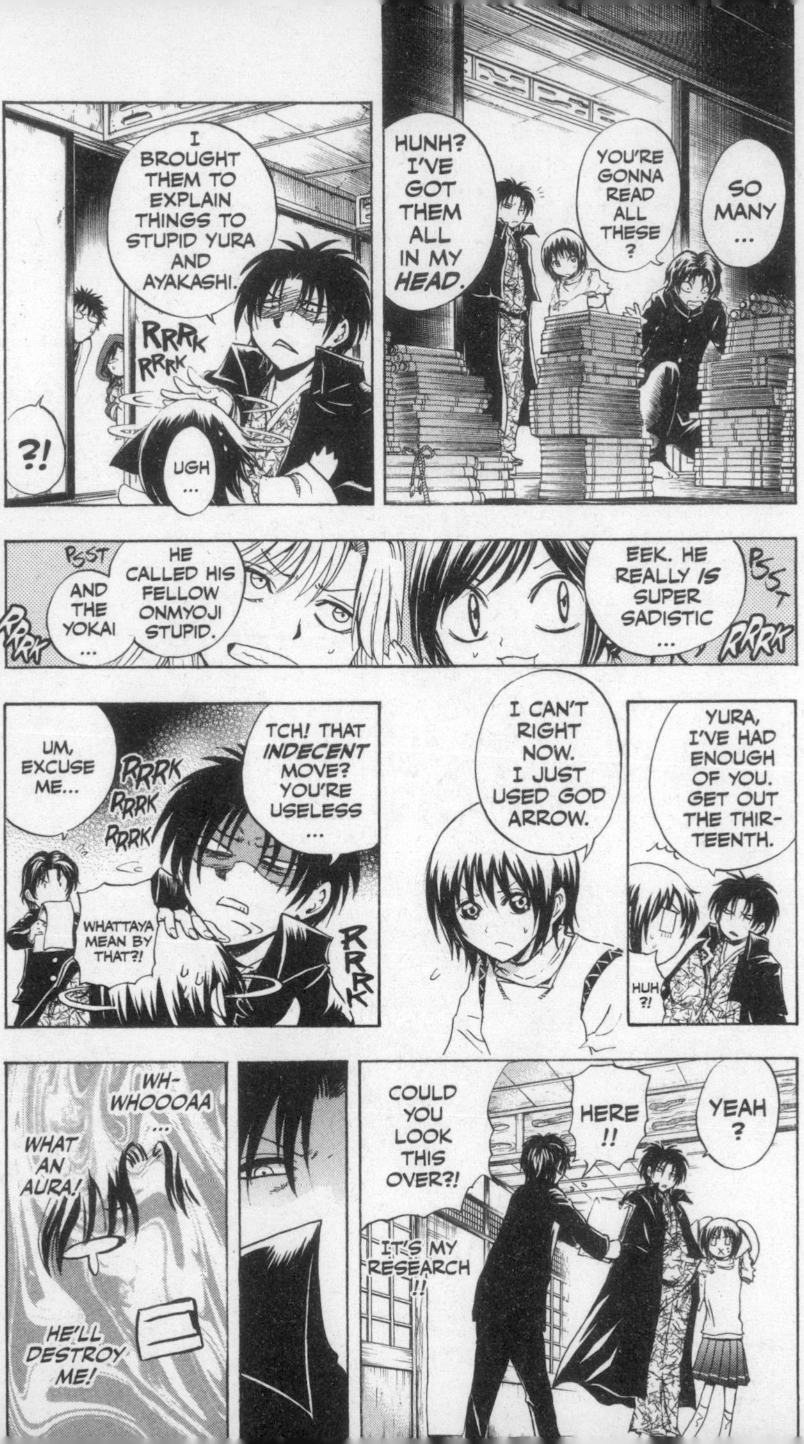
SO MANY ...
YOU'RE GONNA READ ALL THESE?
HUNH? I'VE GOT THEM ALL IN MY *HEAD*.
I BROUGHT THEM TO EXPLAIN THINGS TO STUPID YURA AND AYAKASHI.
RRRK RRRK
?!
UGH ...
PSST
EEK. HE REALLY *IS* SUPER SADISTIC ...
RRRK
HE CALLED HIS FELLOW ONMYOJI STUPID.
AND THE YOKAI ...
PSST
RRRK
YURA, I'VE HAD ENOUGH OF YOU. GET OUT THE THIR-TEENTH.
HUH ?!
I CAN'T RIGHT NOW. I JUST USED GOD ARROW.
TCH! THAT *INDECENT* MOVE? YOU'RE USELESS ...
UM, EXCUSE ME...
RRRK RRRK RRRK
WHATTAYA MEAN BY THAT?!
RRRK
YEAH ?
HERE !!
COULD YOU LOOK THIS OVER?!
IT'S MY RESEARCH !!
WH- WHOOOAA ...
WHAT AN AURA!
HE'LL DESTROY ME!

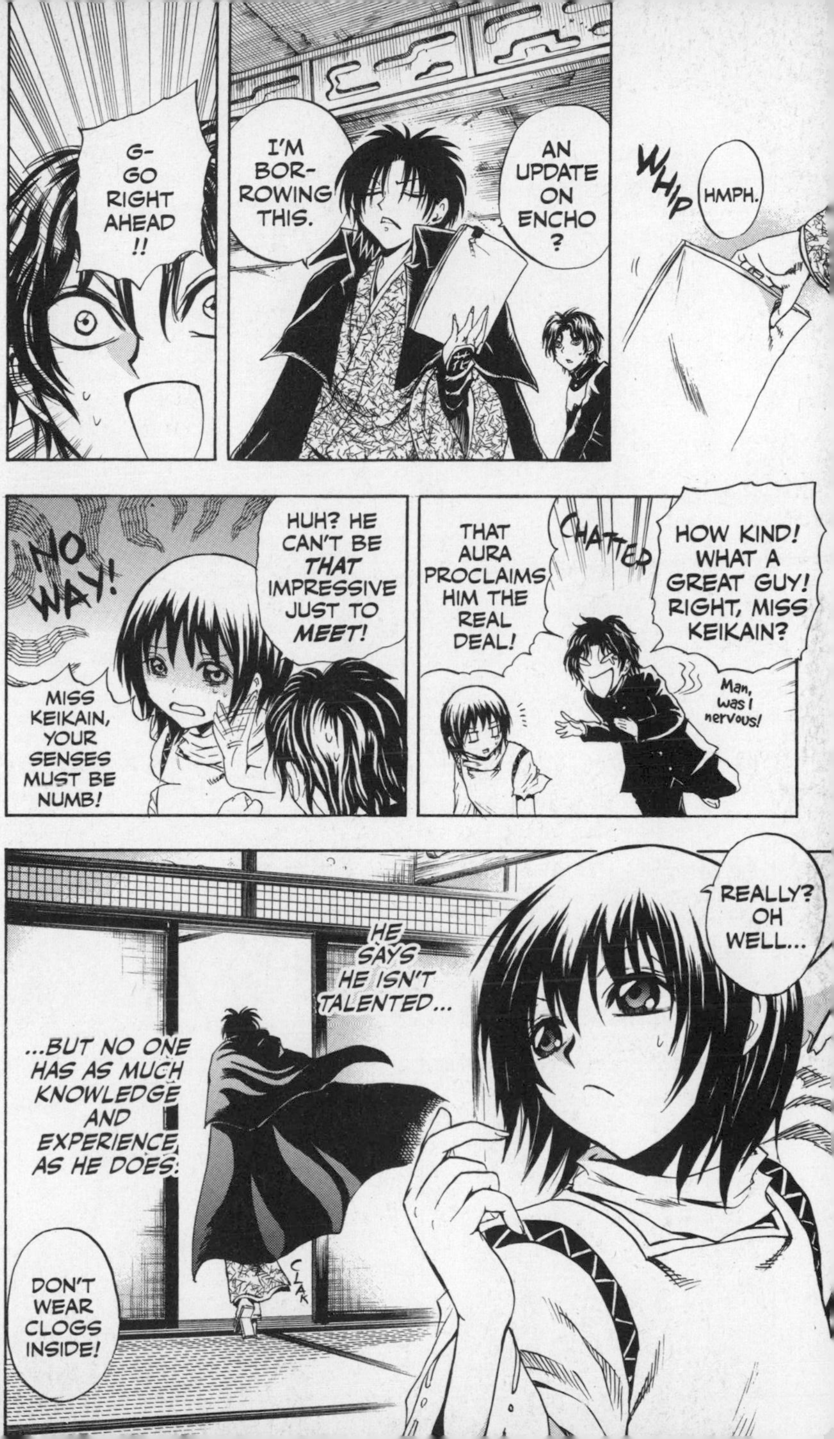
HMPH.
WHIP
AN UPDATE ON ENCHO?
I'M BOR-ROWING THIS.
G-GO RIGHT AHEAD!!
HOW KIND! WHAT A GREAT GUY! RIGHT, MISS KEIKAIN?
CHATTER
Man, was I nervous!
THAT AURA PROCLAIMS HIM THE REAL DEAL!
HUH? HE CAN'T BE *THAT* IMPRESSIVE JUST TO *MEET*!
NO WAY!
MISS KEIKAIN, YOUR SENSES MUST BE NUMB!
REALLY? OH WELL...
HE SAYS HE ISN'T TALENTED...
...BUT NO ONE HAS AS MUCH KNOWLEDGE AND EXPERIENCE AS HE DOES.
CLAK
DON'T WEAR CLOGS INSIDE!

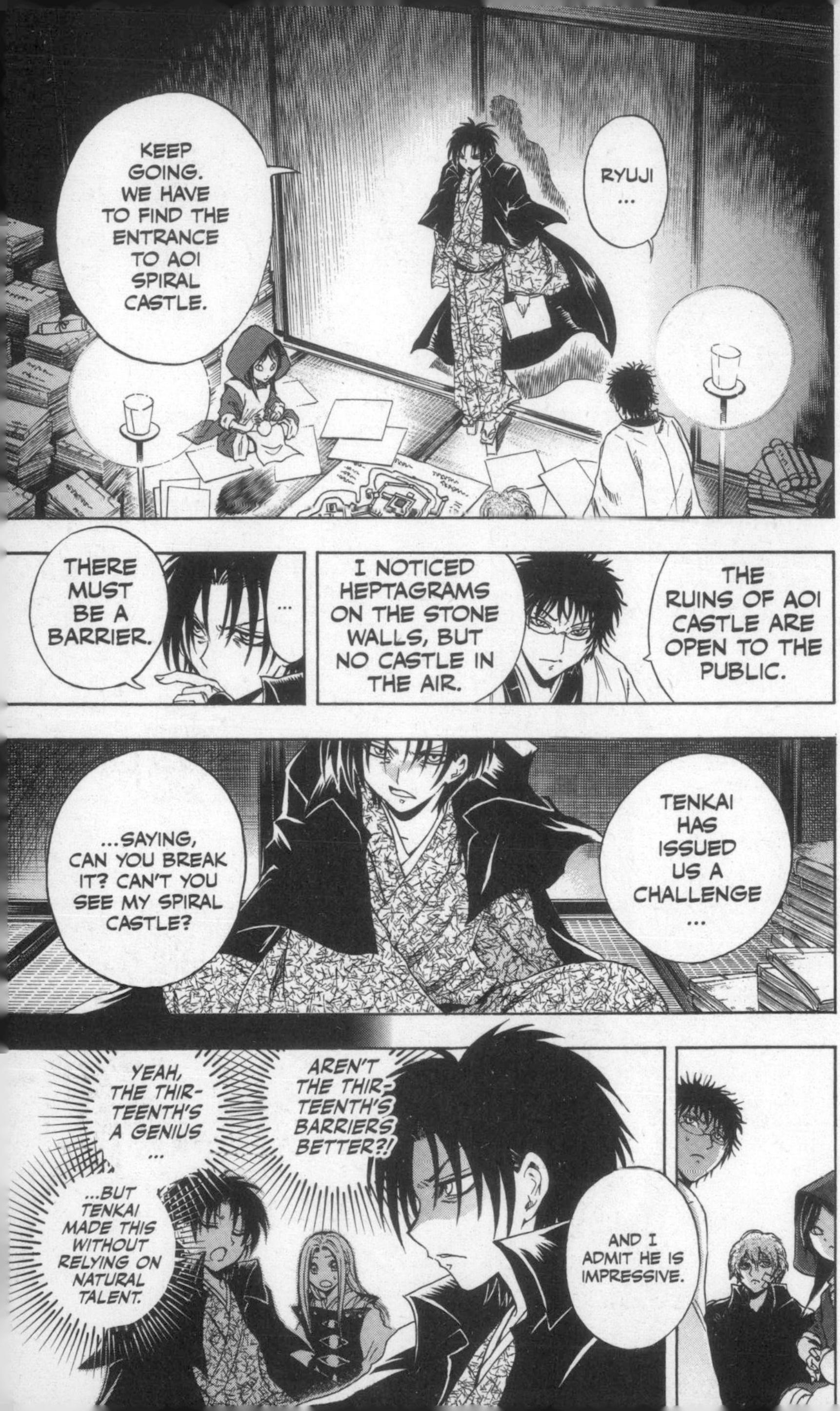
RYUJI ...
KEEP GOING. WE HAVE TO FIND THE ENTRANCE TO AOI SPIRAL CASTLE.
THE RUINS OF AOI CASTLE ARE OPEN TO THE PUBLIC.
I NOTICED HEPTAGRAMS ON THE STONE WALLS, BUT NO CASTLE IN THE AIR.
...
THERE MUST BE A BARRIER.
TENKAI HAS ISSUED US A CHALLENGE ...
...SAYING, CAN YOU BREAK IT? CAN'T YOU SEE MY SPIRAL CASTLE?
AREN'T THE THIRTEENTH'S BARRIERS BETTER?!
YEAH, THE THIRTEENTH'S A GENIUS ...
...BUT TENKAI MADE THIS WITHOUT RELYING ON NATURAL TALENT.
AND I ADMIT HE IS IMPRESSIVE.

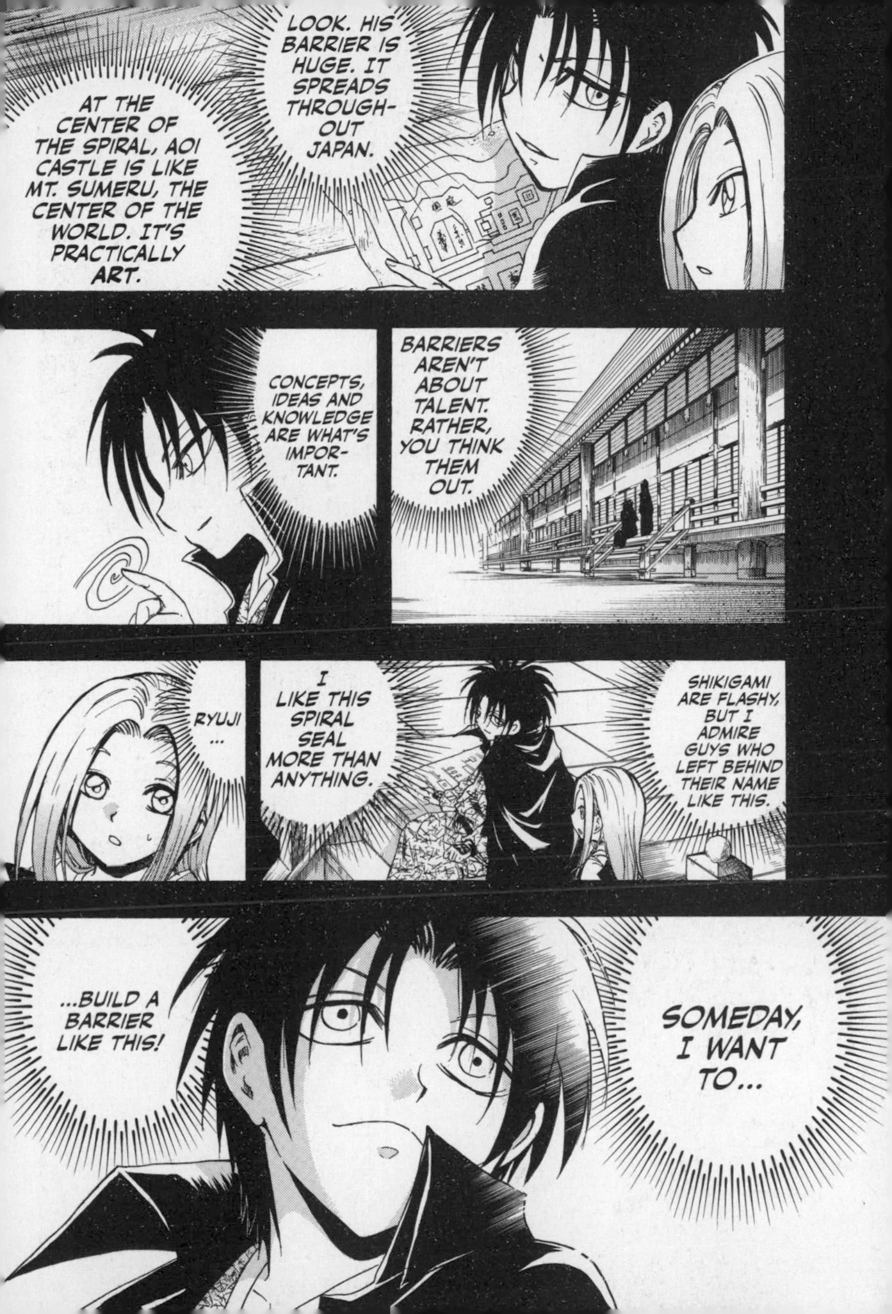
LOOK. HIS BARRIER IS HUGE. IT SPREADS THROUGH-OUT JAPAN.
AT THE CENTER OF THE SPIRAL, AOI CASTLE IS LIKE MT. SUMERU, THE CENTER OF THE WORLD. IT'S PRACTICALLY ART.
BARRIERS AREN'T ABOUT TALENT. RATHER, YOU THINK THEM OUT.
CONCEPTS, IDEAS AND KNOWLEDGE ARE WHAT'S IMPOR-TANT.
SHIKIGAMI ARE FLASHY, BUT I ADMIRE GUYS WHO LEFT BEHIND THEIR NAME LIKE THIS.
I LIKE THIS SPIRAL SEAL MORE THAN ANYTHING.
RYUJI ...
SOMEDAY, I WANT TO...
...BUILD A BARRIER LIKE THIS!

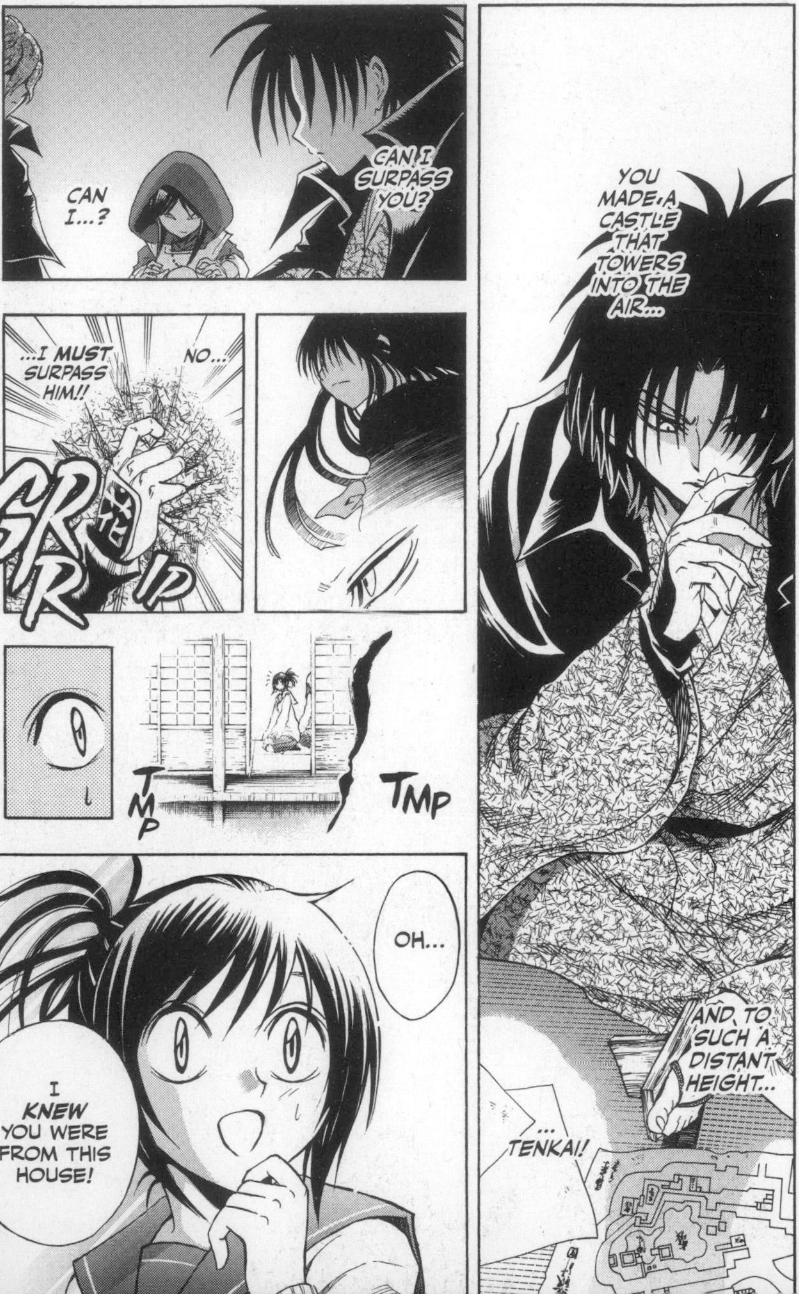
YOU MADE A CASTLE THAT TOWERS INTO THE AIR...
AND TO SUCH A DISTANT HEIGHT...
...TENKAI!
CAN I SURPASS YOU?
CAN I...?
NO...
...I MUST SURPASS HIM!!
GRRIP
TMP
TMP
OH...
I KNEW YOU WERE FROM THIS HOUSE!

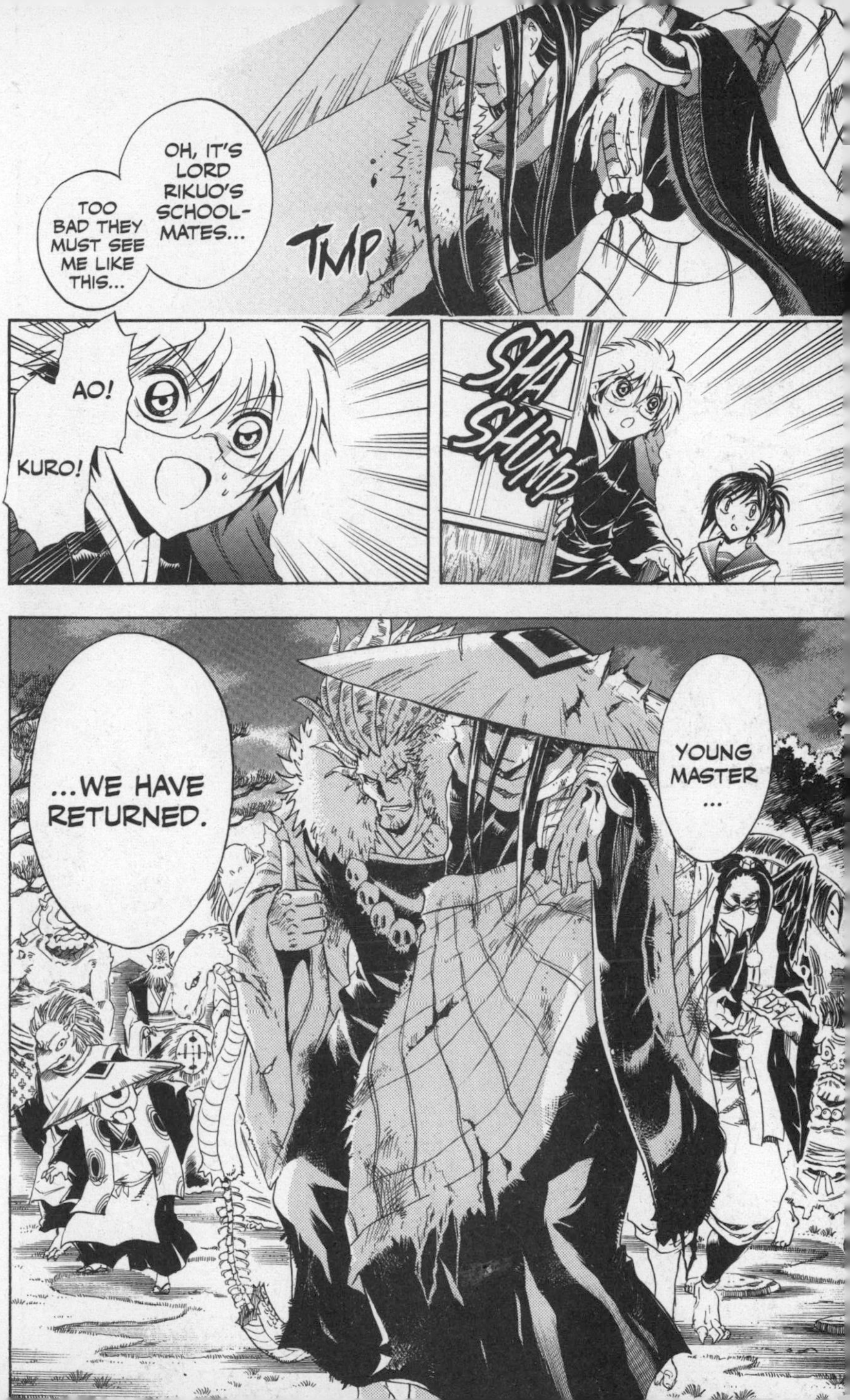
OH, IT'S LORD RIKUO'S SCHOOL-MATES...
TOO BAD THEY MUST SEE ME LIKE THIS...
TMP
SHA SHUMP
AO!
KURO!
YOUNG MASTER ...
...WE HAVE RETURNED.

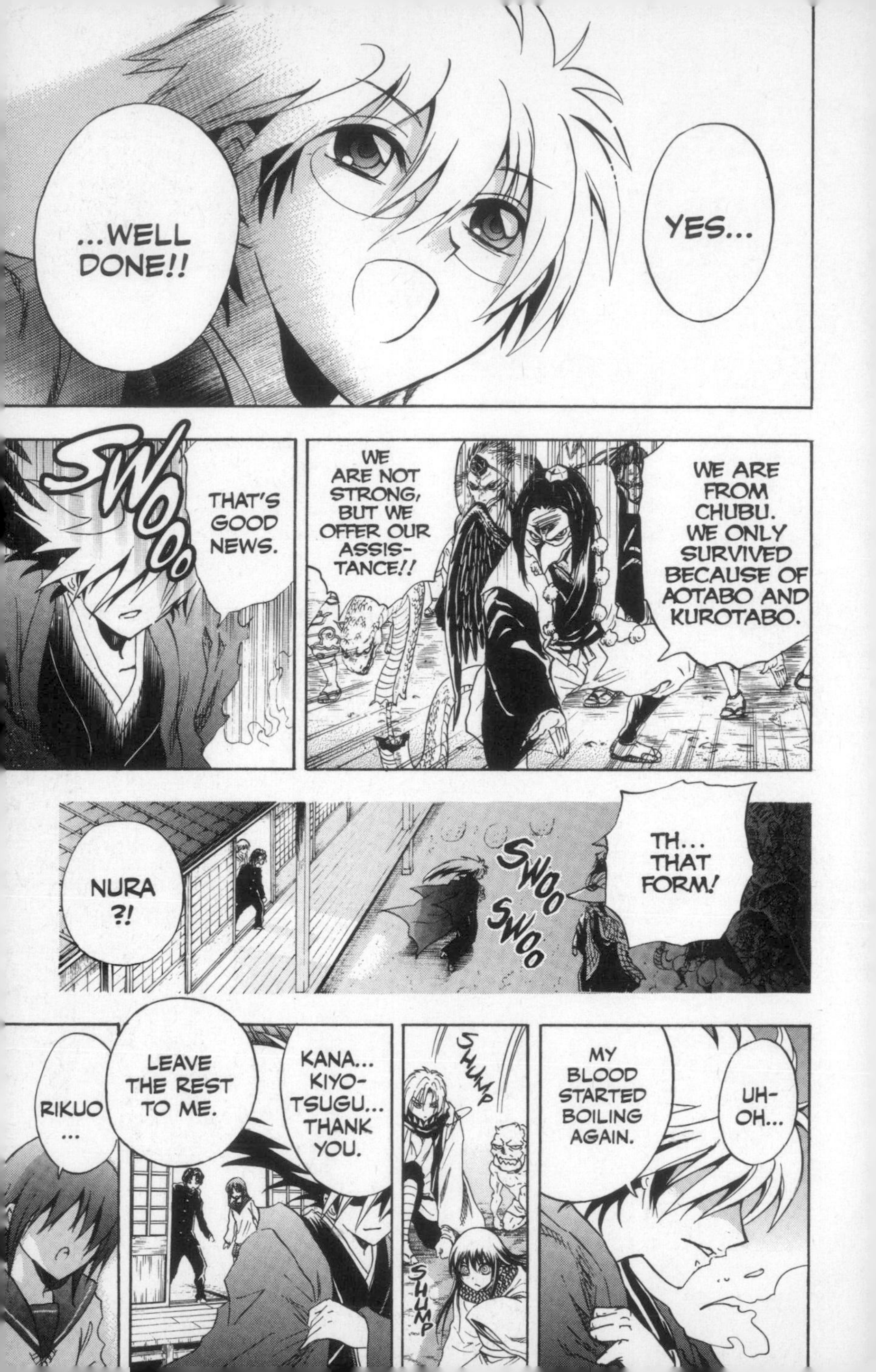
YES...
...WELL DONE!!
WE ARE FROM CHUBU. WE ONLY SURVIVED BECAUSE OF AOTABO AND KUROTABO.
WE ARE NOT STRONG, BUT WE OFFER OUR ASSIS-TANCE!!
SWOOO
THAT'S GOOD NEWS.
TH... THAT FORM!
SWOO SWOO
NURA ?!
UH-OH...
MY BLOOD STARTED BOILING AGAIN.
SHUMP
SHUMP
KANA... KIYO-TSUGU... THANK YOU.
LEAVE THE REST TO ME.
RIKUO ...

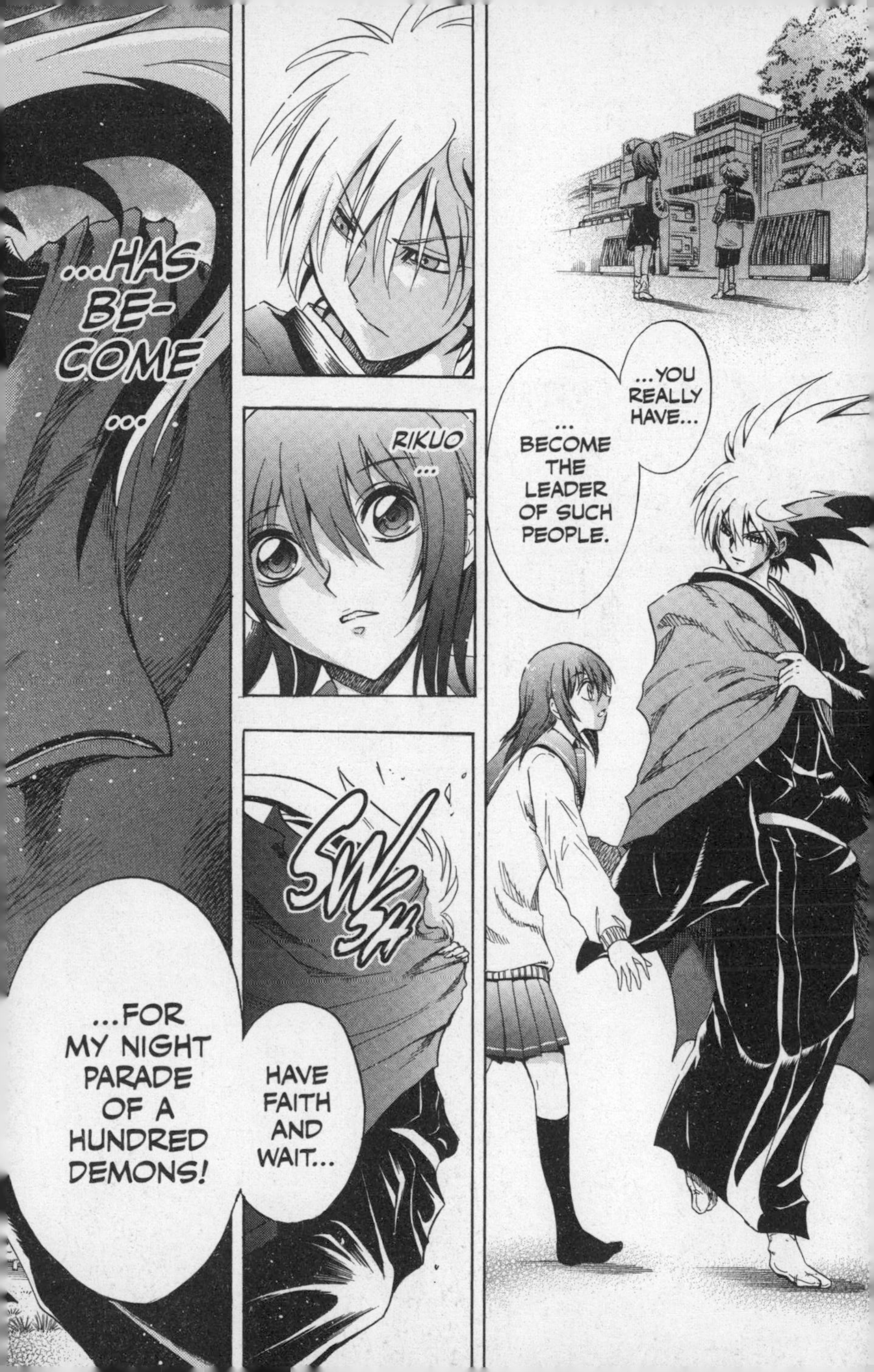
...YOU REALLY HAVE...
...BECOME THE LEADER OF SUCH PEOPLE.
RIKUO...
SWSH
HAVE FAITH AND WAIT...
...HAS BE-COME...
...FOR MY NIGHT PARADE OF A HUNDRED DEMONS!

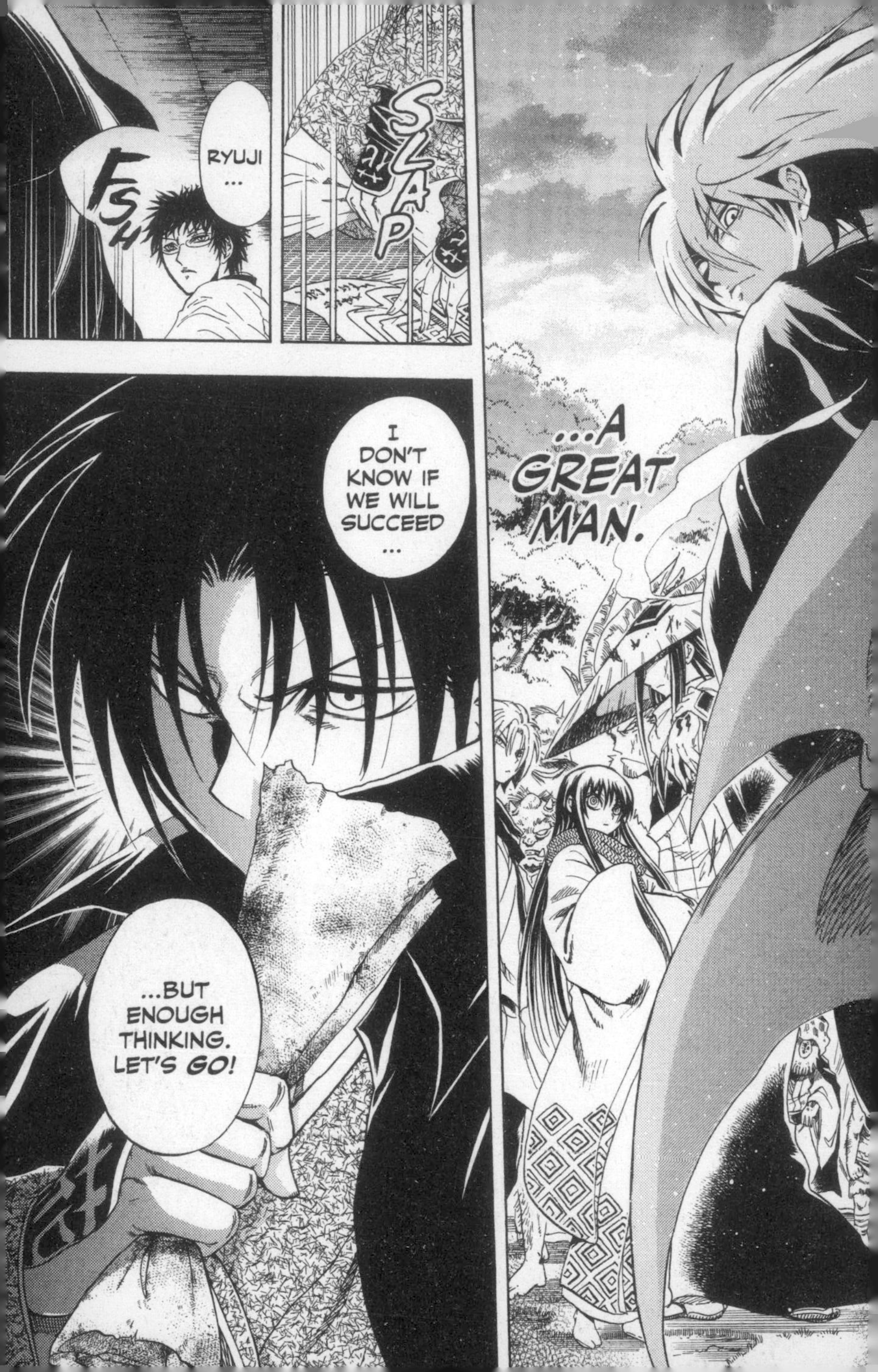
...A GREAT MAN.
SLAP
FSH
RYUJI ...
I DON'T KNOW IF WE WILL SUCCEED ...
...BUT ENOUGH THINKING. LET'S GO!

NURA: RISE OF THE YOKAI CLAN

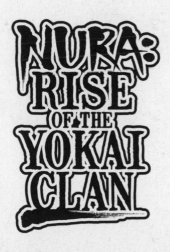

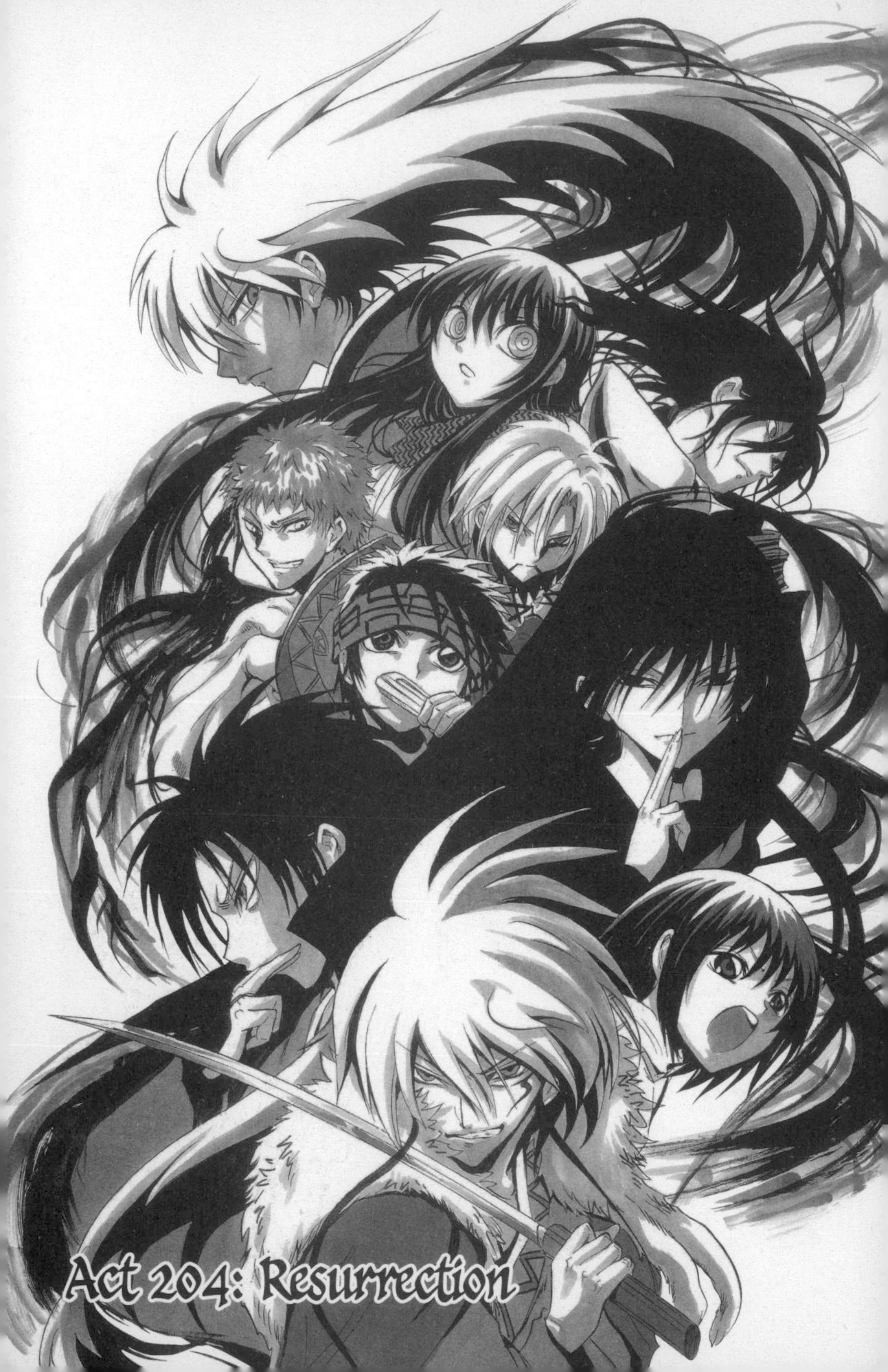
Act 204: Resurrection

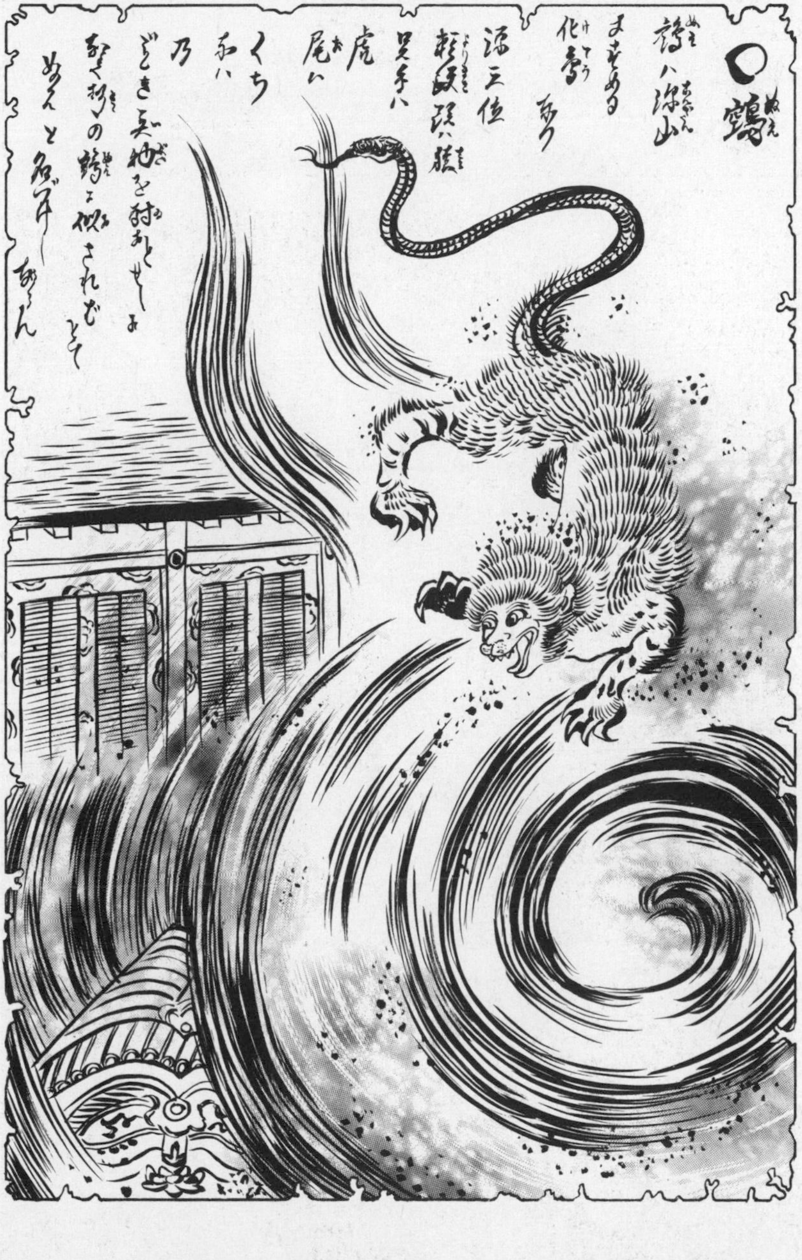
○鵺
鵺ハ深山にすめる化鳥なり
源三位頼政頭ハ猿
足手ハ虎
尾ハくちなハ乃ごとき異物を射おとせしに
なく声の鵺に似たれバとて
ぬえと名づけしならん

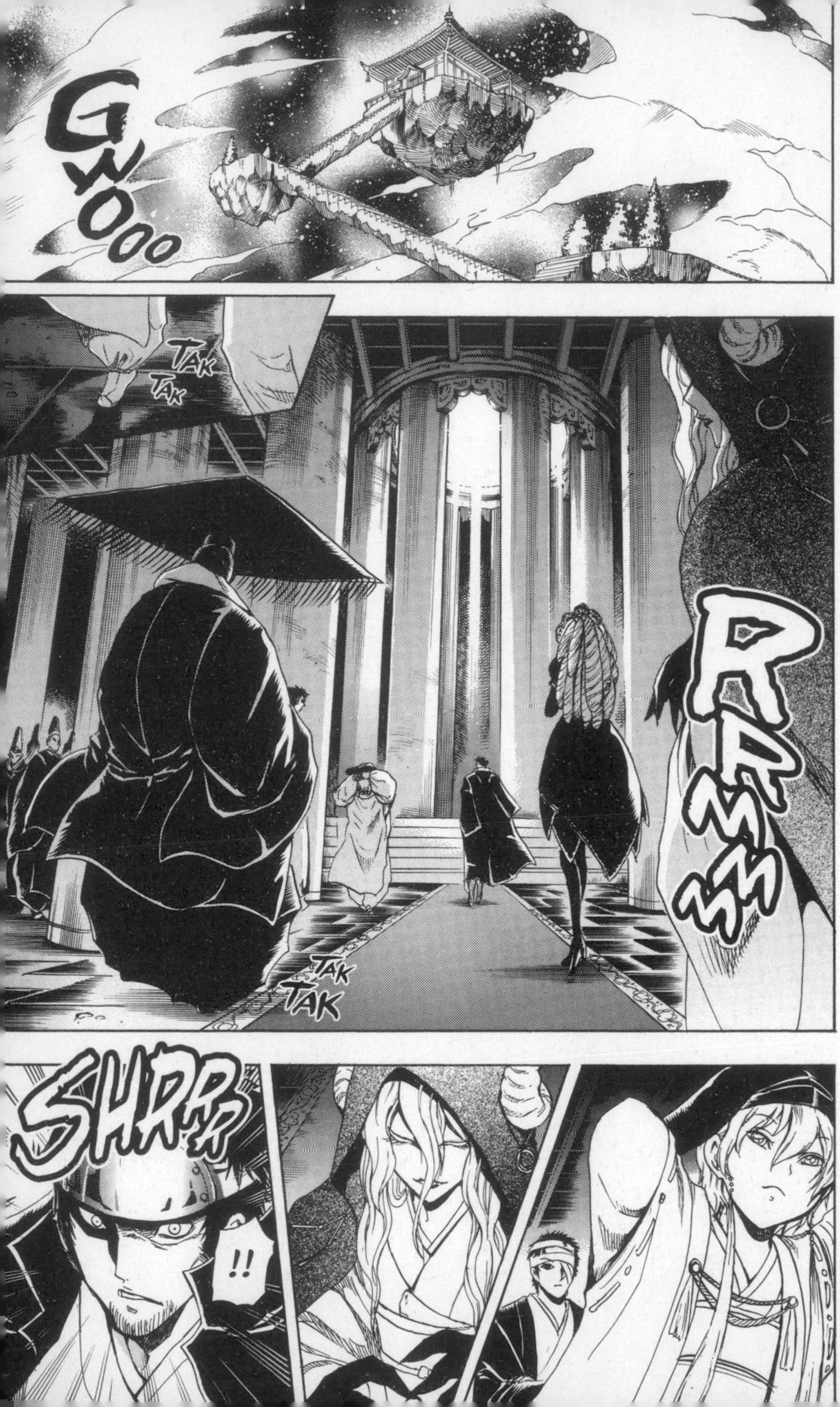
GWOOO
RRMMM
TAK TAK
TAK TAK
SHRR
!!

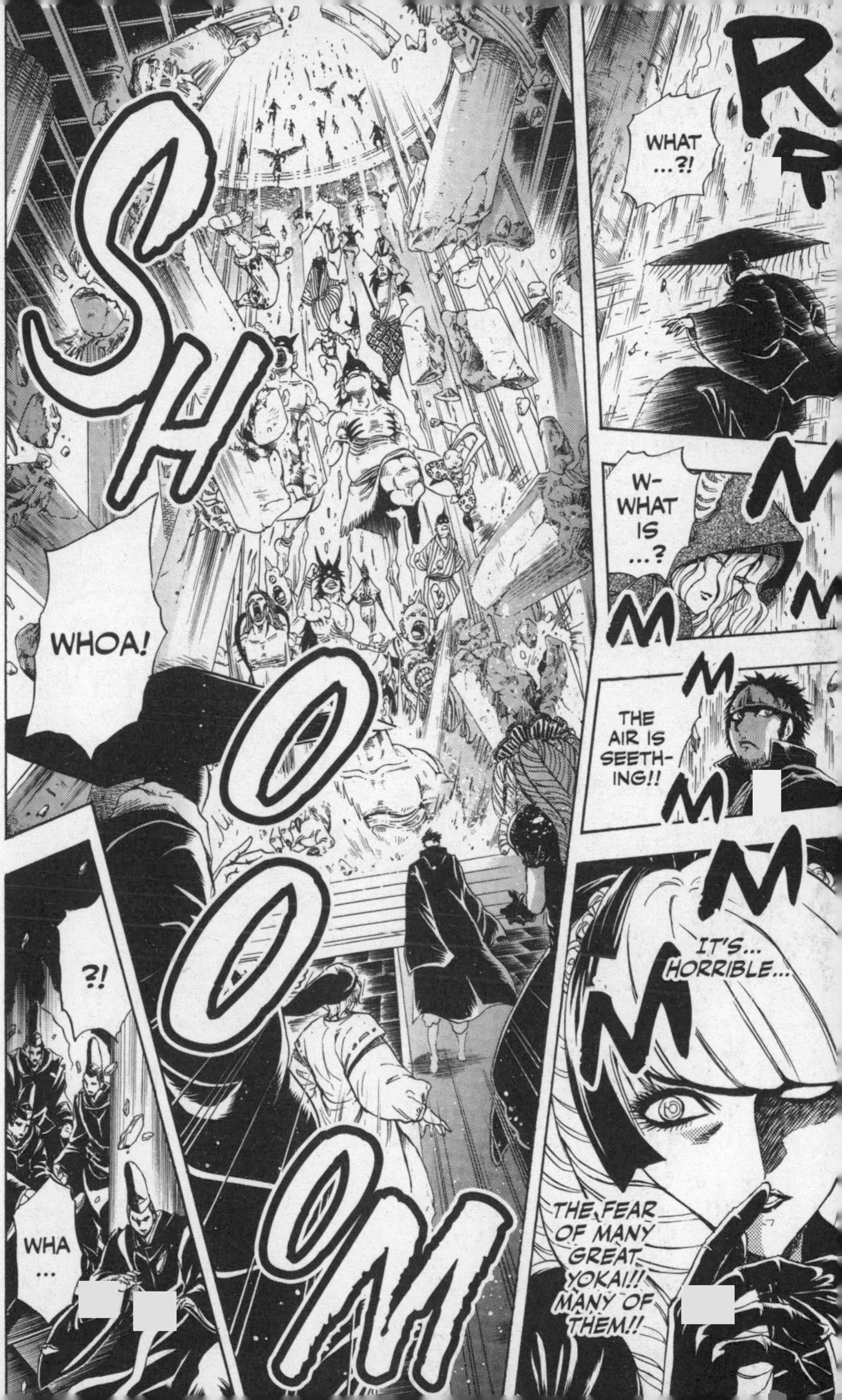

RR
WHAT ...?!
W-WHAT IS ...?
MMMM
THE AIR IS SEETHING!!
IT'S... HORRIBLE...
THE FEAR OF MANY GREAT YOKAI!! MANY OF THEM!!
SHOOOM
WHOA!
?!
WHA ...

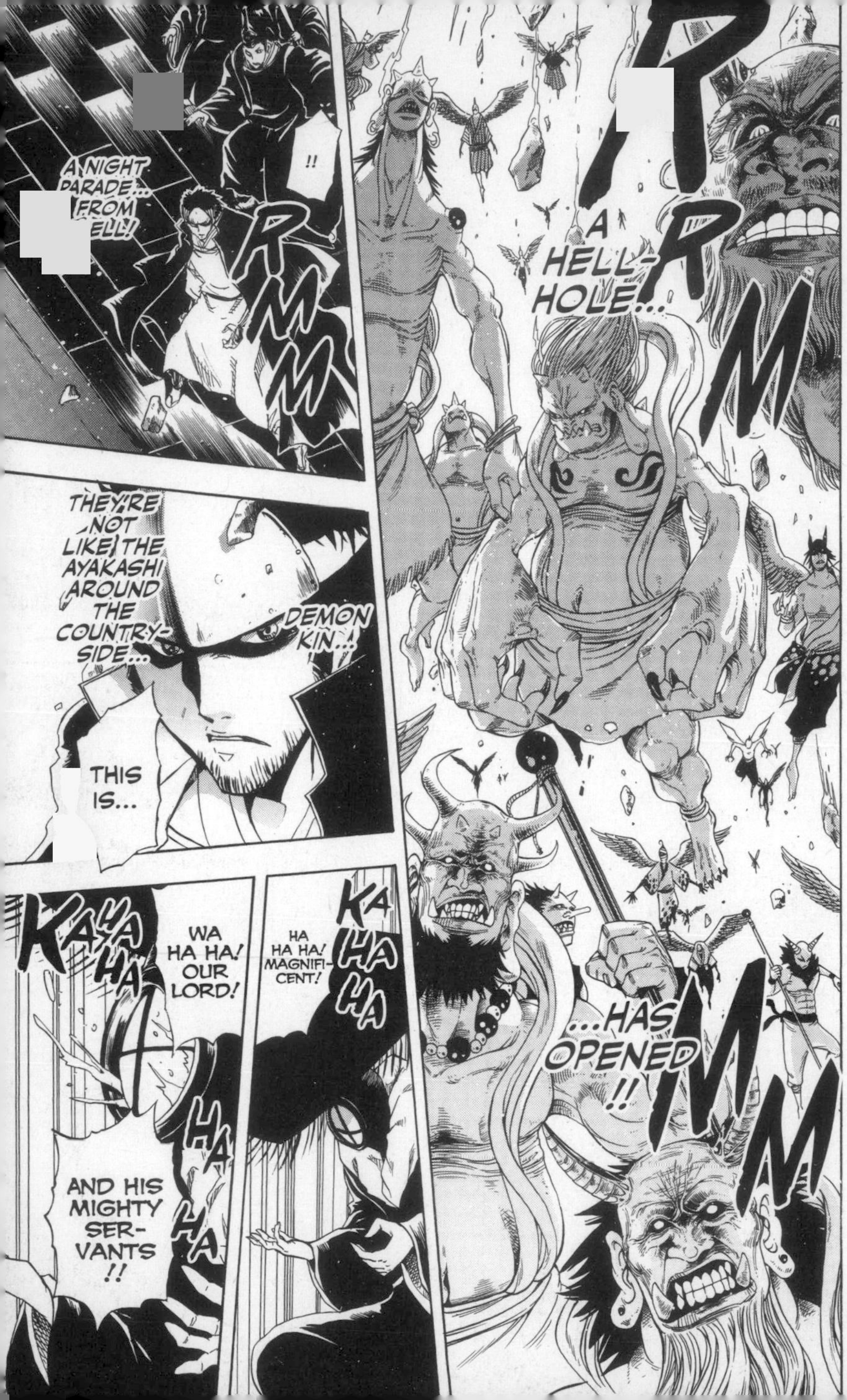
RRRRM
A HELL-HOLE...
...HAS OPENED!!
MM
!!
A NIGHT PARADE... FROM ELL!
RMMM
DEMON KIN...
THEY'RE NOT LIKE THE AYAKASHI AROUND THE COUNTRYSIDE...
THIS IS...
KA HA HA HA
HA HA HA! MAGNIFICENT!
WA HA HA! OUR LORD!
KAHAHA
AND HIS MIGHTY SERVANTS!!
HA HA HA

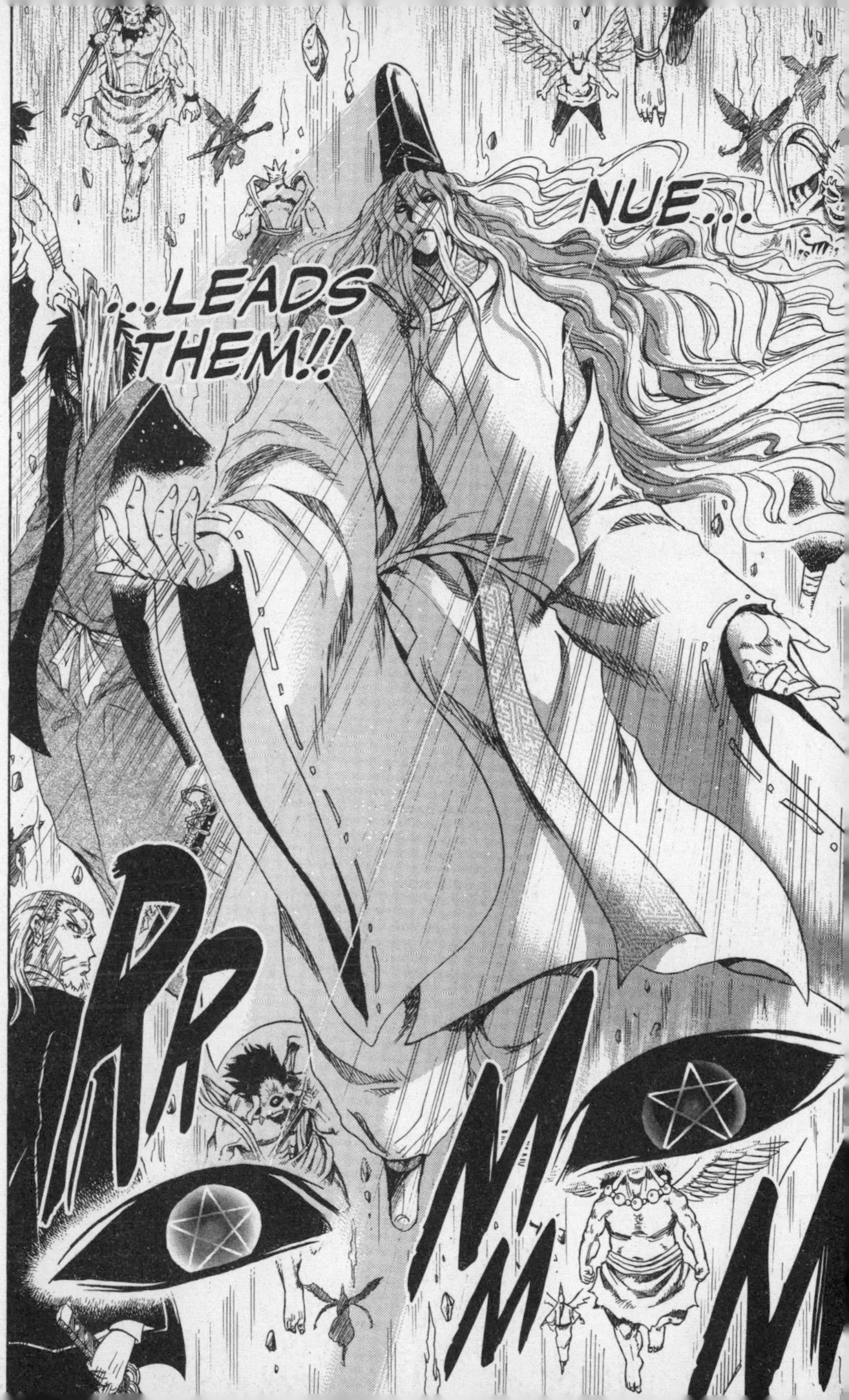
NUE...
...LEADS THEM!!
RRMMM

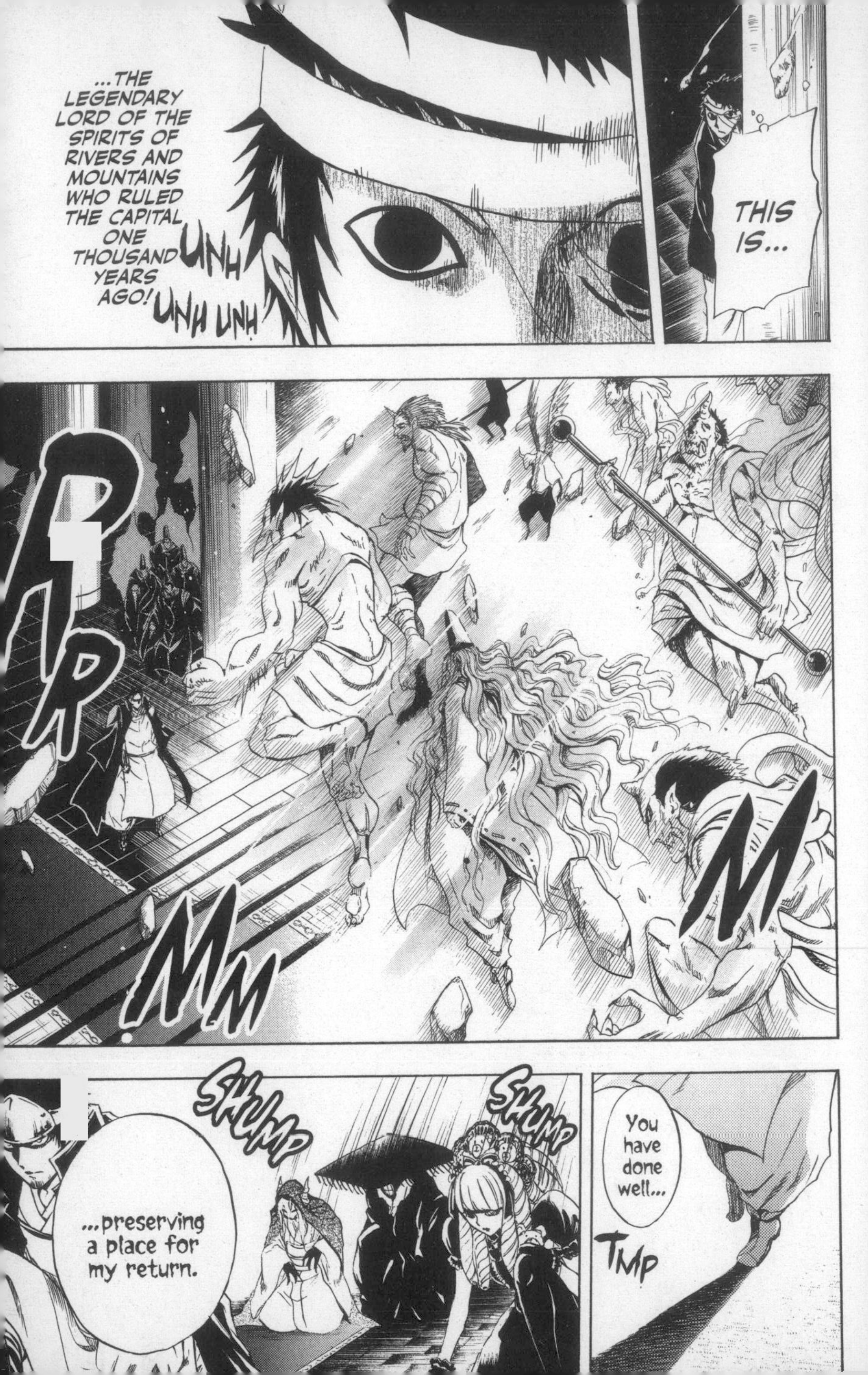
THIS IS...
...THE LEGENDARY LORD OF THE SPIRITS OF RIVERS AND MOUNTAINS WHO RULED THE CAPITAL ONE THOUSAND YEARS AGO!
UNH
UNH UNH
RR
MMM
You have done well...
TMP
SHUMP
SHUMP
...preserving a place for my return.

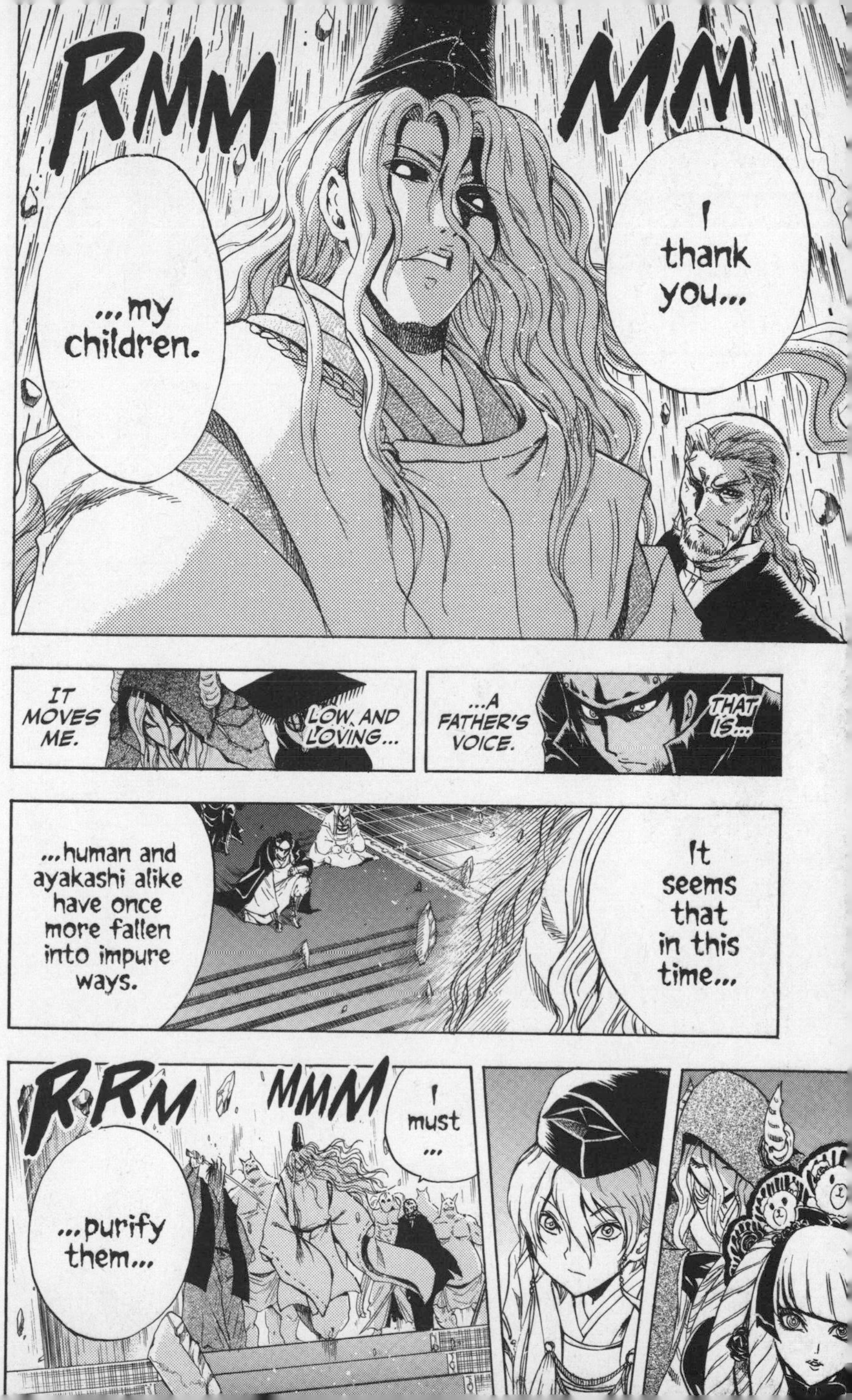
RMM MM
I thank you...
...my children.
THAT IS...
...A FATHER'S VOICE.
LOW AND LOVING...
IT MOVES ME.
It seems that in this time...
...human and ayakashi alike have once more fallen into impure ways.
RRM MMM
I must ...
...purify them...

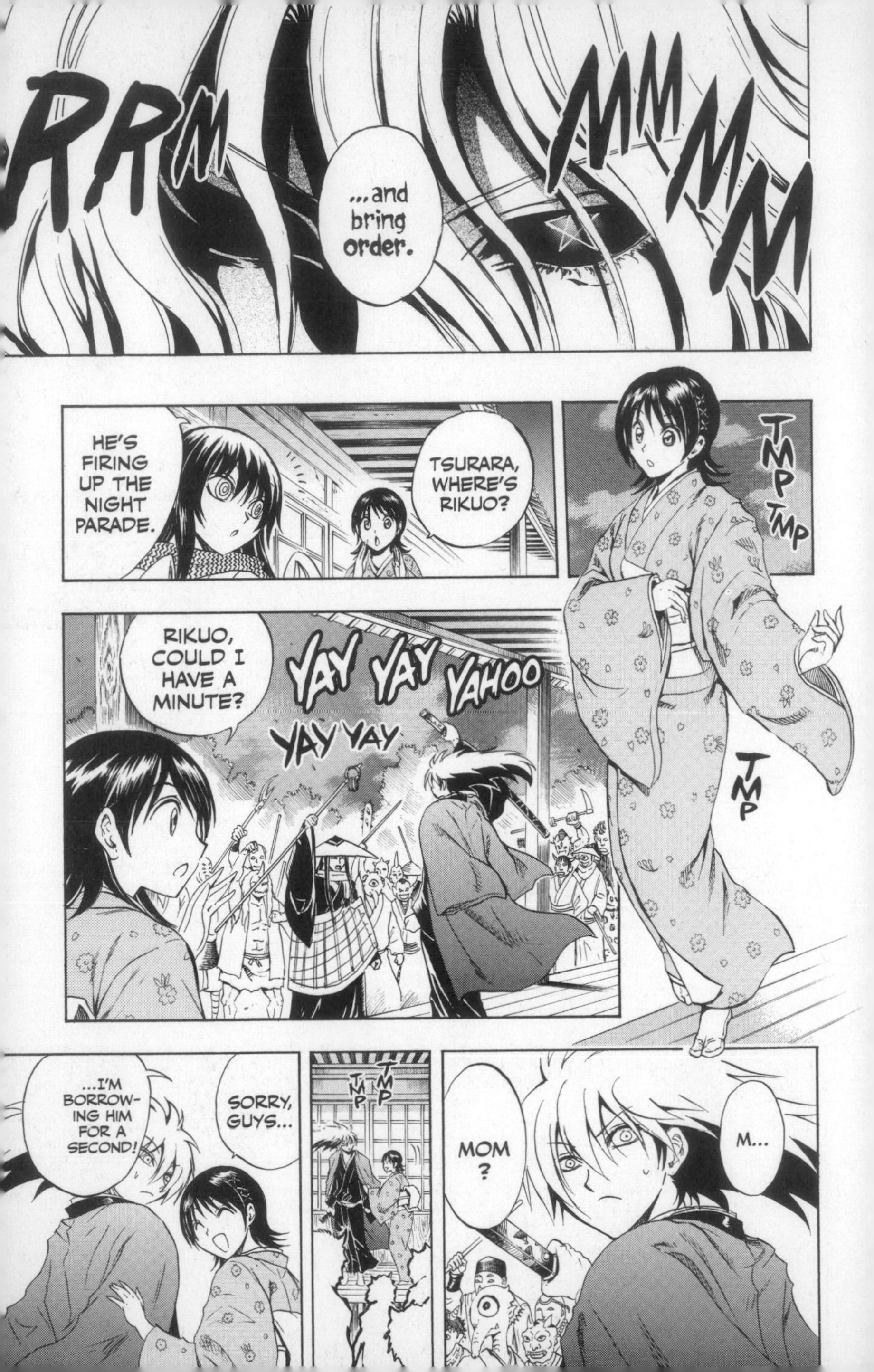
RRM
MMMMM
...and bring order.
TMP TMP TMP
TMP
TSURARA, WHERE'S RIKUO?
HE'S FIRING UP THE NIGHT PARADE.
RIKUO, COULD I HAVE A MINUTE?
YAY YAY YAHOO
YAY YAY
M...
MOM?
TMP TMP
SORRY, GUYS...
...I'M BORROWING HIM FOR A SECOND!

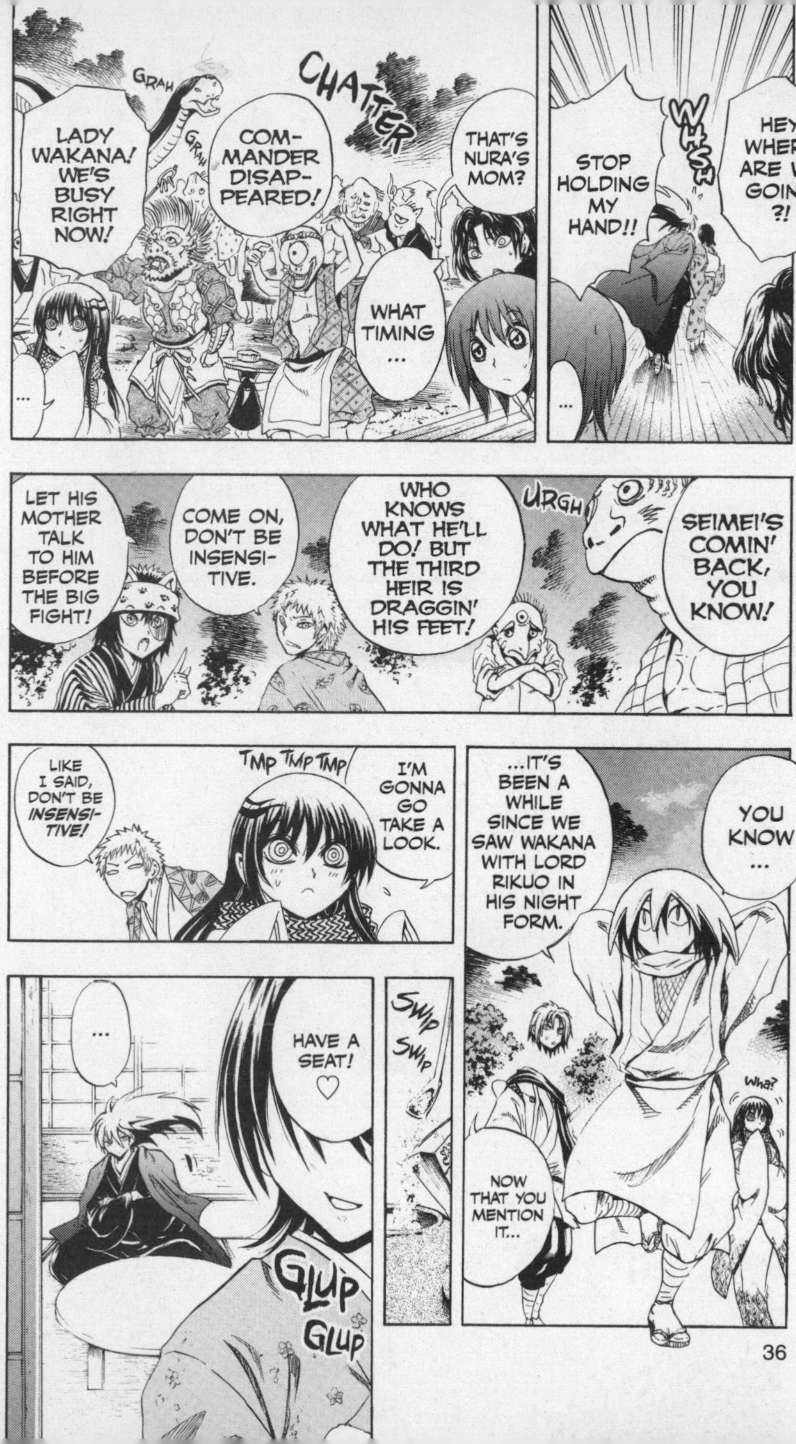

HEY, WHERE ARE WE GOING?!
WHSH
STOP HOLDING MY HAND!!
...
THAT'S NURA'S MOM?
CHATTER
COM-MANDER DISAP-PEARED!
GRAH
GRAH
LADY WAKANA! WE'S BUSY RIGHT NOW!
WHAT TIMING ...
...
SEIMEI'S COMIN' BACK, YOU KNOW!
URGH
WHO KNOWS WHAT HE'LL DO! BUT THE THIRD HEIR IS DRAGGIN' HIS FEET!
COME ON, DON'T BE INSENSI-TIVE.
LET HIS MOTHER TALK TO HIM BEFORE THE BIG FIGHT!
YOU KNOW ...
...IT'S BEEN A WHILE SINCE WE SAW WAKANA WITH LORD RIKUO IN HIS NIGHT FORM.
NOW THAT YOU MENTION IT...
Wha?
I'M GONNA GO TAKE A LOOK.
TMP TMP TMP
LIKE I SAID, DON'T BE *INSENSI-TIVE!*
SWIP
SWIP
HAVE A SEAT! ♡
...
GLUP
GLUP

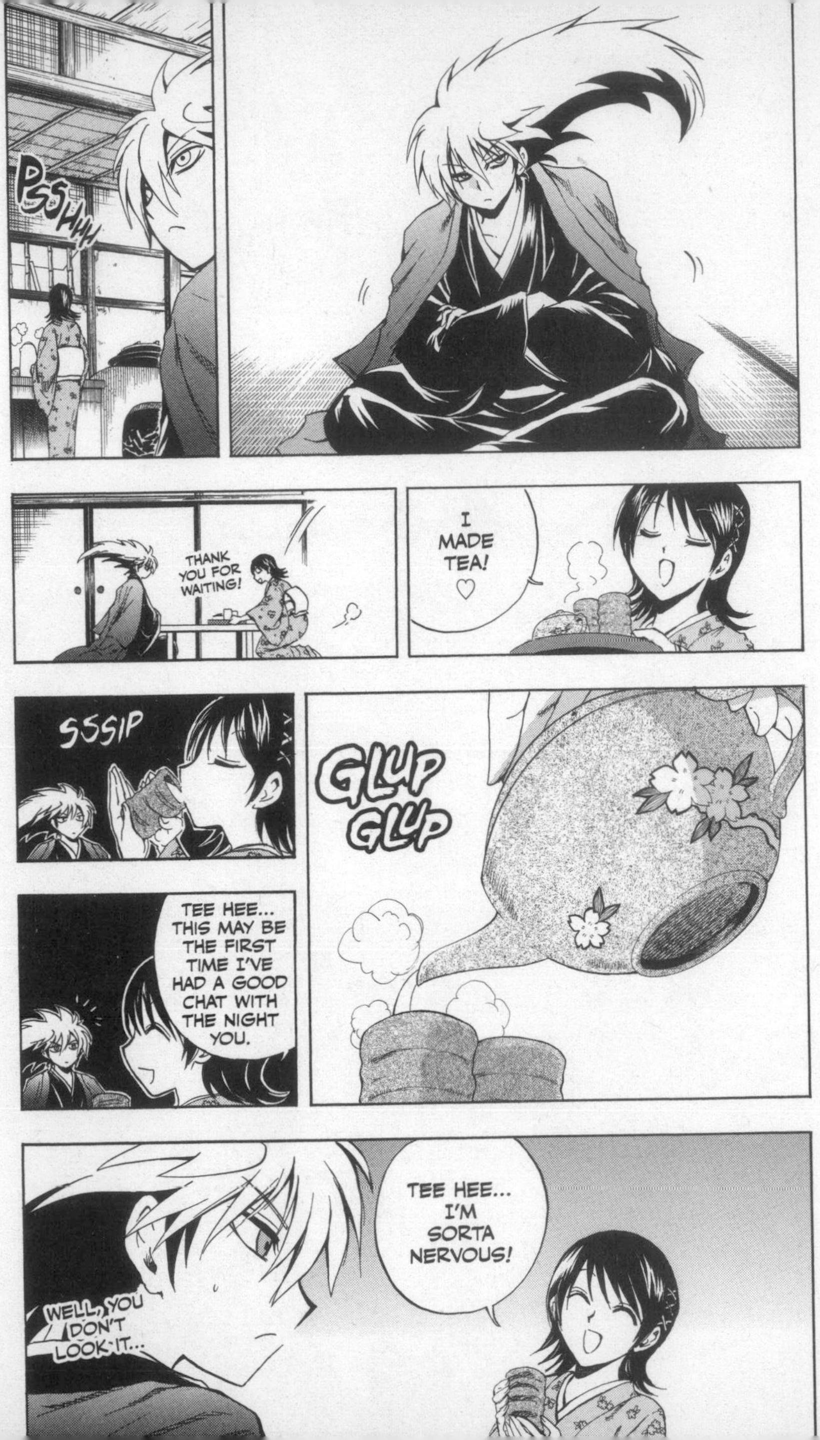
PSSHHH
I MADE TEA! ♡
THANK YOU FOR WAITING!
GLUP GLUP
SSSIP
TEE HEE... THIS MAY BE THE FIRST TIME I'VE HAD A GOOD CHAT WITH THE NIGHT YOU.
TEE HEE... I'M SORTA NERVOUS!
WELL, YOU DON'T LOOK IT...

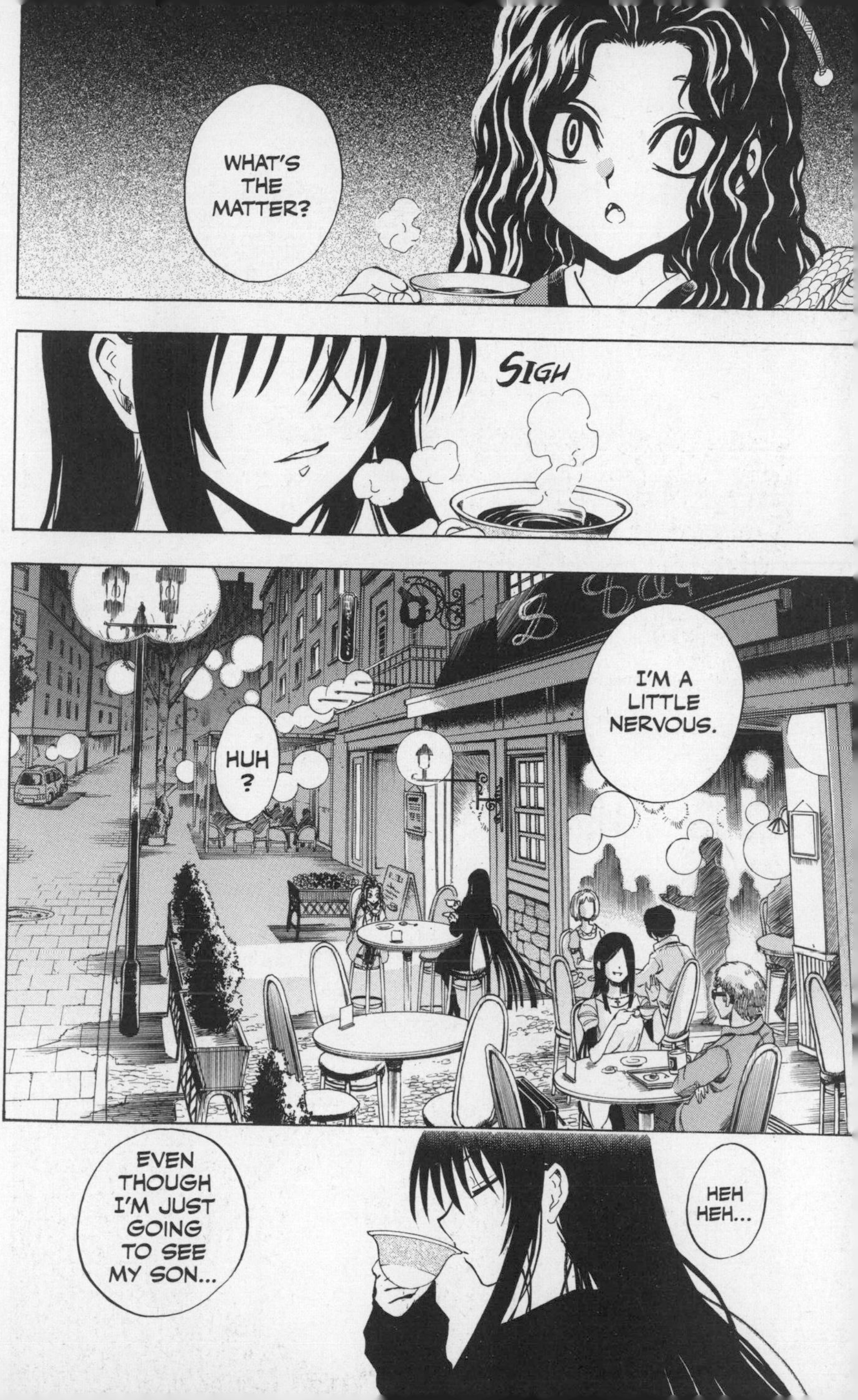
WHAT'S THE MATTER?
SIGH
I'M A LITTLE NERVOUS.
HUH?
HEH HEH...
EVEN THOUGH I'M JUST GOING TO SEE MY SON...

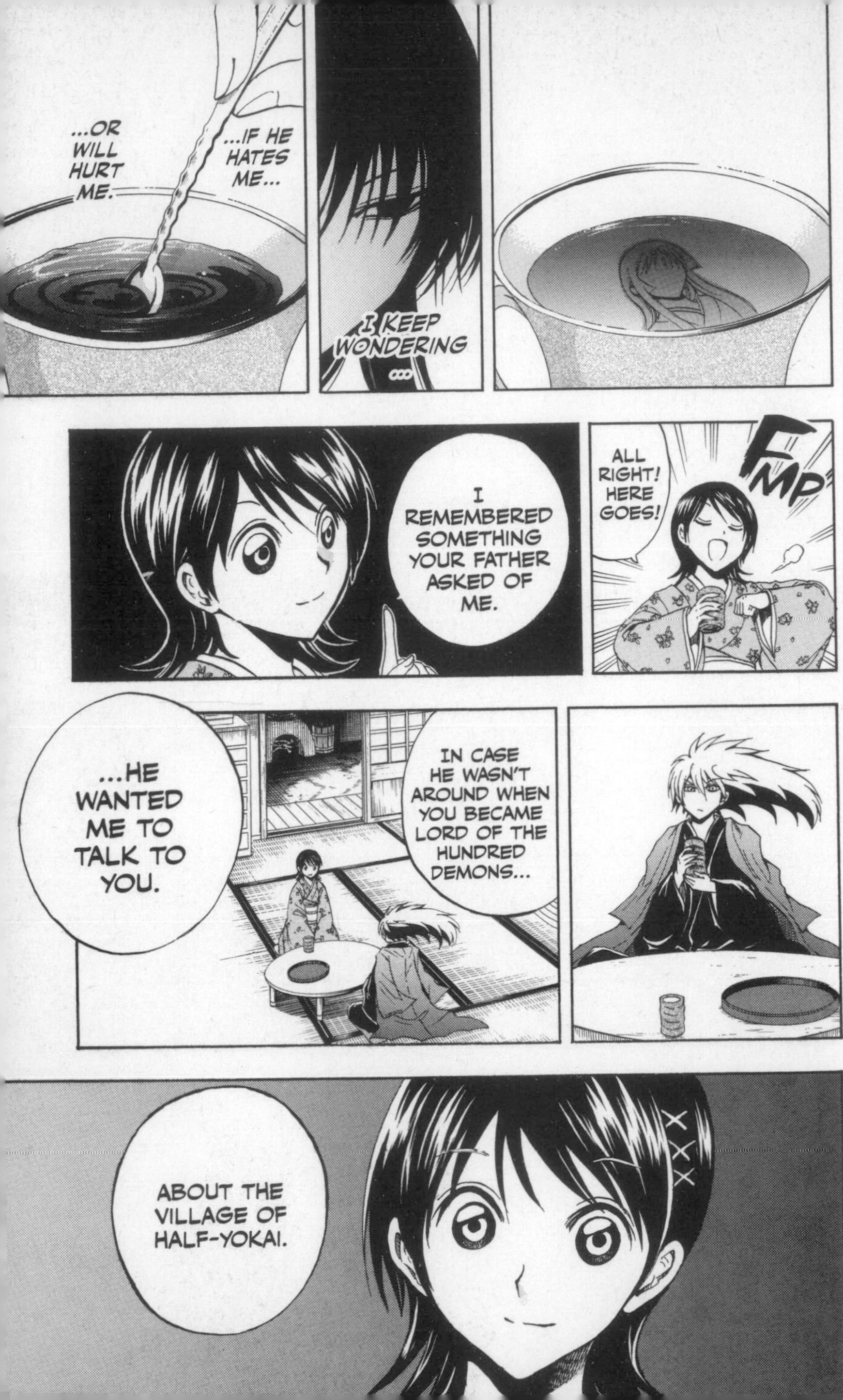
I KEEP WONDERING ...
...IF HE HATES ME...
...OR WILL HURT ME.
ALL RIGHT! HERE GOES!
FMP
I REMEMBERED SOMETHING YOUR FATHER ASKED OF ME.
IN CASE HE WASN'T AROUND WHEN YOU BECAME LORD OF THE HUNDRED DEMONS...
...HE WANTED ME TO TALK TO YOU.
ABOUT THE VILLAGE OF HALF-YOKAI.

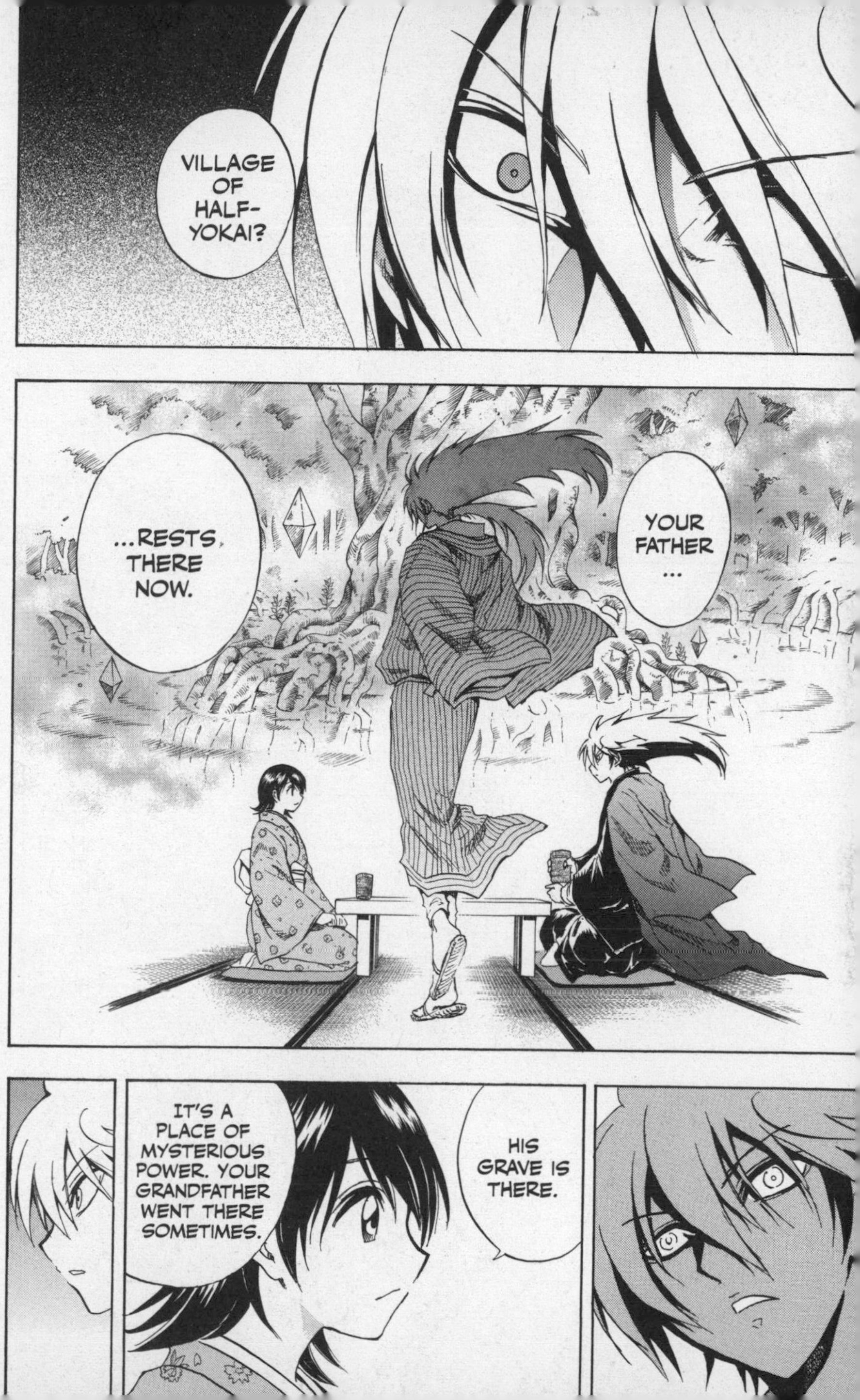
VILLAGE OF HALF-YOKAI?
YOUR FATHER ...
...RESTS THERE NOW.
HIS GRAVE IS THERE.
IT'S A PLACE OF MYSTERIOUS POWER. YOUR GRANDFATHER WENT THERE SOMETIMES.

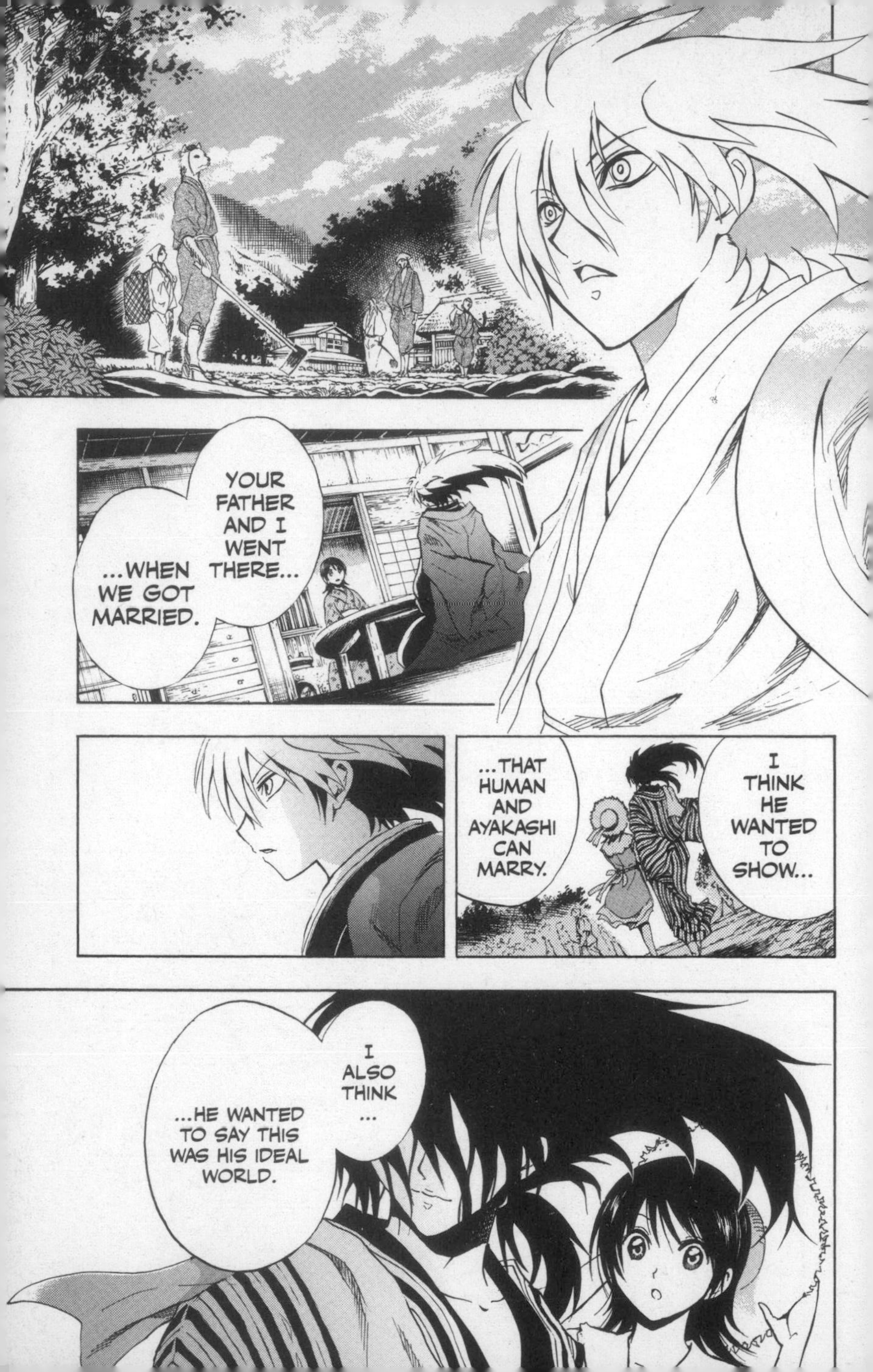
YOUR FATHER AND I WENT THERE...
...WHEN WE GOT MARRIED.
I THINK HE WANTED TO SHOW...
...THAT HUMAN AND AYAKASHI CAN MARRY.
I ALSO THINK ...
...HE WANTED TO SAY THIS WAS HIS IDEAL WORLD.

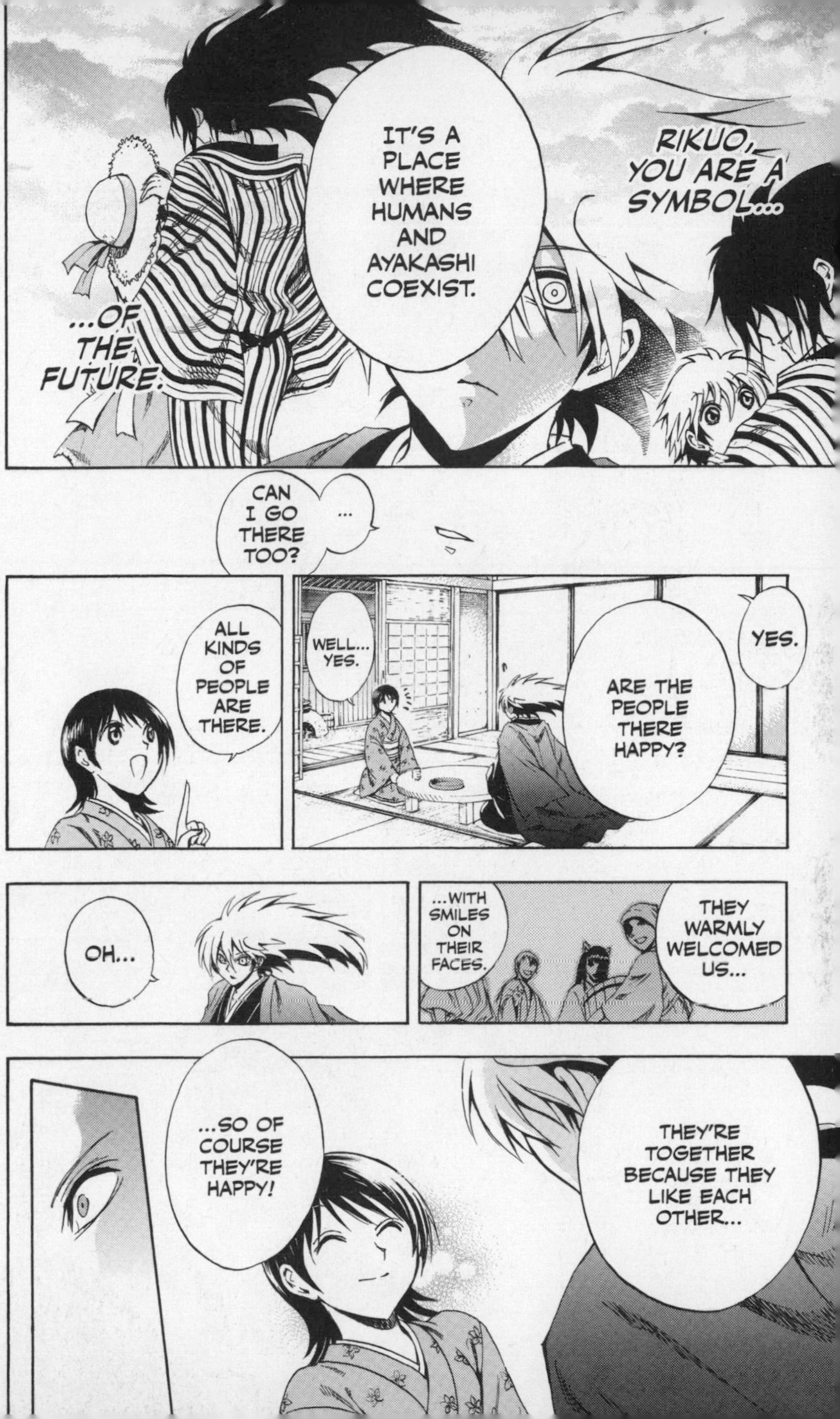
RIKUO, YOU ARE A SYMBOL...
IT'S A PLACE WHERE HUMANS AND AYAKASHI COEXIST.
...OF THE FUTURE.
...
CAN I GO THERE TOO?
YES.
ARE THE PEOPLE THERE HAPPY?
WELL... YES.
ALL KINDS OF PEOPLE ARE THERE.
THEY WARMLY WELCOMED US...
...WITH SMILES ON THEIR FACES.
OH...
THEY'RE TOGETHER BECAUSE THEY LIKE EACH OTHER...
...SO OF COURSE THEY'RE HAPPY!

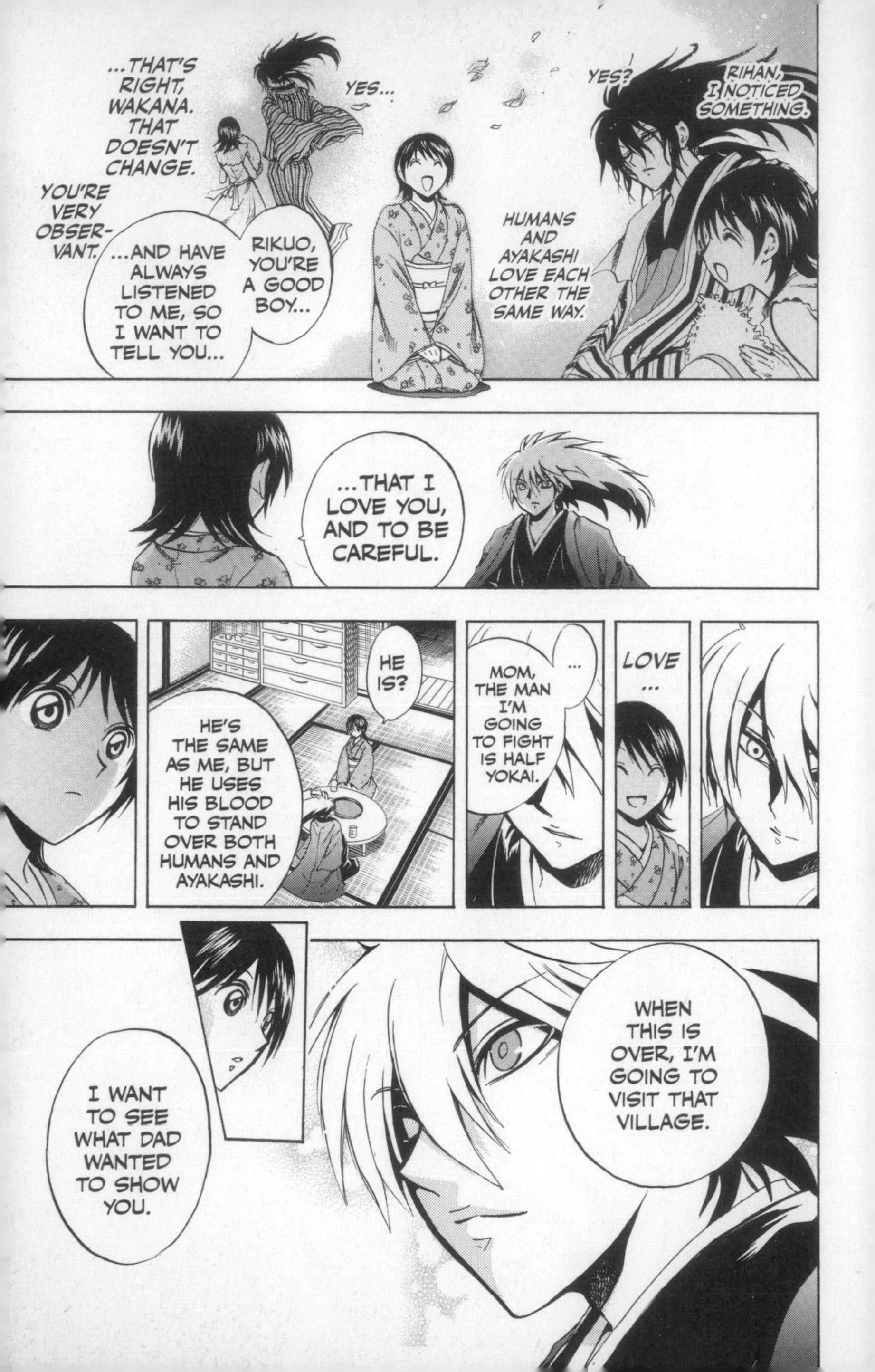
RIHAN, I NOTICED SOMETHING.
YES?
HUMANS AND AYAKASHI LOVE EACH OTHER THE SAME WAY.
YES...
...THAT'S RIGHT, WAKANA. THAT DOESN'T CHANGE.
YOU'RE VERY OBSER-VANT.
RIKUO, YOU'RE A GOOD BOY...
...AND HAVE ALWAYS LISTENED TO ME, SO I WANT TO TELL YOU...
...THAT I LOVE YOU, AND TO BE CAREFUL.
LOVE ...
...
MOM, THE MAN I'M GOING TO FIGHT IS HALF YOKAI.
HE IS?
HE'S THE SAME AS ME, BUT HE USES HIS BLOOD TO STAND OVER BOTH HUMANS AND AYAKASHI.
WHEN THIS IS OVER, I'M GOING TO VISIT THAT VILLAGE.
I WANT TO SEE WHAT DAD WANTED TO SHOW YOU.

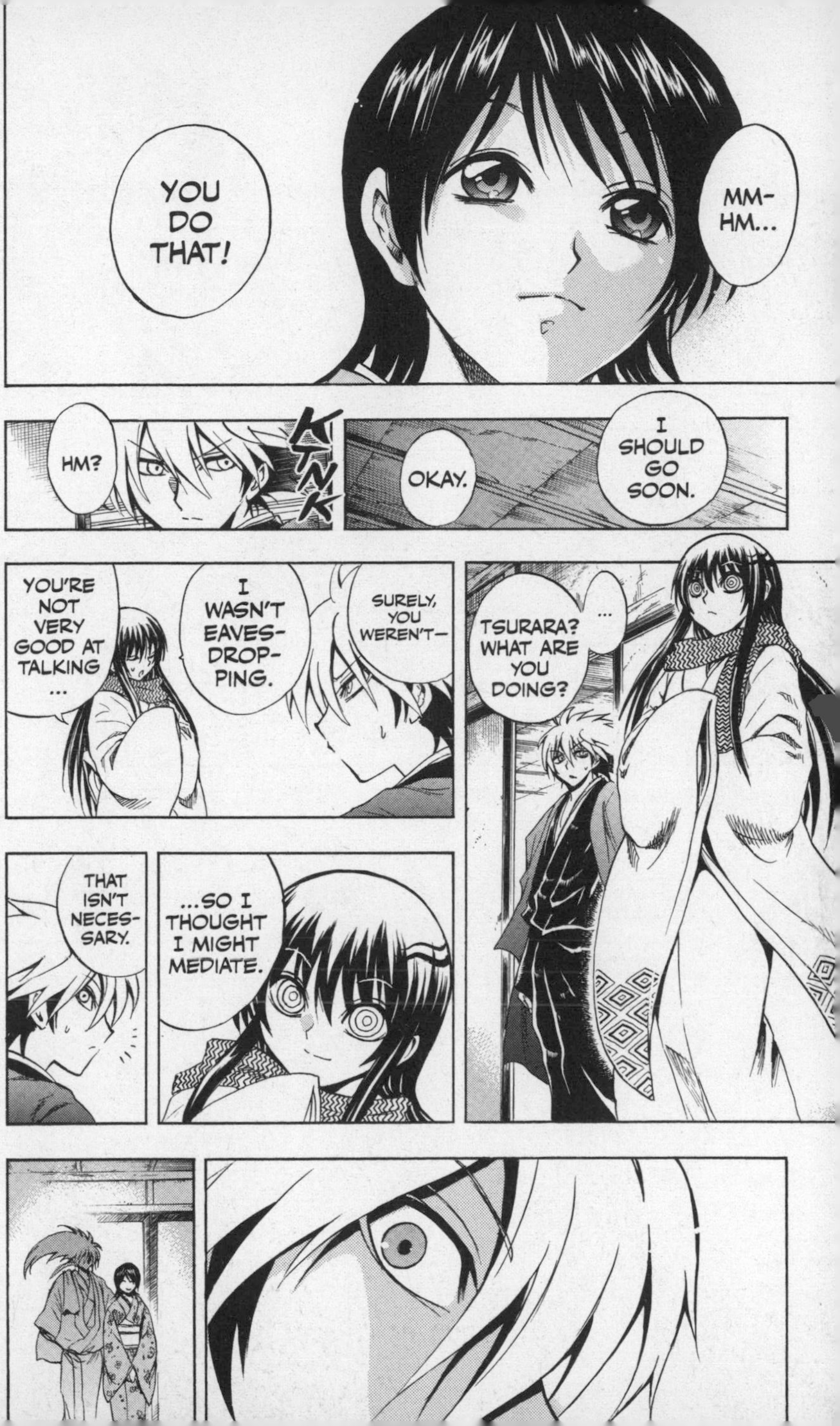
MM-HM...
YOU DO THAT!
I SHOULD GO SOON.
OKAY.
KTNK
HM?
...
TSURARA? WHAT ARE YOU DOING?
SURELY, YOU WEREN'T—
I WASN'T EAVES-DROPPING.
YOU'RE NOT VERY GOOD AT TALKING ...
...SO I THOUGHT I MIGHT MEDIATE.
THAT ISN'T NECES-SARY.

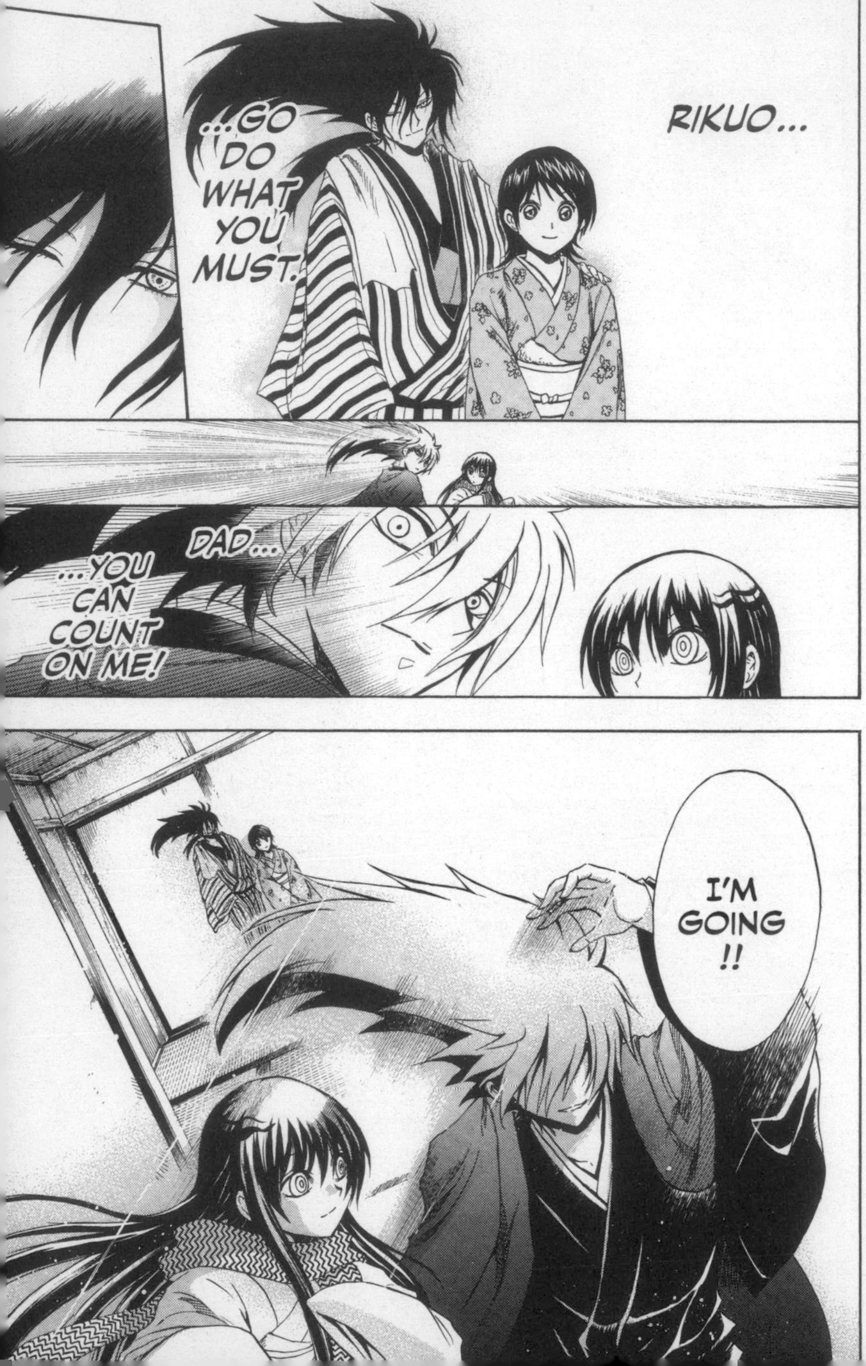
RIKUO...
...GO DO WHAT YOU MUST.
DAD...
...YOU CAN COUNT ON ME!
I'M GOING!!

KIYOTSUGU'S YOKAI BRAIN NO. 25

THE YURA-HAS-MESSY-HAIR-AND-MAMIRU-LIKES-CATS-AND-TSURARA-IS-SENSITIVE-TO-COLD-SO-RIKUO-IS-IN-TROUBLE SPECIAL

Q: I HAVE A QUESTION FOR YURA, WHO NEVER LIES. HOW MANY CENTIMETERS HIGH ARE THE HEELS ON RYUJI'S SANDALS? PLEASE TELL ME!! ALSO, HOW DOES YURA FARE ON APRIL FOOL'S DAY? *–KAIKUKAIN, TOKYO PREFECTURE*

YURA: MY BROTHER IS EXTRA KIND TO ME ON APRIL FOOL'S DAY. AND THAT SCARES ME. HIS SANDAL HEELS?! LET ME CHECK!! KYAH! SANDALS!! WAAAH!! KYOGEN?! GLARRRGH!!

RYUJI: IDIOT. I GOT YOU!

Q: THIS QUESTION IS FOR WAKANA! WHAT IS THE SECRET OF YOUR YOUTH? (I CAN'T BELIEVE YOU'RE 30!) *–EIGETSU, AICHI PREFECTURE*

WAKANA: IT MAY COME AS A SURPRISE, BUT THE SECRET IS TO BE WITH YOKAI! THEY DON'T AGE AND I JUST CAN'T BEAR TO LET THEM SHOW ME UP! ♡

Q: MAMIRU...HOW ARE YOUR INJURIES FROM NIJO CASTLE? *–WAKUI, CHIBA PREFECTURE*

MAMIRU: THEY SURE DID HURT.

Q: THE KEIKAIN SHIKIGAMI ARE GARO, TANRO AND MYAKO. IS MAMIRU THE ONLY ONE WHO LIKES CATS? *–YURA EXPO, CHIBA PREFECTURE*

YURA: YOU'RE RIGHT! WE ALL LIKE DOGS!

RYUJI: HOLD ON, YOU HAVE A DEER AND AN ELEPHANT, TOO. BESIDES, YOU MEAN WOLVES, NOT DOGS.

YURA: MY SHIKIGAMI INCLUDE A JAPANESE WOLF, IRISH ELK AND NAUMANN ELEPHANT. THEY'RE ALL EXTINCT ANIMALS. PRETTY UNUSUAL, HUH?

MAMIRU: ... (I DIDN'T KNOW THAT.)

Q: THE NURA CLAN IS FAIRLY STRONG ON AIR AND LAND. HOW ABOUT WATER? IS THERE ANYONE IN THE AFFILIATED CLANS TO SERVE AS A NAVAL FORCE? *–TADATERU IWASHITA, NAGANO PREFECTURE*

NURARIHYON: UM...COME TO THINK OF IT, THERE'S ONLY KAPPA. GYUKI CAN HANDLE THE SEA, THOUGH. MAYBE I'LL ASK UMIZATO TO JOIN SOMETIME.

Q: HERE'S A QUESTION FOR RIKUO! YOU TALK COOL AT NIGHT. IS THAT ON PURPOSE? OR DOES IT JUST COME NATURALLY? *–MEGANE OBAKA, TOKYO PREFECTURE*

YUKI: WELL?

RIKUO: I THINK...IT JUST COMES NATURALLY.

YURA: BUT IT SOUNDS UNNATURAL! IT CREEPS ME OUT!

RIKUO: I KNOW... YOU DON'T LIKE ME AT NIGHT...

Q: THIS QUESTION'S FOR TSURARA! I ALWAYS FEEL COLD. IN WINTER, MY FEET AND HANDS ARE LIKE DEATH. WHAT SHOULD I DO? *–TOCHISAKIOKA, HIROSHIMA PREFECTURE*

YUKI: TO BE HONEST, I HAVE THE SAME PROBLEM. I DON'T DO ANYTHING SPECIAL FOR IT, BUT YOU COULD WEAR GLOVES OR SOCKS. TAKE CARE!

Q: I HAVE A QUESTION FOR YURA! WHY DOES YOUR HAIR GET LONGER WHEN YOU DO BANISH INTO THE ABYSS YURA MAX: REVISED? *–MEDAKA BOSOZOKU*

YURA: ACCORDING TO MY BROTHER, MY HAIR GETS MESSY IF I DO SOMETHING FORBIDDEN, BUT THAT CAN'T BE TRUE! I DON'T KNOW THE REAL REASON, BUT MAYBE IT'S SIMILAR TO WHAT HAPPENS WHEN YOKAI USE FEAR.

Q: WHAT DID ALL THE TONO YOKAI DO WHILE ITAKU WAS IN TOKYO? AND WHAT DID THEY THINK OF ITAKU GOING TO TOKYO? *–WIND, KANAGAWA PREFECTURE*

AWASHIMA: WE JUST TRAINED LIKE USUAL. YOU KNOW HOW ITAKU WORRIES OVER EVERY LITTLE THING!

Q: THIS ONE'S FOR THE WHOLE NURA CLAN! WHAT WAS THE WORST MISCHIEF RIKUO GOT INTO WHEN HE WAS LITTLE? *–RINRIN, GUNMA PREFECTURE*

TSURARA: HANGING ME UPSIDE DOWN.

KUBINAGHI: USING MY HEAD TO PLAY CATCH WITH AOTABO.

KUROTABO: USING MY UMBRELLA AS A FISHBOWL.

AOTABO: MAKING A PITFALL TRAP ON THE SECOND FLOOR.

KEJORO: STEPPING ON THE HEM OF MY KIMONO ALL THE TIME.

RIKUO: THAT'S ENOUGH!!

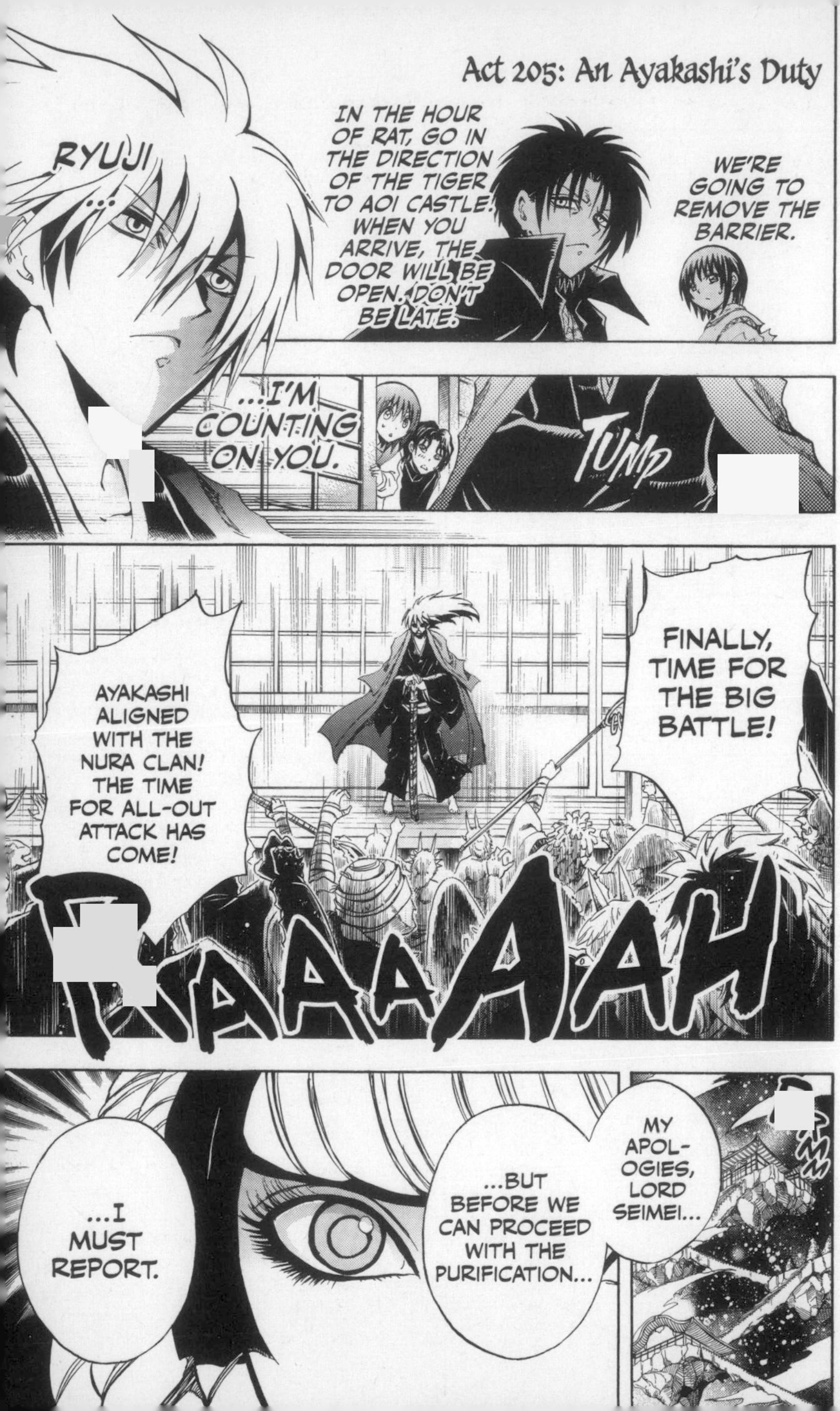
Act 205: An Ayakashi's Duty
WE'RE GOING TO REMOVE THE BARRIER.
IN THE HOUR OF RAT, GO IN THE DIRECTION OF THE TIGER TO AOI CASTLE. WHEN YOU ARRIVE, THE DOOR WILL BE OPEN. DON'T BE LATE.
TUMP
...I'M COUNTING ON YOU.
RYUJI...
FINALLY, TIME FOR THE BIG BATTLE!
AYAKASHI ALIGNED WITH THE NURA CLAN! THE TIME FOR ALL-OUT ATTACK HAS COME!
RAAAAAH
MY APOLOGIES, LORD SEIMEI...
...BUT BEFORE WE CAN PROCEED WITH THE PURIFICATION...
...I MUST REPORT.

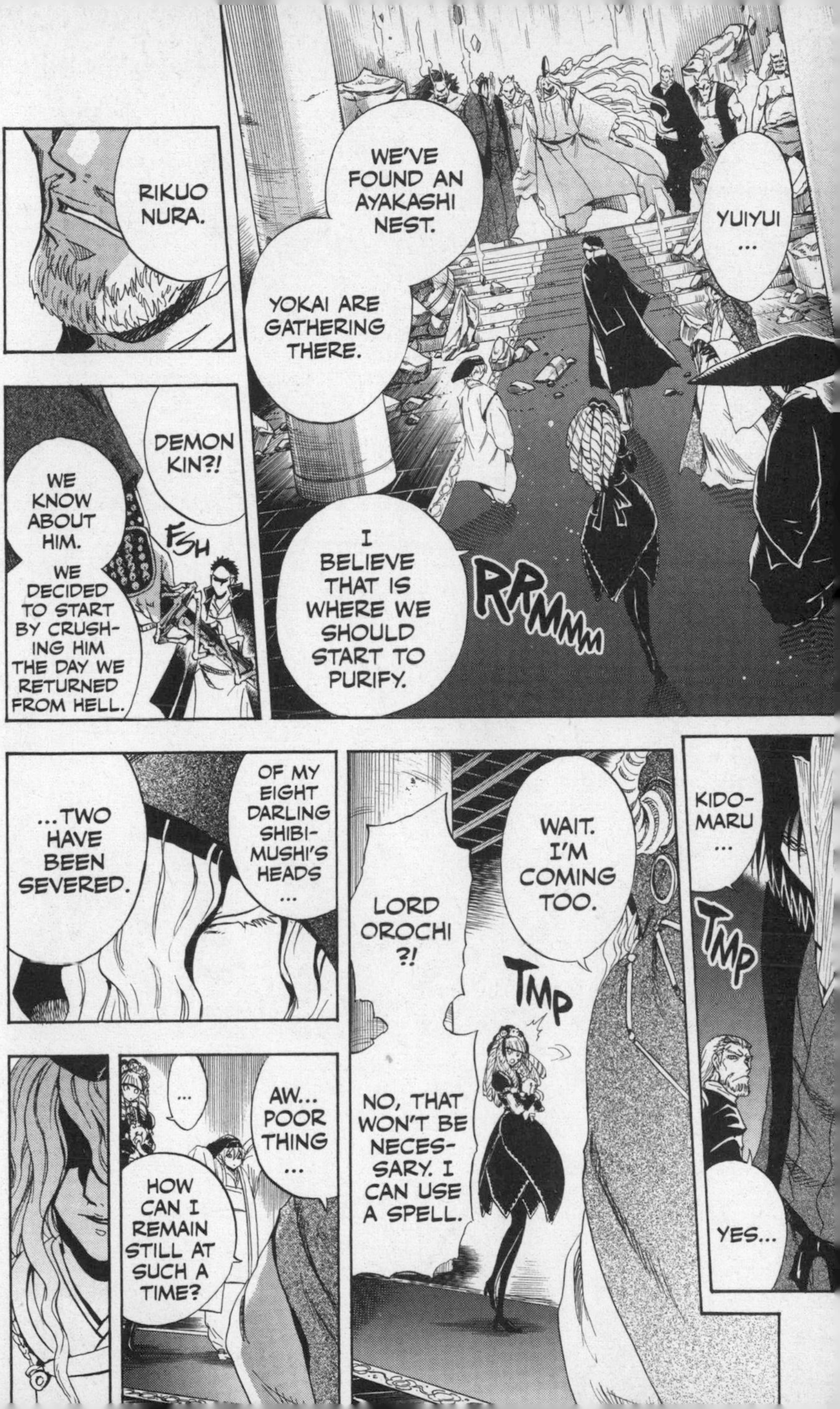
YUIYUI ...
WE'VE FOUND AN AYAKASHI NEST.
YOKAI ARE GATHERING THERE.
I BELIEVE THAT IS WHERE WE SHOULD START TO PURIFY.
RRMMM
RIKUO NURA.
DEMON KIN?!
WE KNOW ABOUT HIM.
FSH
WE DECIDED TO START BY CRUSHING HIM THE DAY WE RETURNED FROM HELL.
KIDO-MARU ...
TMP
YES...
WAIT. I'M COMING TOO.
LORD OROCHI ?!
TMP
NO, THAT WON'T BE NECESSARY. I CAN USE A SPELL.
OF MY EIGHT DARLING SHIBI-MUSHI'S HEADS ...
...TWO HAVE BEEN SEVERED.
AW... POOR THING ...
...
HOW CAN I REMAIN STILL AT SUCH A TIME?

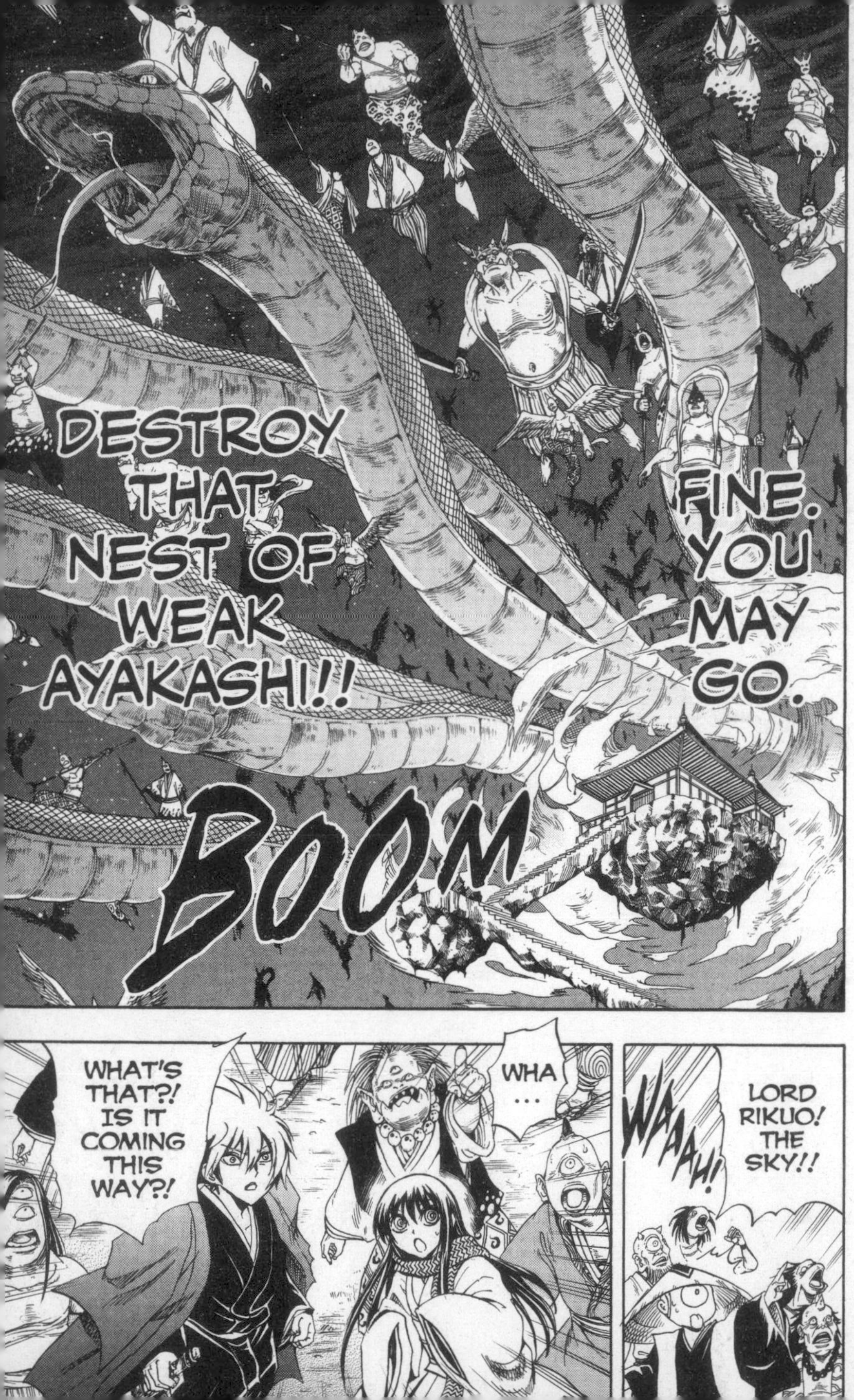
FINE. YOU MAY GO.
DESTROY THAT NEST OF WEAK AYAKASHI!!
BOOM
LORD RIKUO! THE SKY!!
WAAAAH!
WHA...
WHAT'S THAT?! IS IT COMING THIS WAY?!

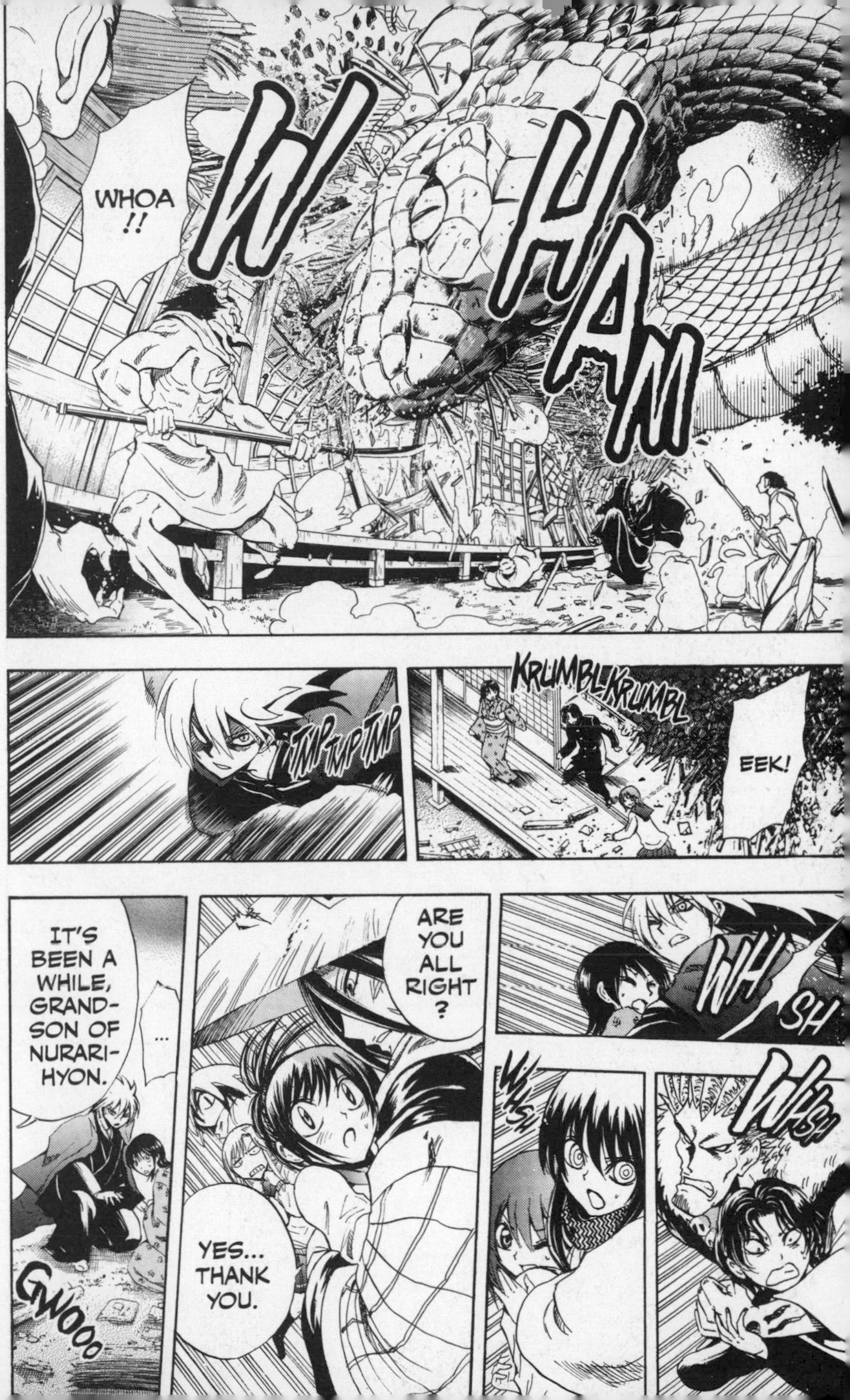
WHAM
WHOA!!
KRUMBL KRUMBL
EEK!
TMP TMP TMP
WHSH
WHSH
WHSH
ARE YOU ALL RIGHT?
YES... THANK YOU.
IT'S BEEN A WHILE, GRANDSON OF NURARIHYON.
...
GWOOO

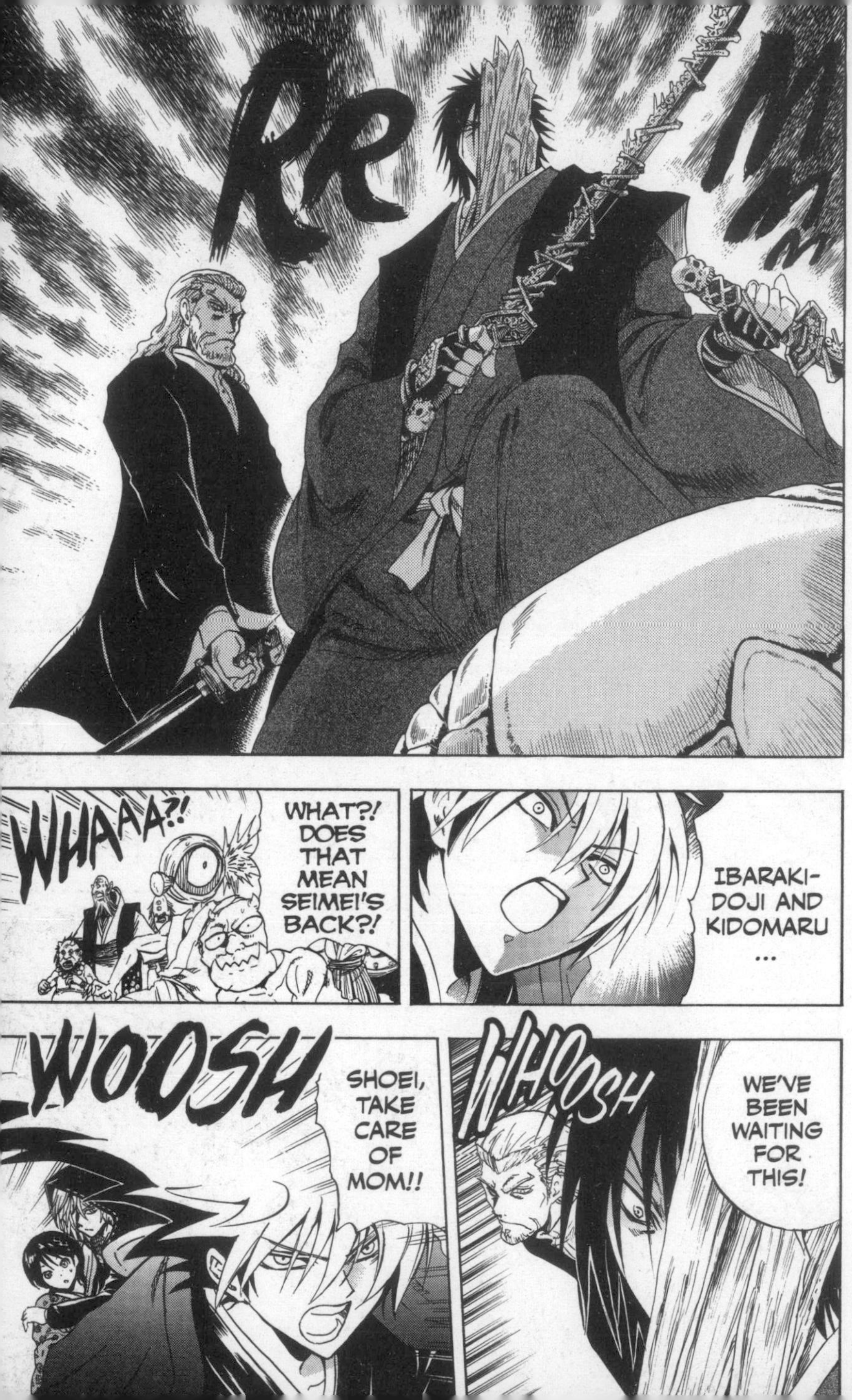
IBARAKI-DOJI AND KIDOMARU ...
WHAT?! DOES THAT MEAN SEIMEI'S BACK?!
WHAAA?!
WHOOSH
WE'VE BEEN WAITING FOR THIS!
WOOSH
SHOEI, TAKE CARE OF MOM!!

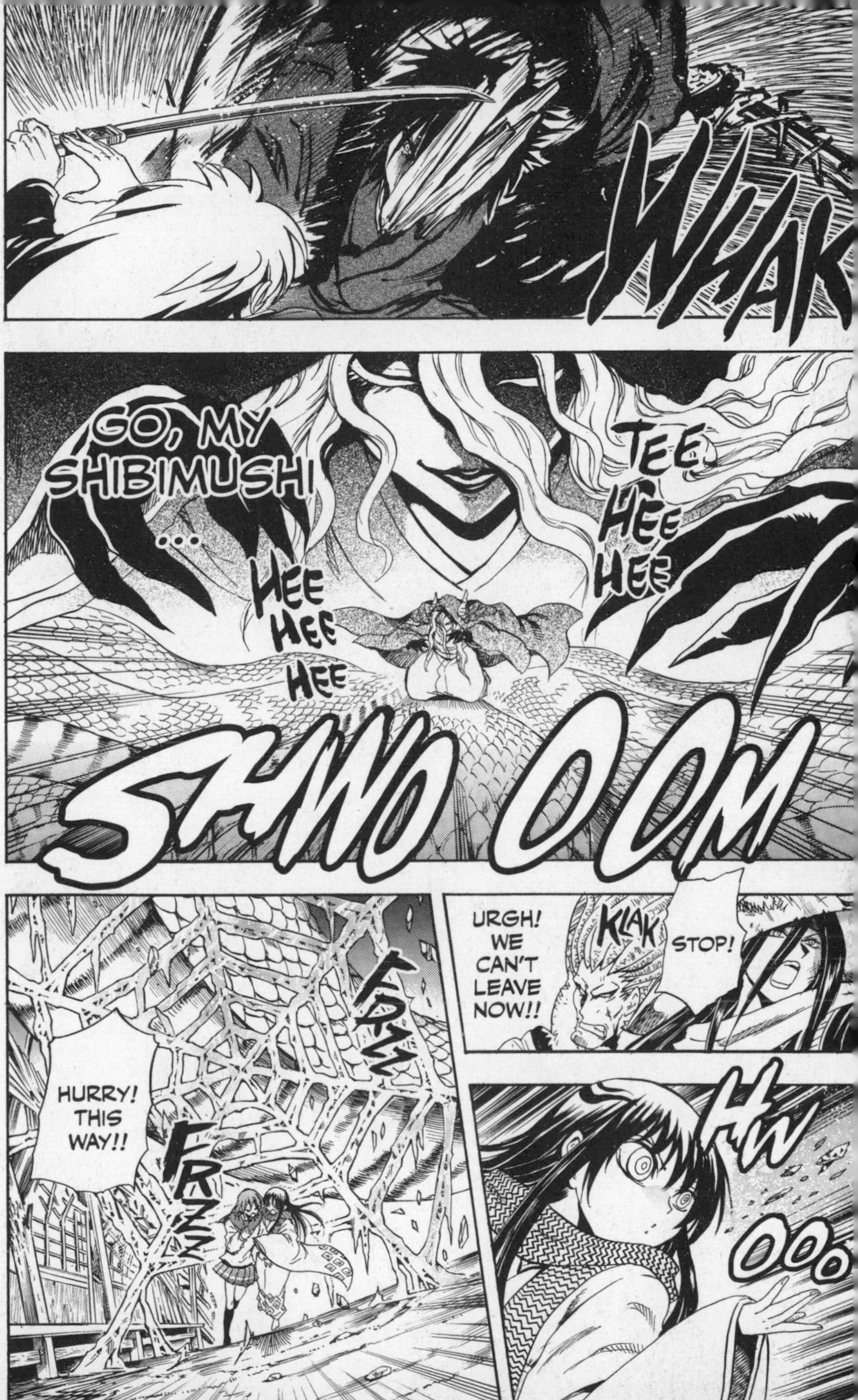
WHAK
TEE HEE HEE
GO, MY SHIBIMUSHI...
HEE HEE HEE
SHWOOOM
STOP!
KLAK
URGH! WE CAN'T LEAVE NOW!!
HW
OOO
FZZZ
HURRY! THIS WAY!!
FRZZZ

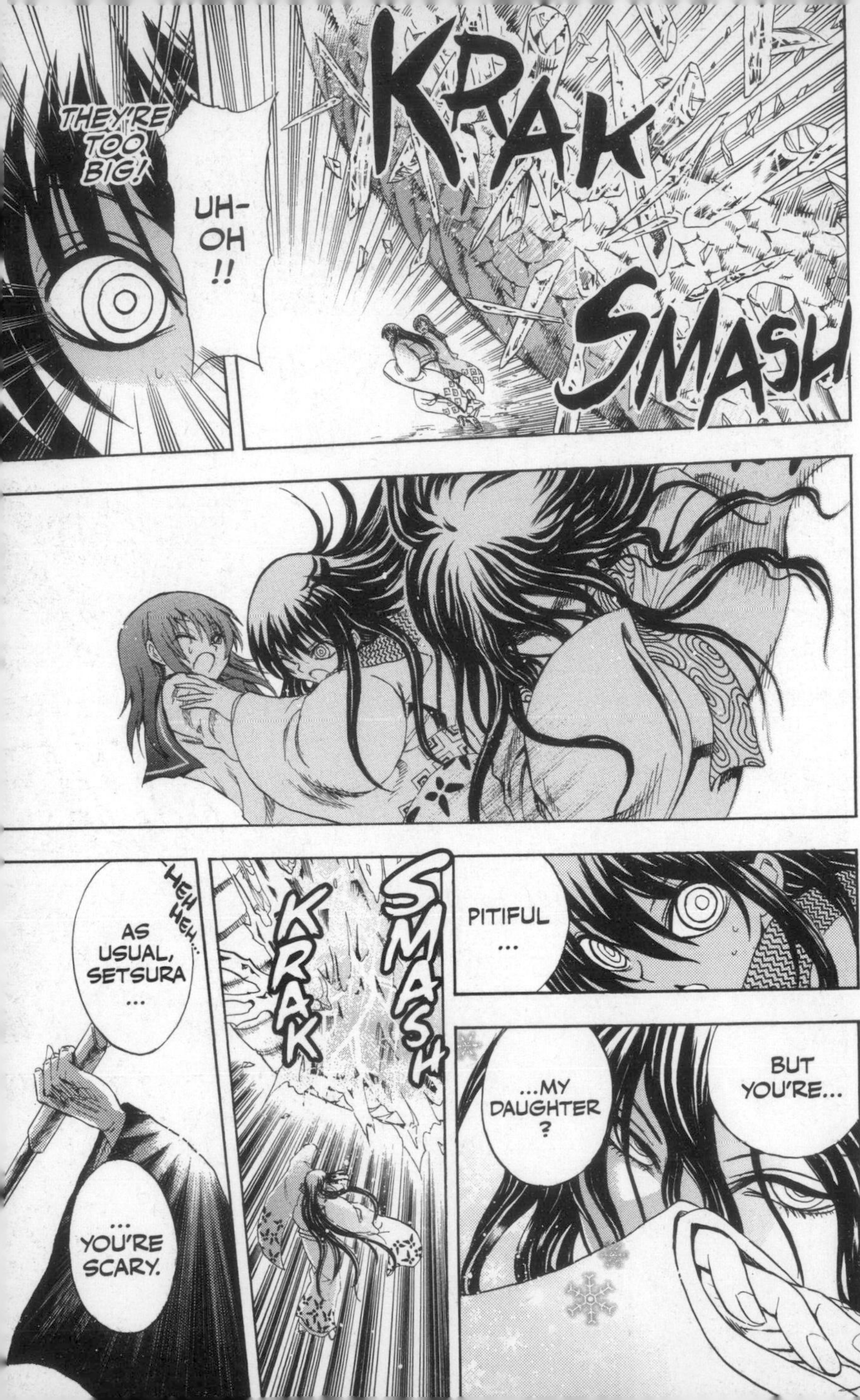
KRAK
SMASH
UH-OH !!
THEY'RE TOO BIG!
PITIFUL ...
BUT YOU'RE...
...MY DAUGHTER ?
SMASH
KRAK
HEH HEH...
AS USUAL, SETSURA ...
... YOU'RE SCARY.

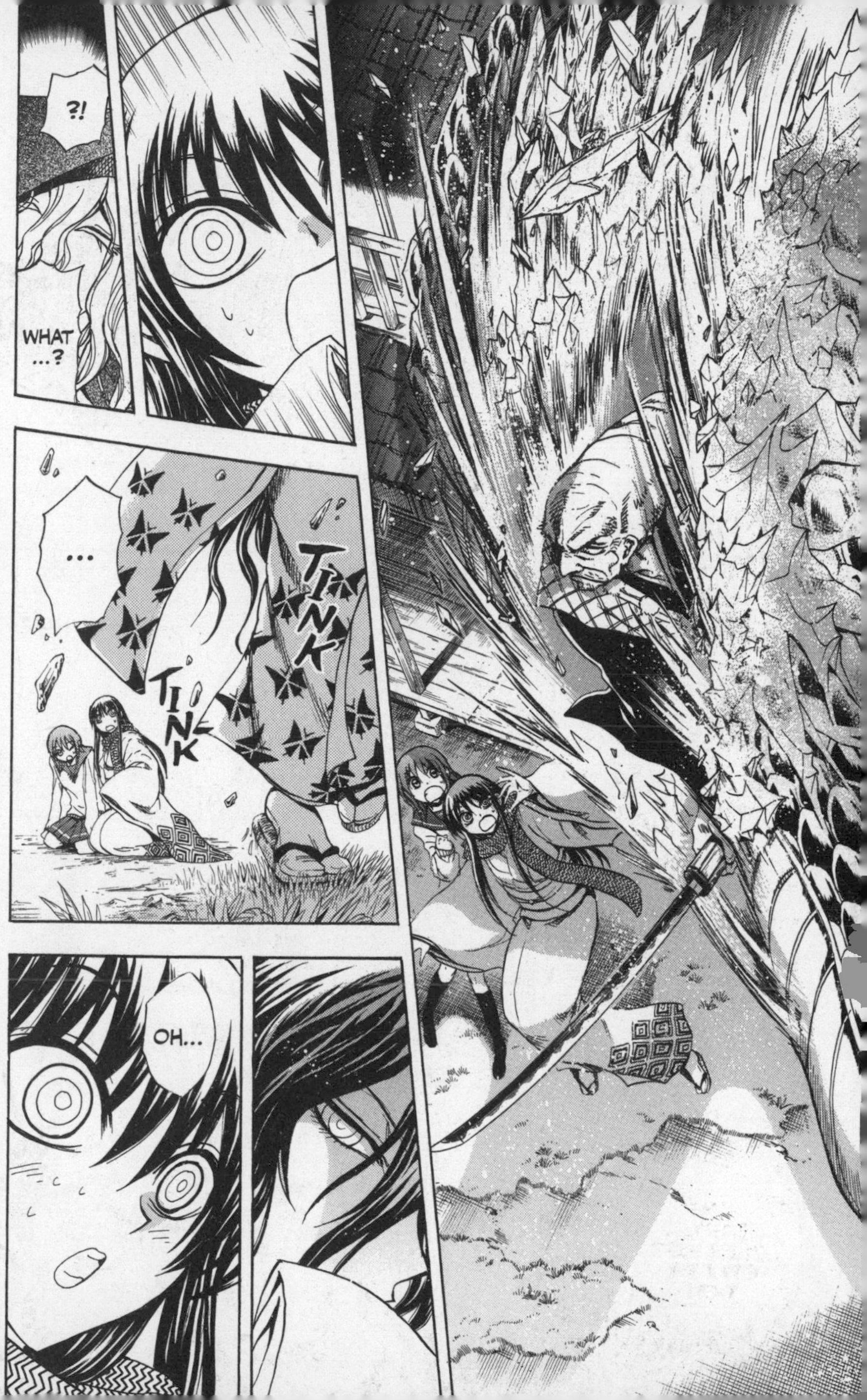
?!
WHAT ...?
...
TINK
TINK
OH...

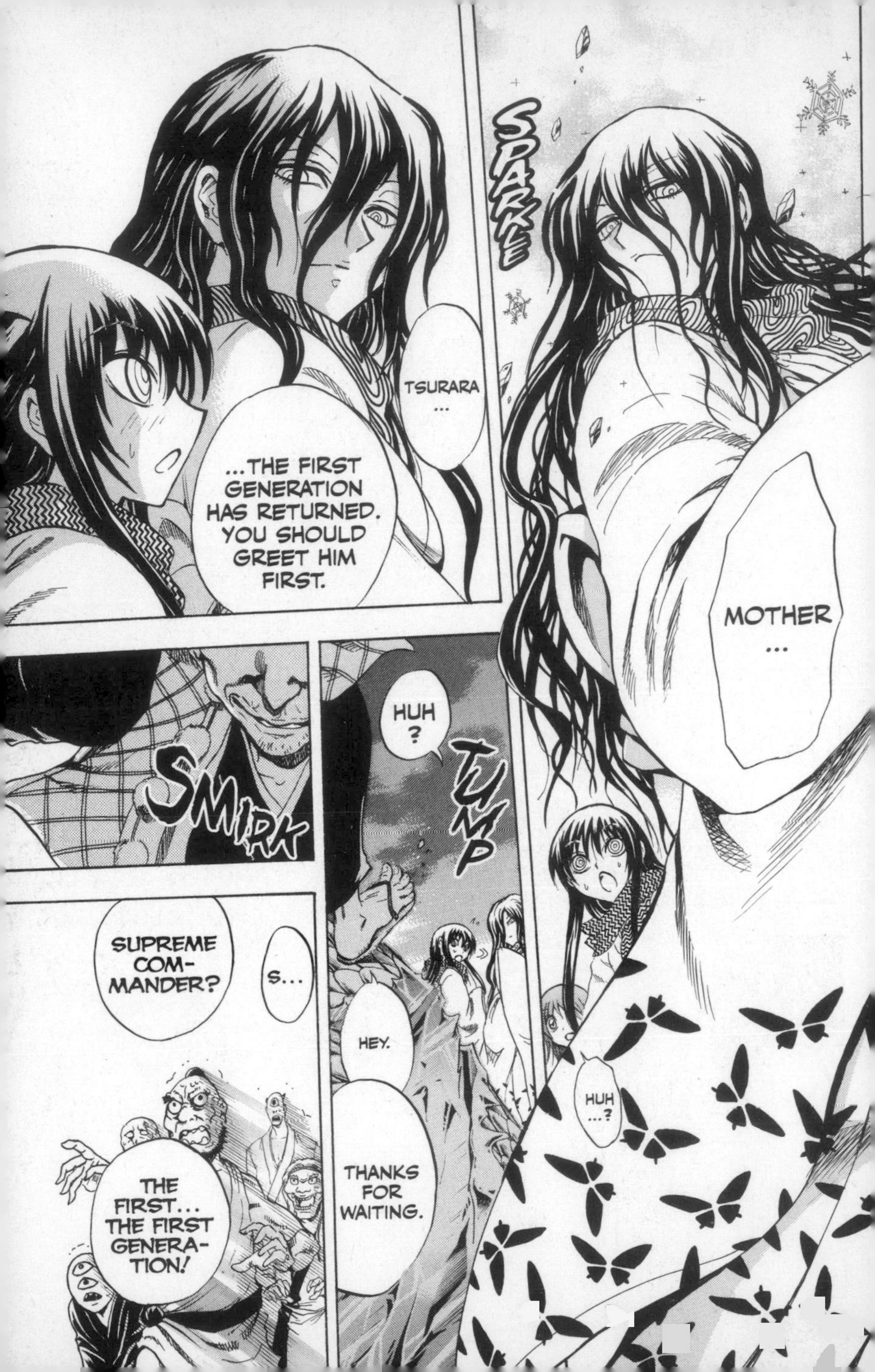
SPARKLE
MOTHER...
TSURARA...
...THE FIRST GENERATION HAS RETURNED. YOU SHOULD GREET HIM FIRST.
HUH?
TUMP
SMIRK
HUH...?
HEY.
THANKS FOR WAITING.
S...
SUPREME COMMANDER?
THE FIRST... THE FIRST GENERATION!

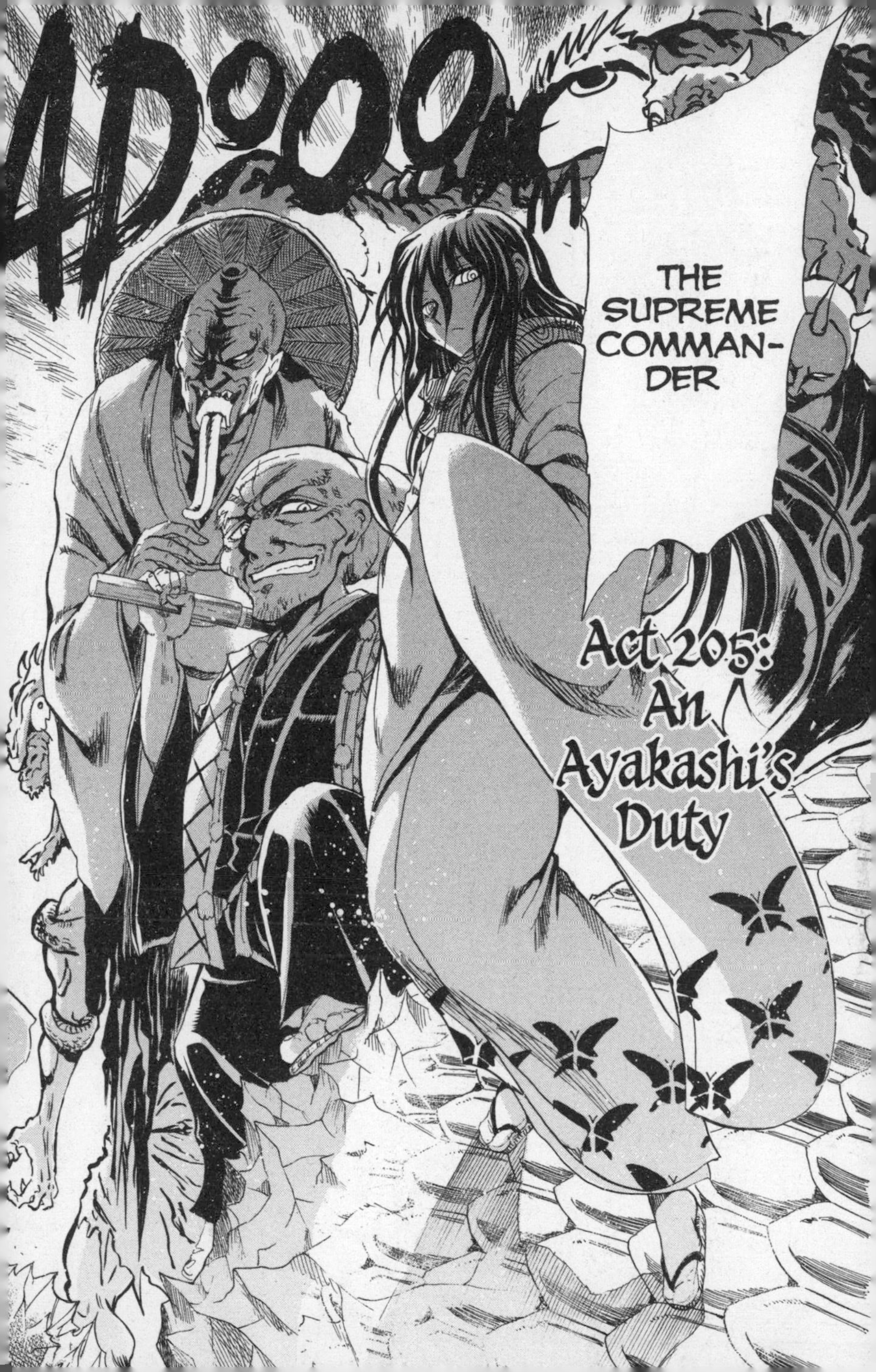
THE SUPREME COMMAN-DER
Act 205: An Ayakashi's Duty

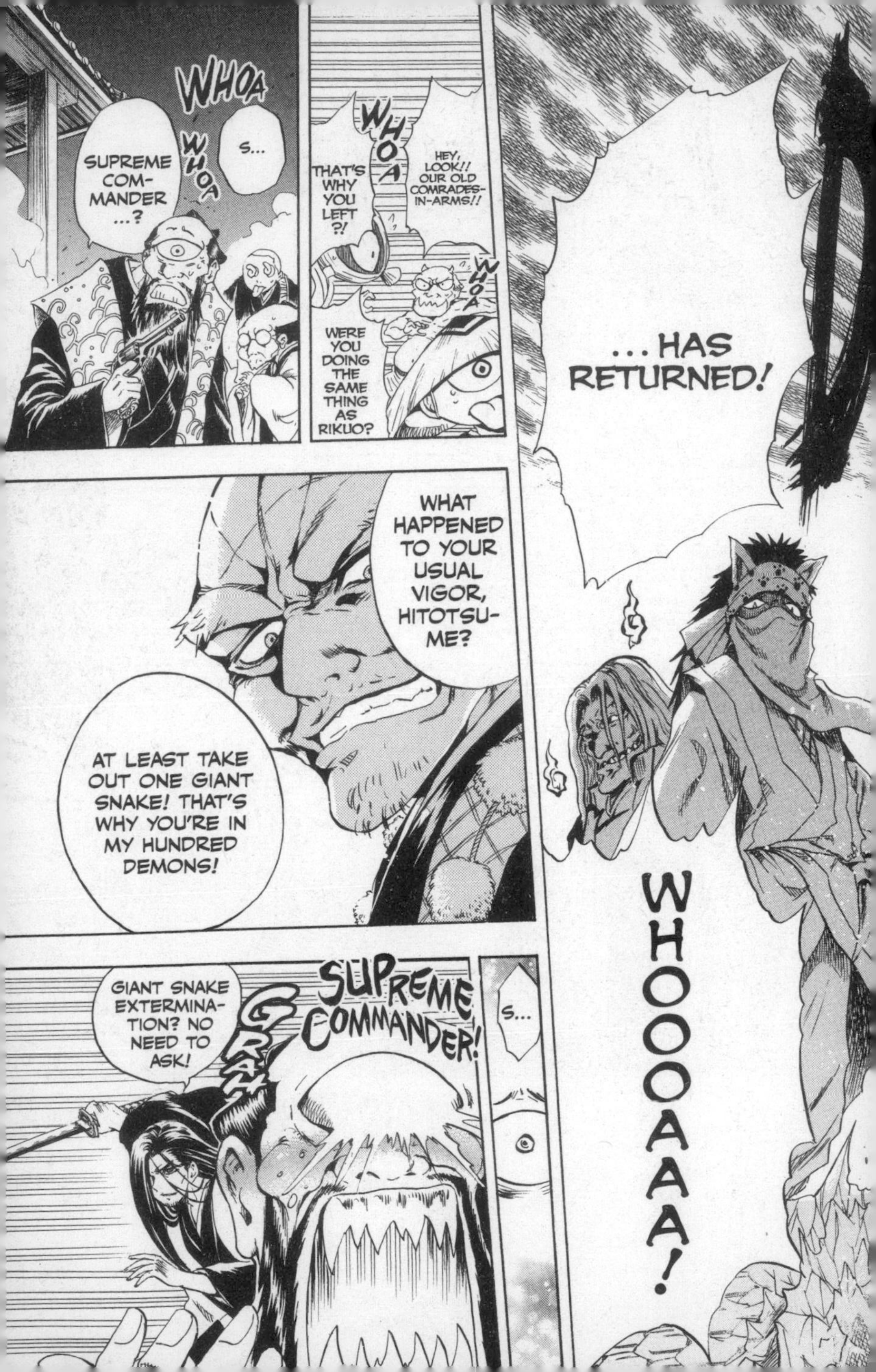
...HAS RETURNED!
WHOOOAAA!
HEY, LOOK!! OUR OLD COMRADES-IN-ARMS!!
WHOA
THAT'S WHY YOU LEFT ?!
WHOA
WHOA
WERE YOU DOING THE SAME THING AS RIKUO?
WHOA
S...
WHOA
SUPREME COMMANDER ...?
WHAT HAPPENED TO YOUR USUAL VIGOR, HITOTSUME?
AT LEAST TAKE OUT ONE GIANT SNAKE! THAT'S WHY YOU'RE IN MY HUNDRED DEMONS!
S...
SUPREME COMMANDER!
GRAH
GIANT SNAKE EXTERMINATION? NO NEED TO ASK!

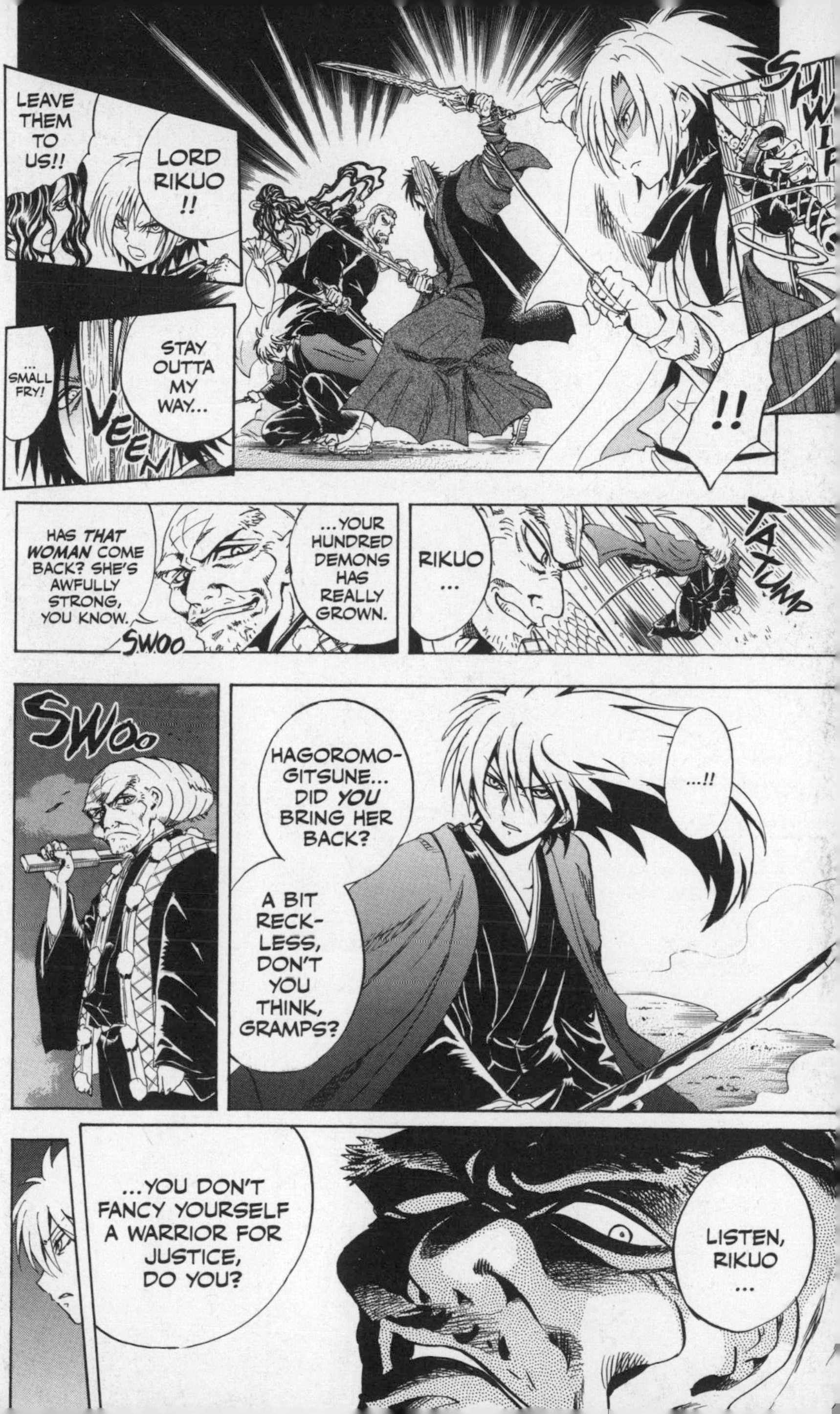
SHWIP
LORD RIKUO !!
LEAVE THEM TO US!!
!!
STAY OUTTA MY WAY...
...SMALL FRY!
VEEEN
TATUMP
RIKUO ...
...YOUR HUNDRED DEMONS HAS REALLY GROWN.
HAS *THAT WOMAN* COME BACK? SHE'S AWFULLY STRONG, YOU KNOW.
SWOO
...!!
HAGOROMO-GITSUNE... DID *YOU* BRING HER BACK?
A BIT RECK-LESS, DON'T YOU THINK, GRAMPS?
SWOO
LISTEN, RIKUO ...
...YOU DON'T FANCY YOURSELF A WARRIOR FOR JUSTICE, DO YOU?

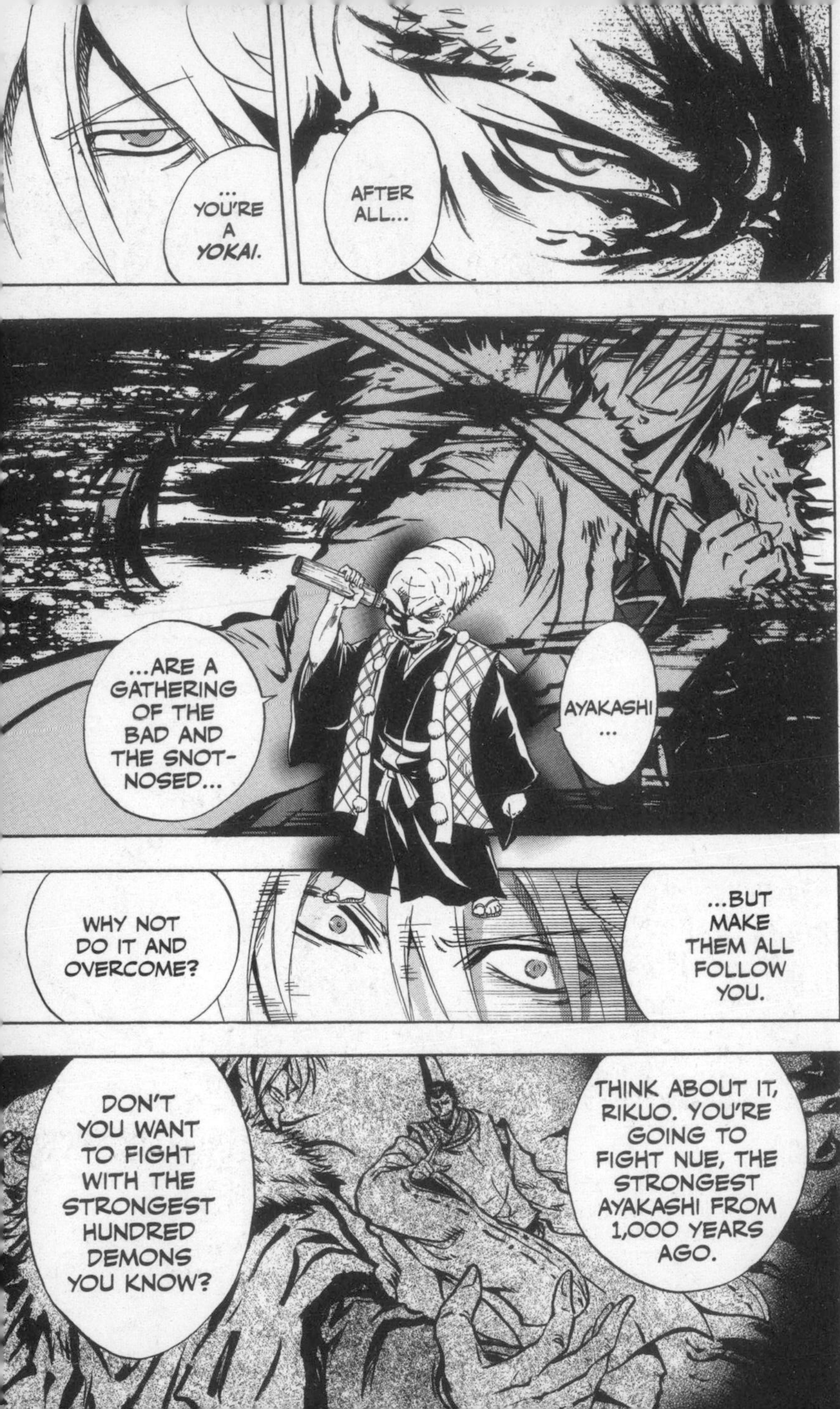
AFTER ALL...
...YOU'RE A *YOKAI*.
AYAKASHI ...
...ARE A GATHERING OF THE BAD AND THE SNOT-NOSED...
...BUT MAKE THEM ALL FOLLOW YOU.
WHY NOT DO IT AND OVERCOME?
THINK ABOUT IT, RIKUO. YOU'RE GOING TO FIGHT NUE, THE STRONGEST AYAKASHI FROM 1,000 YEARS AGO.
DON'T YOU WANT TO FIGHT WITH THE STRONGEST HUNDRED DEMONS YOU KNOW?

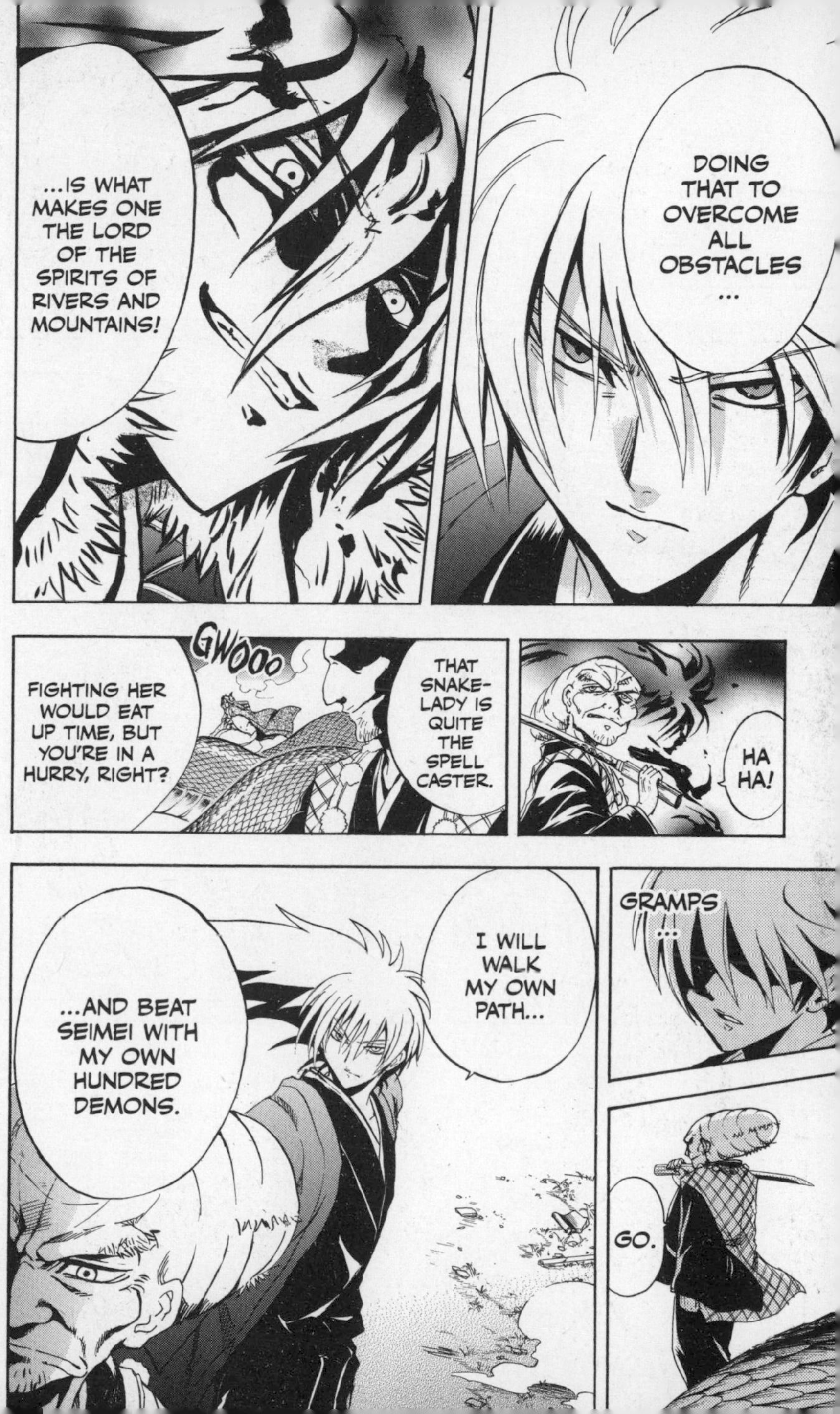
DOING THAT TO OVERCOME ALL OBSTACLES...
...IS WHAT MAKES ONE THE LORD OF THE SPIRITS OF RIVERS AND MOUNTAINS!
HA HA!
THAT SNAKE-LADY IS QUITE THE SPELL CASTER.
GWOOO
FIGHTING HER WOULD EAT UP TIME, BUT YOU'RE IN A HURRY, RIGHT?
GRAMPS...
GO.
I WILL WALK MY OWN PATH...
...AND BEAT SEIMEI WITH MY OWN HUNDRED DEMONS.

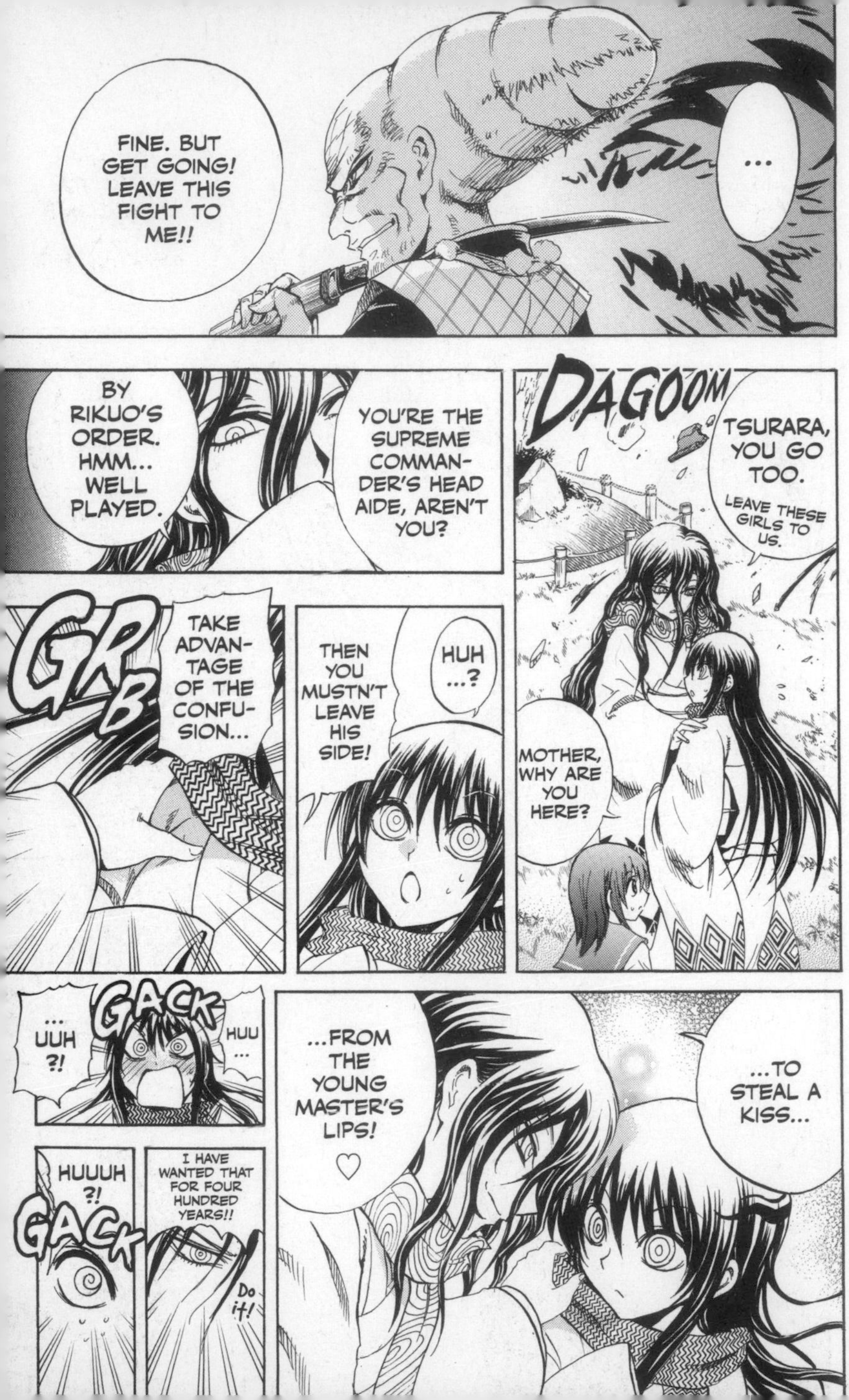
...
FINE. BUT GET GOING! LEAVE THIS FIGHT TO ME!!
DAGOOM
TSURARA, YOU GO TOO.
LEAVE THESE GIRLS TO US.
MOTHER, WHY ARE YOU HERE?
YOU'RE THE SUPREME COMMANDER'S HEAD AIDE, AREN'T YOU?
BY RIKUO'S ORDER. HMM... WELL PLAYED.
HUH ...?
THEN YOU MUSTN'T LEAVE HIS SIDE!
GRB
TAKE ADVANTAGE OF THE CONFUSION...
...TO STEAL A KISS...
...FROM THE YOUNG MASTER'S LIPS! ♡
HUU ...
GACK
... UUH ?!
I HAVE WANTED THAT FOR FOUR HUNDRED YEARS!!
Do it!
HUUUH ?!
GACK

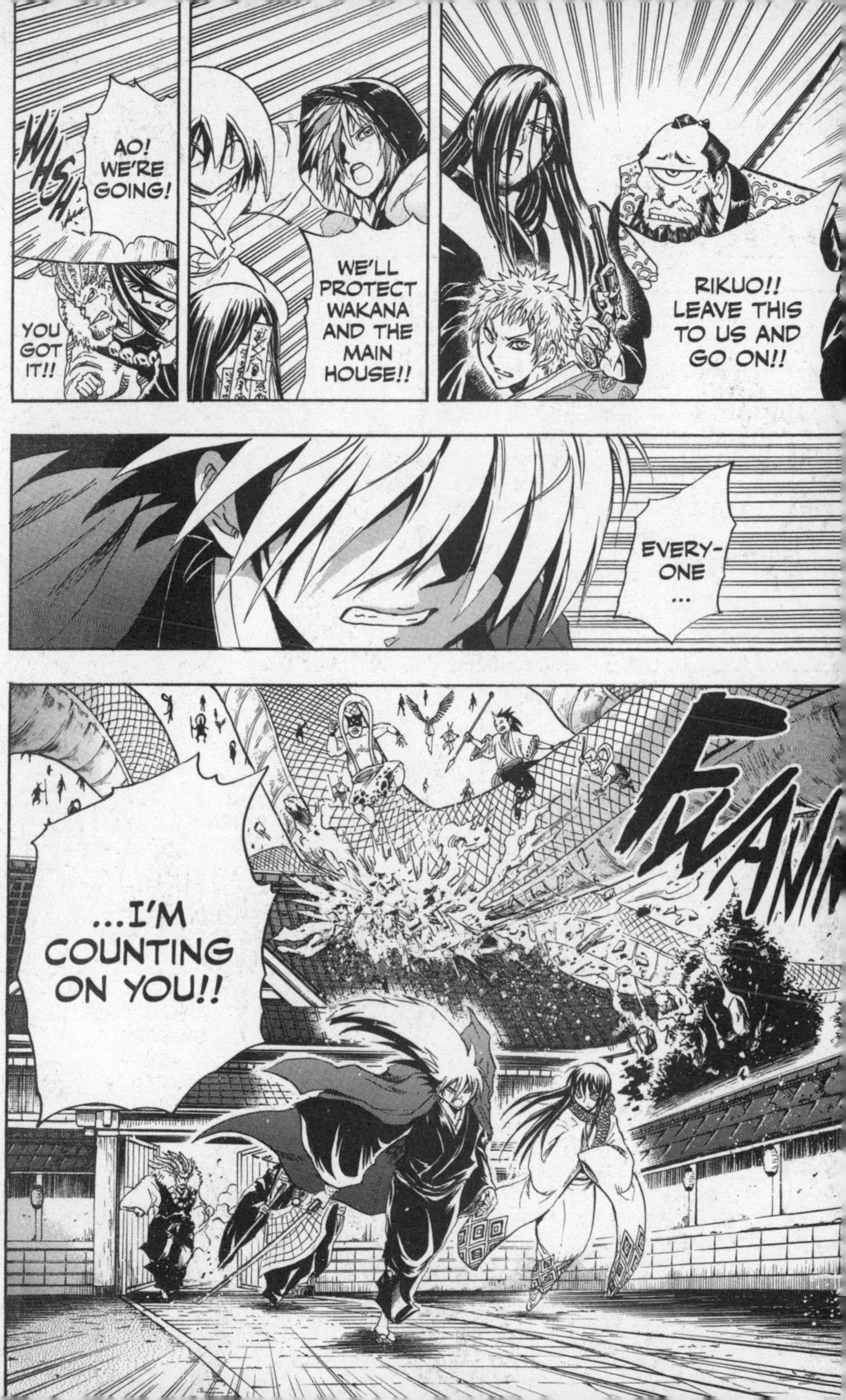
RIKUO!! LEAVE THIS TO US AND GO ON!!
WE'LL PROTECT WAKANA AND THE MAIN HOUSE!!
AO! WE'RE GOING!
YOU GOT IT!!
EVERY-ONE ...
...I'M COUNTING ON YOU!!

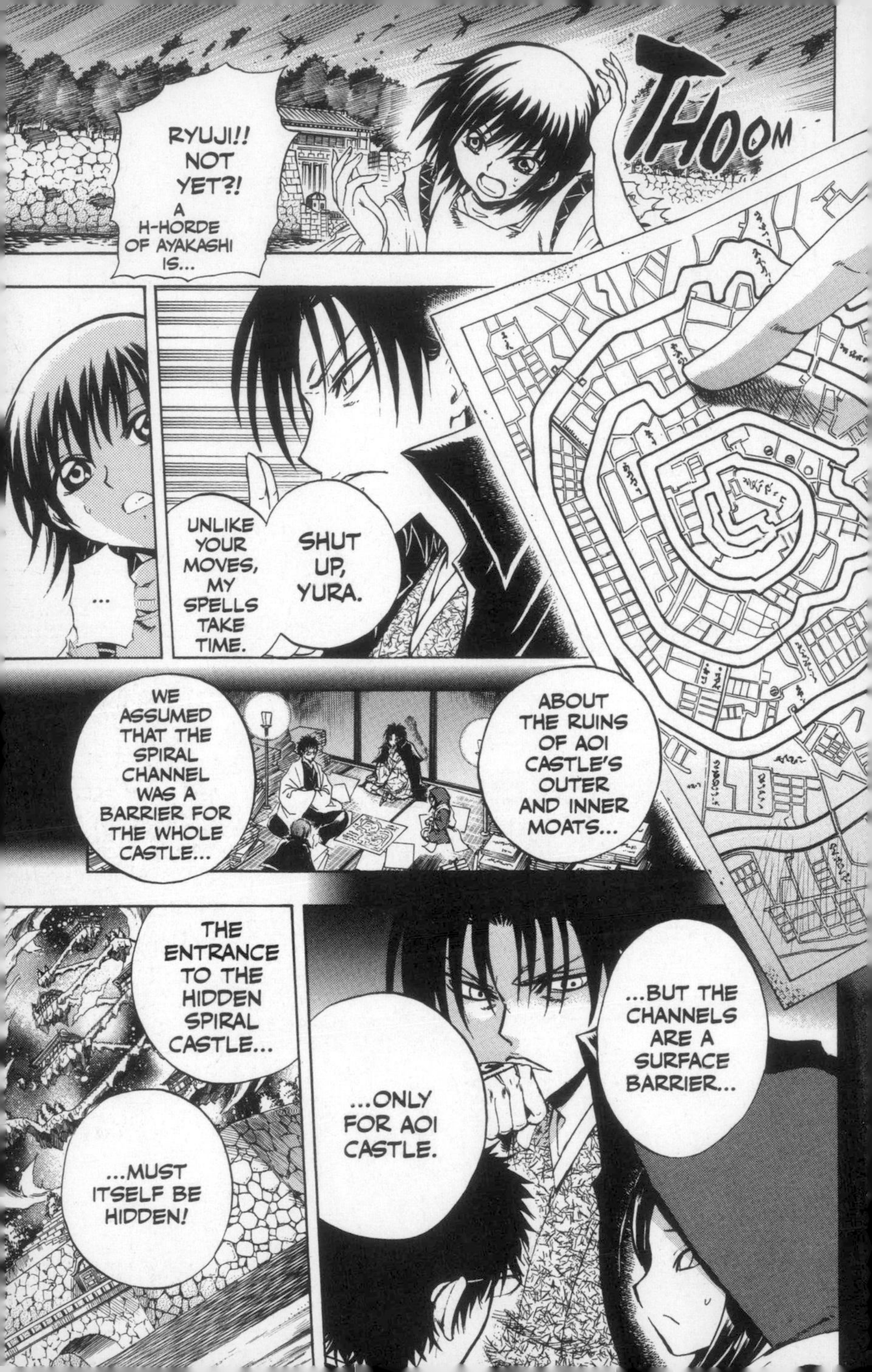
THOOM
RYUJI!! NOT YET?! A H-HORDE OF AYAKASHI IS...
SHUT UP, YURA.
UNLIKE YOUR MOVES, MY SPELLS TAKE TIME.
...
ABOUT THE RUINS OF AOI CASTLE'S OUTER AND INNER MOATS...
WE ASSUMED THAT THE SPIRAL CHANNEL WAS A BARRIER FOR THE WHOLE CASTLE...
...BUT THE CHANNELS ARE A SURFACE BARRIER...
...ONLY FOR AOI CASTLE.
THE ENTRANCE TO THE HIDDEN SPIRAL CASTLE...
...MUST ITSELF BE HIDDEN!

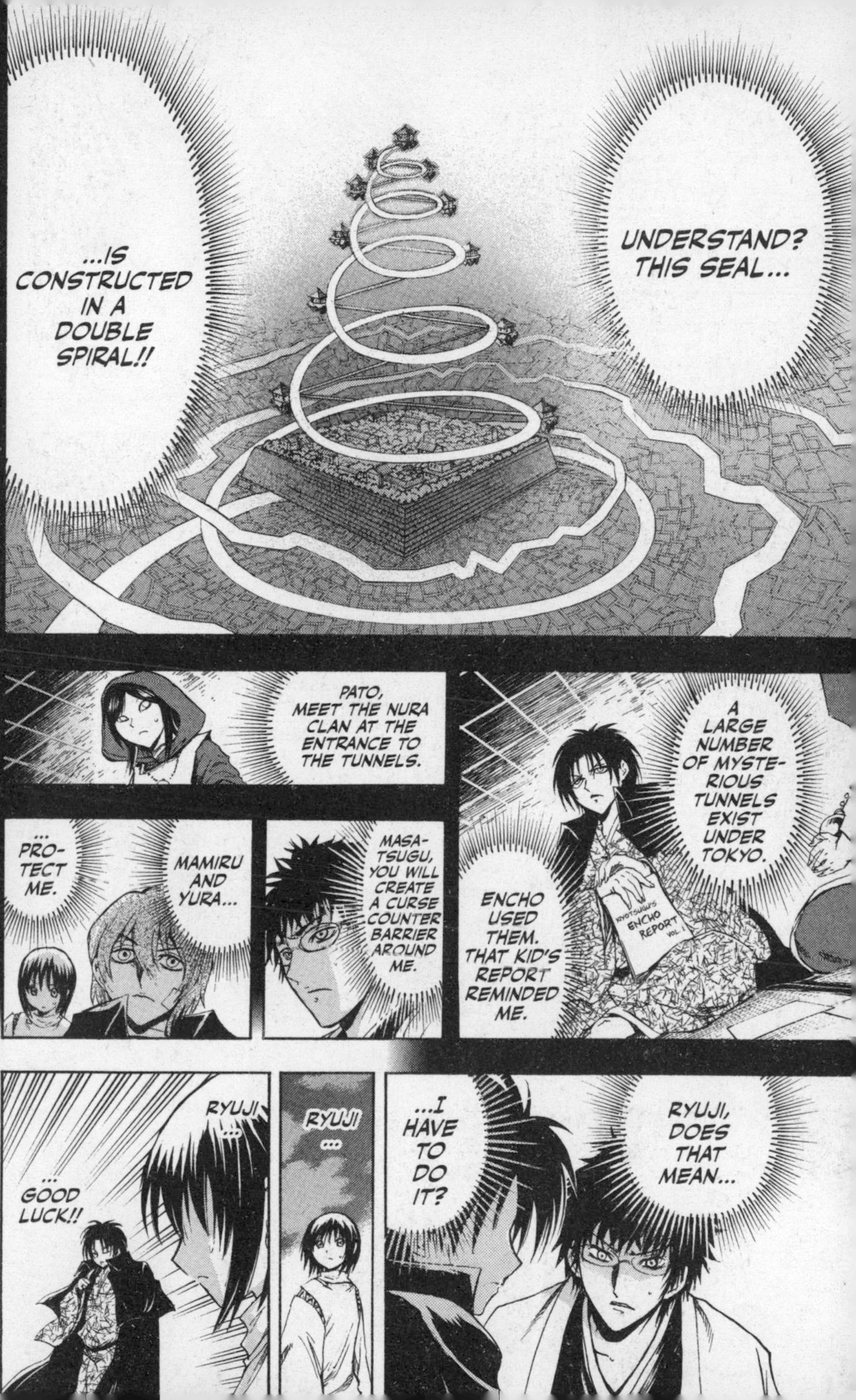
UNDERSTAND? THIS SEAL...
...IS CONSTRUCTED IN A DOUBLE SPIRAL!!
A LARGE NUMBER OF MYSTE-RIOUS TUNNELS EXIST UNDER TOKYO.
ENCHO USED THEM. THAT KID'S REPORT REMINDED ME.
KIYOTSUGU'S ENCHO REPORT VOL. 1
PATO, MEET THE NURA CLAN AT THE ENTRANCE TO THE TUNNELS.
MASA-TSUGU, YOU WILL CREATE A CURSE COUNTER BARRIER AROUND ME.
MAMIRU AND YURA...
...PROTECT ME.
RYUJI, DOES THAT MEAN...
...I HAVE TO DO IT?
RYUJI ...
RYUJI ...
...GOOD LUCK!!

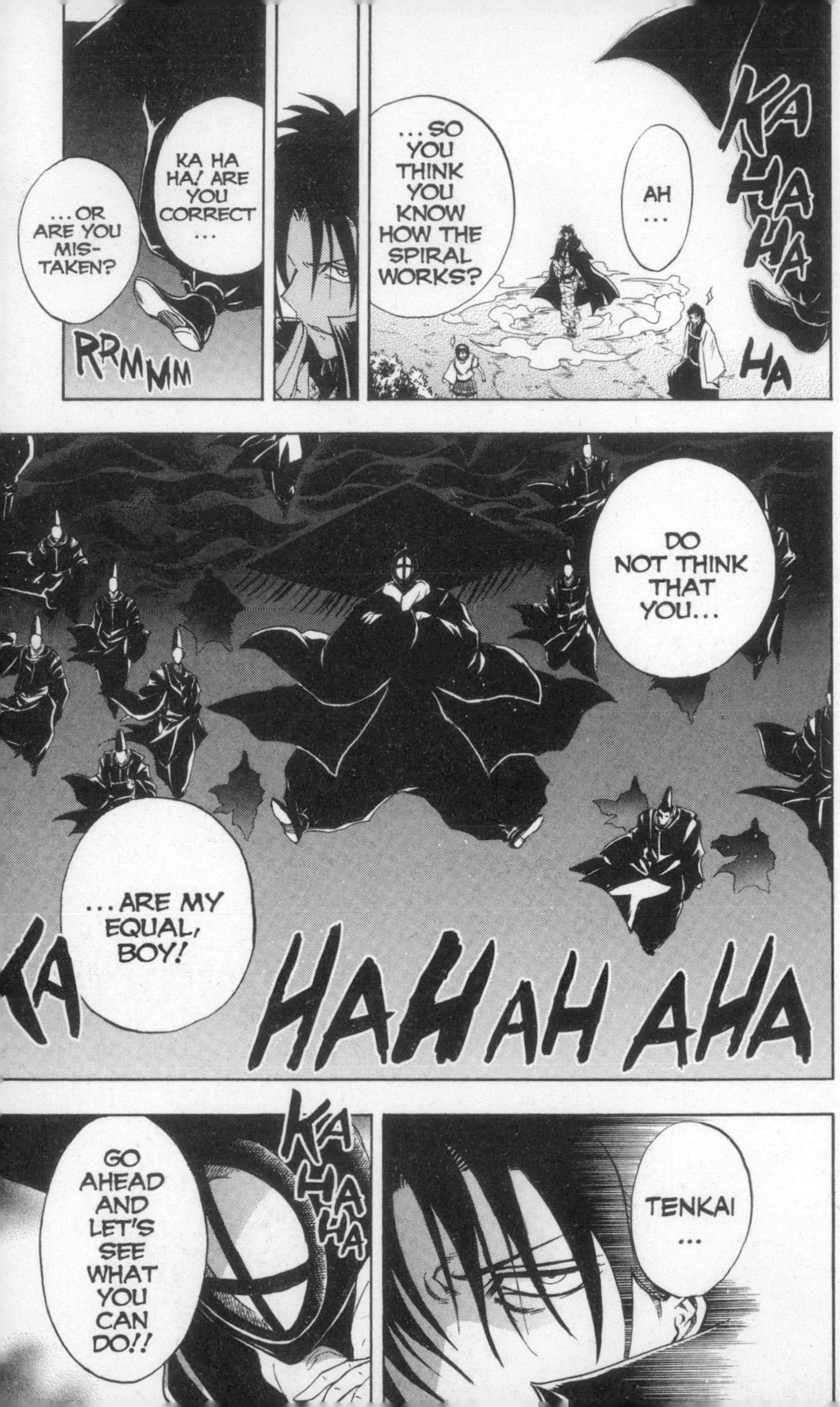
KA HA HA HA
HA
AH ...
...SO YOU THINK YOU KNOW HOW THE SPIRAL WORKS?
KA HA HA! ARE YOU CORRECT ...
...OR ARE YOU MIS-TAKEN?
RRMMMM
DO NOT THINK THAT YOU...
...ARE MY EQUAL, BOY!
KA HAHAH AHA
TENKAI ...
KA HA HA HA
GO AHEAD AND LET'S SEE WHAT YOU CAN DO!!

NURA: RISE OF THE YOKAI CLAN

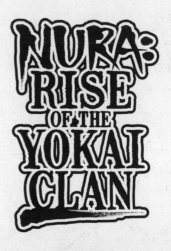

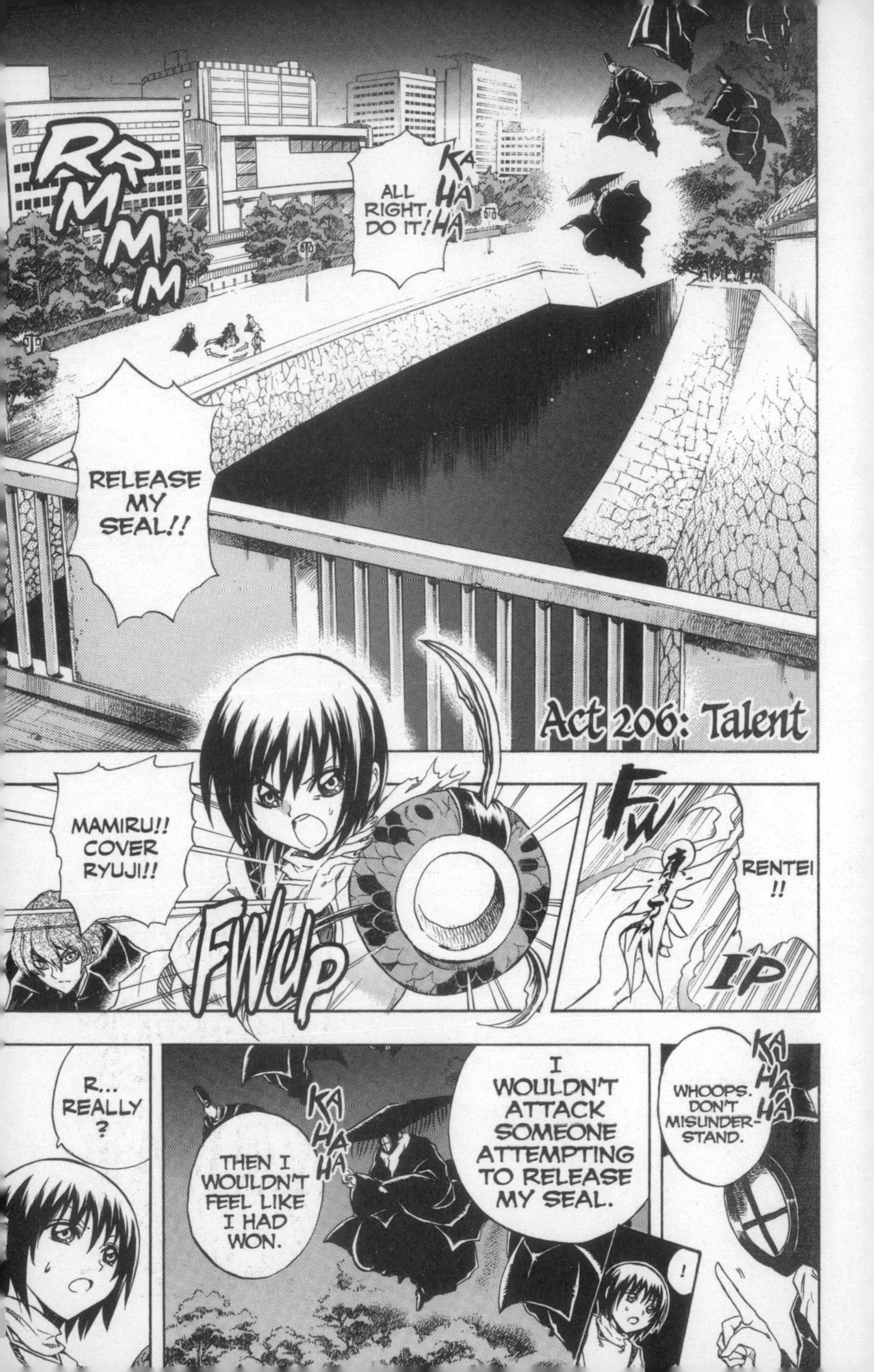
KA HA HA
ALL RIGHT, DO IT!
RRMMM
RELEASE MY SEAL!!
Act 206: Talent
FW
RENTEI!!
IP
MAMIRU!! COVER RYUJI!!
FWUP
KA HA HA
WHOOPS. DON'T MISUNDER-STAND.
!
I WOULDN'T ATTACK SOMEONE ATTEMPTING TO RELEASE MY SEAL.
KA HA HA
THEN I WOULDN'T FEEL LIKE I HAD WON.
R... REALLY?

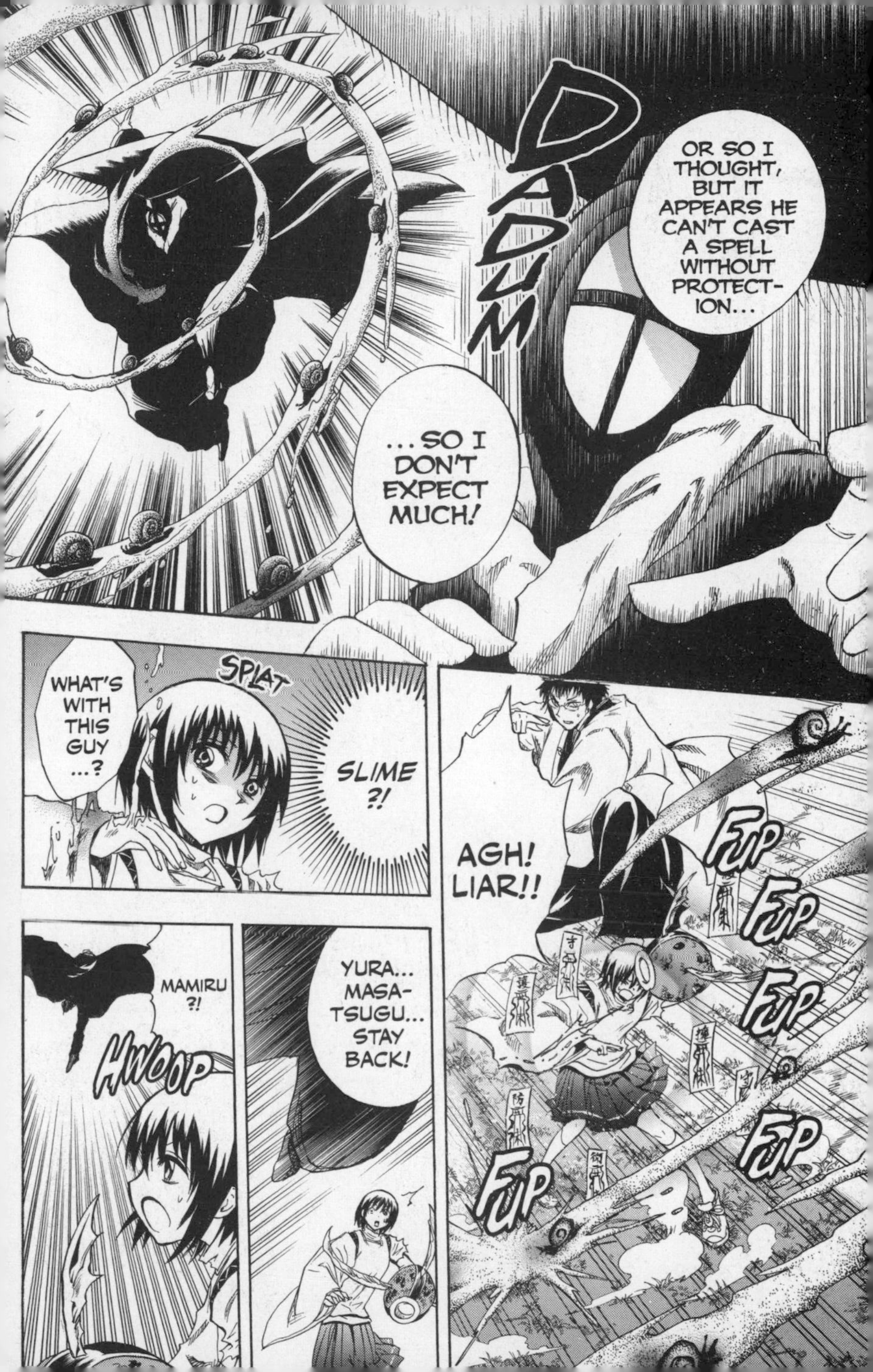
DADUM
OR SO I THOUGHT, BUT IT APPEARS HE CAN'T CAST A SPELL WITHOUT PROTECTION...
...SO I DON'T EXPECT MUCH!
AGH! LIAR!!
FUP
FUP
FUP
FUP
FUP
SPLAT
SLIME?!
WHAT'S WITH THIS GUY...?
YURA... MASATSUGU... STAY BACK!
MAMIRU?!
HWOOP

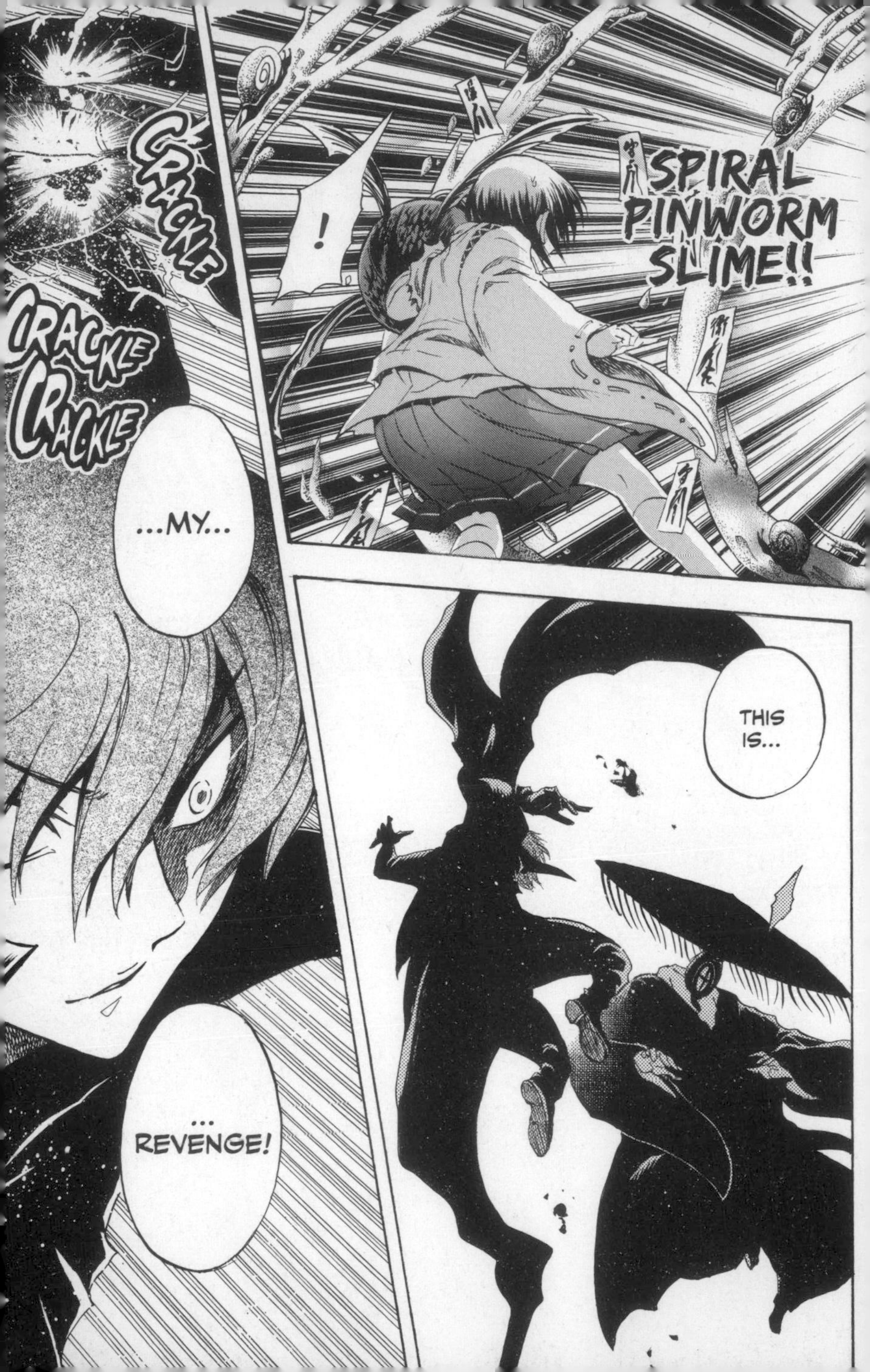
SPIRAL PINWORM SLIME!!
!
THIS IS...
CRACKLE
CRACKLE CRACKLE
...MY...
... REVENGE!

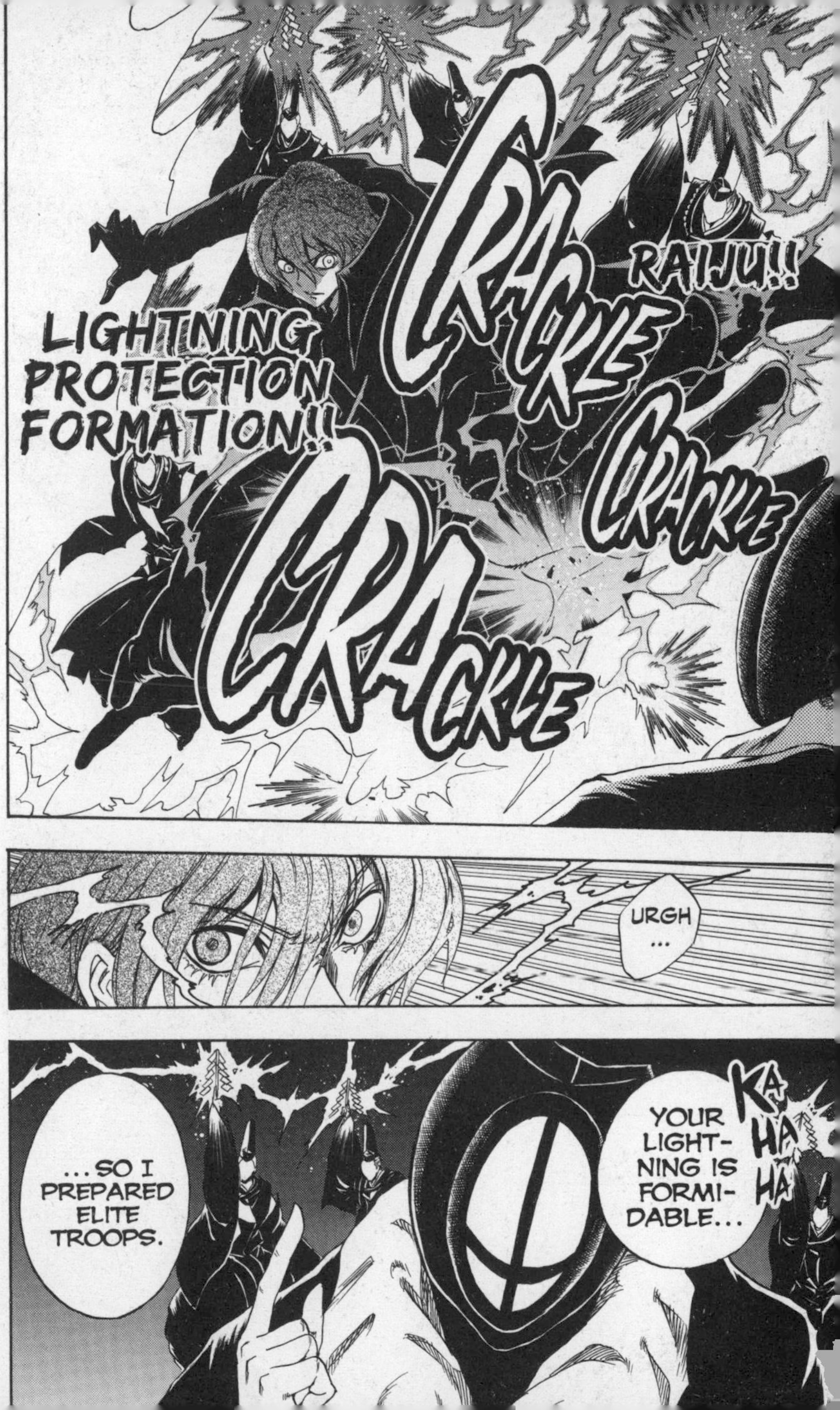
RAIJU!!
CRACKLE CRACKLE
CRACKLE
LIGHTNING PROTECTION FORMATION!!
CRACKLE
URGH ...
KA HA HA
YOUR LIGHTNING IS FORMIDABLE...
...SO I PREPARED ELITE TROOPS.

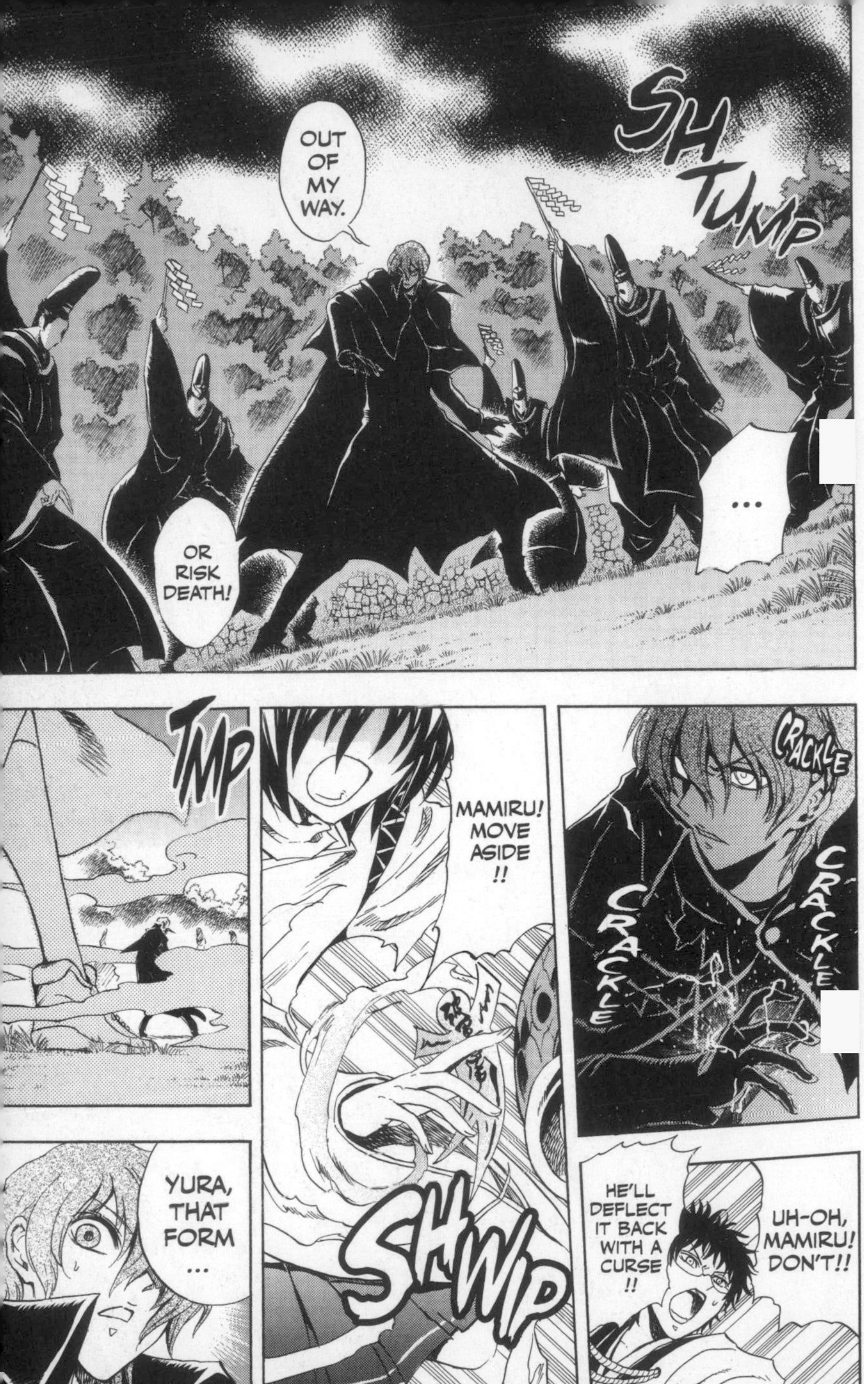
SH TUMP
OUT OF MY WAY.
...
OR RISK DEATH!
CRACKLE
CRACKLE
CRACKLE
UH-OH, MAMIRU! DON'T!!
HE'LL DEFLECT IT BACK WITH A CURSE!!
MAMIRU! MOVE ASIDE!!
SHWIP
TMP
YURA, THAT FORM...

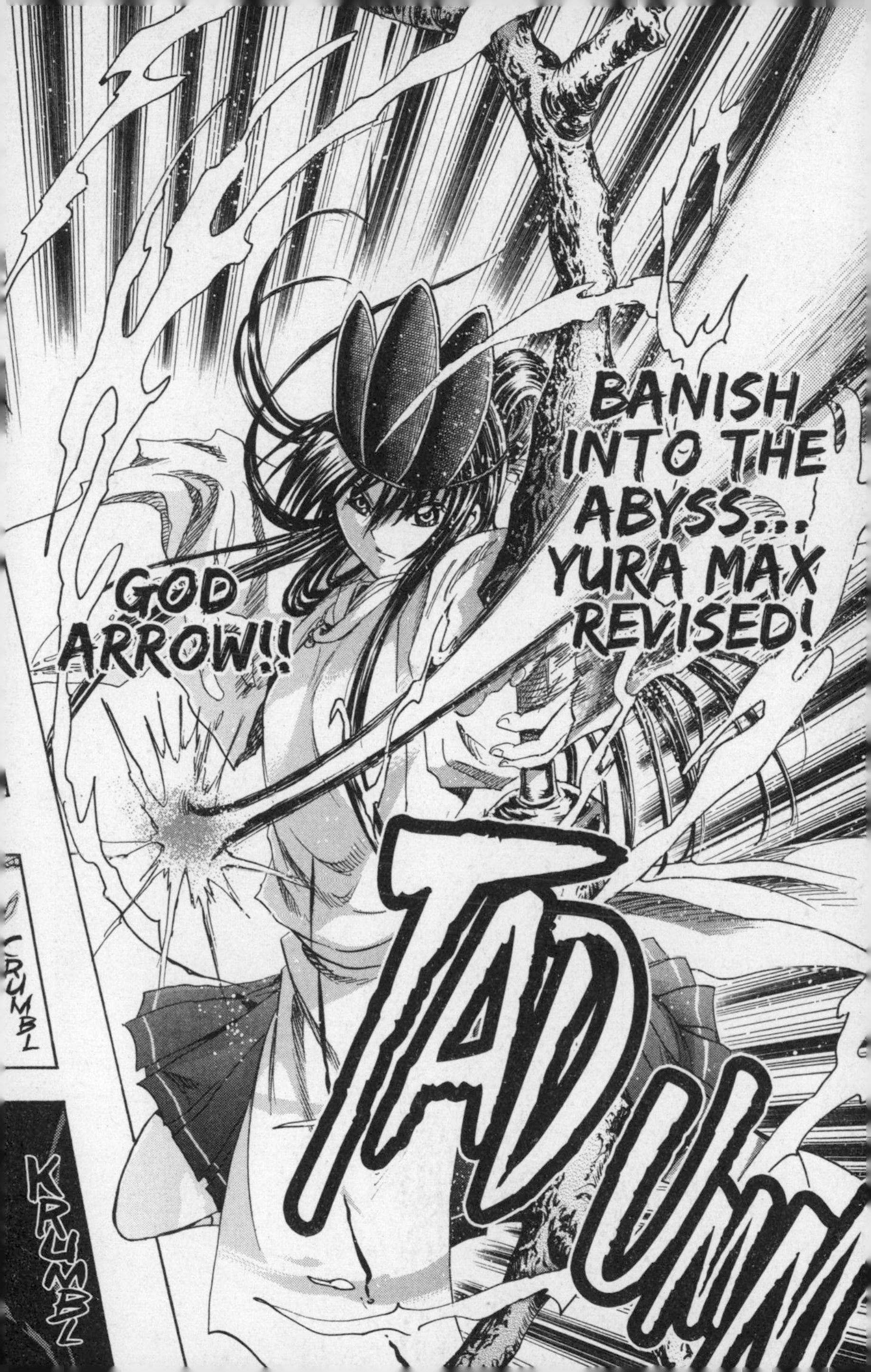
BANISH INTO THE ABYSS... YURA MAX REVISED!
GOD ARROW!!
TADUM
CRUMBL
KRUMBL

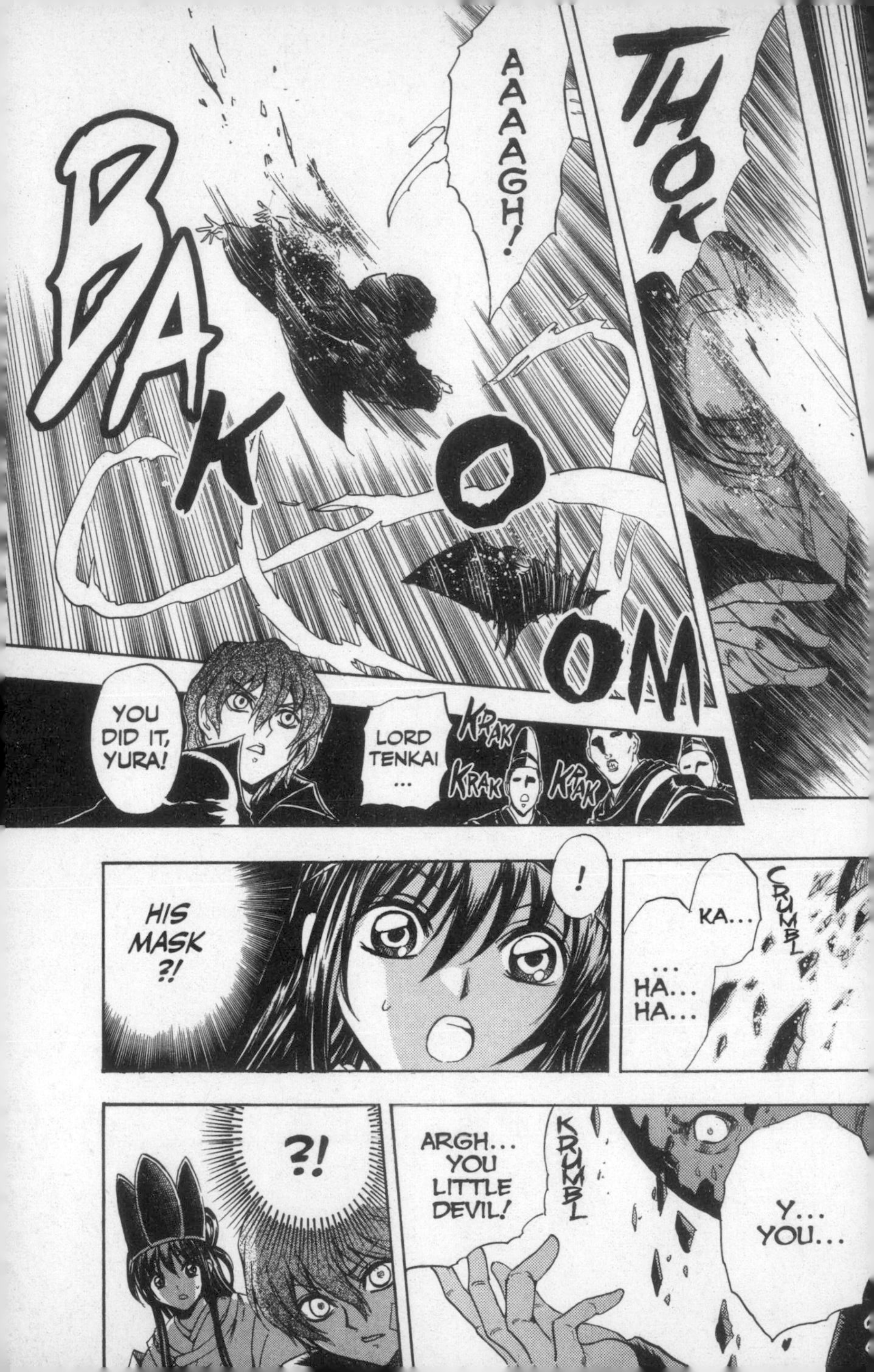
THOK
AAAAGH!
BAKOOOM
KRAK KRAK KRAK
LORD TENKAI ...
YOU DID IT, YURA!
KA... ... HA... HA...
CRUMBL
!
HIS MASK ?!
Y... YOU...
KRUMBL
ARGH... YOU LITTLE DEVIL!
?!

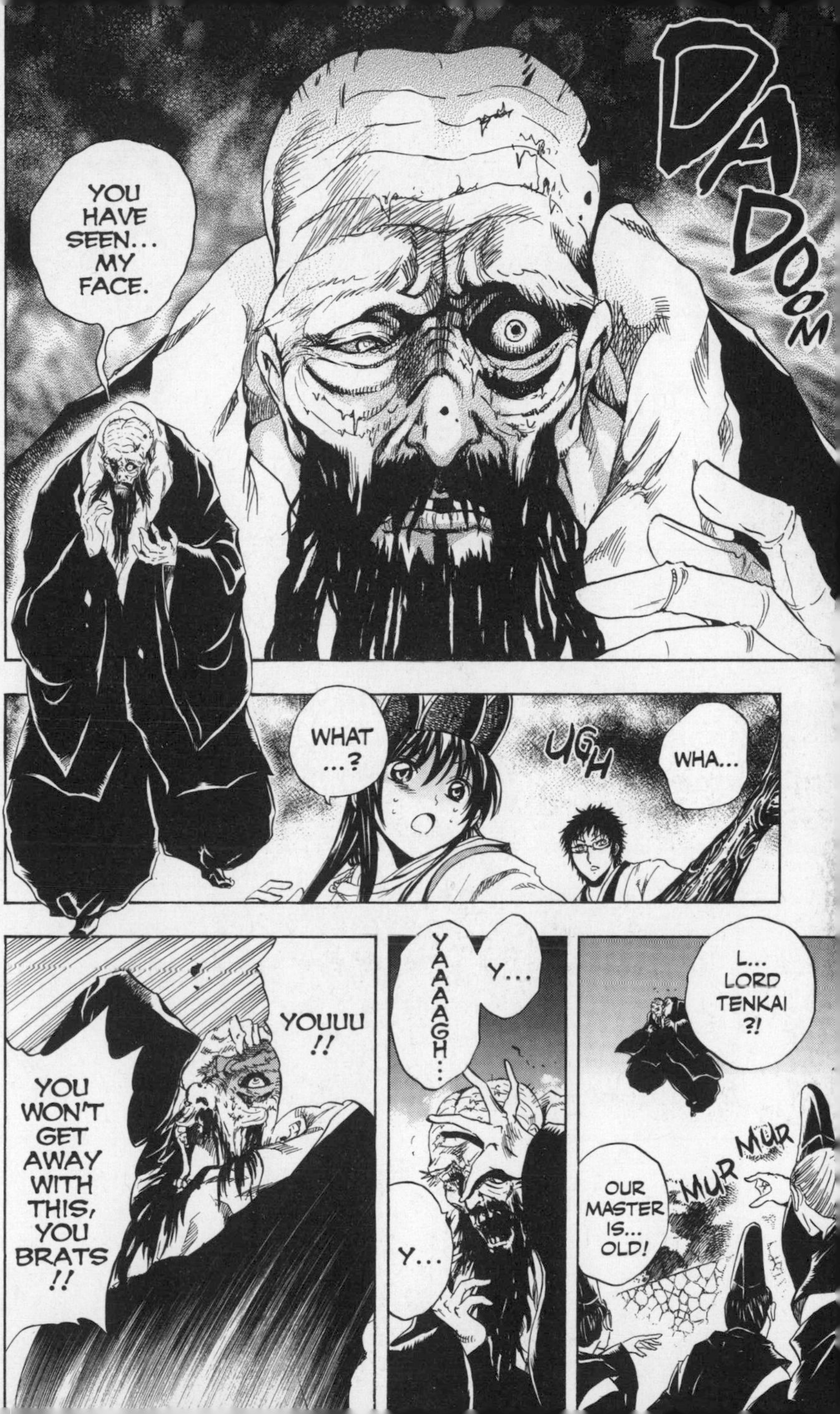
DADOOM
YOU HAVE SEEN... MY FACE.
WHA...
UGH
WHAT ...?
L... LORD TENKAI ?!
MUR MUR
OUR MASTER IS... OLD!
Y...
YAAAAGH...
Y...
YOUUU !!
YOU WON'T GET AWAY WITH THIS, YOU BRATS !!

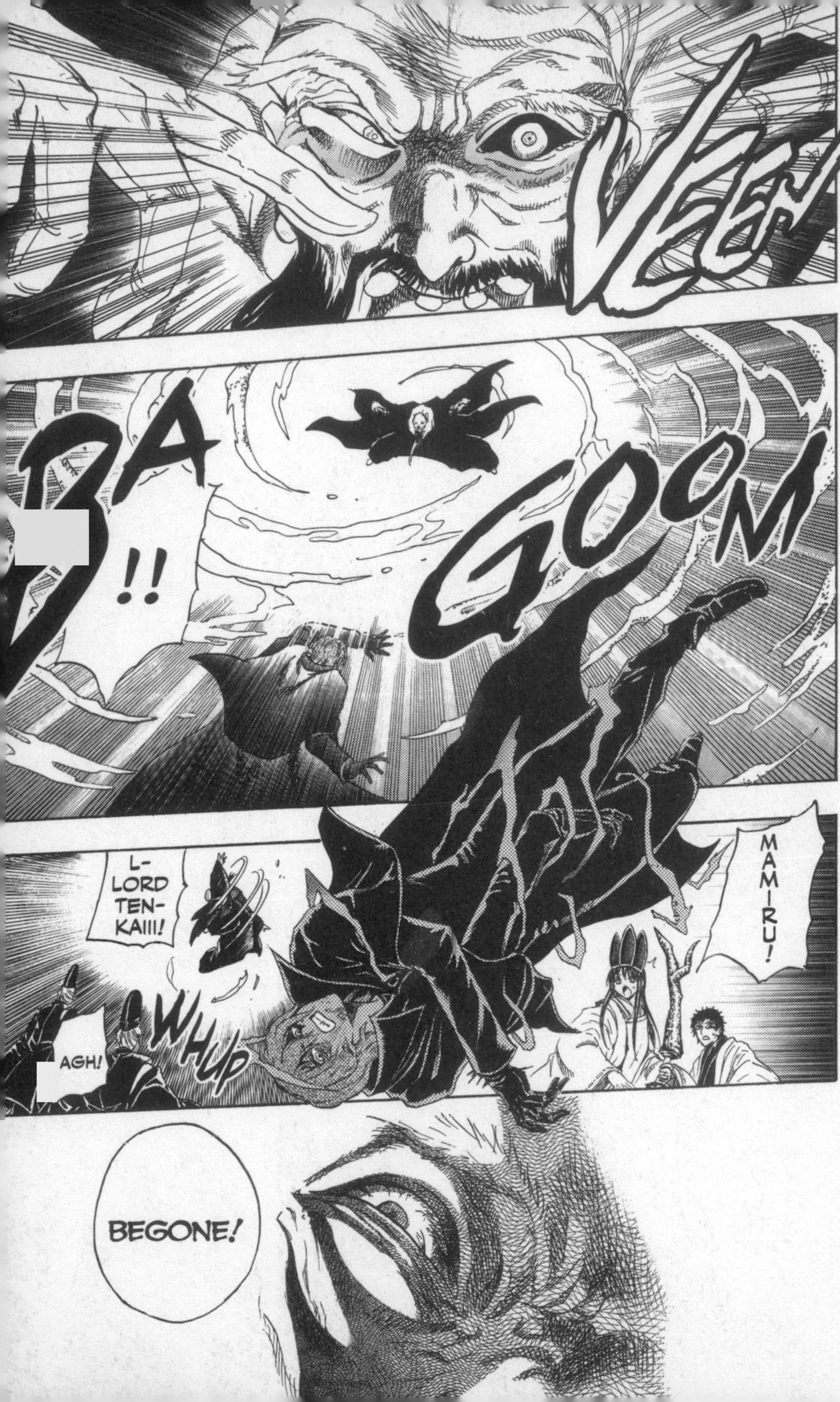
BA GOOM!!
MAMIRU!
L-LORD TEN-KAIII!
WHUP
AGH!
BEGONE!

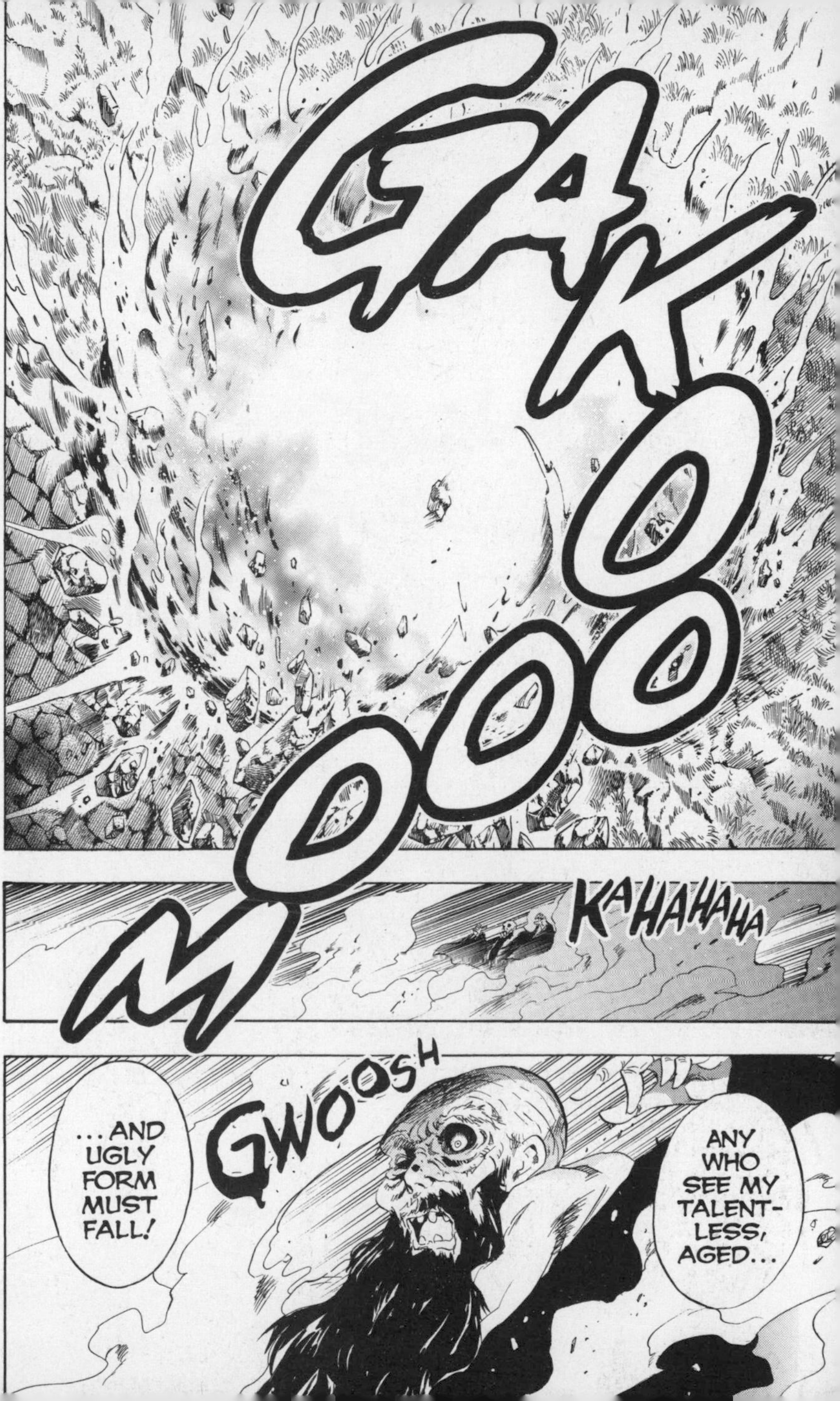
KAHAHAHA
GWOOSH
ANY WHO SEE MY TALENT-LESS, AGED...
...AND UGLY FORM MUST FALL!

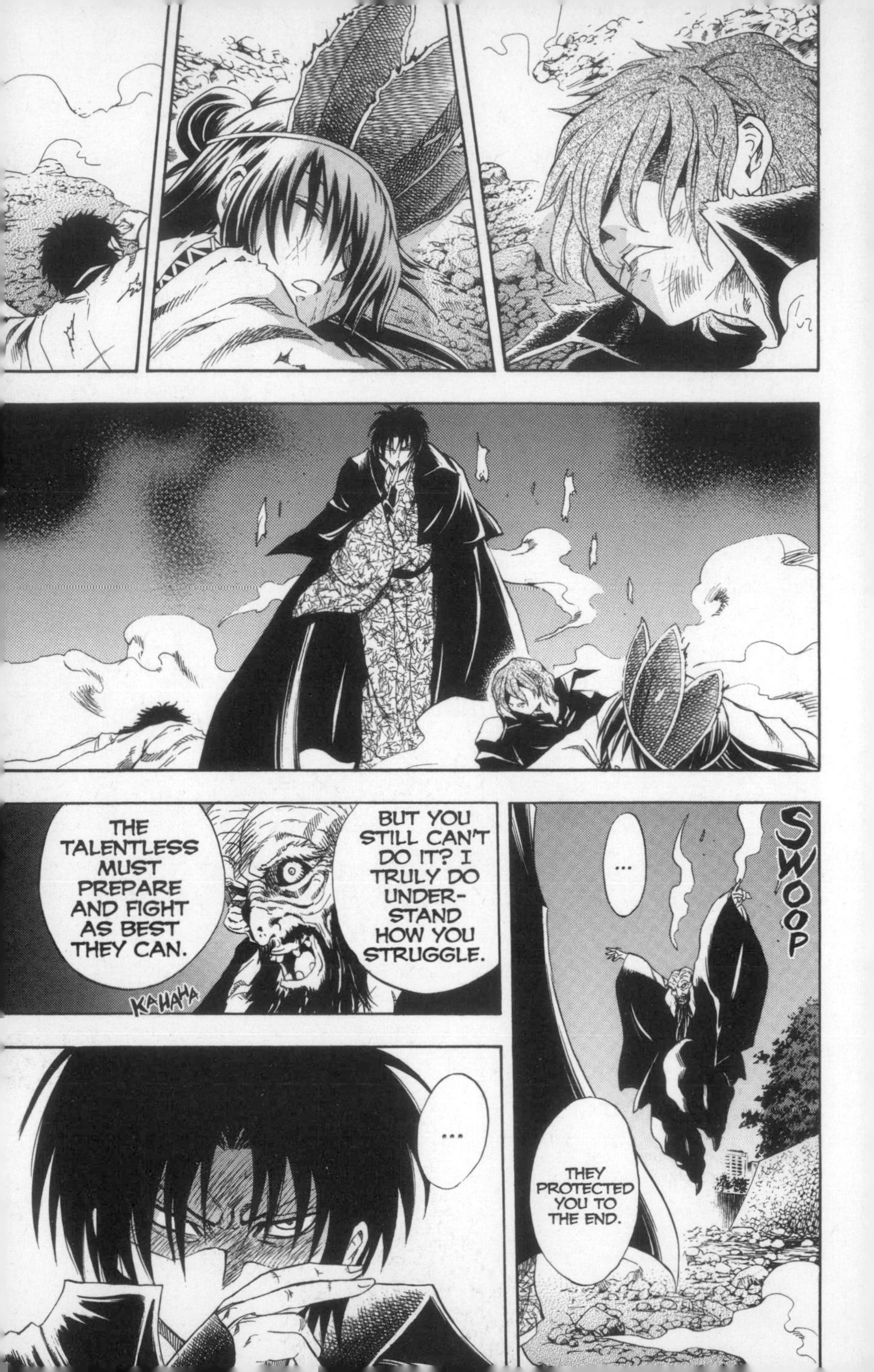
...
SWOOP
THEY PROTECTED YOU TO THE END.
BUT YOU STILL CAN'T DO IT? I TRULY DO UNDER-STAND HOW YOU STRUGGLE.
THE TALENTLESS MUST PREPARE AND FIGHT AS BEST THEY CAN.
KAHAHA
...

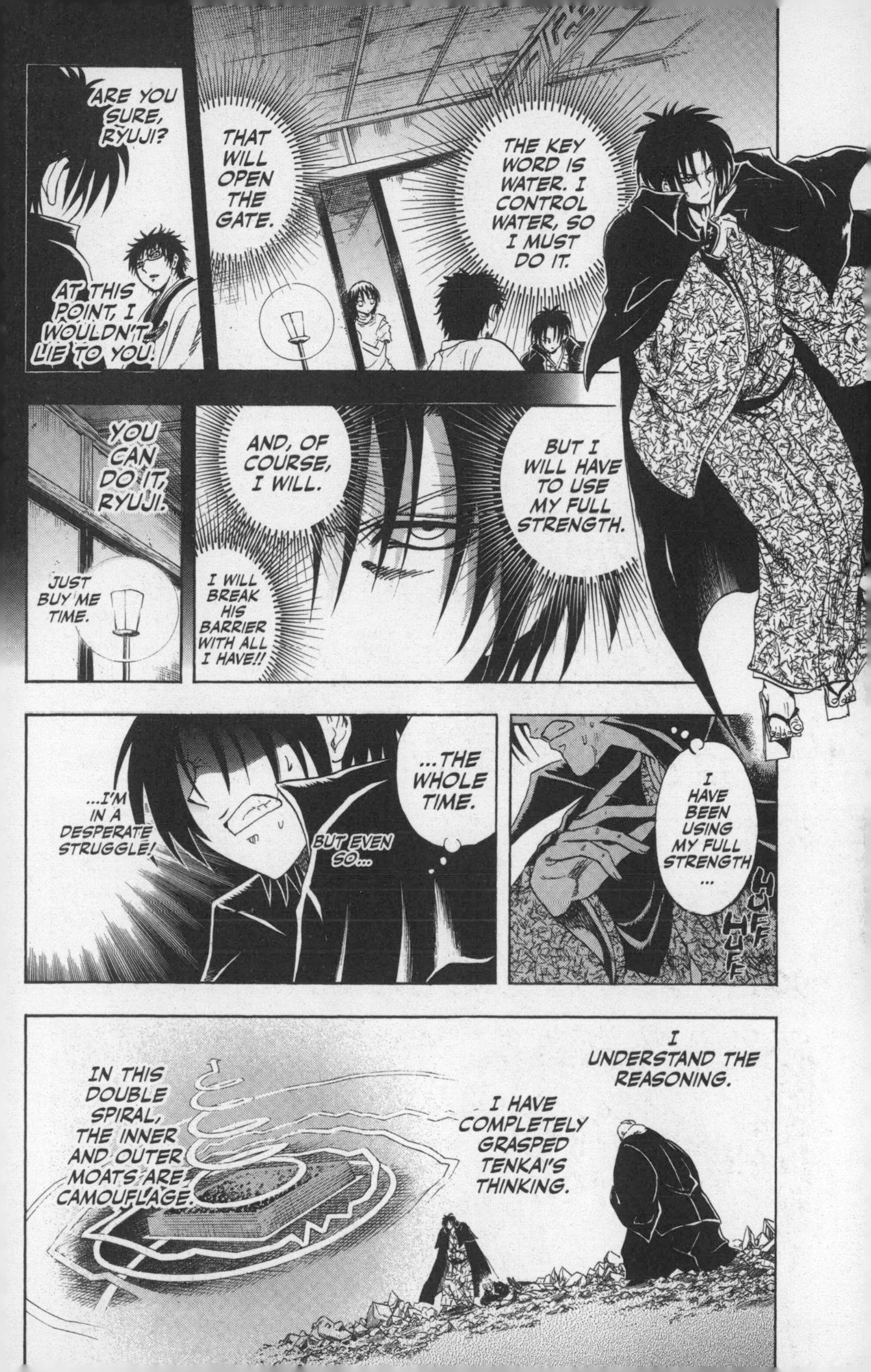
THE KEY WORD IS WATER. I CONTROL WATER, SO I MUST DO IT.
THAT WILL OPEN THE GATE.
ARE YOU SURE, RYUJI?
AT THIS POINT, I WOULDN'T LIE TO YOU.
BUT I WILL HAVE TO USE MY FULL STRENGTH.
AND, OF COURSE, I WILL.
I WILL BREAK HIS BARRIER WITH ALL I HAVE!!
YOU CAN DO IT, RYUJI.
JUST BUY ME TIME.
I HAVE BEEN USING MY FULL STRENGTH...
HUFF HUFF
...THE WHOLE TIME.
BUT EVEN SO...
...I'M IN A DESPERATE STRUGGLE!
I UNDERSTAND THE REASONING.
I HAVE COMPLETELY GRASPED TENKAI'S THINKING.
IN THIS DOUBLE SPIRAL, THE INNER AND OUTER MOATS ARE CAMOUFLAGE.

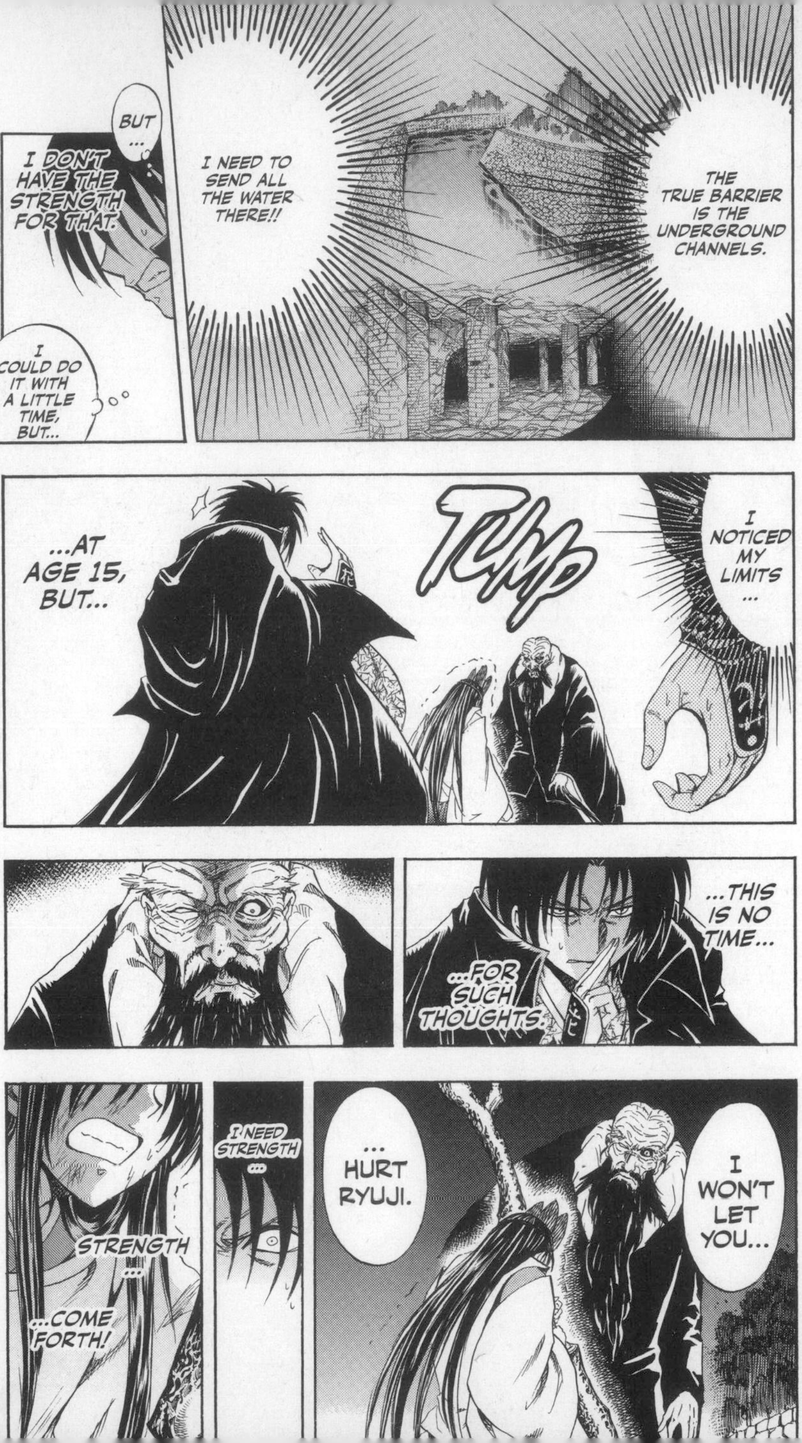
THE TRUE BARRIER IS THE UNDERGROUND CHANNELS.
I NEED TO SEND ALL THE WATER THERE!!
BUT...
I DON'T HAVE THE STRENGTH FOR THAT.
I COULD DO IT WITH A LITTLE TIME, BUT...
I NOTICED MY LIMITS...
TUMP
...AT AGE 15, BUT...
...THIS IS NO TIME...
...FOR SUCH THOUGHTS.
I WON'T LET YOU...
...HURT RYUJI.
I NEED STRENGTH...
STRENGTH...
...COME FORTH!

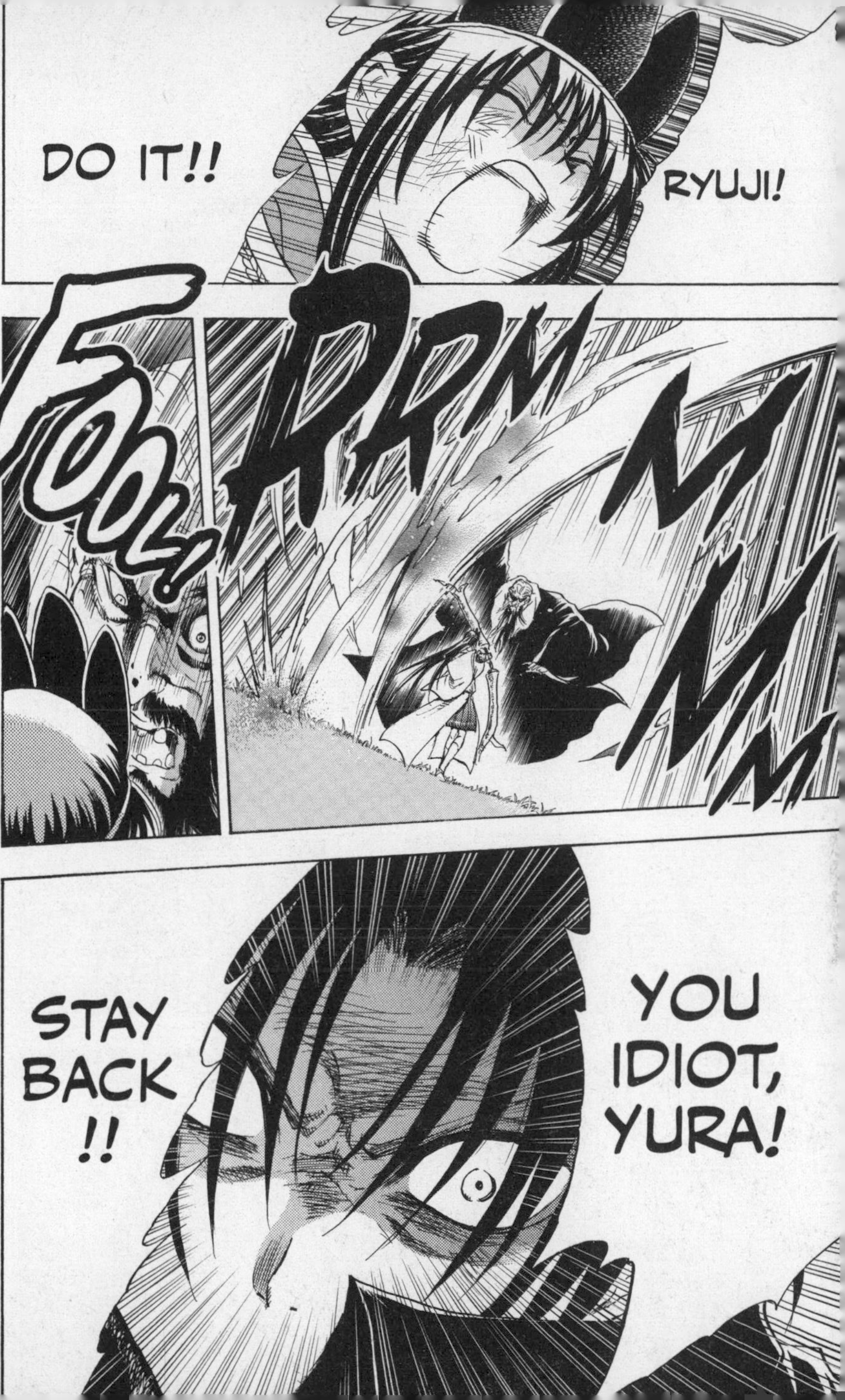
RYUJI!
DO IT!!
KRRMMMM
FOOL!
YOU IDIOT, YURA!
STAY BACK!!

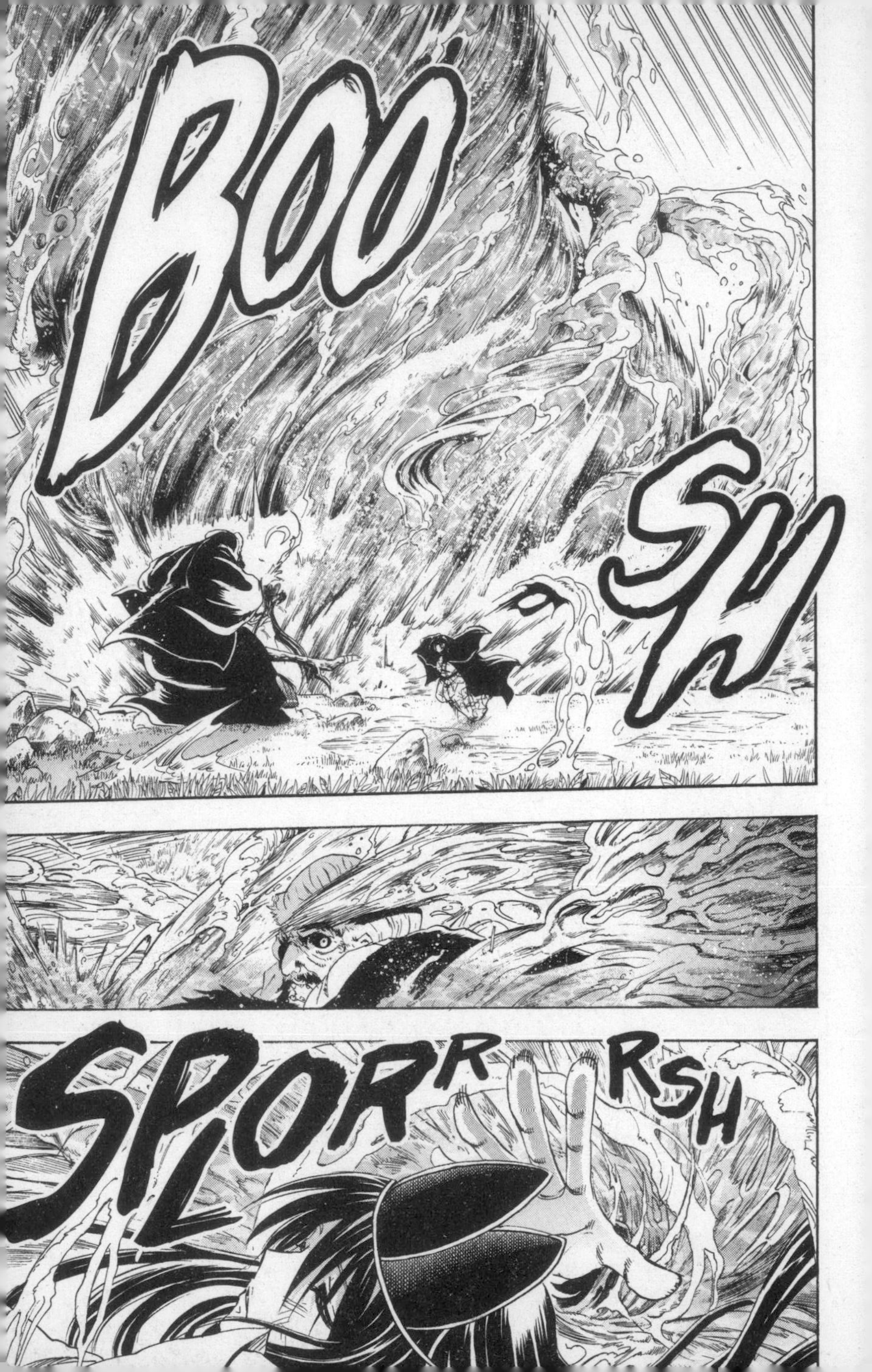
BOOO
SHH
SPORR
RSH

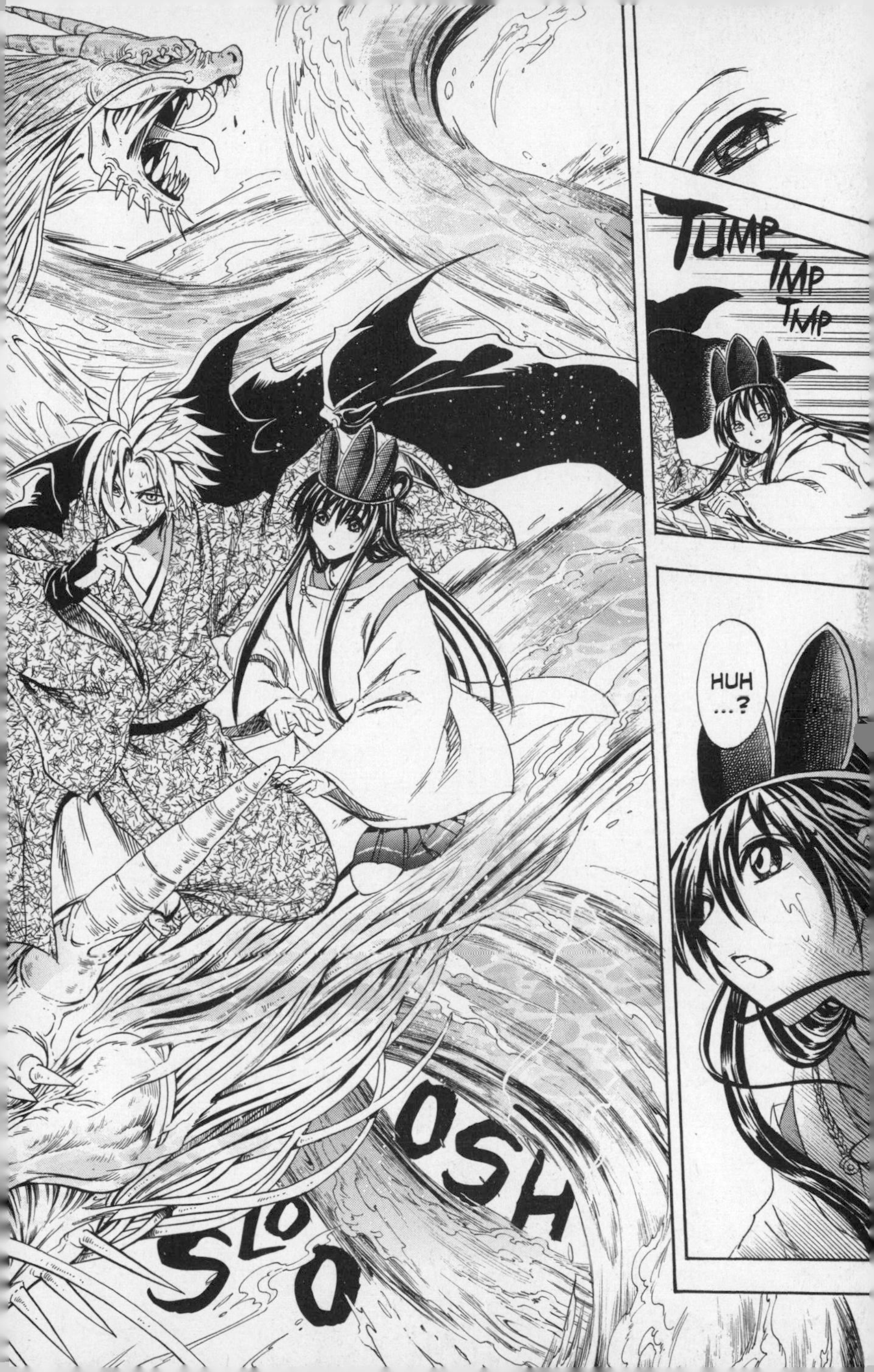
TUMP TMP TMP
HUH ...?
SLOOOSH

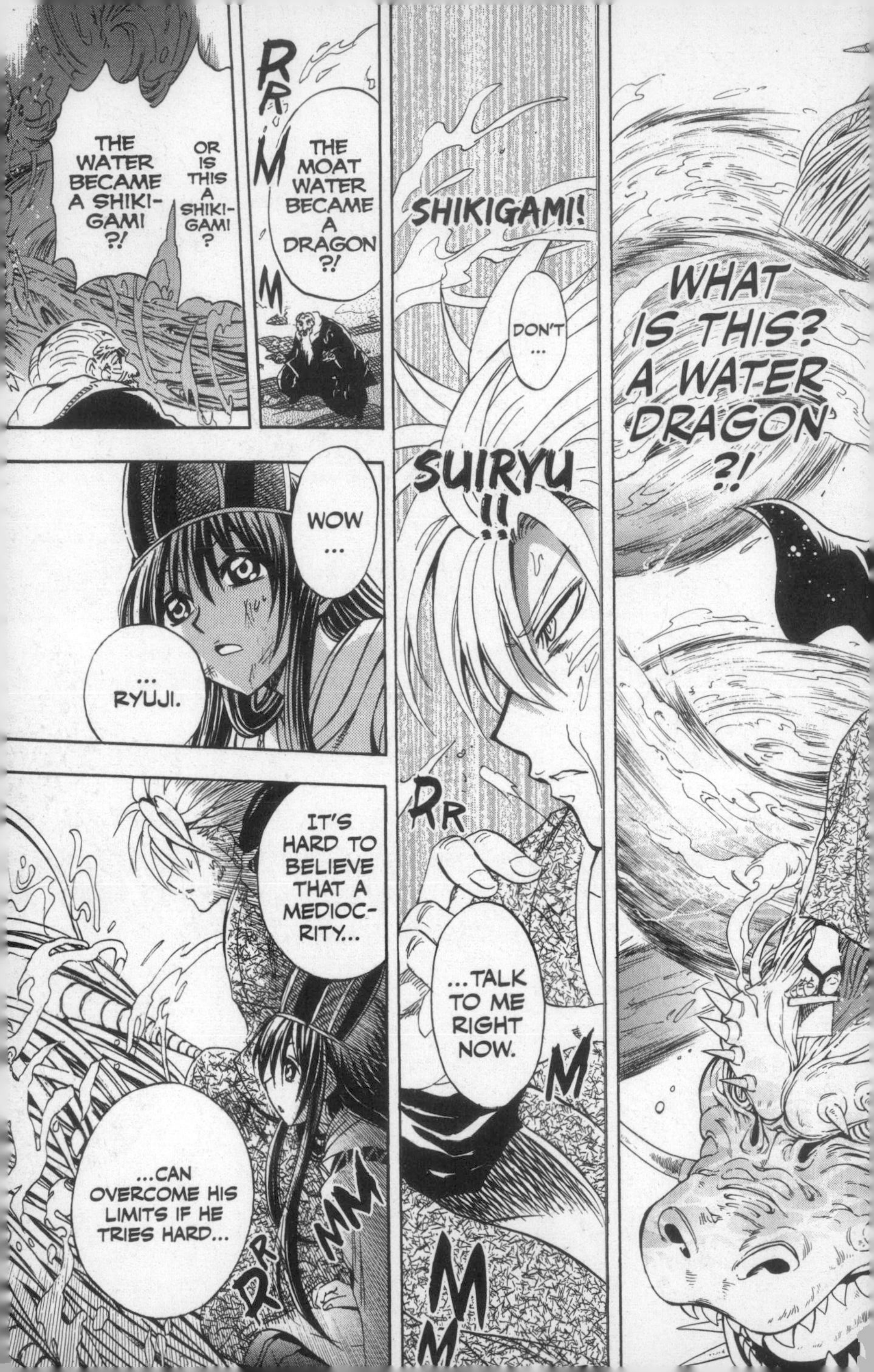
WHAT IS THIS? A WATER DRAGON ?!
SHIKIGAMI!
DON'T ...
SUIRYU !!
DR
...TALK TO ME RIGHT NOW.
M
MMM
DRRRMM
THE MOAT WATER BECAME A DRAGON ?!
M
OR IS THIS A SHIKIGAMI ?
THE WATER BECAME A SHIKIGAMI ?!
WOW ...
... RYUJI.
IT'S HARD TO BELIEVE THAT A MEDIOC-RITY...
...CAN OVERCOME HIS LIMITS IF HE TRIES HARD...
DRMM

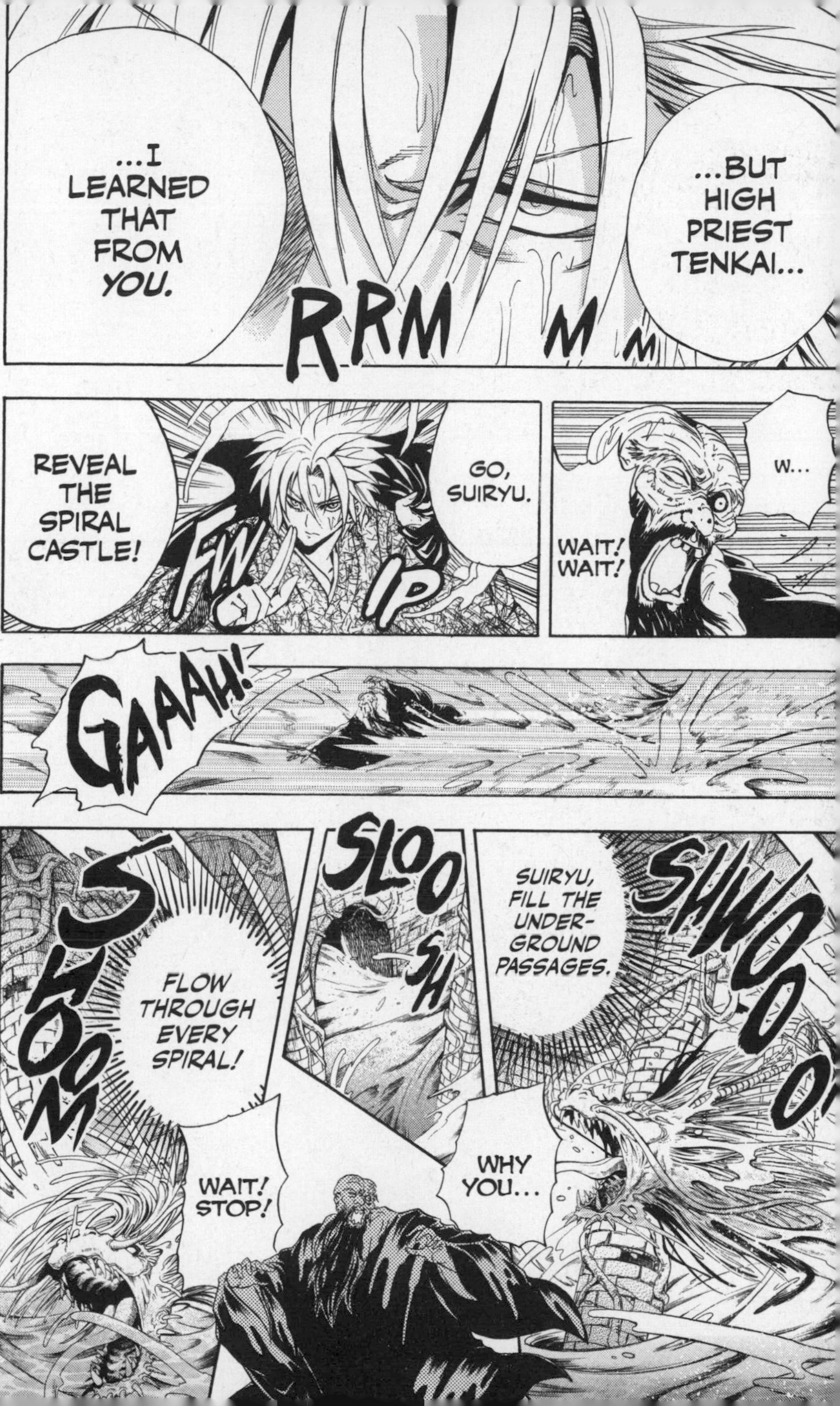
...BUT HIGH PRIEST TENKAI...
...I LEARNED THAT FROM YOU.
RRM M M
W...
WAIT! WAIT!
GO, SUIRYU.
FWIP
REVEAL THE SPIRAL CASTLE!
GAAAH!
SHWOOO
SUIRYU, FILL THE UNDER-GROUND PASSAGES.
WHY YOU...
SLOOSH
SHOOM
FLOW THROUGH EVERY SPIRAL!
WAIT! STOP!

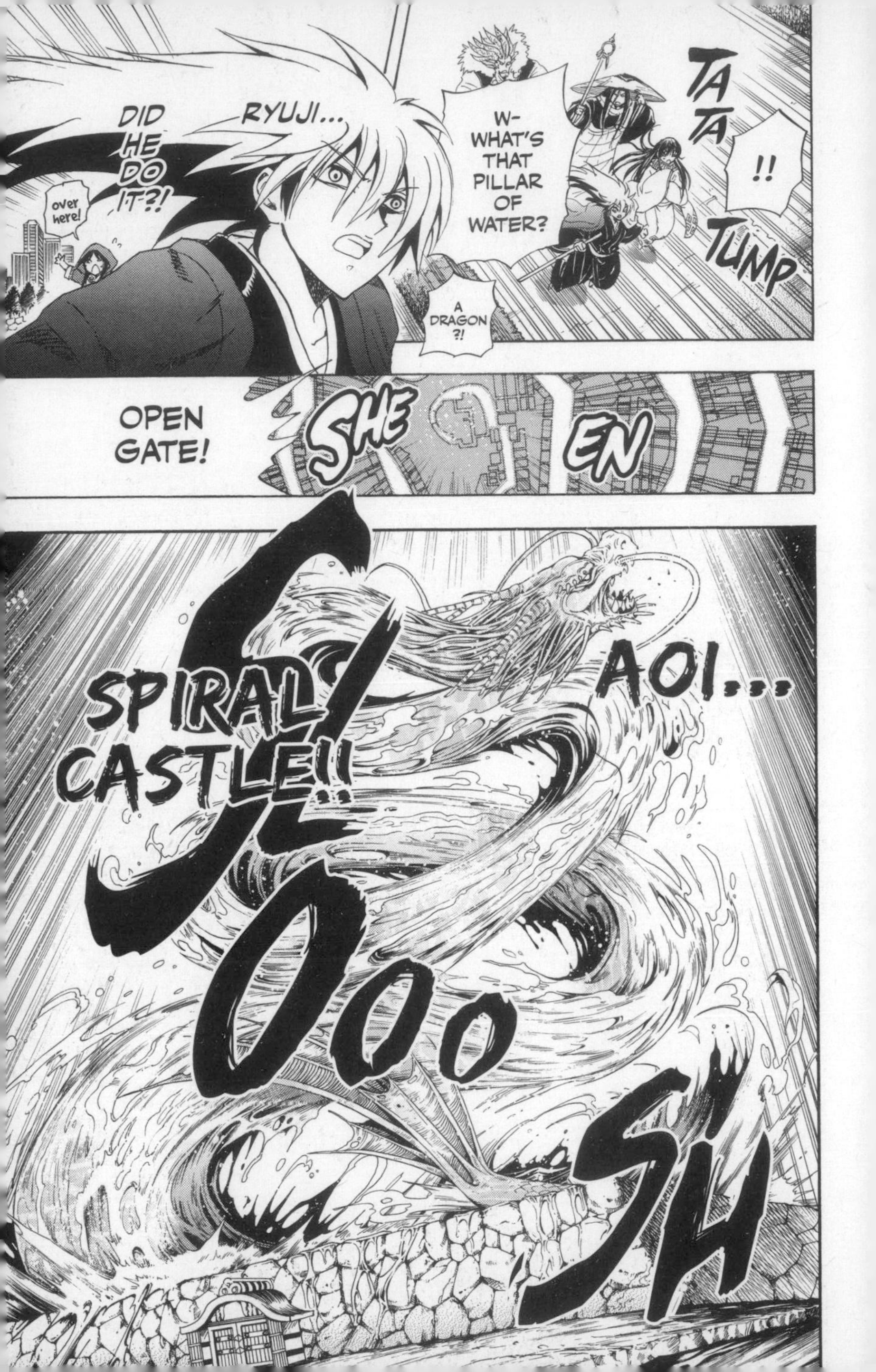
TA TA
!!
TUMP
W- WHAT'S THAT PILLAR OF WATER?
A DRAGON ?!
RYUJI...
DID HE DO IT?!
over here!
SHE
EN
OPEN GATE!
AOI...
SPIRAL CASTLE!!
SOOOSH

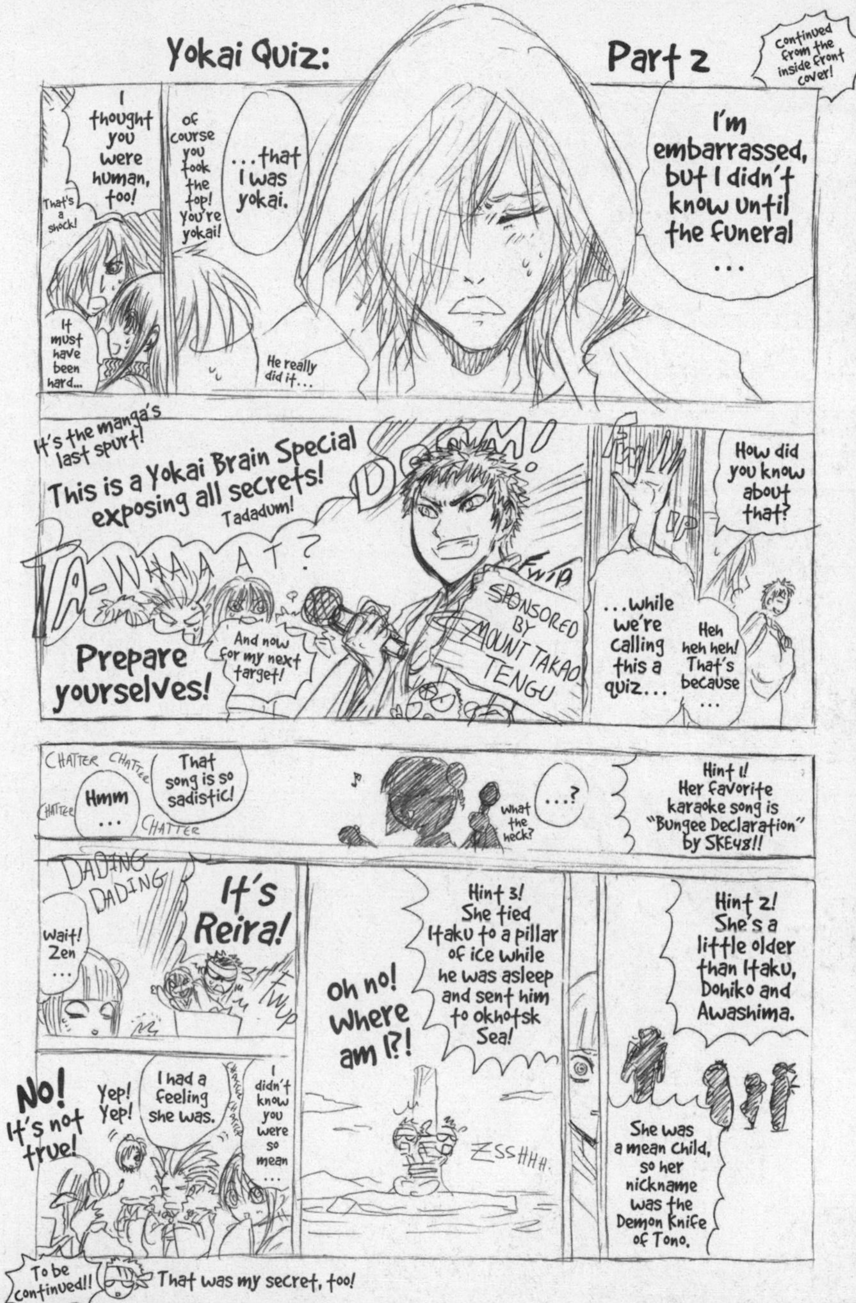
Yokai Quiz: Part 2
Continued from the inside front cover!
I'm embarrassed, but I didn't know until the funeral...
...that I was yokai.
He really did it...
Of course you took the top! You're yokai!
I thought you were human, too!
That's a shock!
It must have been hard...
How did you know about that?
Fwip
...while we're calling this a quiz...
Heh heh heh! That's because...
DOOM!
It's the manga's last spurt!
This is a Yokai Brain Special exposing all secrets!
Tadadum!
TA-WHAAAAT?
Fwip
SPONSORED BY MOUNT TAKAO TENGU
And now for my next target!
Prepare yourselves!
Hint 1! Her favorite karaoke song is "Bungee Declaration" by SKE48!!
...?
What the heck?
That song is so sadistic!
Hmm...
CHATTER CHATTER CHATTER CHATTER
Hint 2! She's a little older than Itaku, Dohiko and Awashima.
She was a mean child, so her nickname was the Demon Knife of Tono.
Hint 3! She tied Itaku to a pillar of ice while he was asleep and sent him to Okhotsk Sea!
Oh no! Where am I?!
ZSSHHH.
It's Reira!
DADING DADING
Wait! Zen...
FWUP
I didn't know you were so mean...
I had a feeling she was.
Yep! Yep!
No! It's not true!
To be continued!!
That was my secret, too!

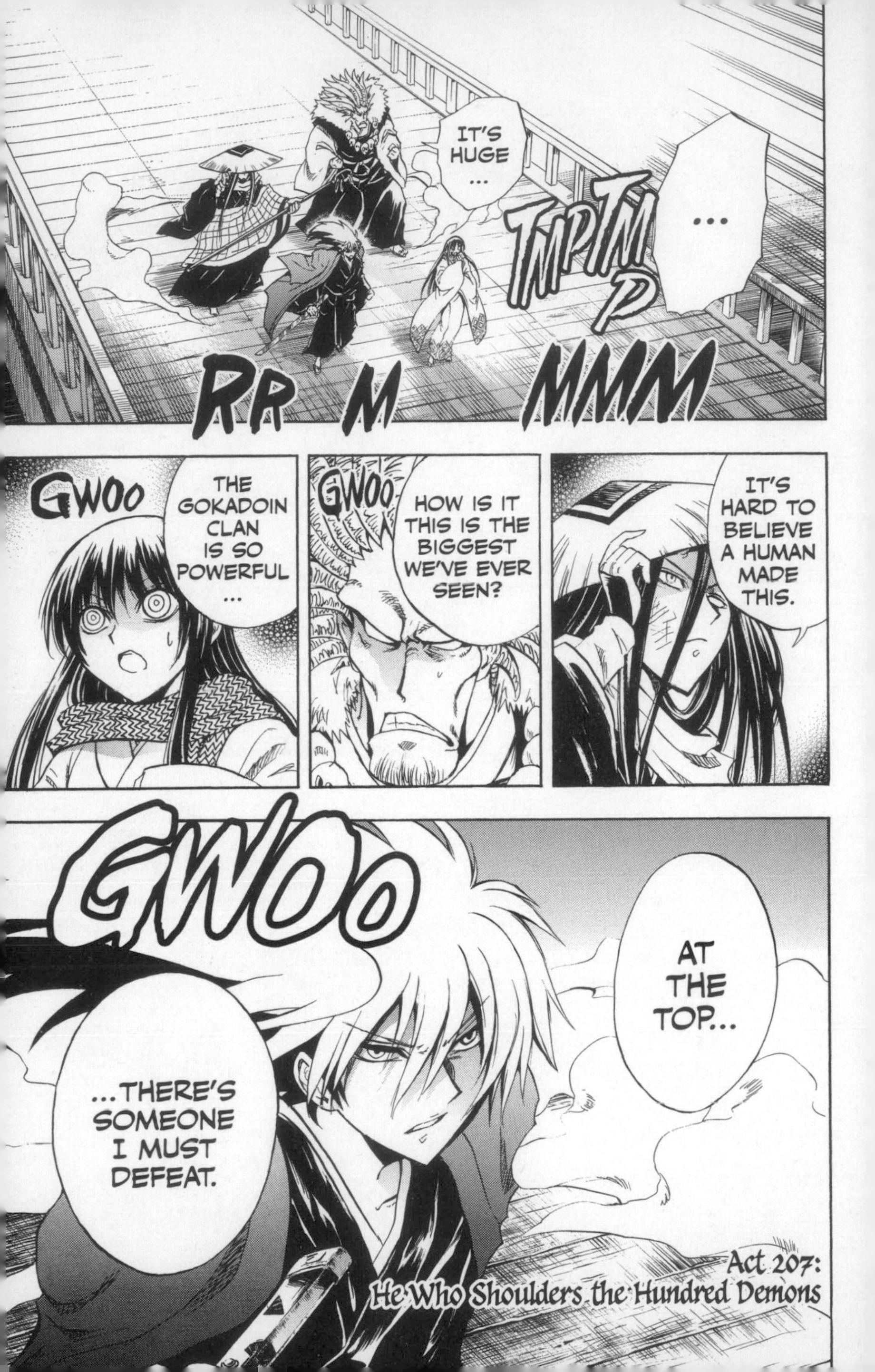
...
IT'S HUGE ...
RR M MMM
IT'S HARD TO BELIEVE A HUMAN MADE THIS.
GWOO
HOW IS IT THIS IS THE BIGGEST WE'VE EVER SEEN?
GWOO
THE GOKADOIN CLAN IS SO POWERFUL ...
GWOO
AT THE TOP...
...THERE'S SOMEONE I MUST DEFEAT.
Act 207:
He Who Shoulders the Hundred Demons

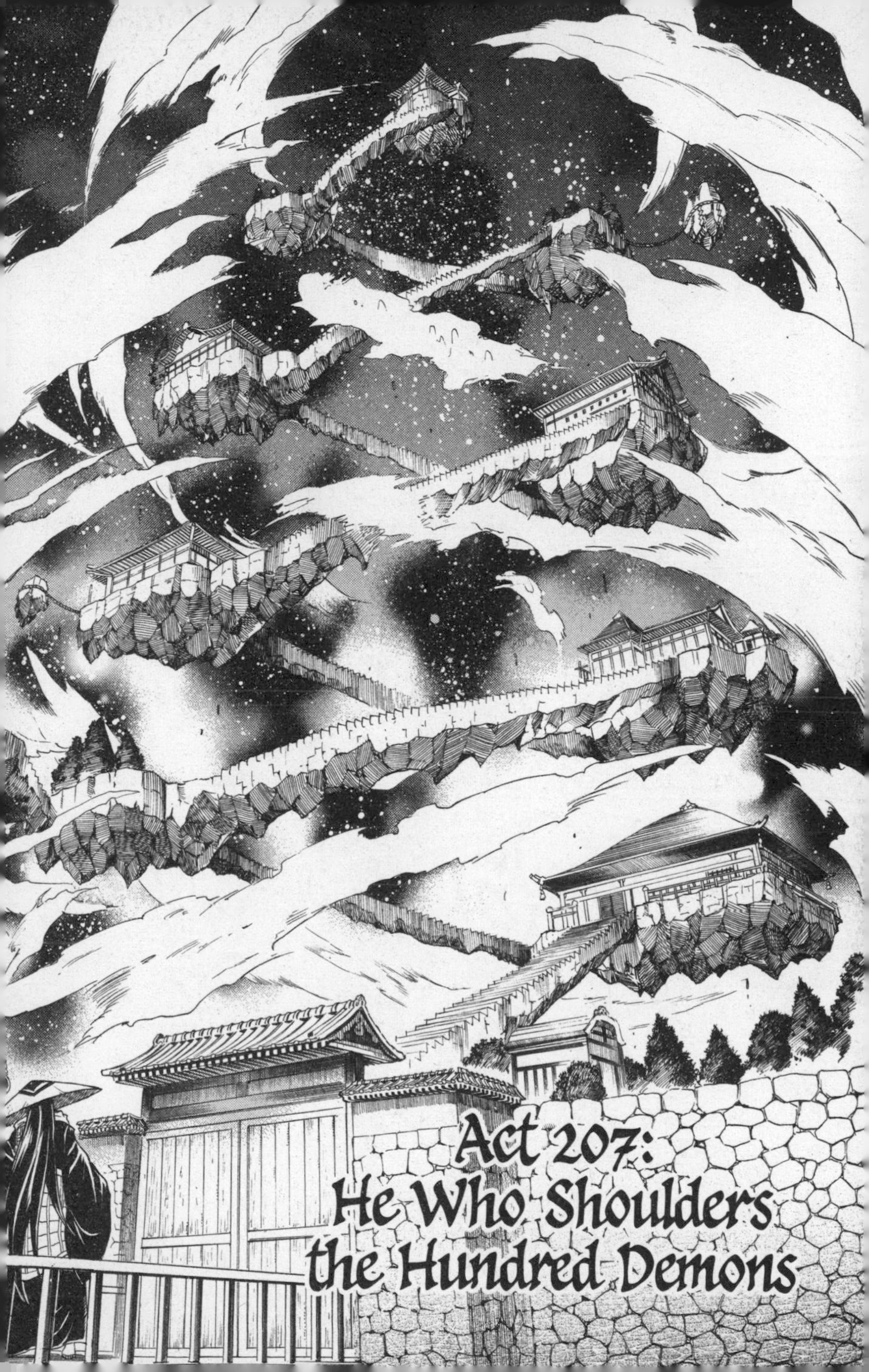
Act 207:
He Who Shoulders the Hundred Demons

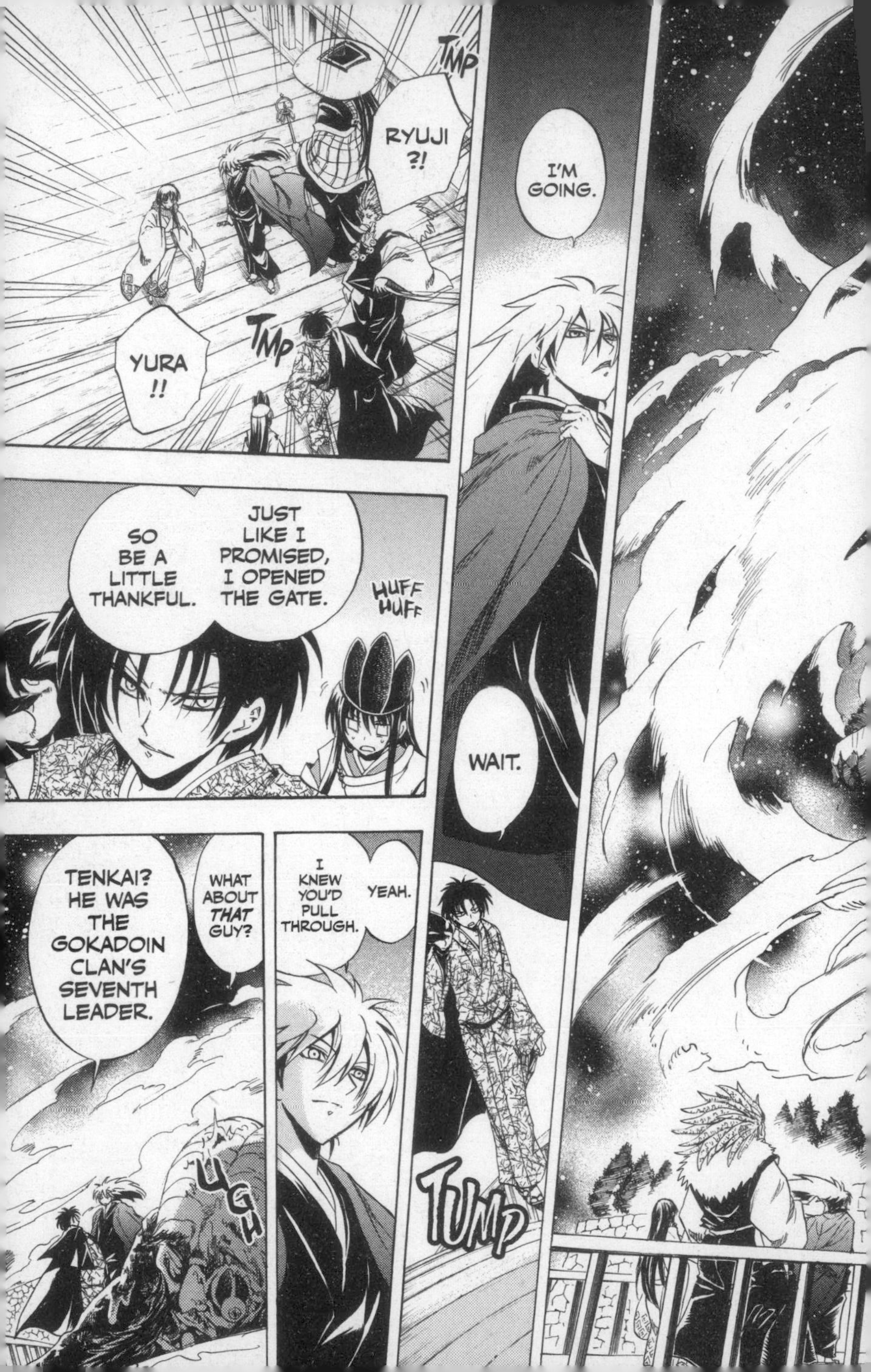
I'M GOING.
WAIT.
TUMP
TMP
RYUJI ?!
TMP
YURA !!
JUST LIKE I PROMISED, I OPENED THE GATE.
SO BE A LITTLE THANKFUL.
HUFF HUFF
I KNEW YOU'D PULL THROUGH.
YEAH.
WHAT ABOUT *THAT* GUY?
TENKAI? HE WAS THE GOKADOIN CLAN'S SEVENTH LEADER.
UGH

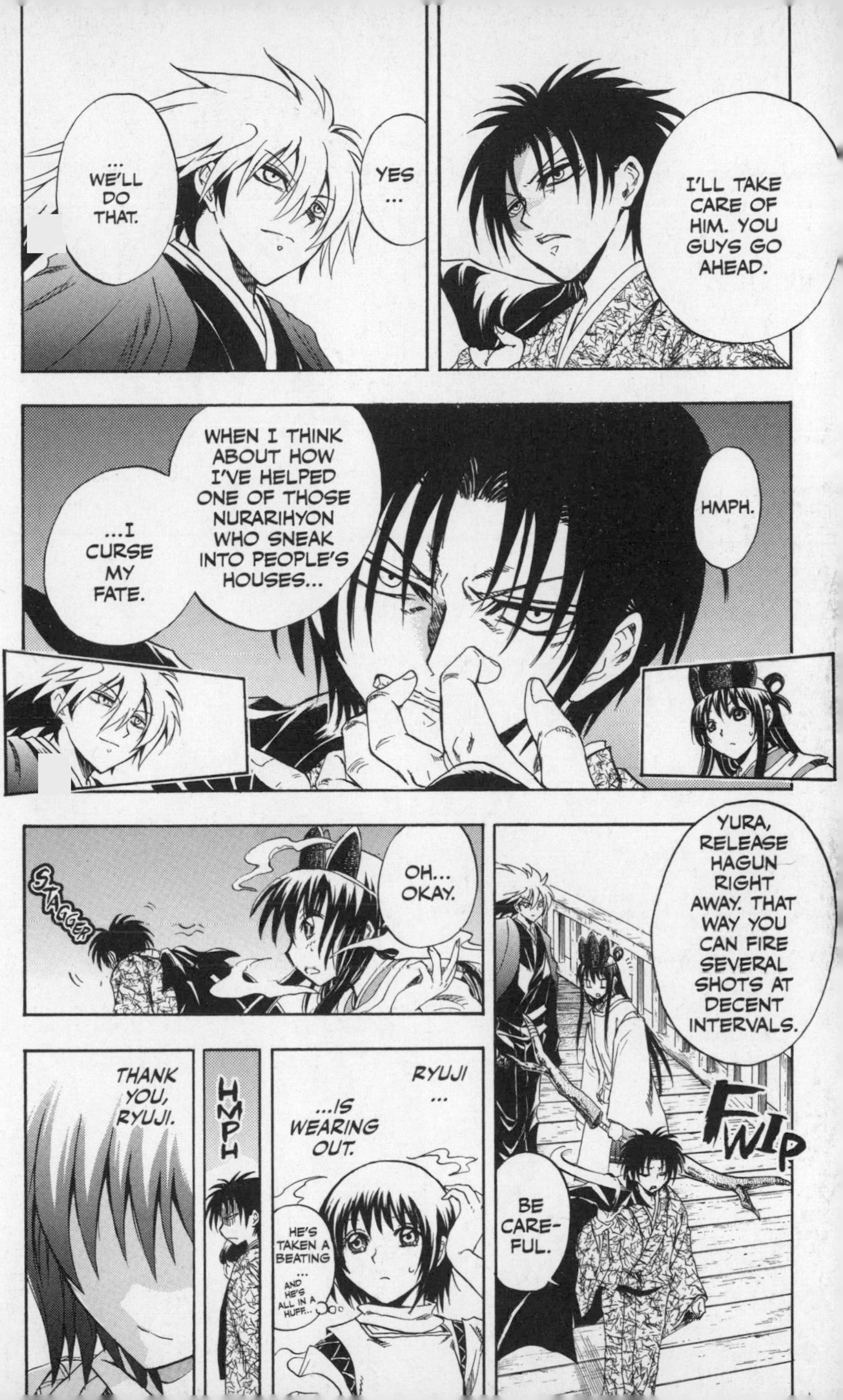

I'LL TAKE CARE OF HIM. YOU GUYS GO AHEAD.
YES ...
... WE'LL DO THAT.
HMPH.
WHEN I THINK ABOUT HOW I'VE HELPED ONE OF THOSE NURARIHYON WHO SNEAK INTO PEOPLE'S HOUSES...
...I CURSE MY FATE.
YURA, RELEASE HAGUN RIGHT AWAY. THAT WAY YOU CAN FIRE SEVERAL SHOTS AT DECENT INTERVALS.
FWIP
BE CARE-FUL.
OH... OKAY.
STAGGER
RYUJI ...
...IS WEARING OUT.
HE'S TAKEN A BEATING ...
AND HE'S ALL IN A HUFF...
HMPH
THANK YOU, RYUJI.

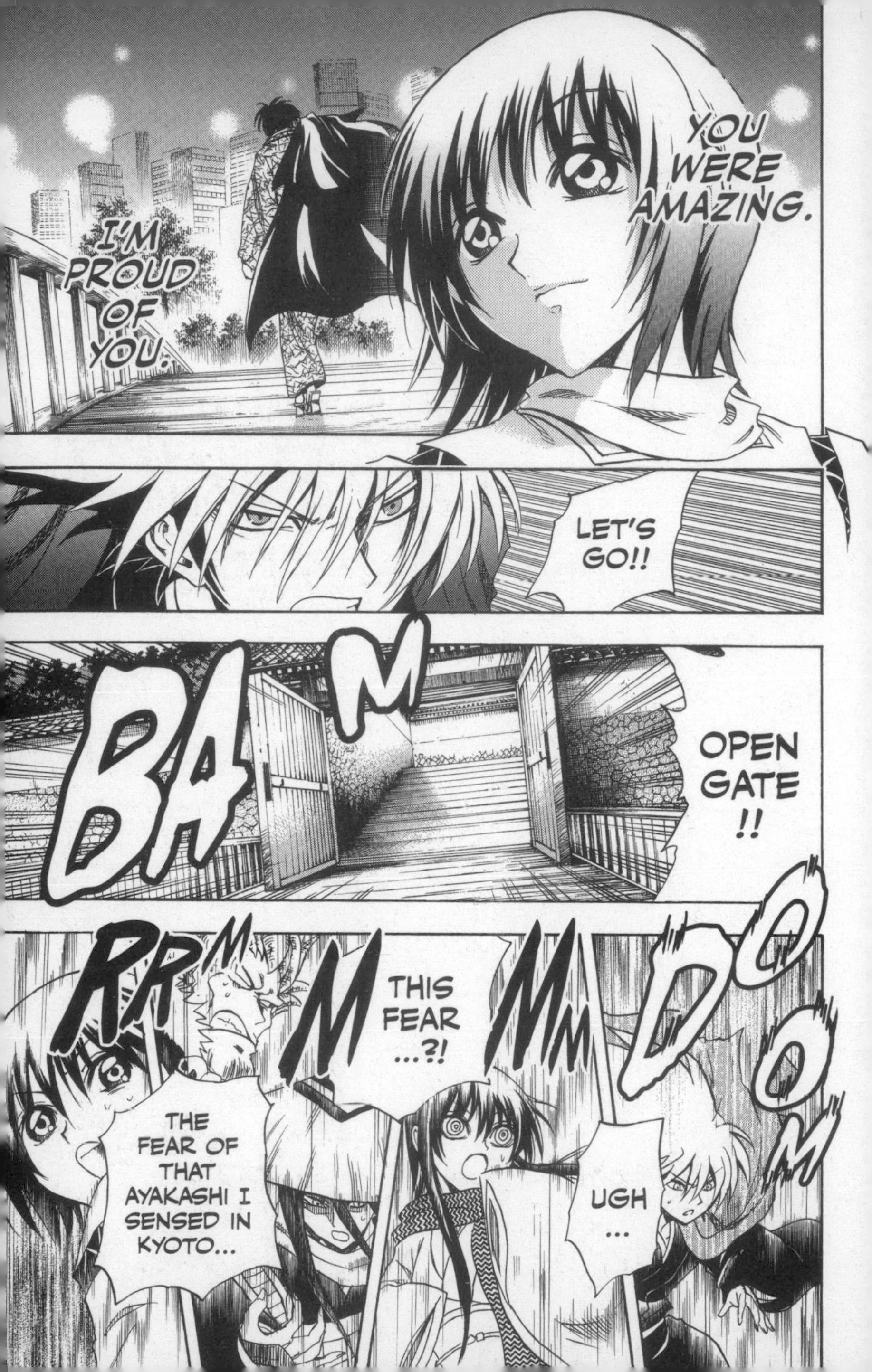
YOU WERE AMAZING.
I'M PROUD OF YOU.
LET'S GO!!
OPEN GATE!!
BAMM
DOOOM
RRMMMMM
THIS FEAR ...?!
UGH ...
THE FEAR OF THAT AYAKASHI I SENSED IN KYOTO...

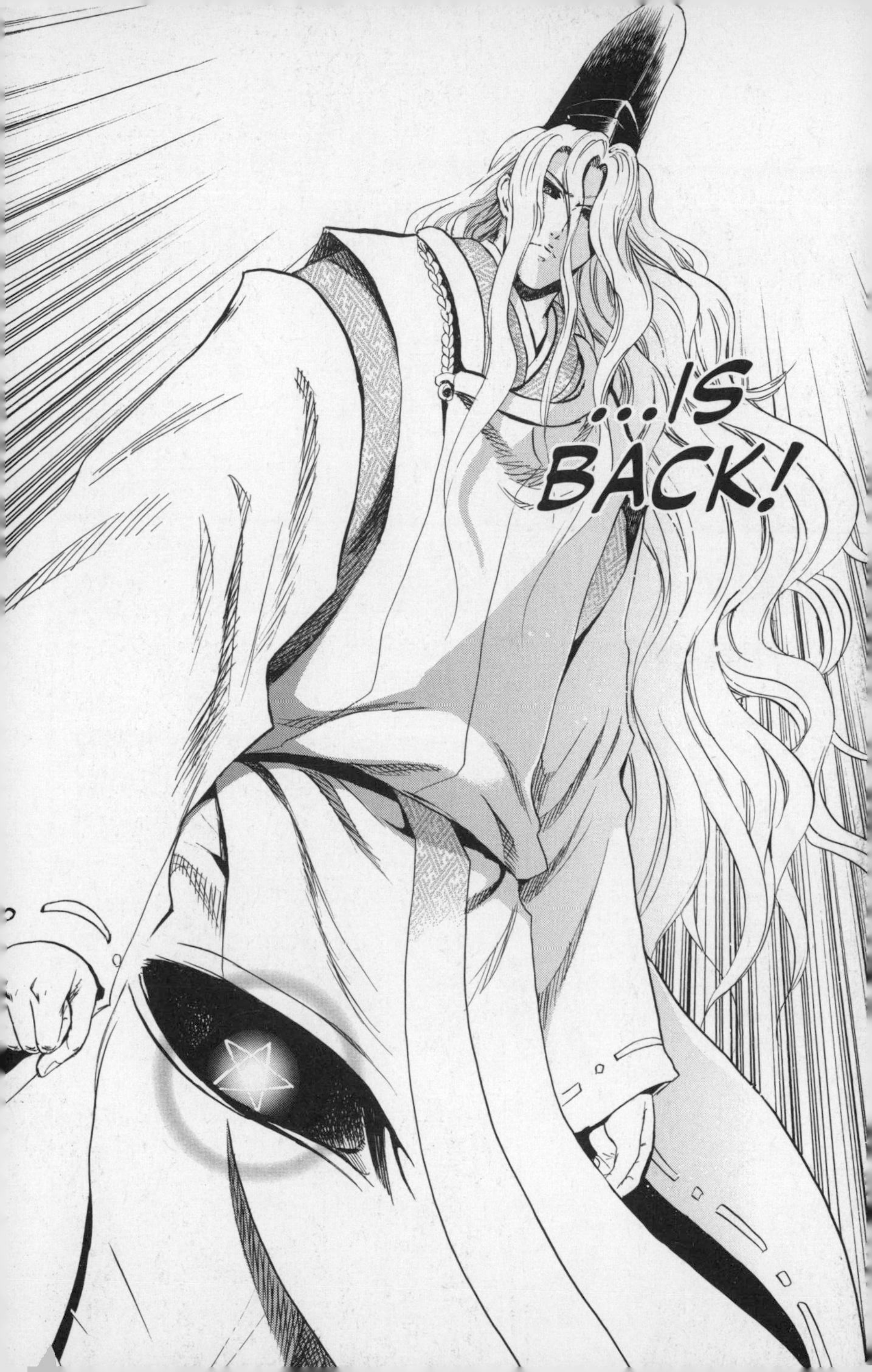
...IS BACK!

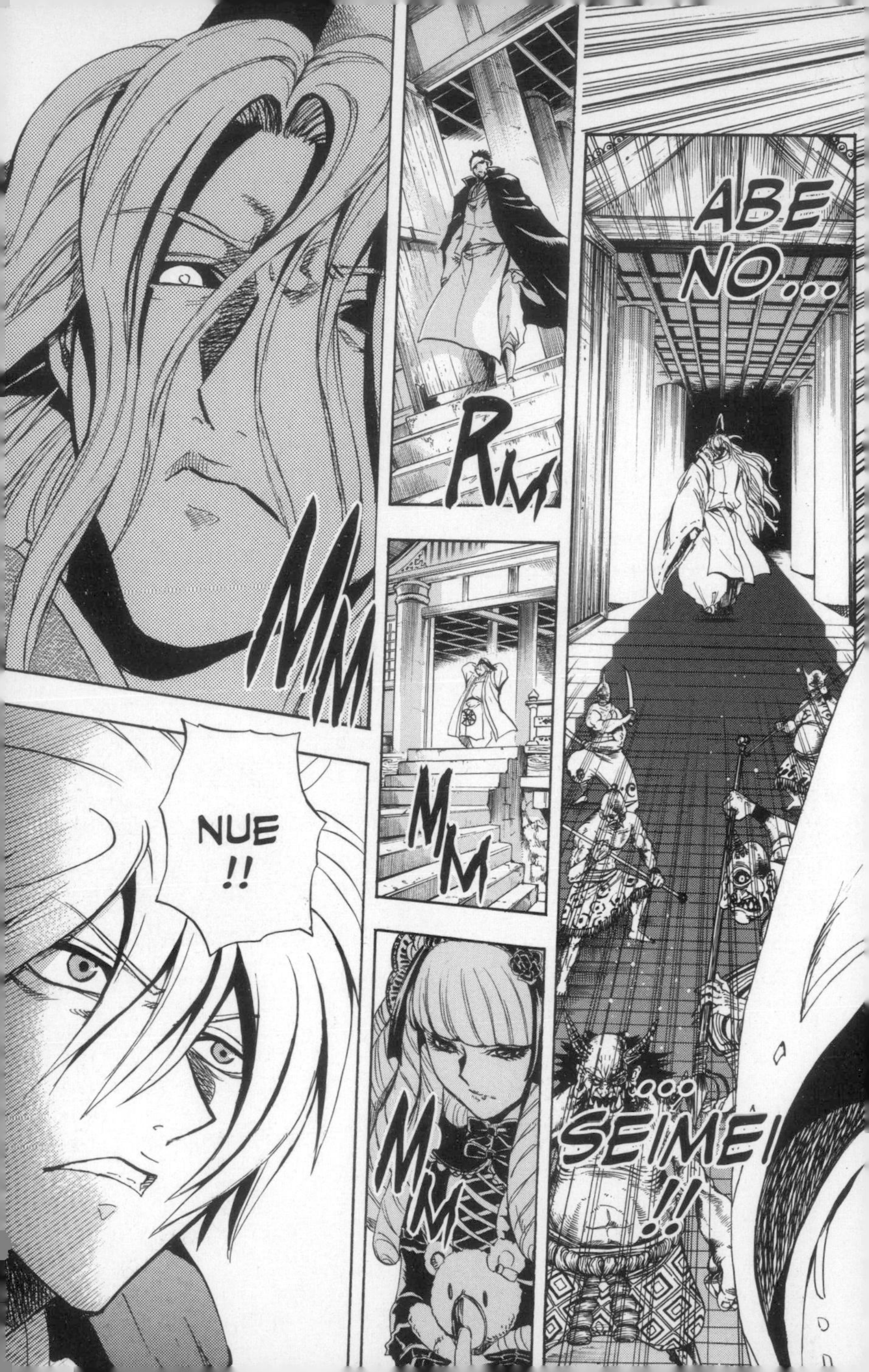
ABE NO...
...SEIMEI !!
RM
MM
MM
MM
NUE !!

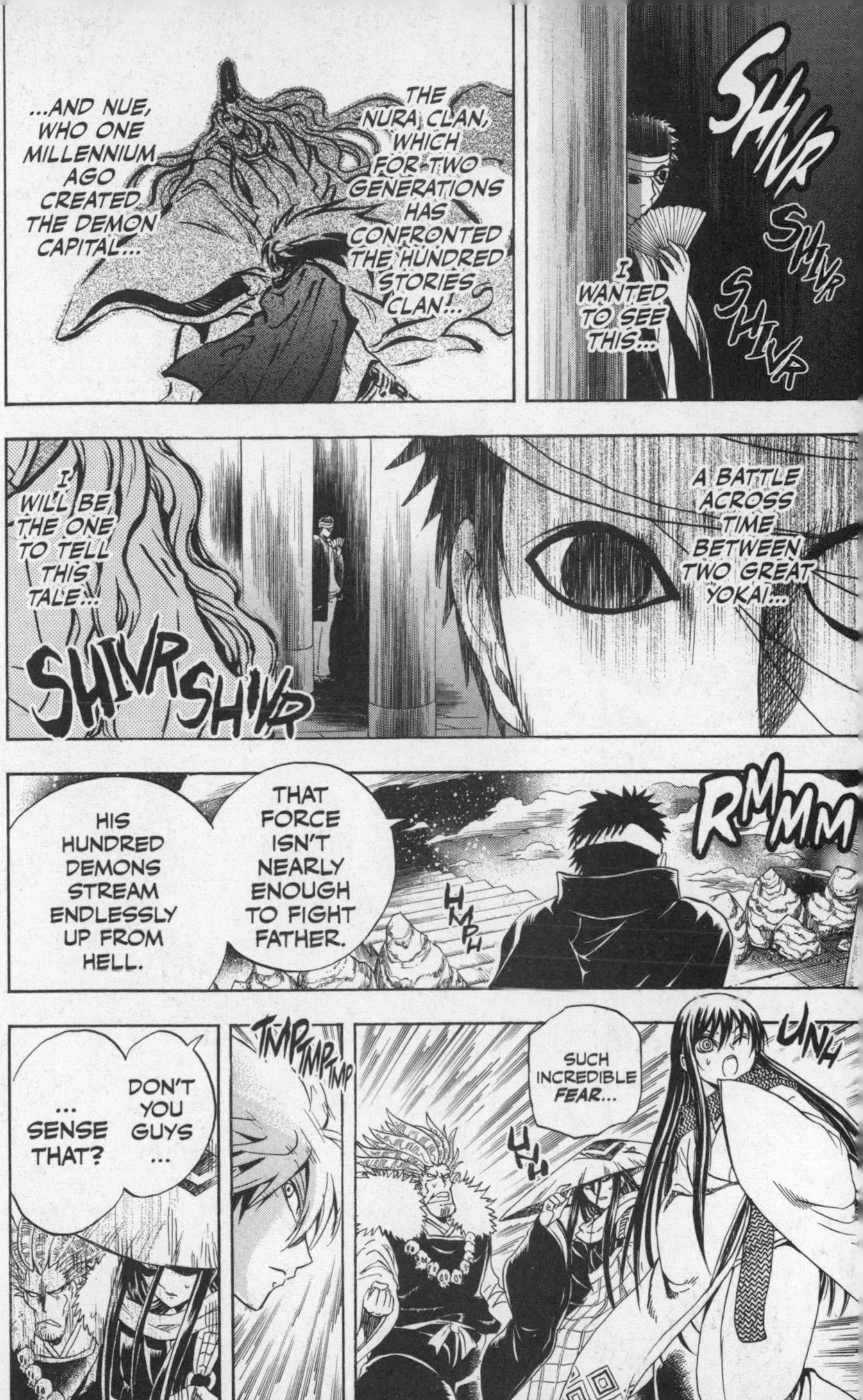
SHIVR
SHIVR
SHIVR
SHIVR
I WANTED TO SEE THIS...
THE NURA CLAN, WHICH FOR TWO GENERATIONS HAS CONFRONTED THE HUNDRED STORIES CLAN!...
...AND NUE, WHO ONE MILLENNIUM AGO CREATED THE DEMON CAPITAL...
A BATTLE ACROSS TIME BETWEEN TWO GREAT YOKAI...
I WILL BE THE ONE TO TELL THIS TALE...
SHIVR SHIVR
RMMMM
HMPH
THAT FORCE ISN'T NEARLY ENOUGH TO FIGHT FATHER.
HIS HUNDRED DEMONS STREAM ENDLESSLY UP FROM HELL.
UNH
SUCH INCREDIBLE FEAR...
UHH
TMP TMP TMP TMP
DON'T YOU GUYS...
...SENSE THAT?

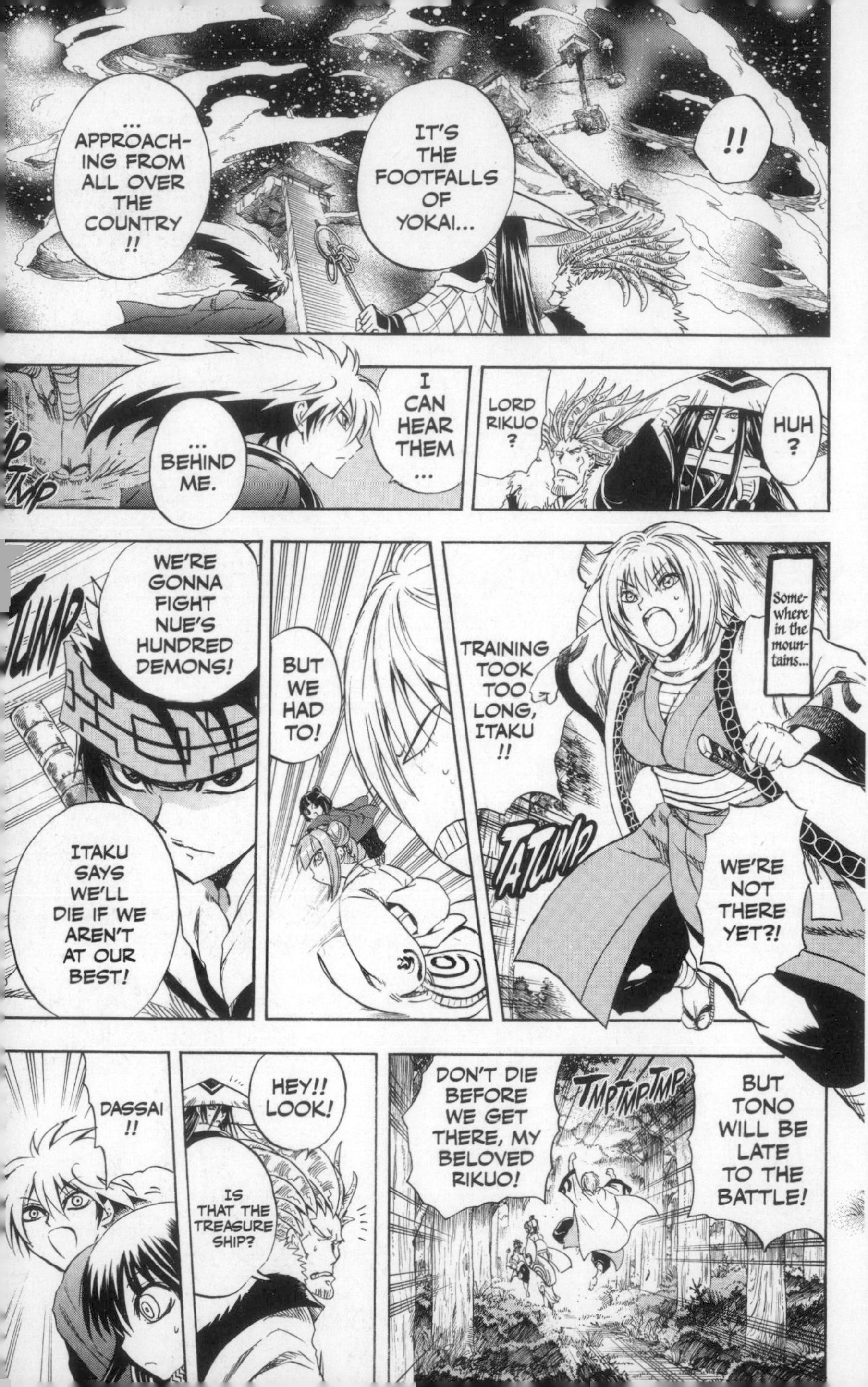
!!
IT'S THE FOOTFALLS OF YOKAI...
...APPROACHING FROM ALL OVER THE COUNTRY!!
HUH?
LORD RIKUO?
I CAN HEAR THEM...
...BEHIND ME.
TMP TMP
Somewhere in the mountains...
TRAINING TOOK TOO LONG, ITAKU!!
TATUMP
WE'RE NOT THERE YET?!
BUT WE HAD TO!
TUMP
WE'RE GONNA FIGHT NUE'S HUNDRED DEMONS!
ITAKU SAYS WE'LL DIE IF WE AREN'T AT OUR BEST!
BUT TONO WILL BE LATE TO THE BATTLE!
TMPTMPTMP
DON'T DIE BEFORE WE GET THERE, MY BELOVED RIKUO!
HEY!! LOOK!
IS THAT THE TREASURE SHIP?
DASSAI!!

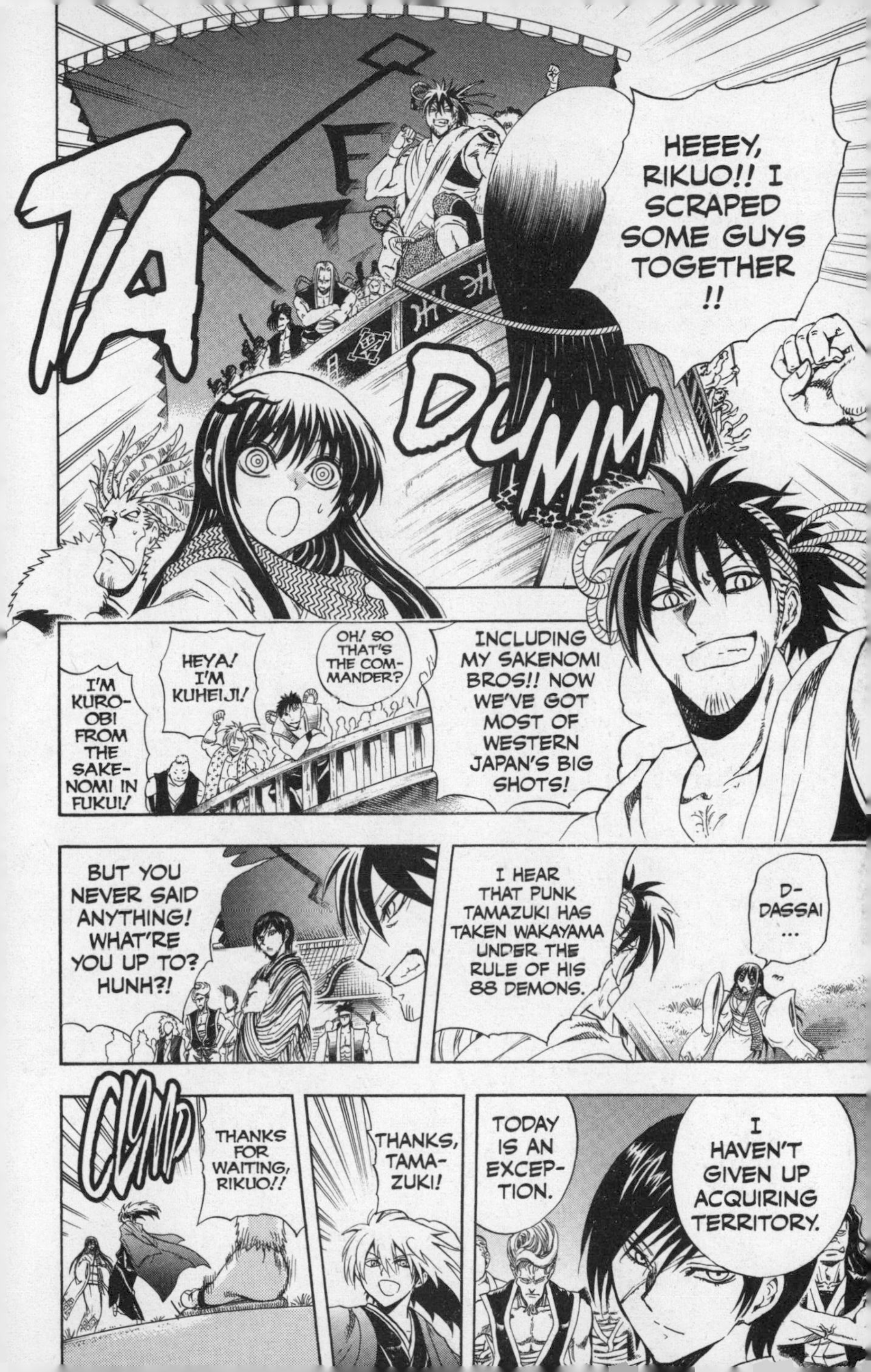
HEEEY, RIKUO!! I SCRAPED SOME GUYS TOGETHER!!
DUMM
TA
INCLUDING MY SAKENOMI BROS!! NOW WE'VE GOT MOST OF WESTERN JAPAN'S BIG SHOTS!
OH! SO THAT'S THE COM-MANDER?
HEYA! I'M KUHEIJI!
I'M KURO-OBI FROM THE SAKE-NOMI IN FUKUI!
D-DASSAI ...
I HEAR THAT PUNK TAMAZUKI HAS TAKEN WAKAYAMA UNDER THE RULE OF HIS 88 DEMONS.
BUT YOU NEVER SAID ANYTHING! WHAT'RE YOU UP TO? HUNH?!
I HAVEN'T GIVEN UP ACQUIRING TERRITORY.
TODAY IS AN EXCEP-TION.
THANKS, TAMA-ZUKI!
THANKS FOR WAITING, RIKUO!!

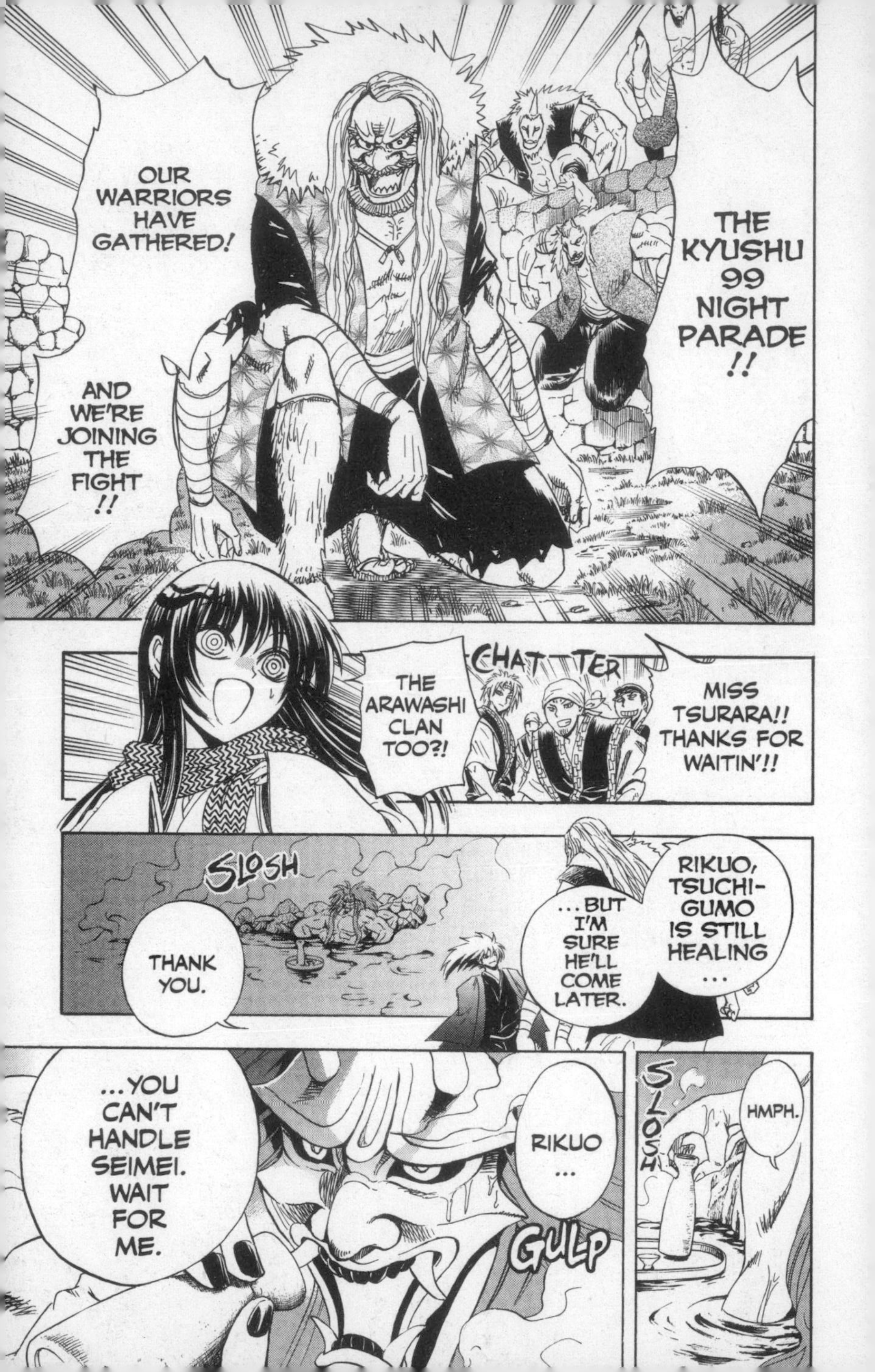
THE KYUSHU 99 NIGHT PARADE!!
OUR WARRIORS HAVE GATHERED!
AND WE'RE JOINING THE FIGHT!!
MISS TSURARA!! THANKS FOR WAITIN'!!
CHATTER
THE ARAWASHI CLAN TOO?!
RIKUO, TSUCHI-GUMO IS STILL HEALING...
...BUT I'M SURE HE'LL COME LATER.
SLOSH
THANK YOU.
SLOSH
HMPH.
RIKUO...
...YOU CAN'T HANDLE SEIMEI. WAIT FOR ME.
GULP

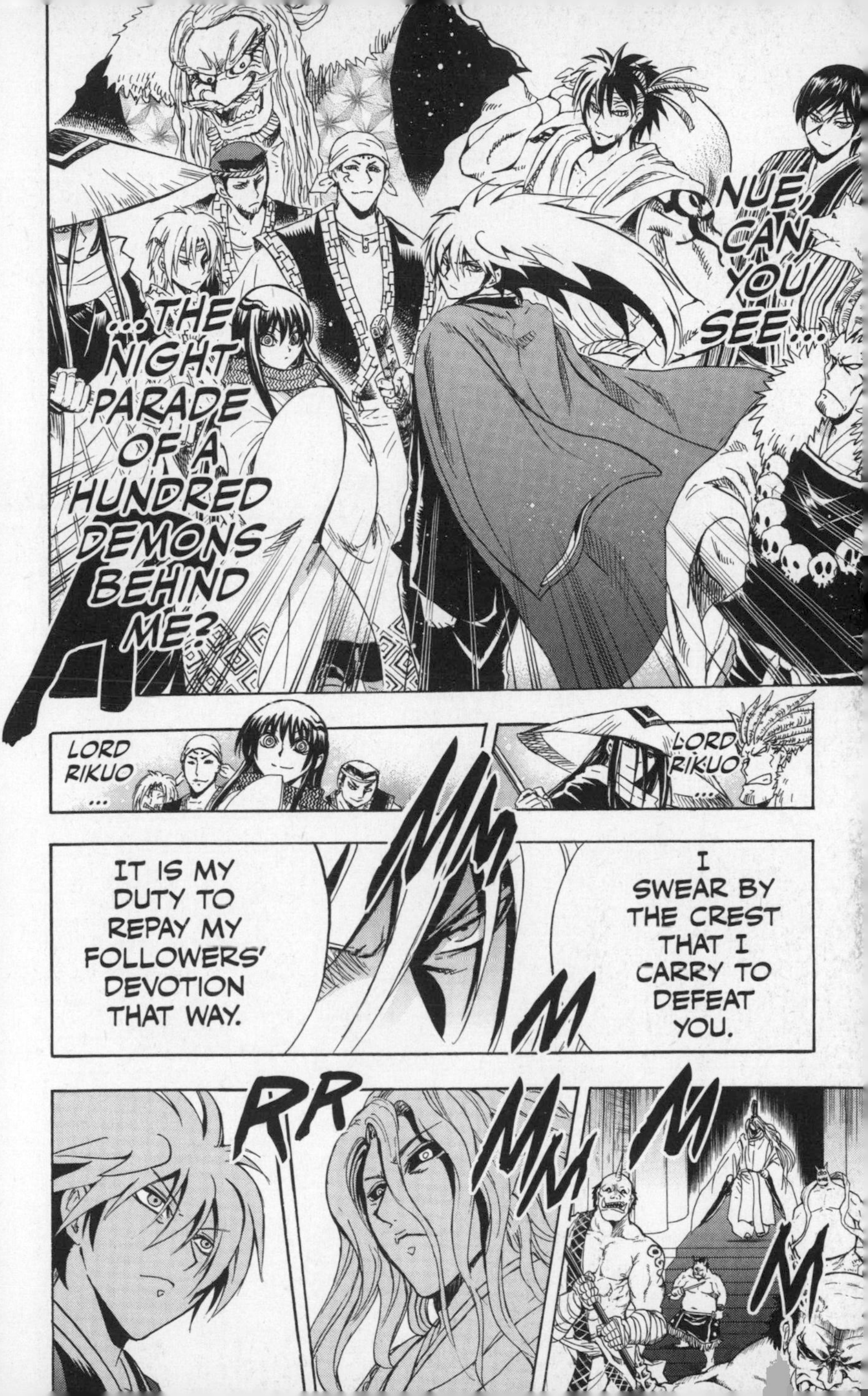
NUE, CAN YOU SEE...
...THE NIGHT PARADE OF A HUNDRED DEMONS BEHIND ME?
LORD RIKUO...
LORD RIKUO...
MM
M
I SWEAR BY THE CREST THAT I CARRY TO DEFEAT YOU.
IT IS MY DUTY TO REPAY MY FOLLOWERS' DEVOTION THAT WAY.
RR
MMMM
M

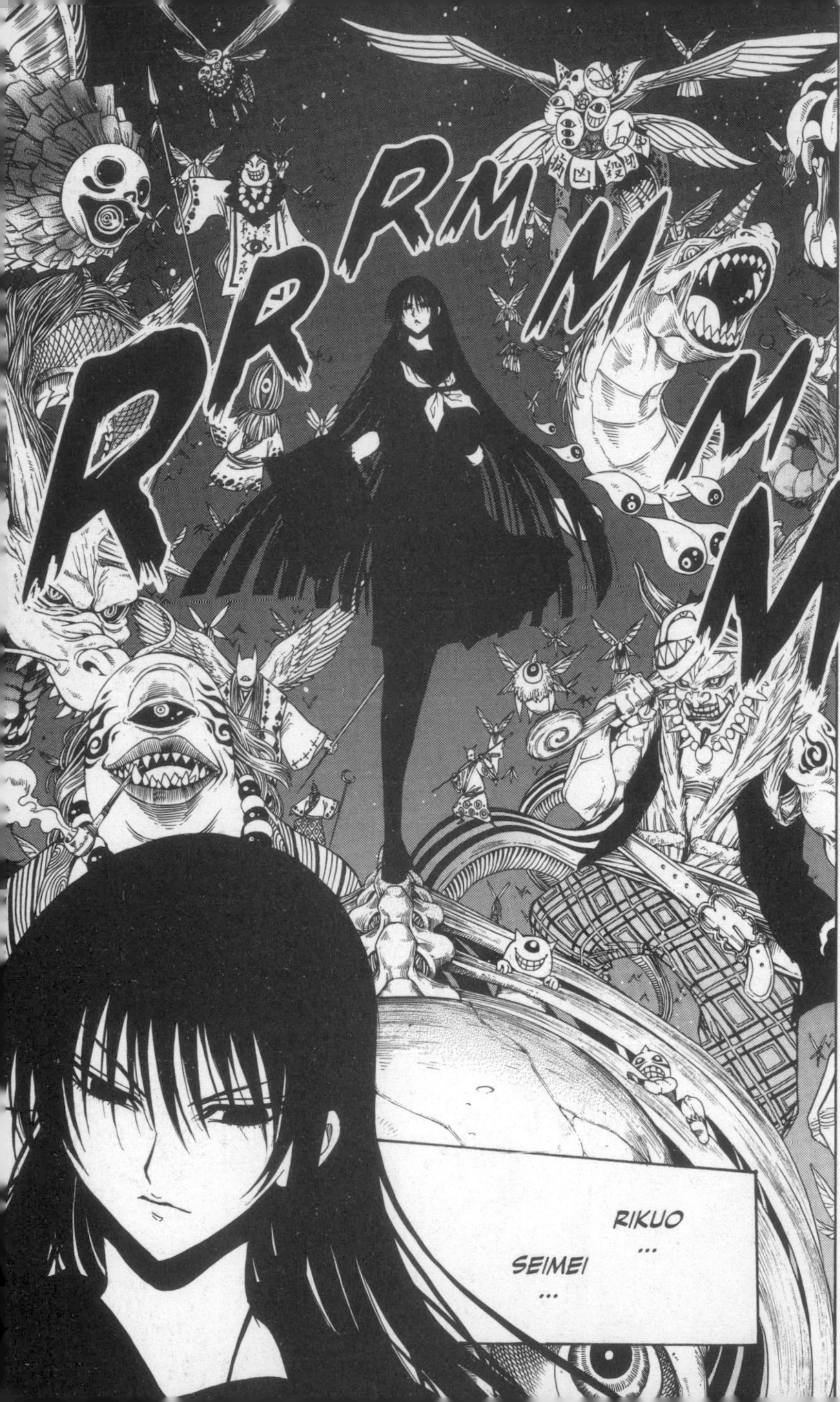
RRRMMMM
RIKUO ...
SEIMEI ...

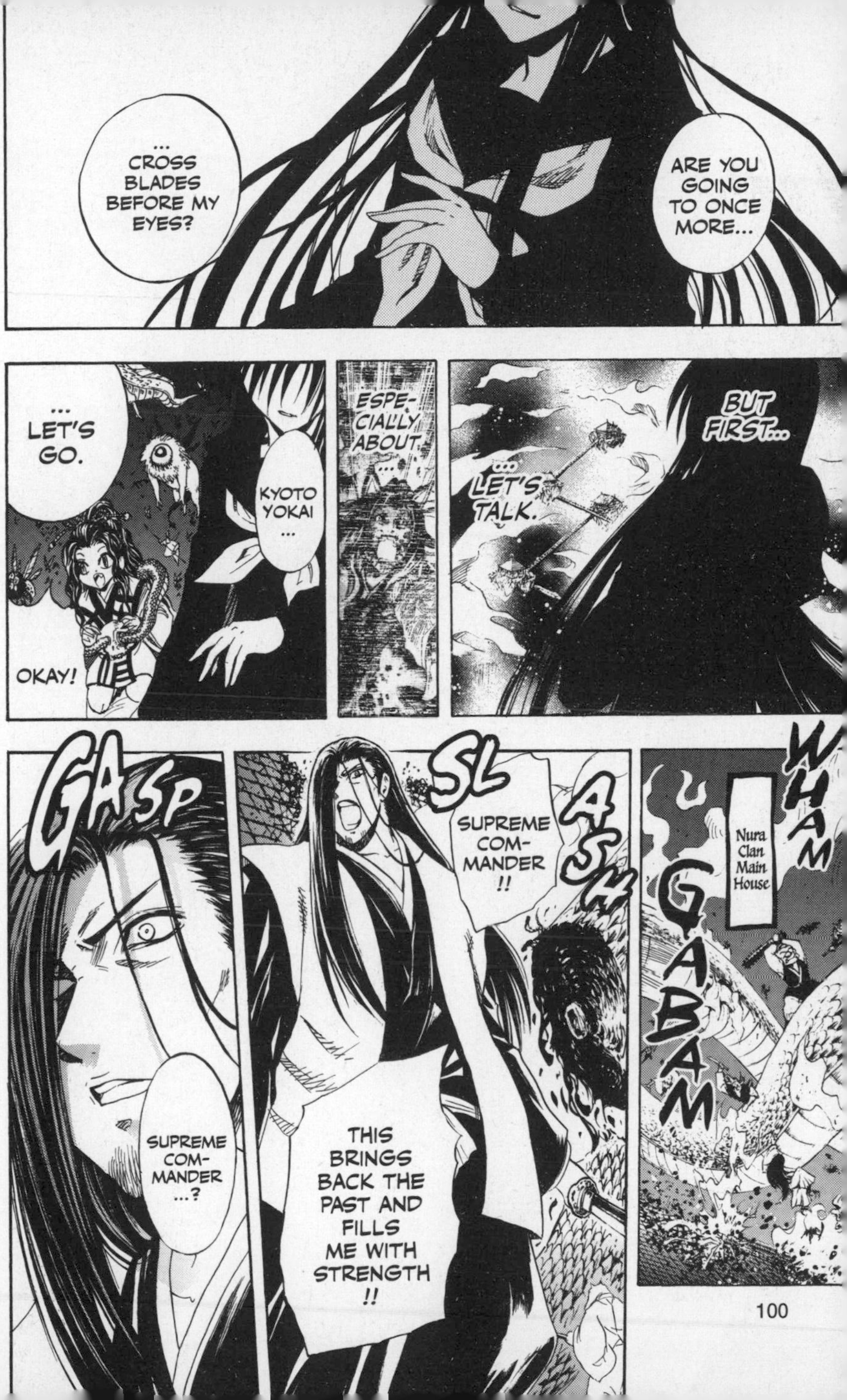
ARE YOU GOING TO ONCE MORE...
... CROSS BLADES BEFORE MY EYES?
BUT FIRST...
... LET'S TALK.
ESPE-CIALLY ABOUT ...
KYOTO YOKAI ...
... LET'S GO.
OKAY!
WHAM
GABAM
Nura Clan Main House
SLASH
SUPREME COM-MANDER !!
THIS BRINGS BACK THE PAST AND FILLS ME WITH STRENGTH !!
GASP
SUPREME COM-MANDER ...?

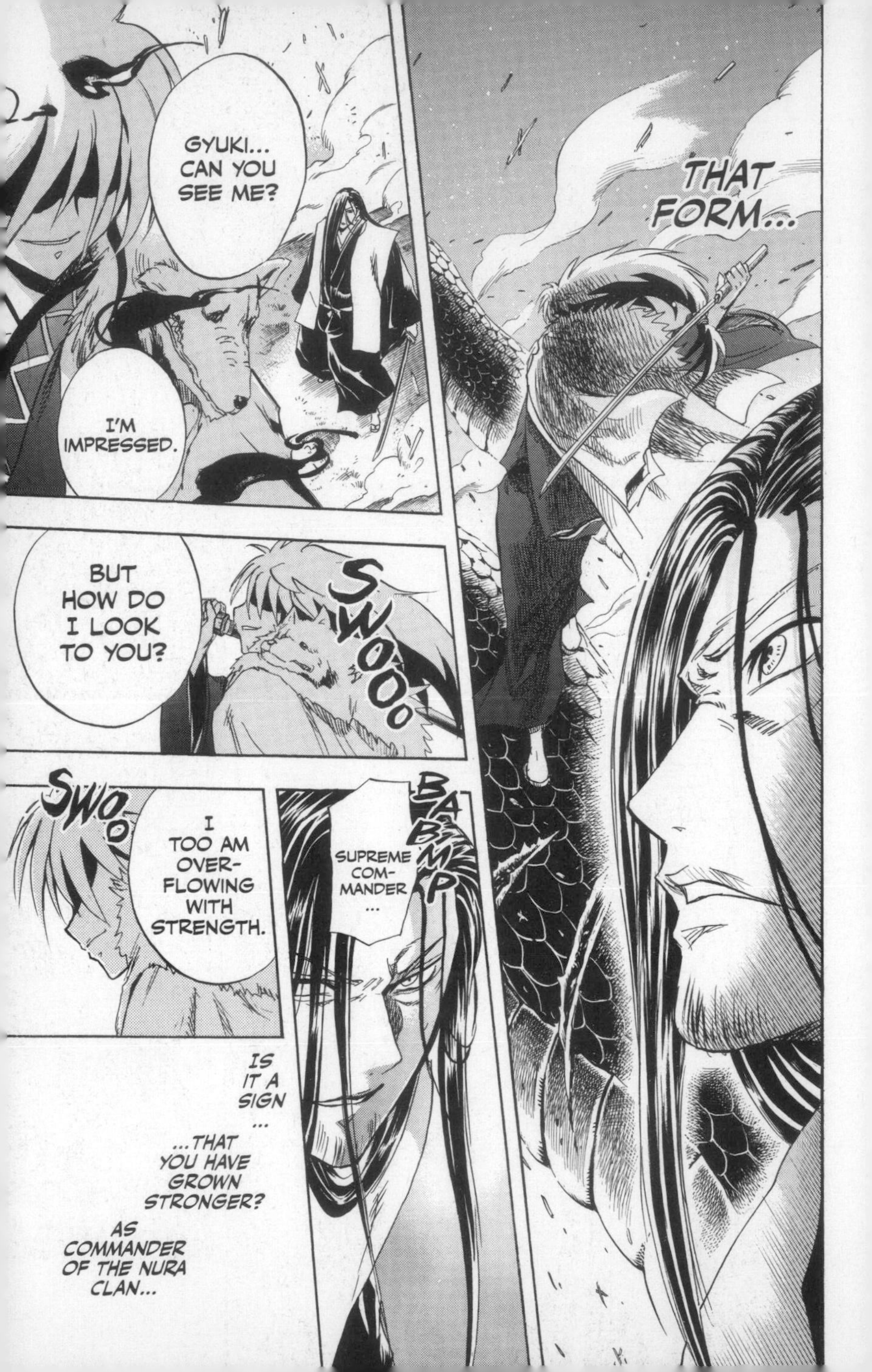
THAT FORM...
GYUKI... CAN YOU SEE ME?
I'M IMPRESSED.
BUT HOW DO I LOOK TO YOU?
SWOOO
SWOO
I TOO AM OVER-FLOWING WITH STRENGTH.
BABUMP
SUPREME COM-MANDER...
IS IT A SIGN...
...THAT YOU HAVE GROWN STRONGER?
AS COMMANDER OF THE NURA CLAN...

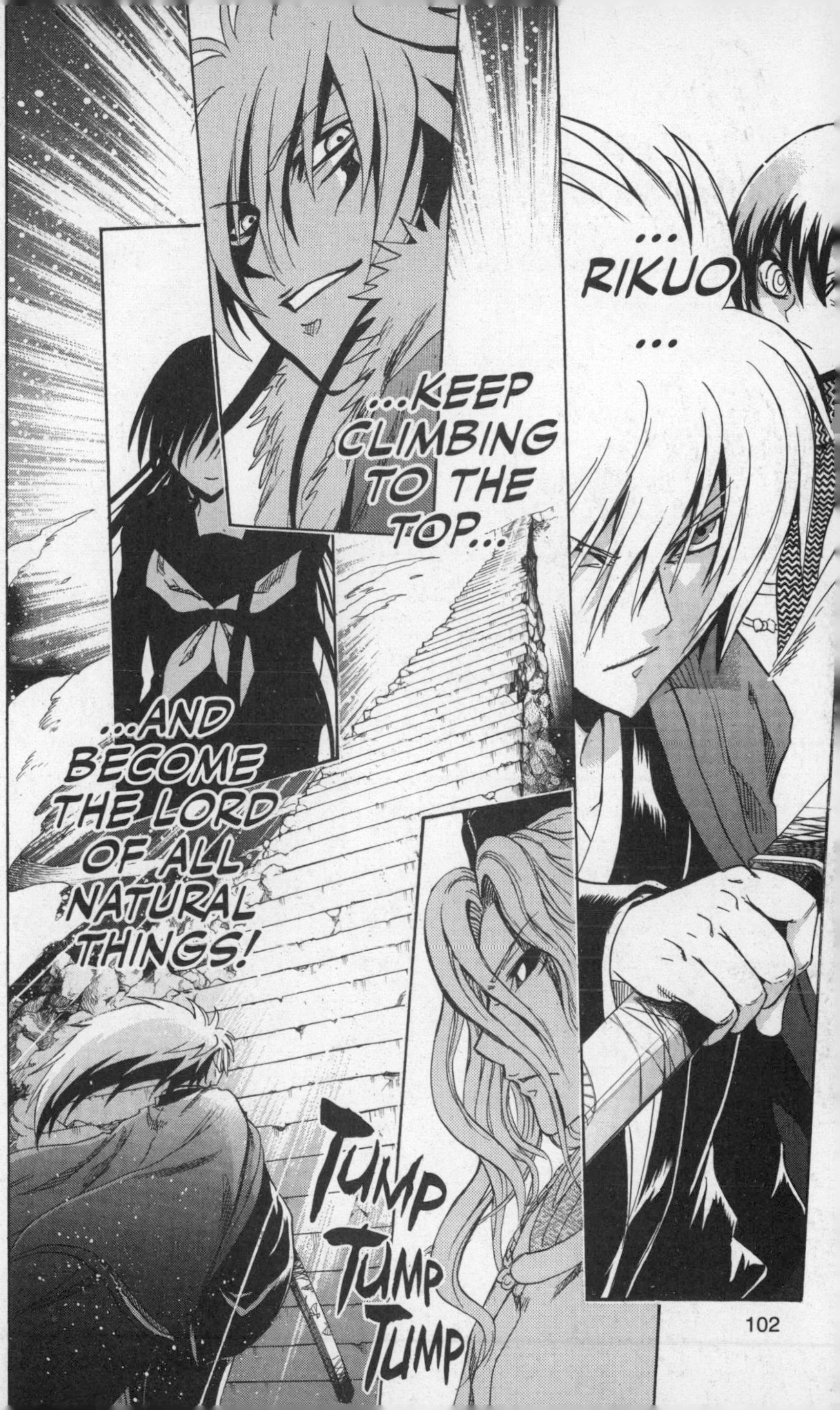
...RIKUO...
...KEEP CLIMBING TO THE TOP...
...AND BECOME THE LORD OF ALL NATURAL THINGS!
TUMP TUMP TUMP

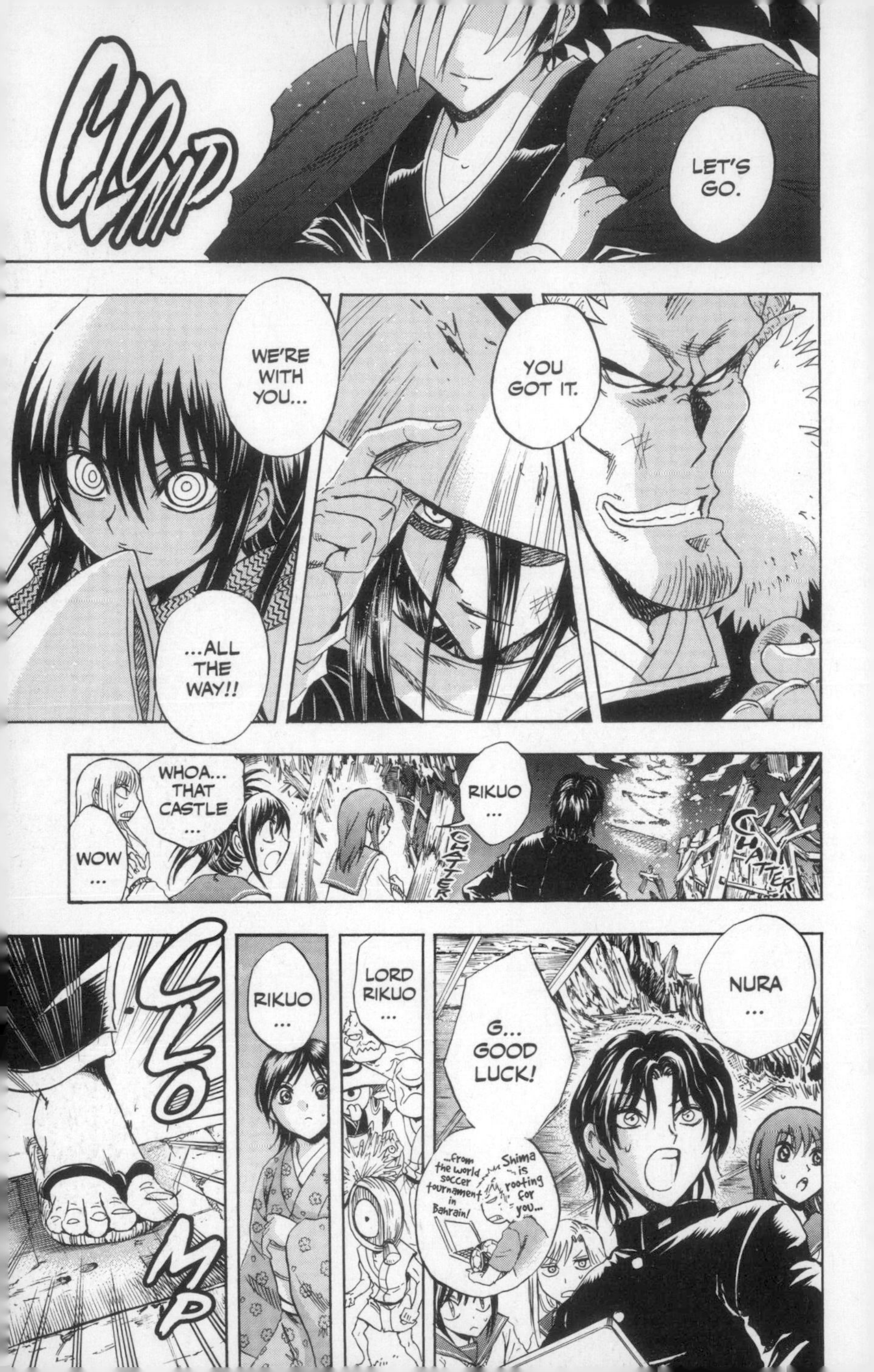
LET'S GO.
CLOMP
YOU GOT IT.
WE'RE WITH YOU...
...ALL THE WAY!!
CHATTER
RIKUO ...
CHATTER
WHOA... THAT CASTLE ...
WOW ...
NURA ...
G... GOOD LUCK!
Shima is rooting for you...
...from the world soccer tournament in Bahrain!
LORD RIKUO ...
RIKUO ...
CLOMP

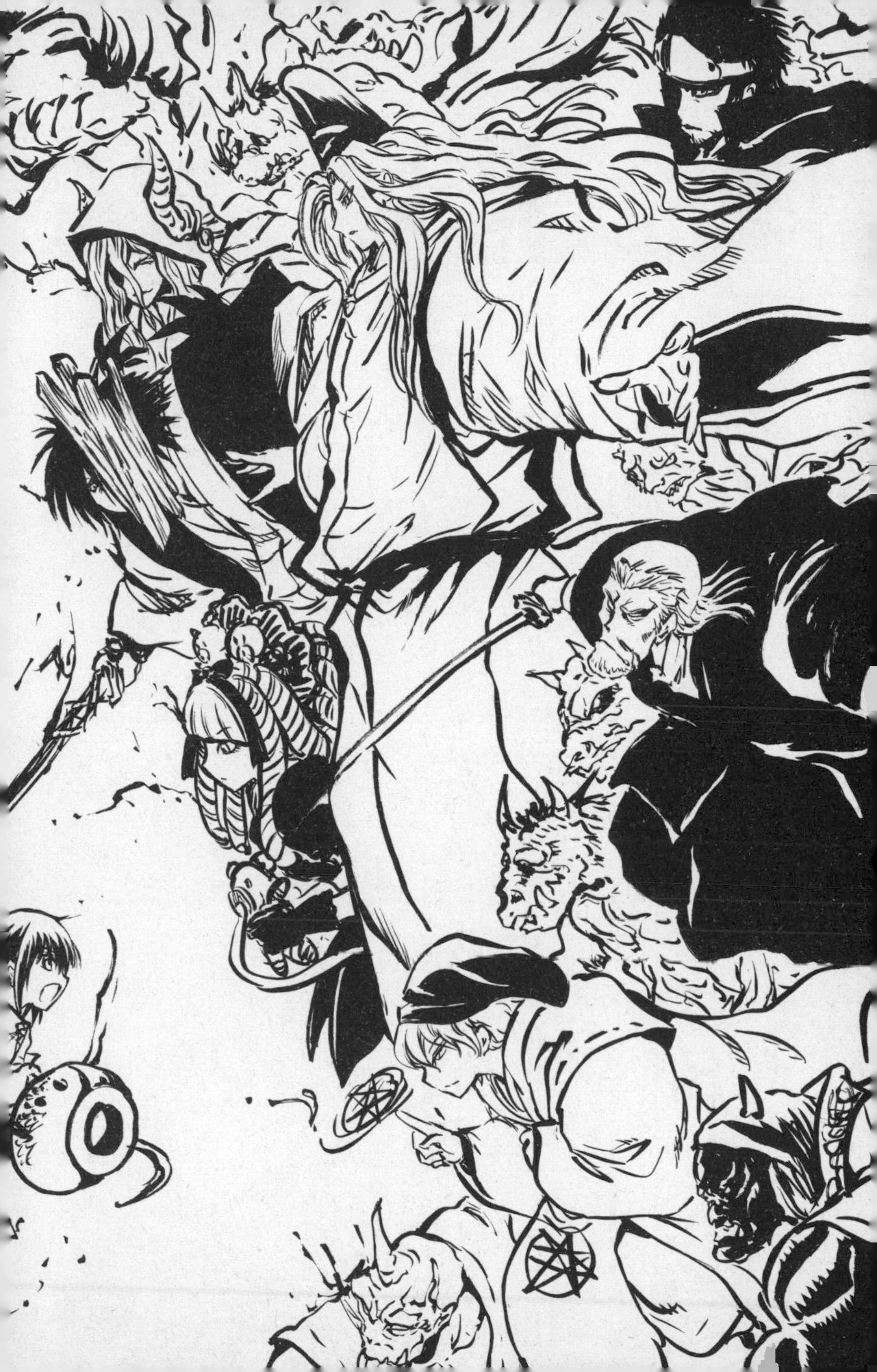

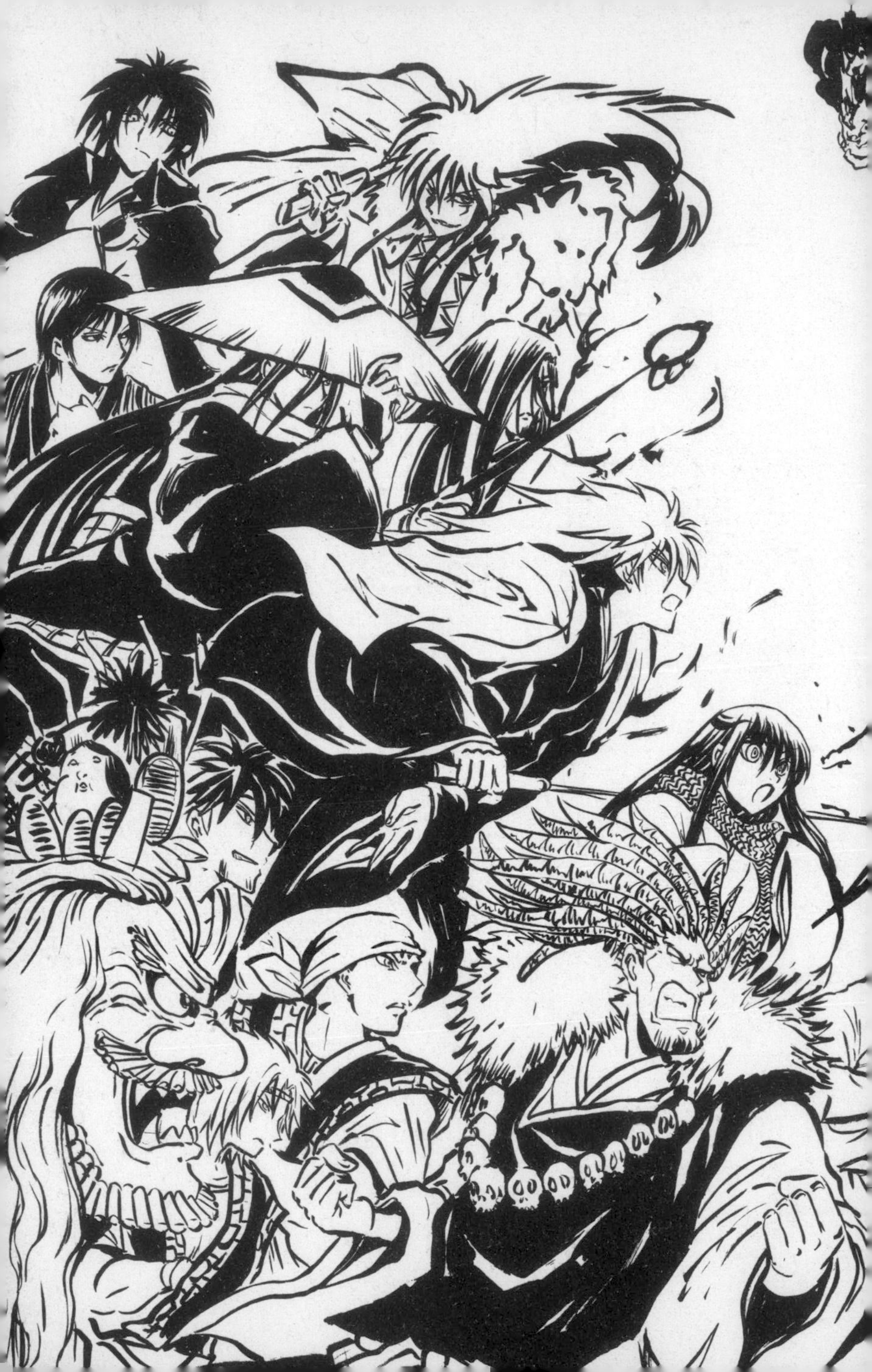

Yokai Quiz: Part 3

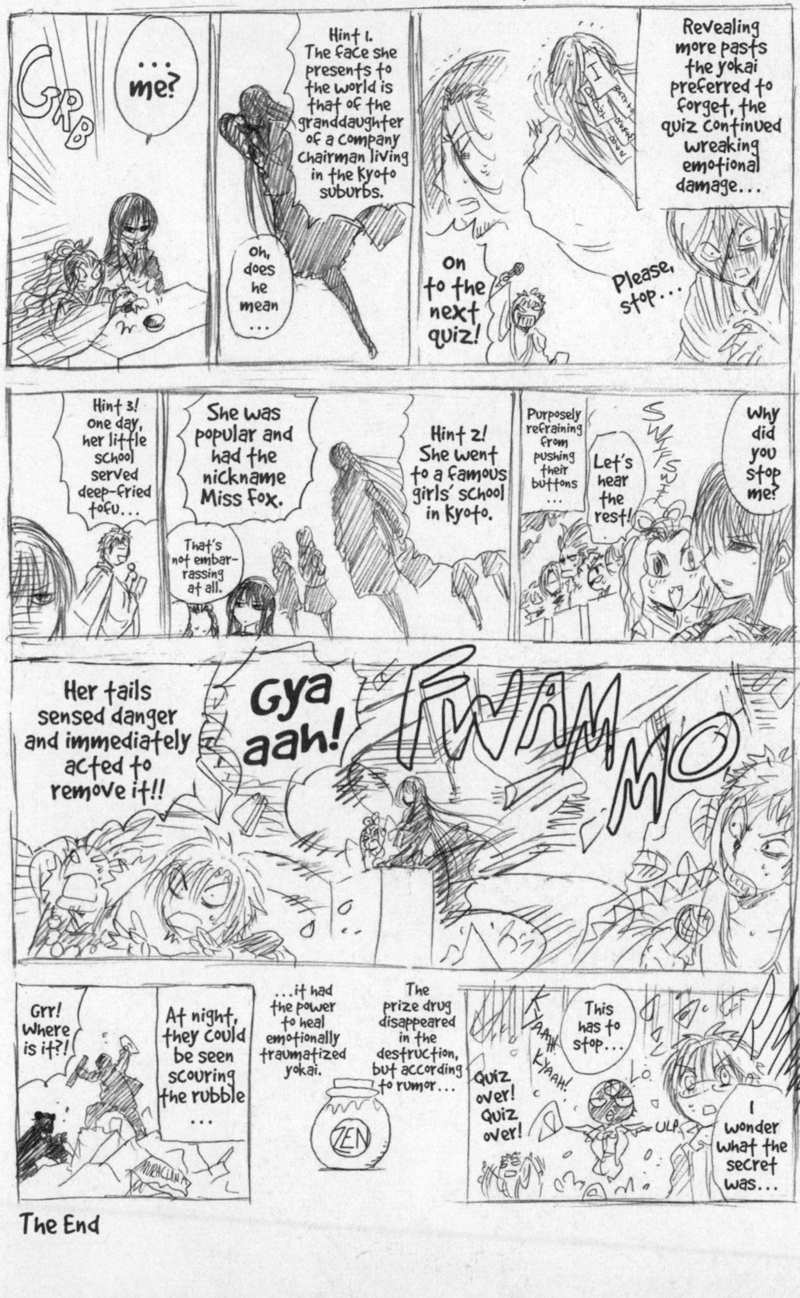
Revealing more pasts the yokai preferred to forget, the quiz continued wreaking emotional damage...
Please, stop...
On to the next quiz!
Hint 1. The face she presents to the world is that of the granddaughter of a company chairman living in the Kyoto suburbs.
Oh, does he mean...
... me?
Why did you stop me?
Let's hear the rest!
Purposely refraining from pushing their buttons...
Hint 2! She went to a famous girls' school in Kyoto.
She was popular and had the nickname Miss Fox.
That's not embarrassing at all.
Hint 3! One day, her little school served deep-fried tofu...
Gya aah!
Her tails sensed danger and immediately acted to remove it!!
I wonder what the secret was...
ULP.
This has to stop...
KYAAH!
Quiz over! Quiz over!
The prize drug disappeared in the destruction, but according to rumor...
...it had the power to heal emotionally traumatized yokai.
ZEN
At night, they could be seen scouring the rubble...
Grr! Where is it?!

The End

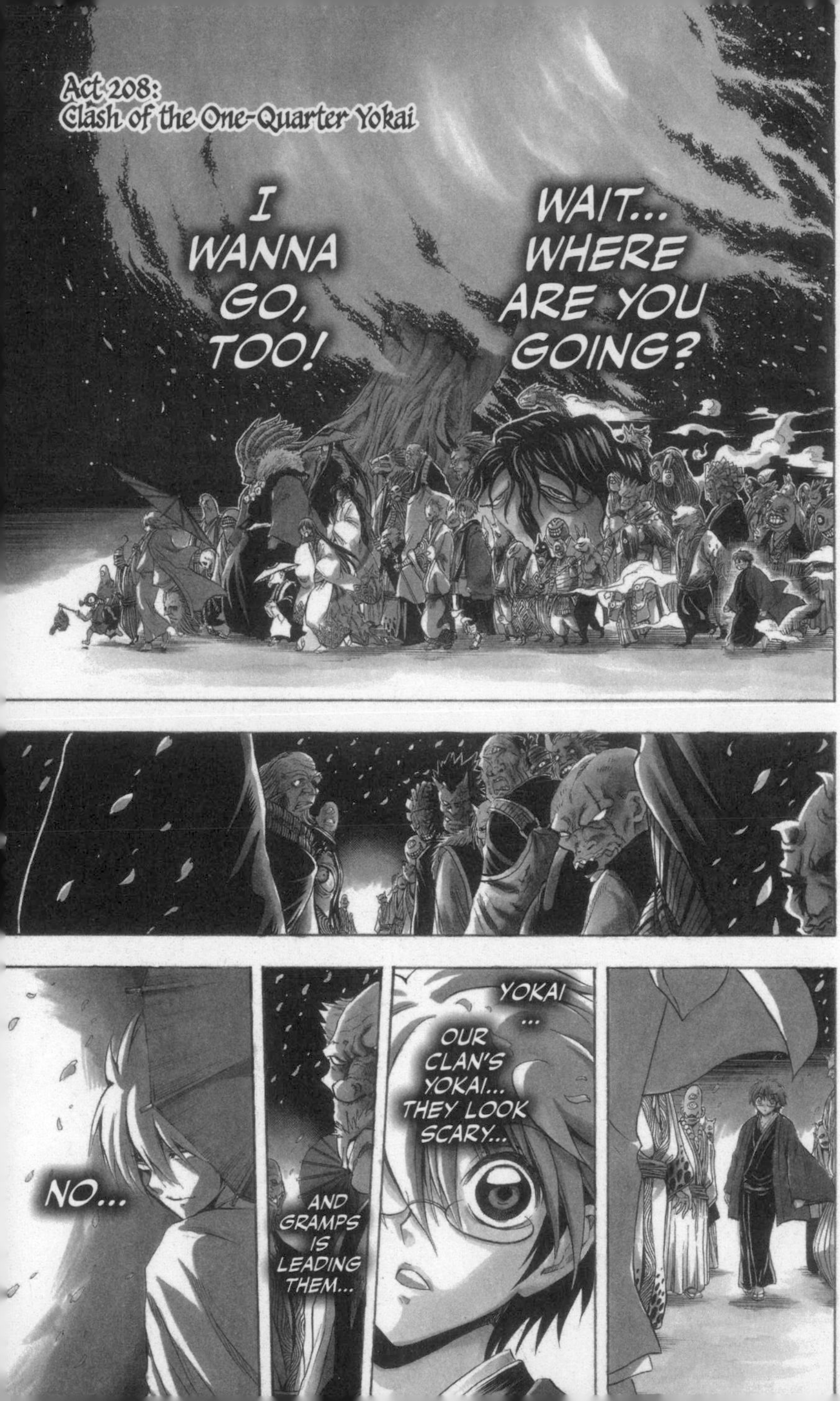
Act 208:
Clash of the One-Quarter Yokai
WAIT... WHERE ARE YOU GOING?
I WANNA GO, TOO!
YOKAI...
OUR CLAN'S YOKAI... THEY LOOK SCARY...
AND GRAMPS IS LEADING THEM...
NO...

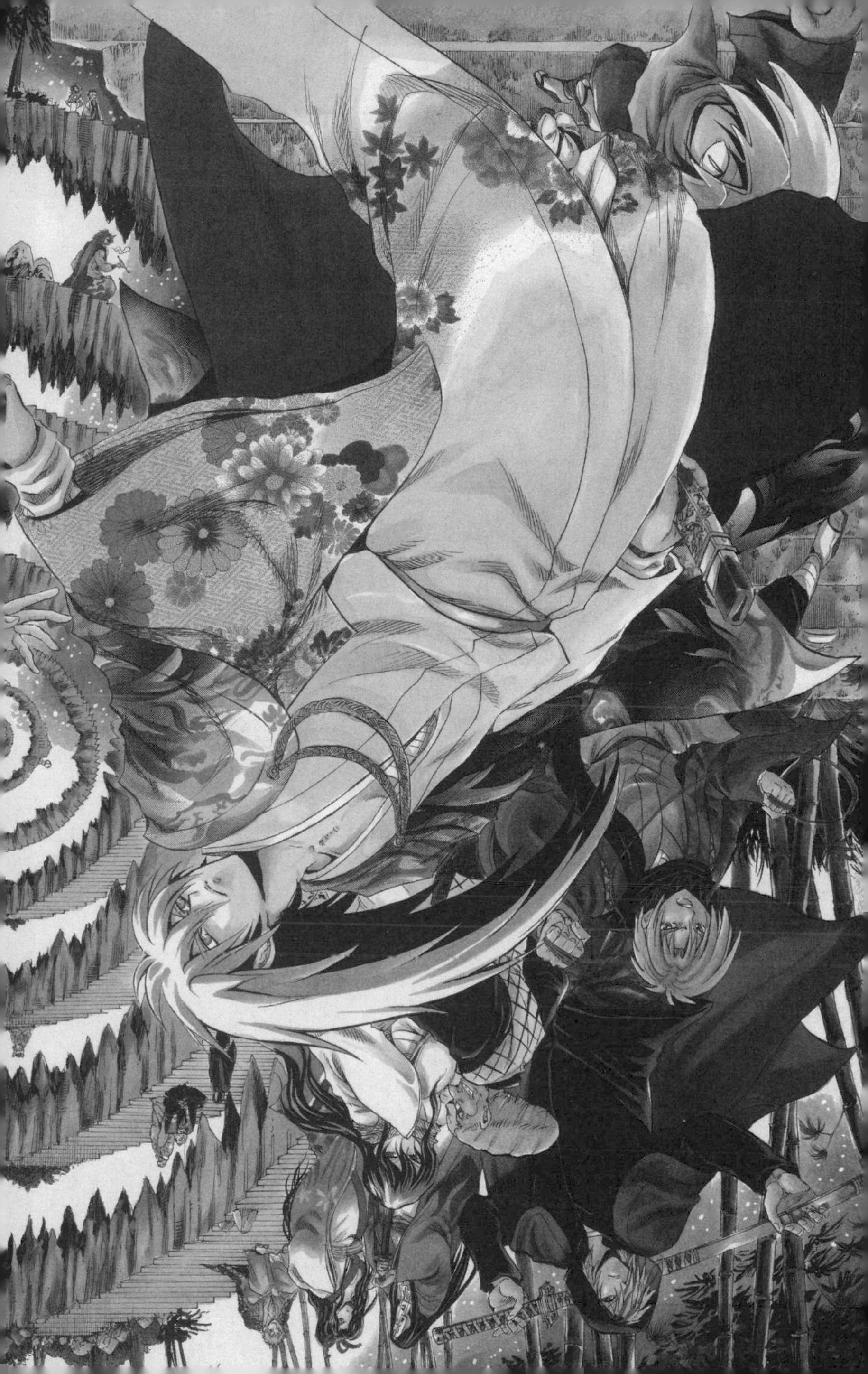

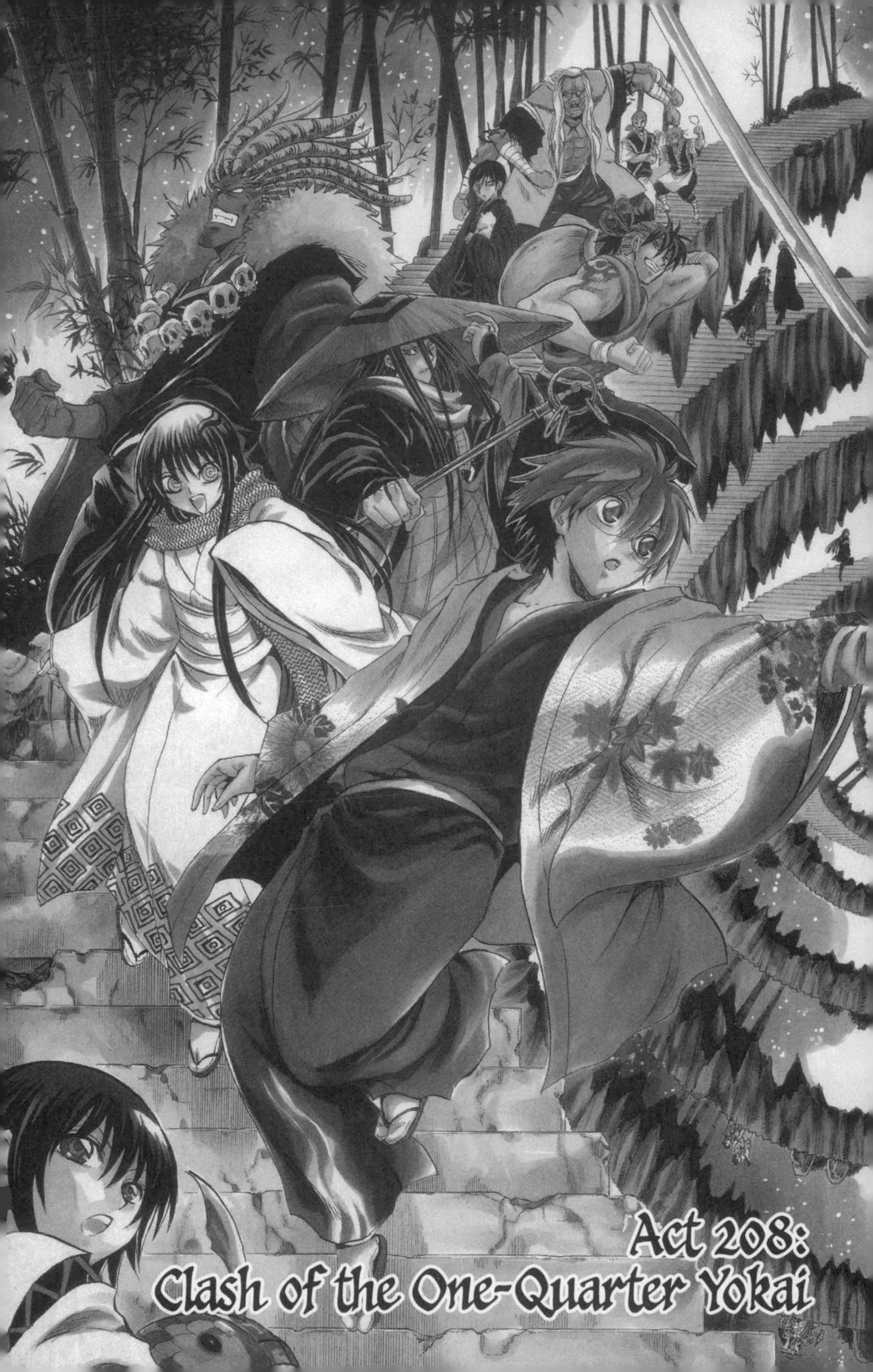
Act 208:
Clash of the One-Quarter Yokai

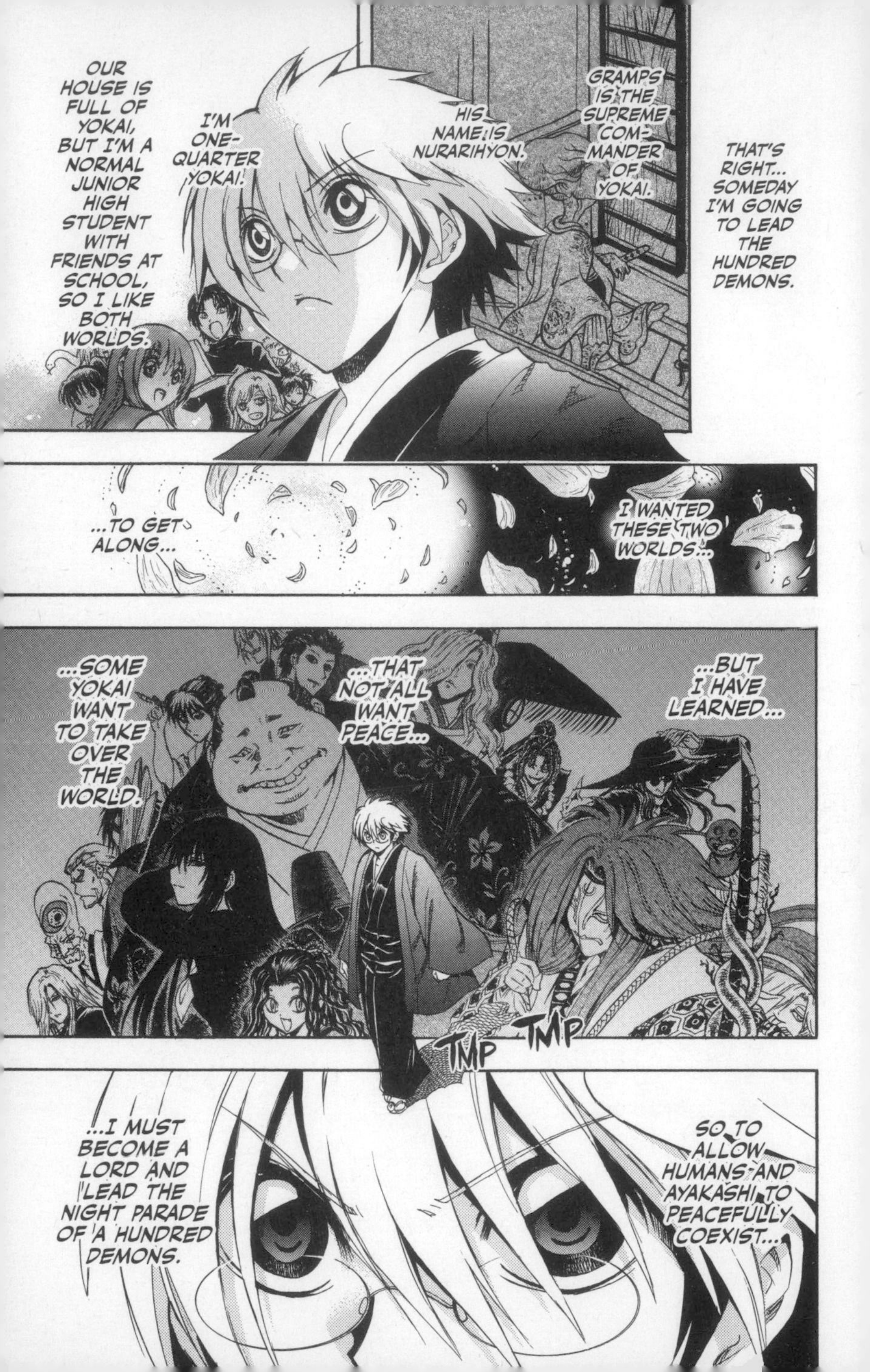
THAT'S RIGHT... SOMEDAY I'M GOING TO LEAD THE HUNDRED DEMONS.
GRAMPS IS THE SUPREME COMMANDER OF YOKAI.
HIS NAME IS NURARIHYON.
I'M ONE-QUARTER YOKAI.
OUR HOUSE IS FULL OF YOKAI, BUT I'M A NORMAL JUNIOR HIGH STUDENT WITH FRIENDS AT SCHOOL, SO I LIKE BOTH WORLDS.
I WANTED THESE TWO WORLDS...
...TO GET ALONG...
...BUT I HAVE LEARNED...
...THAT NOT ALL WANT PEACE...
...SOME YOKAI WANT TO TAKE OVER THE WORLD.
TMP
TMP
SO TO ALLOW HUMANS AND AYAKASHI TO PEACEFULLY COEXIST...
...I MUST BECOME A LORD AND LEAD THE NIGHT PARADE OF A HUNDRED DEMONS.

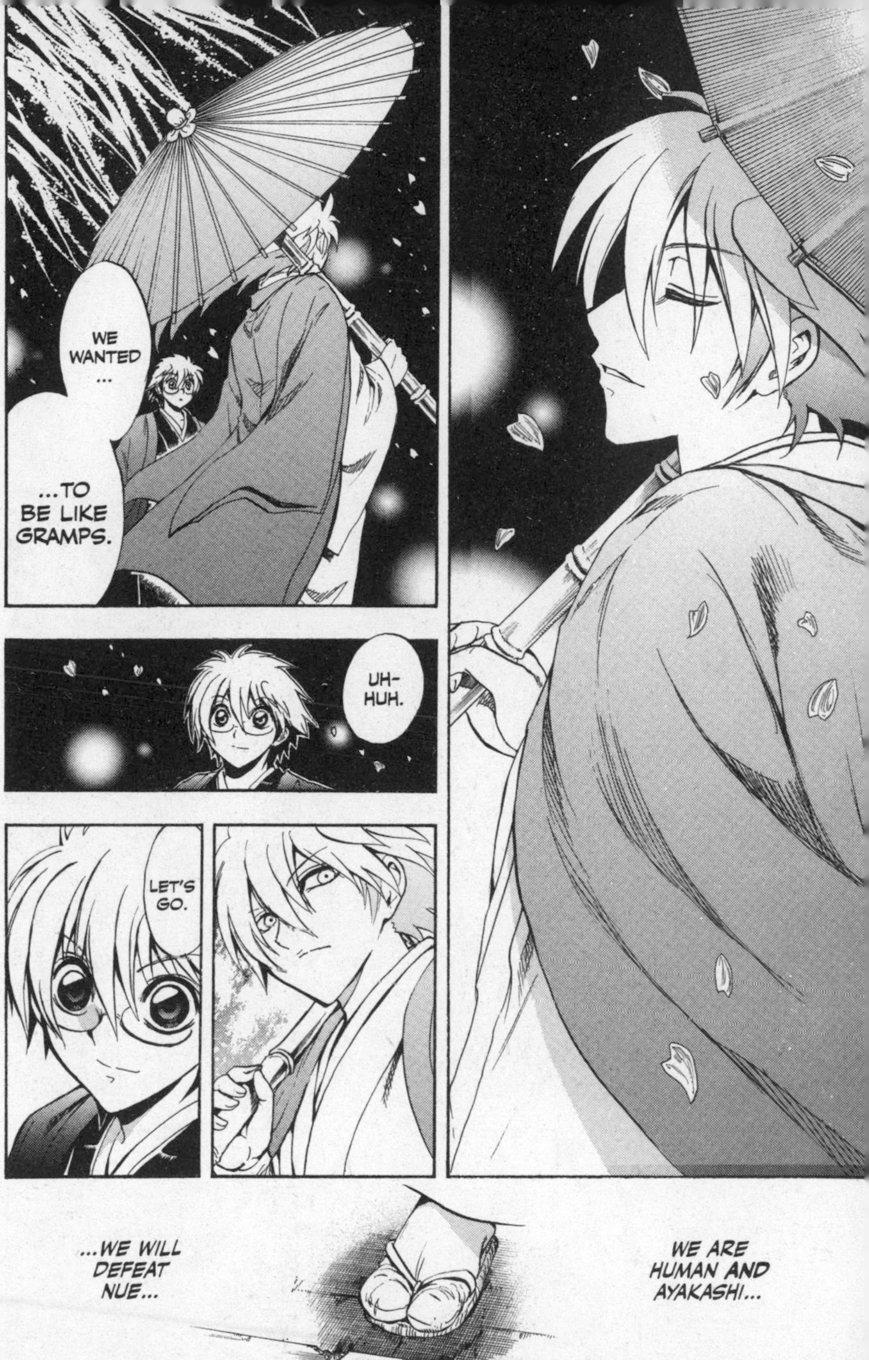
WE WANTED ...
...TO BE LIKE GRAMPS.
UH-HUH.
LET'S GO.
WE ARE HUMAN AND AYAKASHI...
...WE WILL DEFEAT NUE...

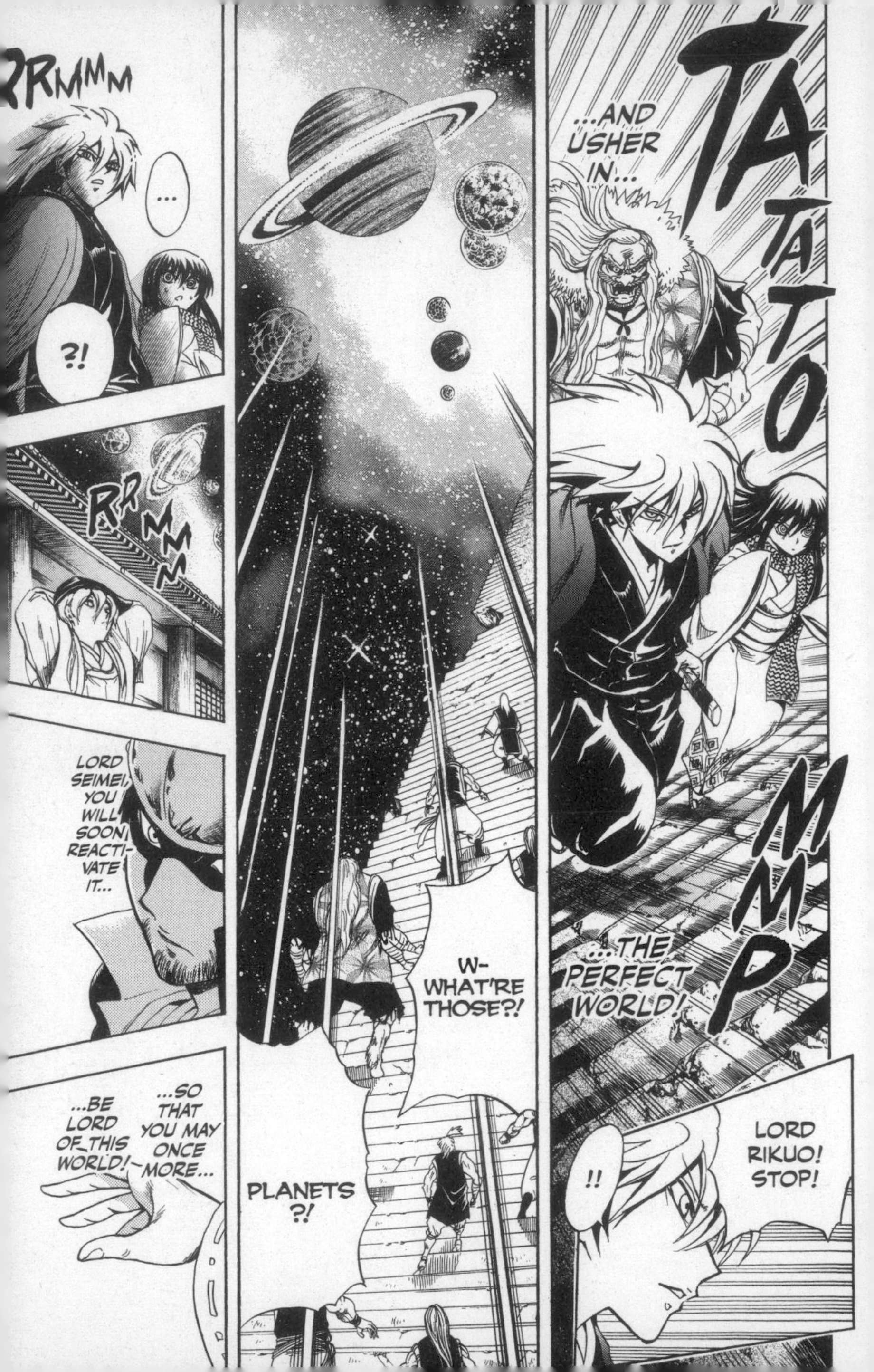
TATATO
...AND USHER IN...
...THE PERFECT WORLD!
MMMP
LORD RIKUO! STOP!
!!
W- WHAT'RE THOSE?!
PLANETS ?!
RMMMM
...
?!
RRMMMM
LORD SEIMEI, YOU WILL SOON REACTIVATE IT...
...SO THAT YOU MAY ONCE MORE...
...BE LORD OF THIS WORLD!

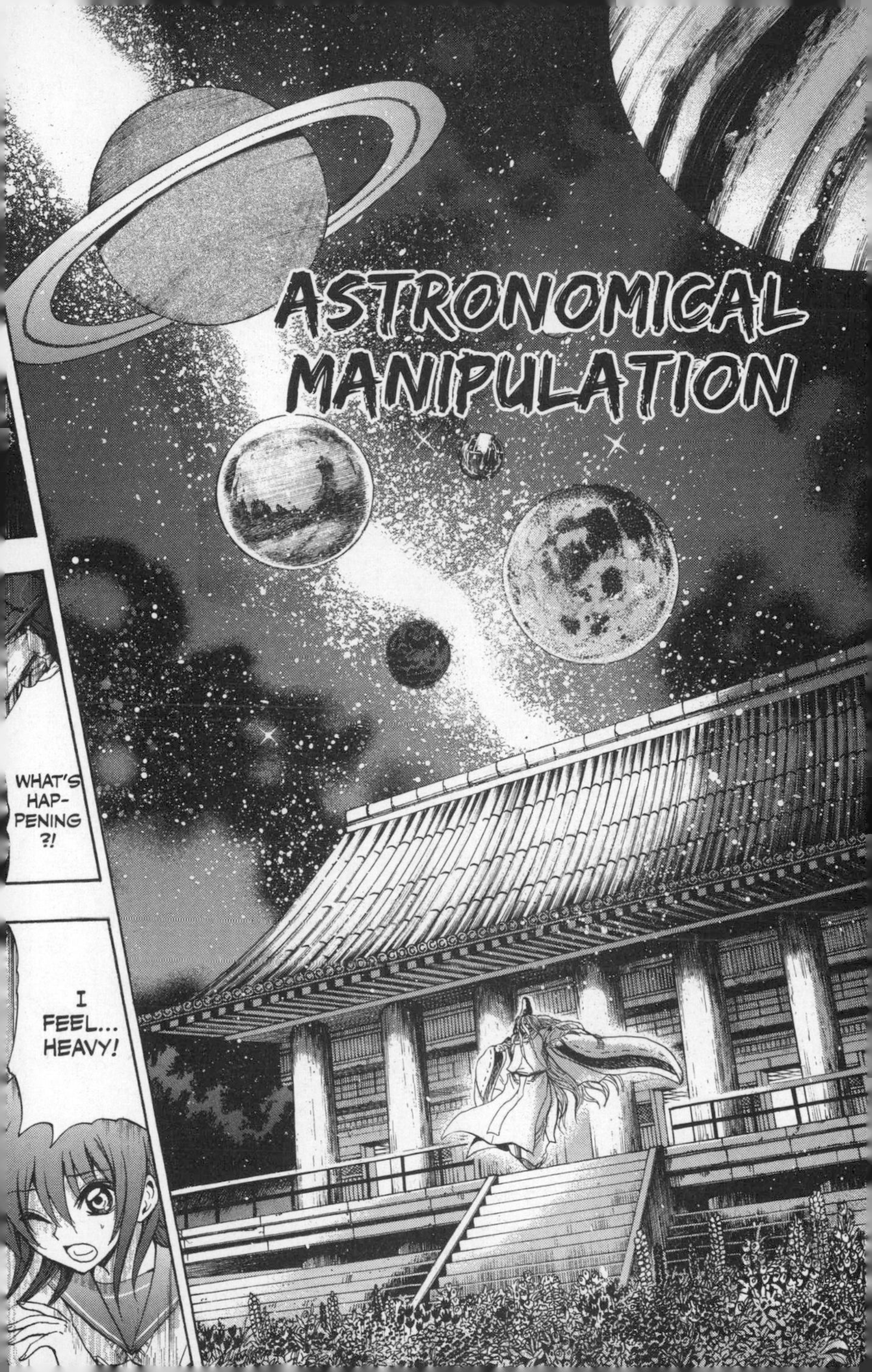
ASTRONOMICAL MANIPULATION
WHAT'S HAP-PENING ?!
I FEEL... HEAVY!

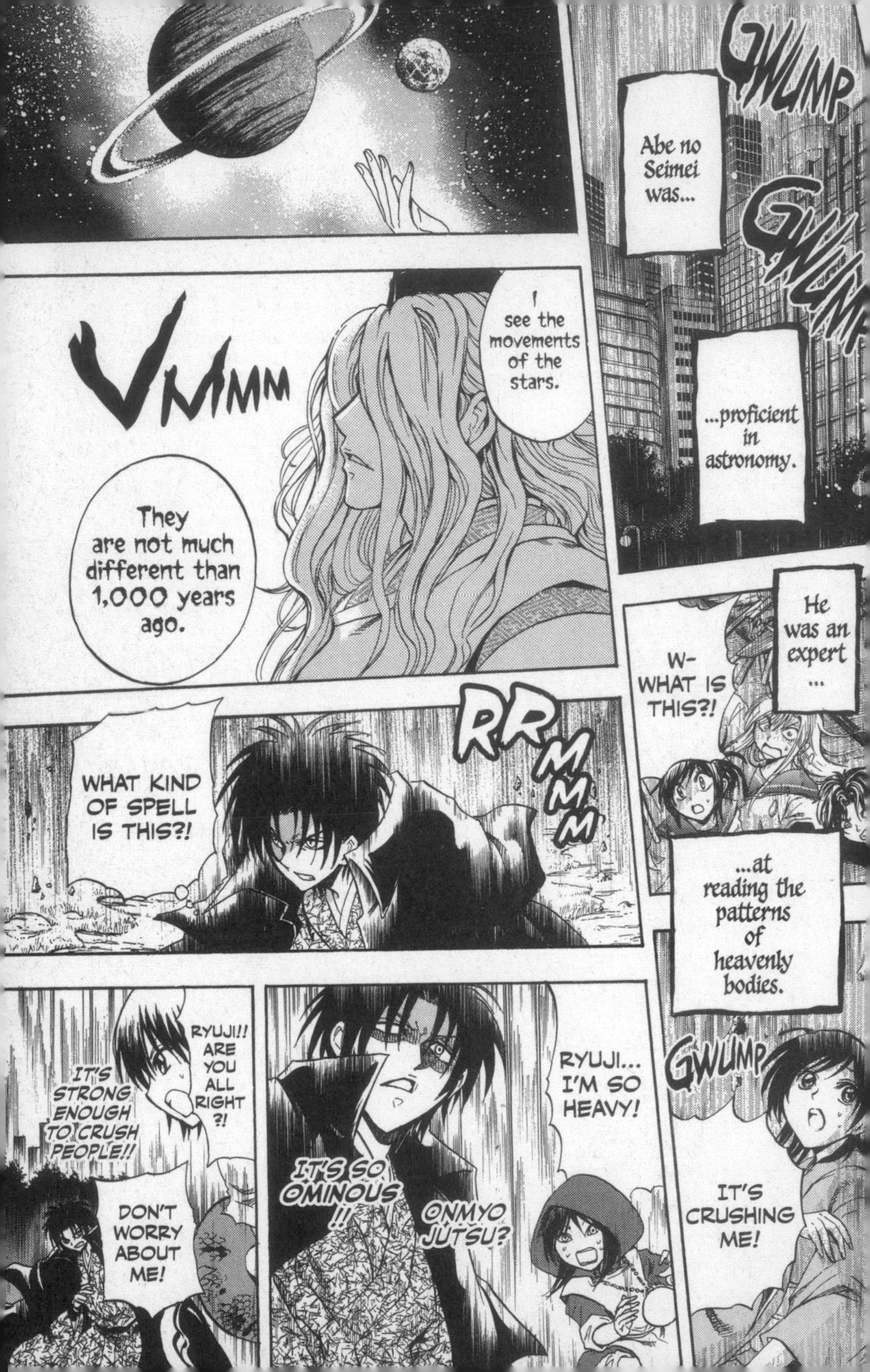
GWUMP
Abe no Seimei was...
GWUMP
...proficient in astronomy.
I see the movements of the stars.
VMMM
They are not much different than 1,000 years ago.
He was an expert...
W-WHAT IS THIS?!
...at reading the patterns of heavenly bodies.
RRMMM
WHAT KIND OF SPELL IS THIS?!
GWUMP
IT'S CRUSHING ME!
RYUJI... I'M SO HEAVY!
ONMYO JUTSU?
IT'S SO OMINOUS!!
RYUJI!! ARE YOU ALL RIGHT?!
IT'S STRONG ENOUGH TO CRUSH PEOPLE!!
DON'T WORRY ABOUT ME!

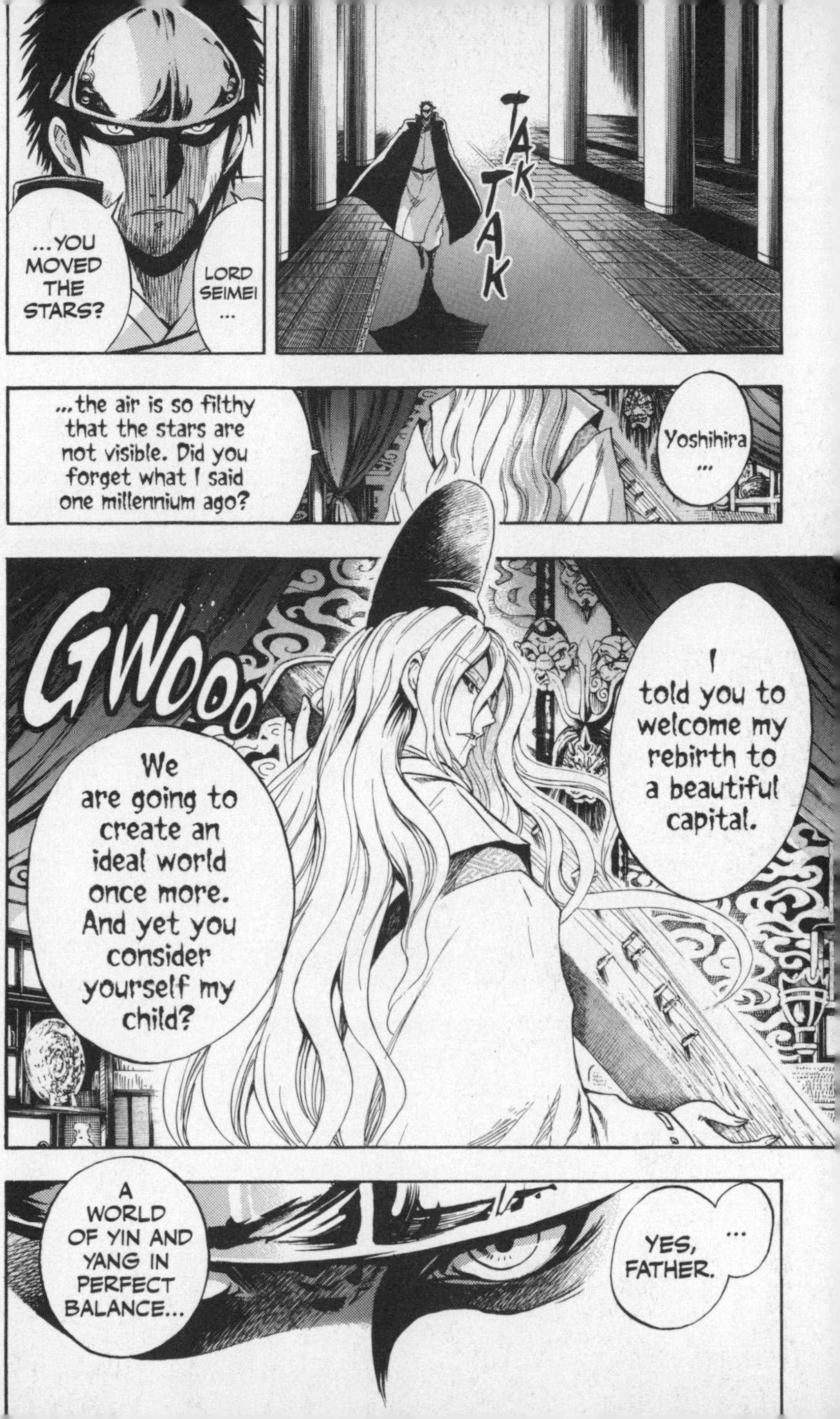
TAK TAK
LORD SEIMEI ...
...YOU MOVED THE STARS?
Yoshihira ...
...the air is so filthy that the stars are not visible. Did you forget what I said one millennium ago?
I told you to welcome my rebirth to a beautiful capital.
GWOOO
We are going to create an ideal world once more. And yet you consider yourself my child?
A WORLD OF YIN AND YANG IN PERFECT BALANCE...
... YES, FATHER.

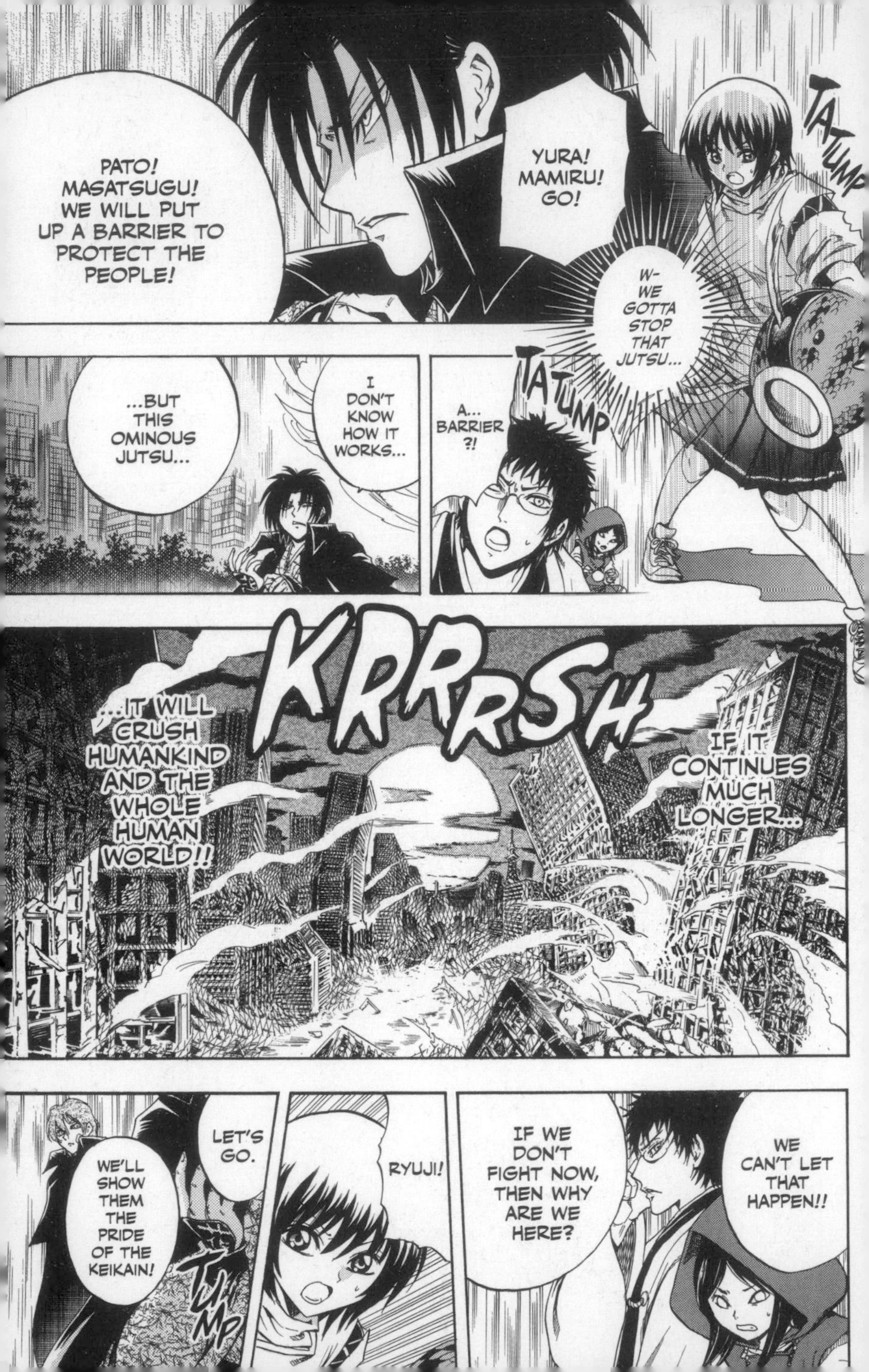
YURA! MAMIRU! GO!
PATO! MASATSUGU! WE WILL PUT UP A BARRIER TO PROTECT THE PEOPLE!
TATUMP
W-WE GOTTA STOP THAT JUTSU...
TATUMP
A... BARRIER?!
I DON'T KNOW HOW IT WORKS...
...BUT THIS OMINOUS JUTSU...
KRRRSH
IF IT CONTINUES MUCH LONGER...
...IT WILL CRUSH HUMANKIND AND THE WHOLE HUMAN WORLD!!
WE CAN'T LET THAT HAPPEN!!
IF WE DON'T FIGHT NOW, THEN WHY ARE WE HERE?
RYUJI!
LET'S GO.
WE'LL SHOW THEM THE PRIDE OF THE KEIKAIN!
TUMP

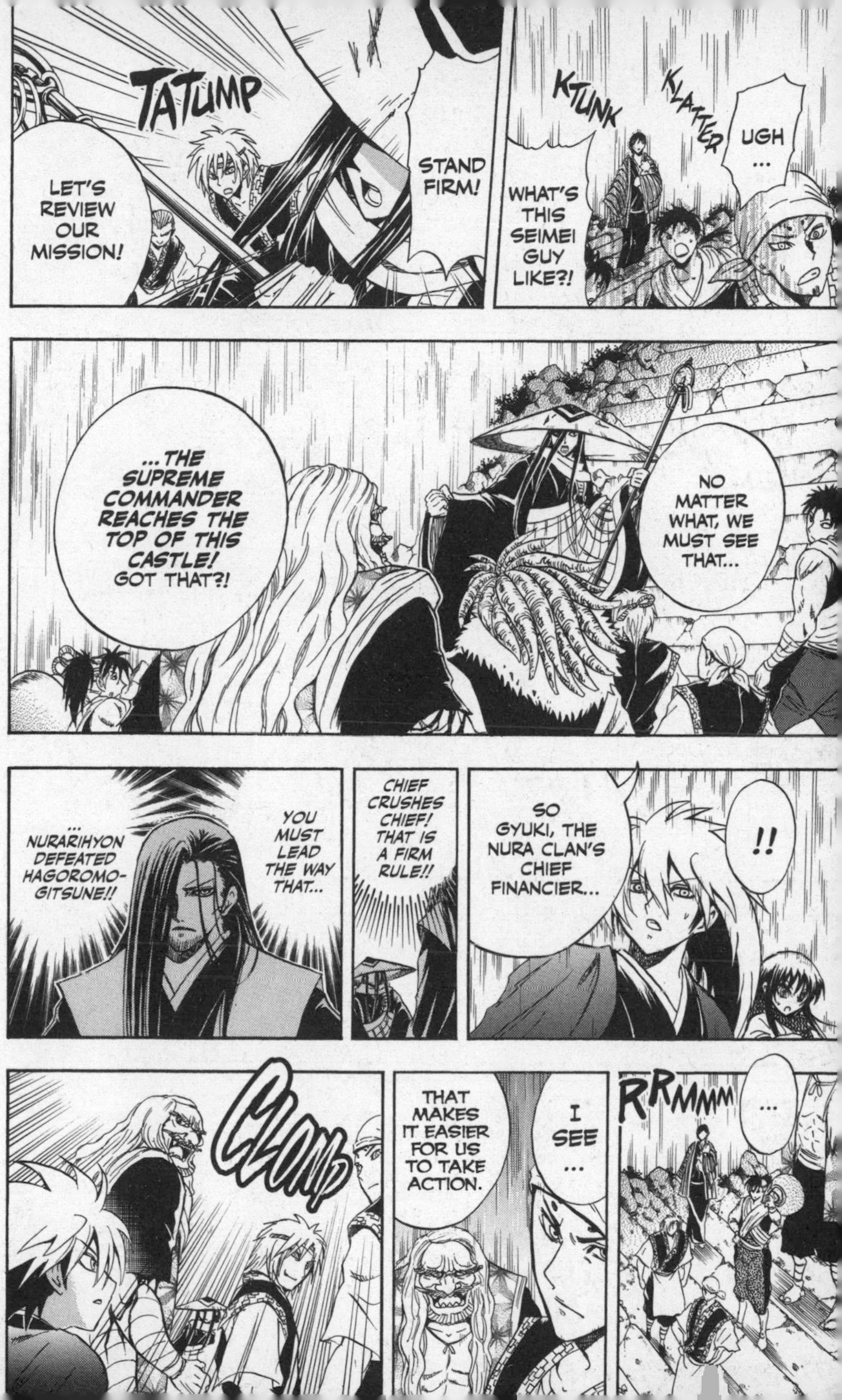
UGH ...
KLATTER
KTUNK
WHAT'S THIS SEIMEI GUY LIKE?!
STAND FIRM!
TATUMP
LET'S REVIEW OUR MISSION!
NO MATTER WHAT, WE MUST SEE THAT...
...THE SUPREME COMMANDER REACHES THE TOP OF THIS CASTLE! GOT THAT?!
!!
SO GYUKI, THE NURA CLAN'S CHIEF FINANCIER...
CHIEF CRUSHES CHIEF! THAT IS A FIRM RULE!!
YOU MUST LEAD THE WAY THAT...
... NURARIHYON DEFEATED HAGOROMO-GITSUNE!!
...
RRMMM
I SEE ...
THAT MAKES IT EASIER FOR US TO TAKE ACTION.
CLOMP

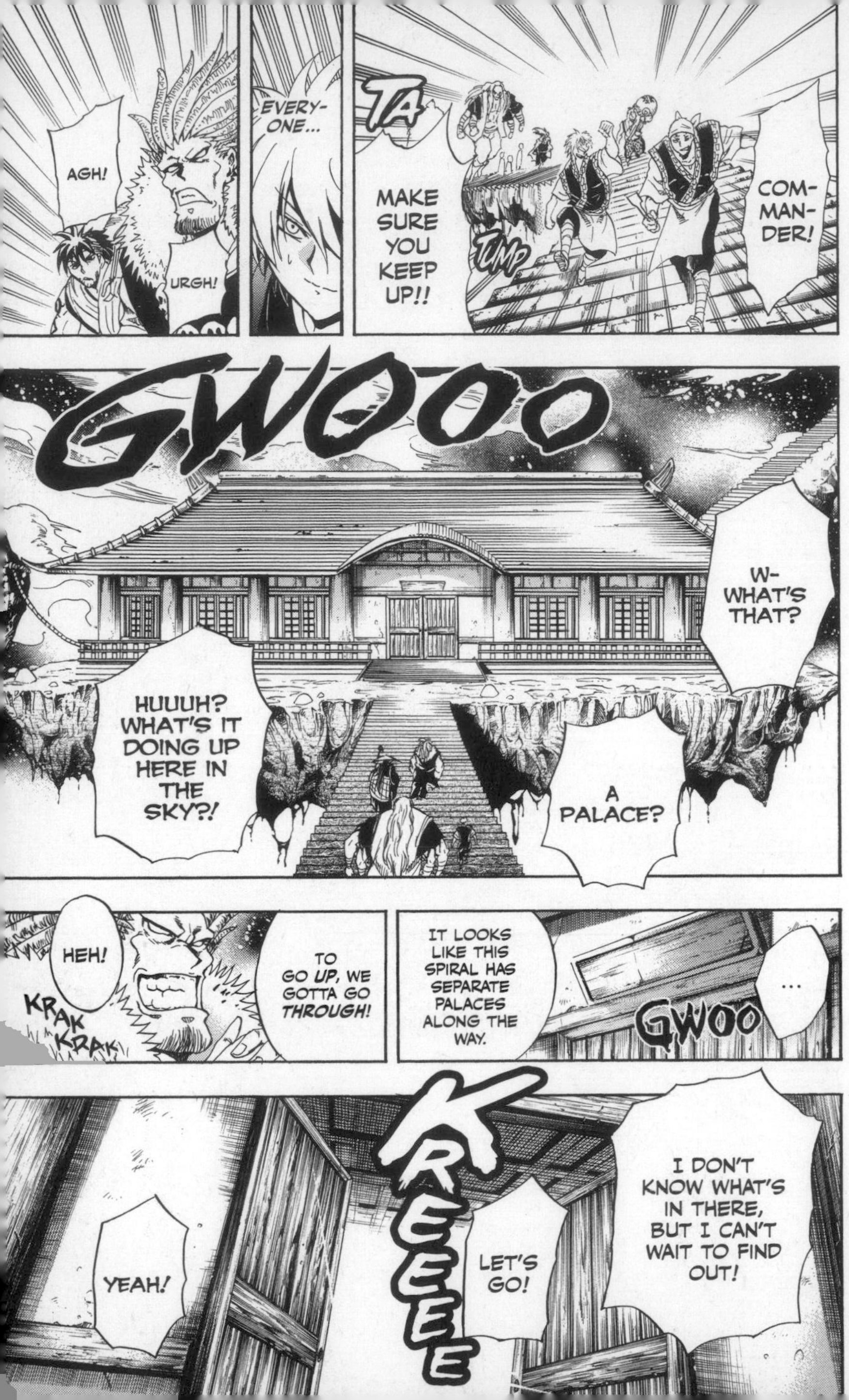
COM-MAN-DER!
TA
TUMP
EVERY-ONE...
MAKE SURE YOU KEEP UP!!
AGH!
URGH!
GWOOO
W-WHAT'S THAT?
A PALACE?
HUUUH? WHAT'S IT DOING UP HERE IN THE SKY?!
...
GWOO
IT LOOKS LIKE THIS SPIRAL HAS SEPARATE PALACES ALONG THE WAY.
TO GO UP, WE GOTTA GO THROUGH!
HEH!
KRAK KRAK
KREEEE
I DON'T KNOW WHAT'S IN THERE, BUT I CAN'T WAIT TO FIND OUT!
LET'S GO!
YEAH!

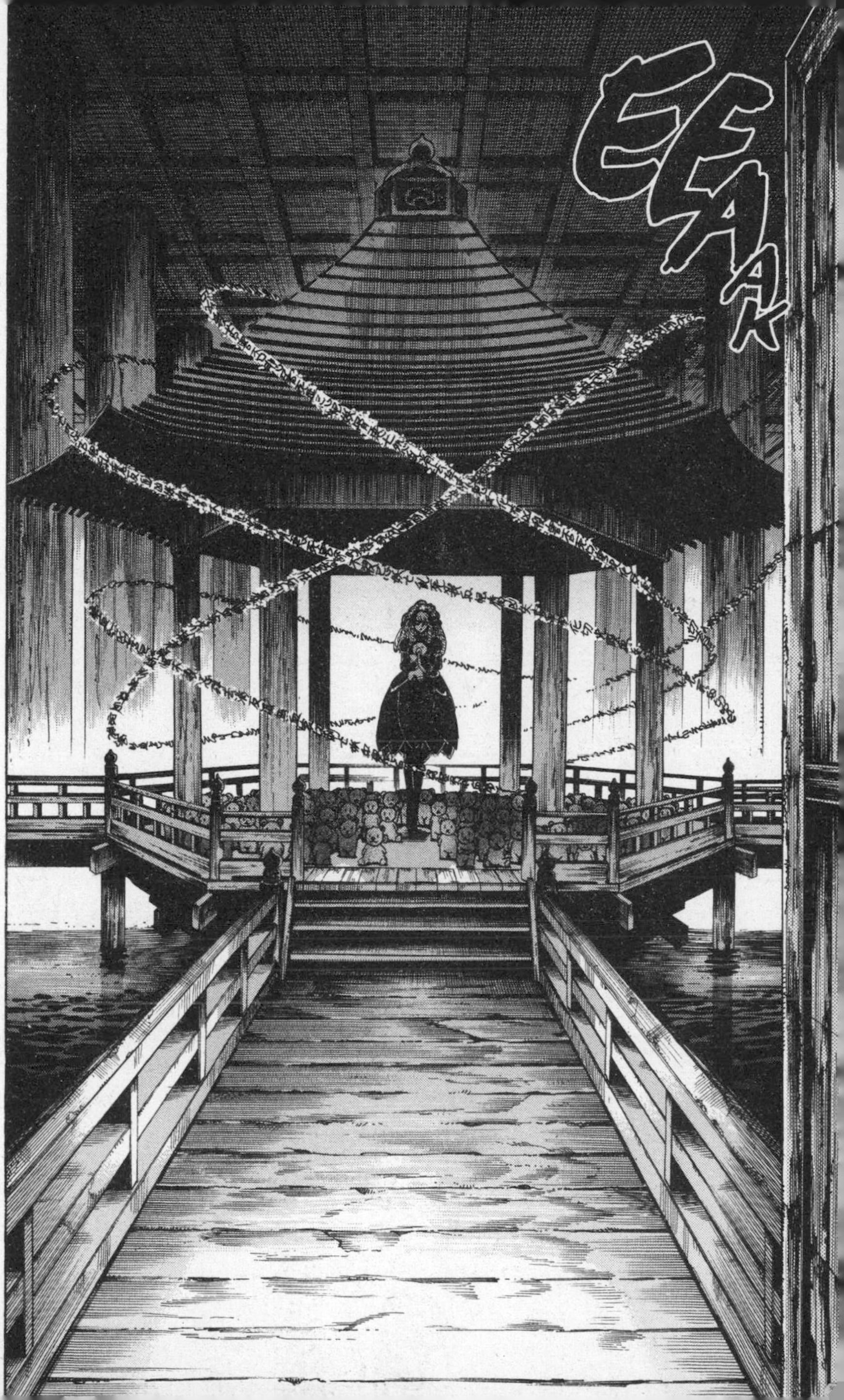
EEAAK

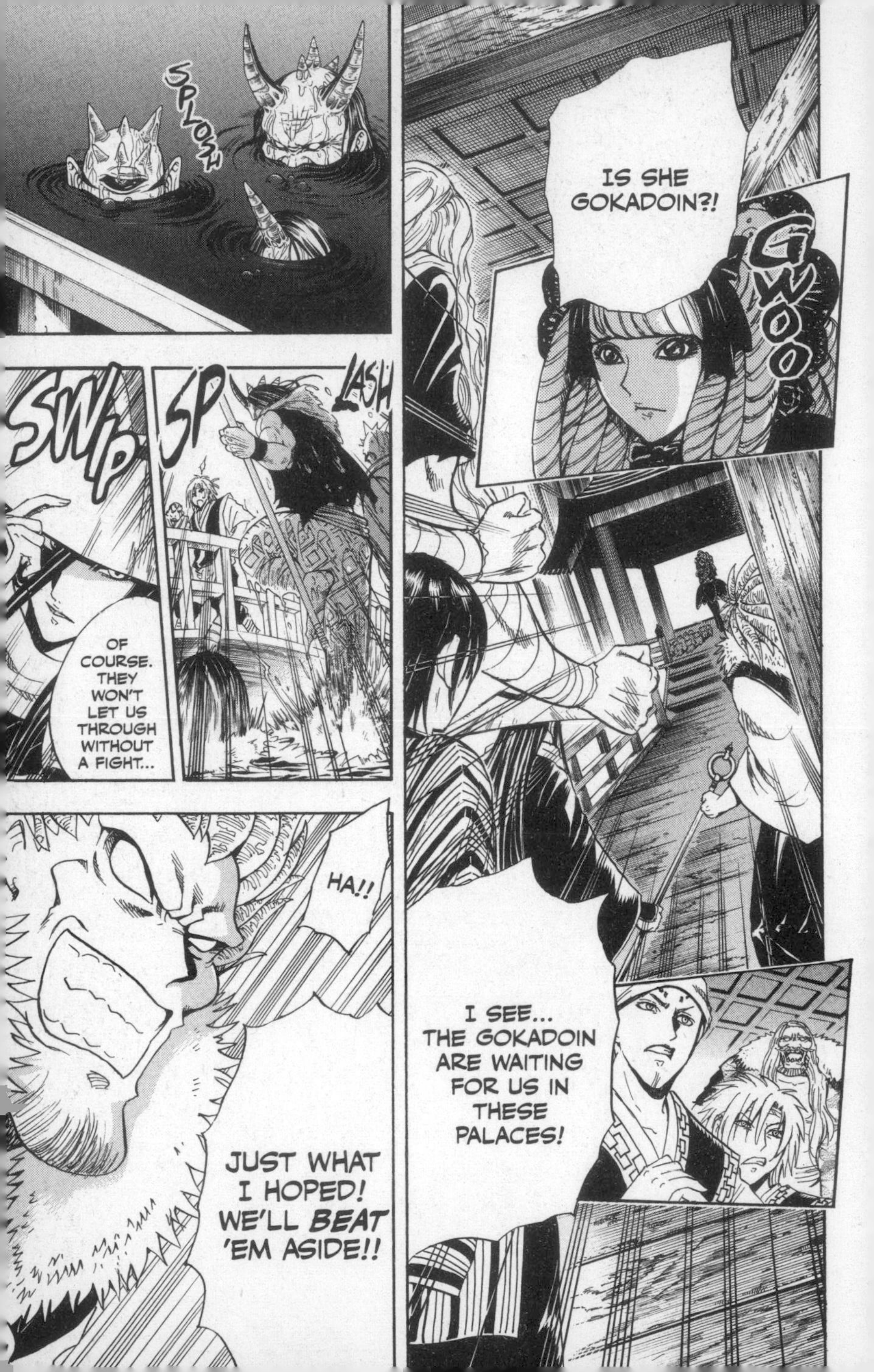

IS SHE GOKADOIN?!
GWOO
I SEE... THE GOKADOIN ARE WAITING FOR US IN THESE PALACES!
SPLOSH
SPLASH
SWIP
OF COURSE. THEY WON'T LET US THROUGH WITHOUT A FIGHT...
HA!!
JUST WHAT I HOPED! WE'LL *BEAT* 'EM ASIDE!!

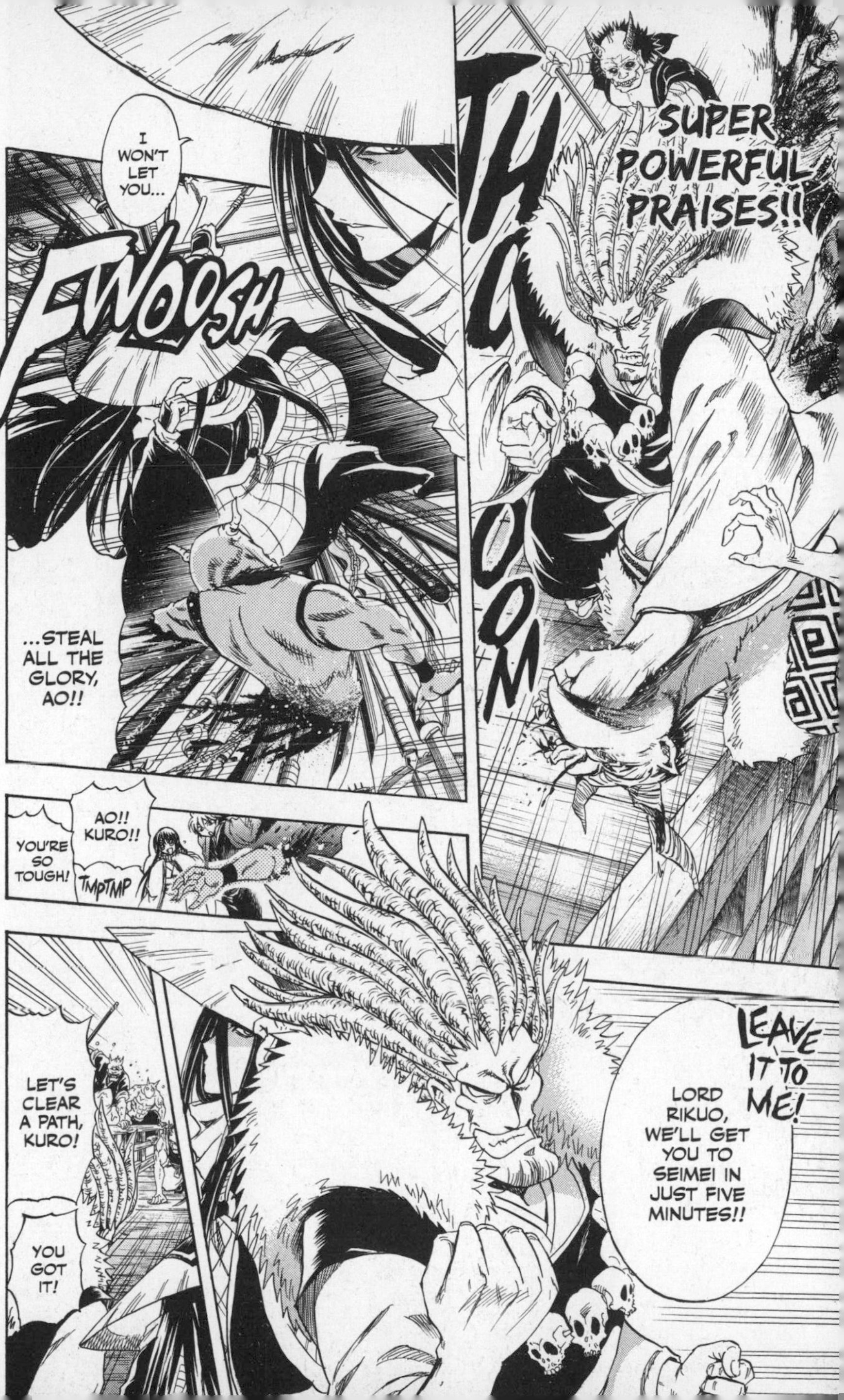
SUPER POWERFUL PRAISES!!
THUOOOM
I WON'T LET YOU...
FWOOSH
...STEAL ALL THE GLORY, AO!!
AO!! KURO!!
YOU'RE SO TOUGH!
TMPTMP
LEAVE IT TO ME!
LORD RIKUO, WE'LL GET YOU TO SEIMEI IN JUST FIVE MINUTES!!
LET'S CLEAR A PATH, KURO!
YOU GOT IT!

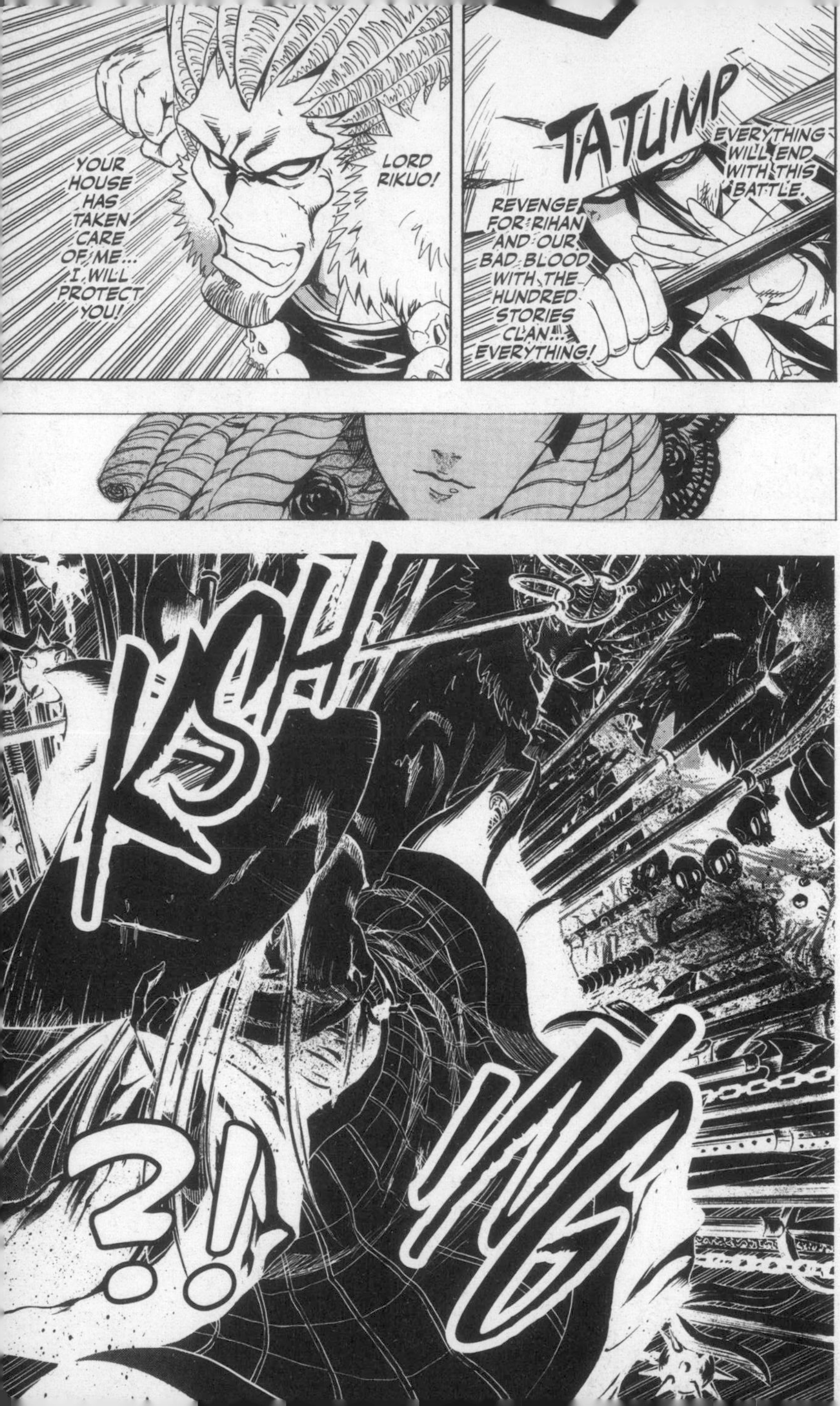
TATUMP
EVERYTHING WILL END WITH THIS BATTLE.
REVENGE FOR RIHAN AND OUR BAD BLOOD WITH THE HUNDRED STORIES CLAN... EVERYTHING!
LORD RIKUO!
YOUR HOUSE HAS TAKEN CARE OF ME... I WILL PROTECT YOU!
?!

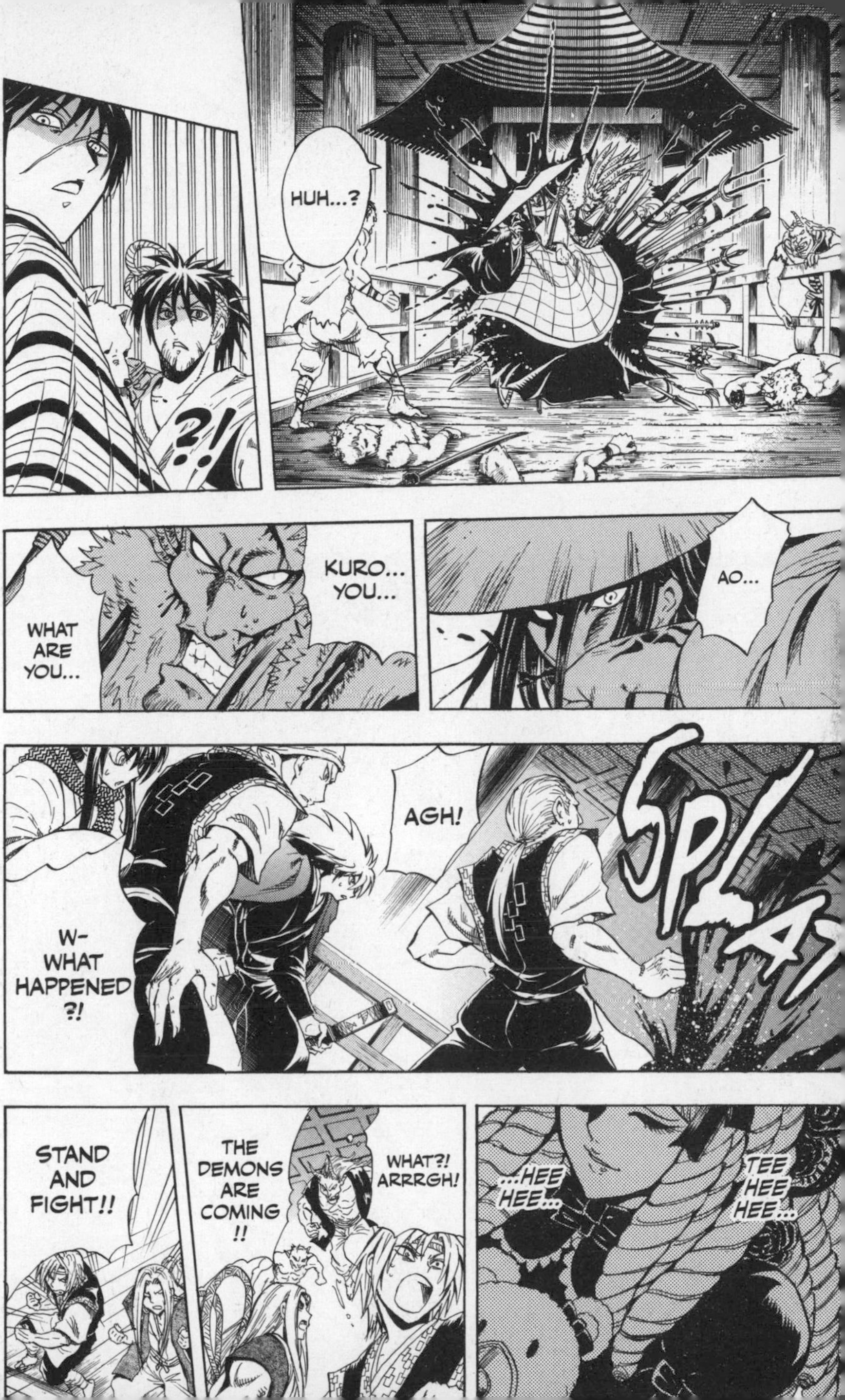
HUH...?
?!
AO...
KURO... YOU...
WHAT ARE YOU...
SPLA
AGH!
W-WHAT HAPPENED?!
TEE HEE HEE...
...HEE HEE...
WHAT?! ARRRGH!
THE DEMONS ARE COMING!!
STAND AND FIGHT!!

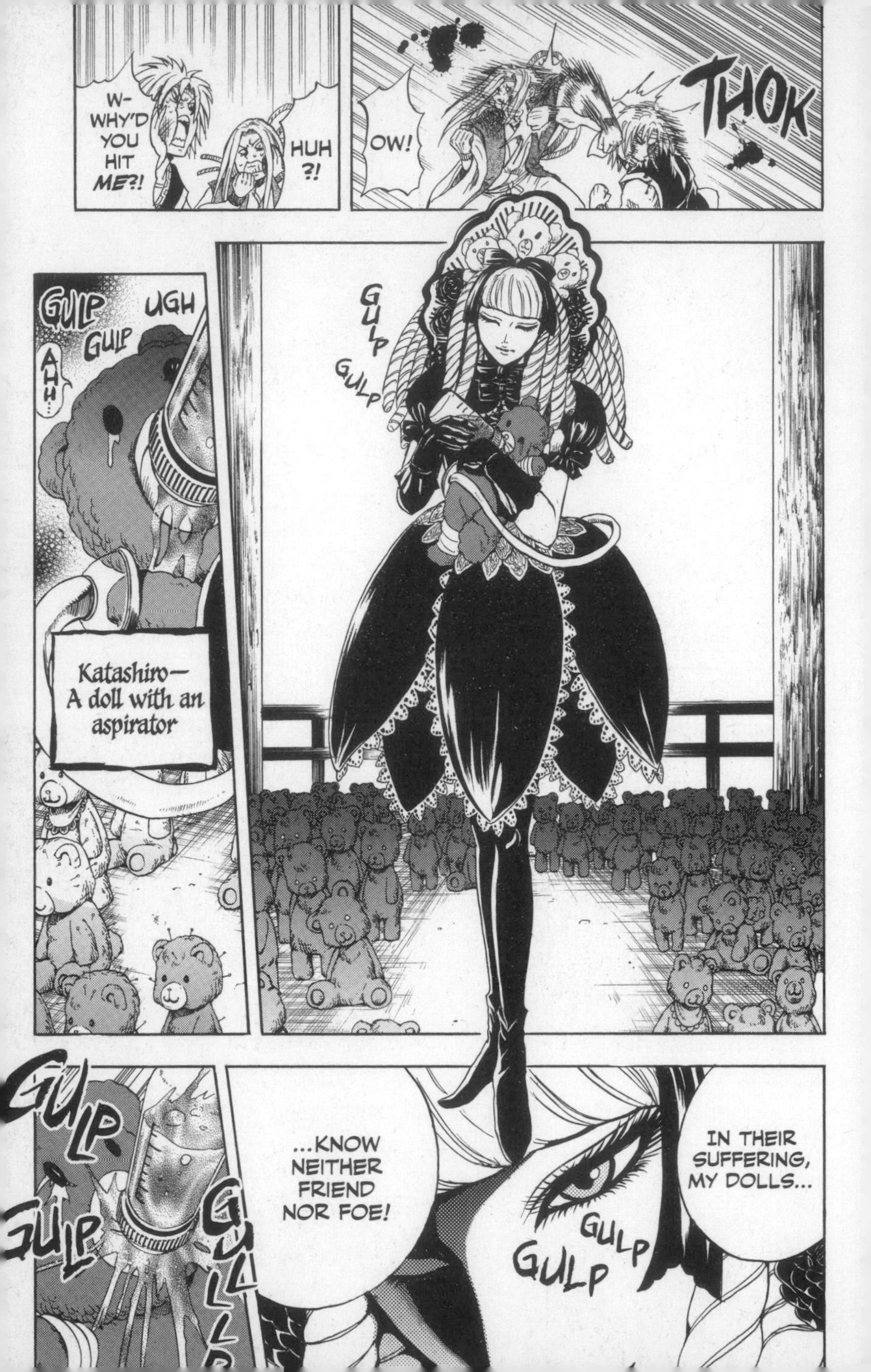
THOK
OW!
W-WHY'D YOU HIT ME?!
HUH ?!
GULP
GULP
UGH
GULP
GULP
AHH...
Katashiro—
A doll with an aspirator
IN THEIR SUFFERING, MY DOLLS...
GULP
GULP
...KNOW NEITHER FRIEND NOR FOE!
GULP
GULP

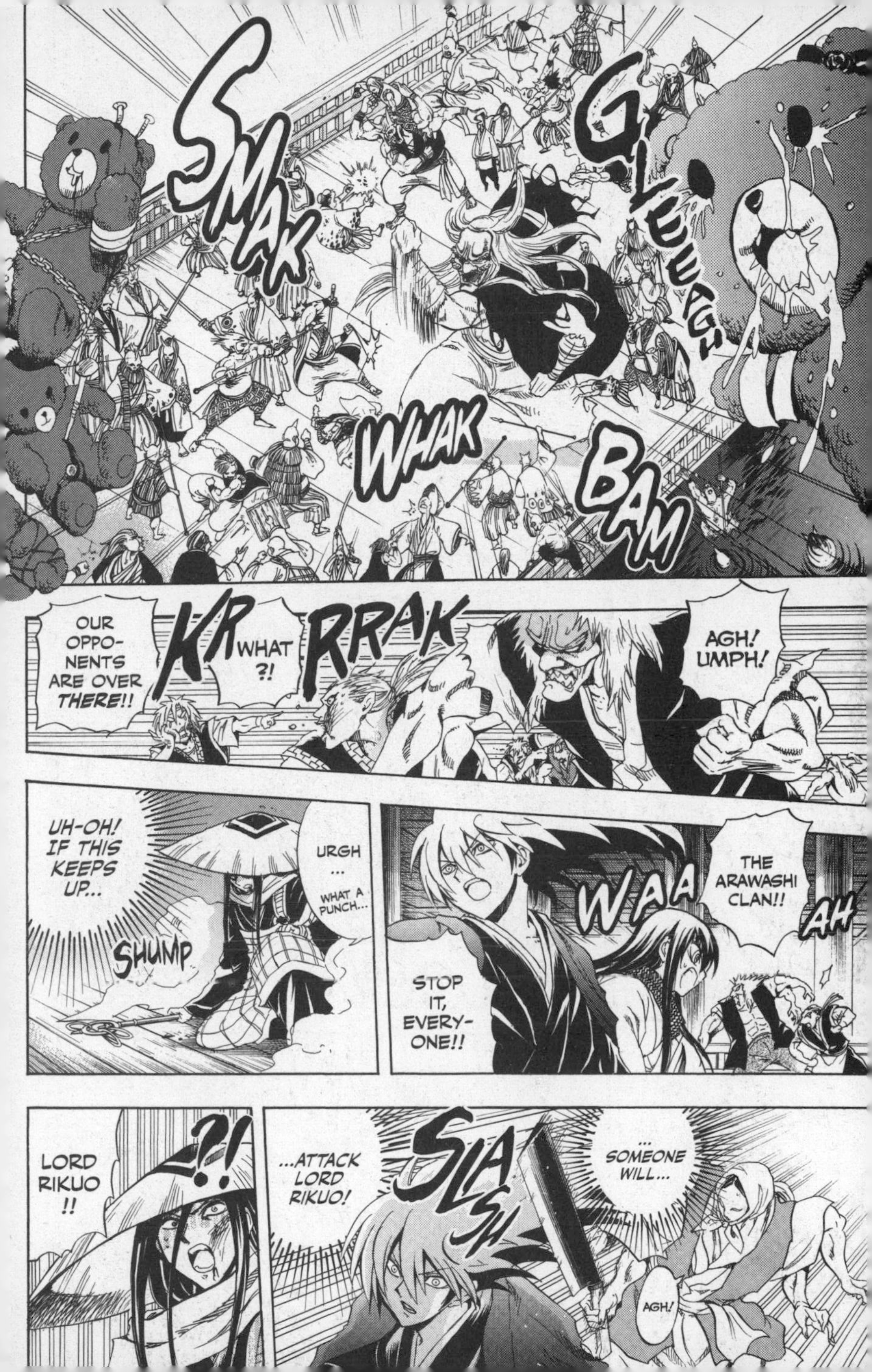
GLEEAGH
SMAK
BAM
WHAK
AGH! UMPH!
KRRRAK
WHAT?!
OUR OPPONENTS ARE OVER THERE!!
THE ARAWASHI CLAN!!
AH
WAA
STOP IT, EVERYONE!!
URGH ... WHAT A PUNCH...
UH-OH! IF THIS KEEPS UP...
SHUMP
... SOMEONE WILL...
SLASH
...ATTACK LORD RIKUO!
AGH!
?!
LORD RIKUO!!

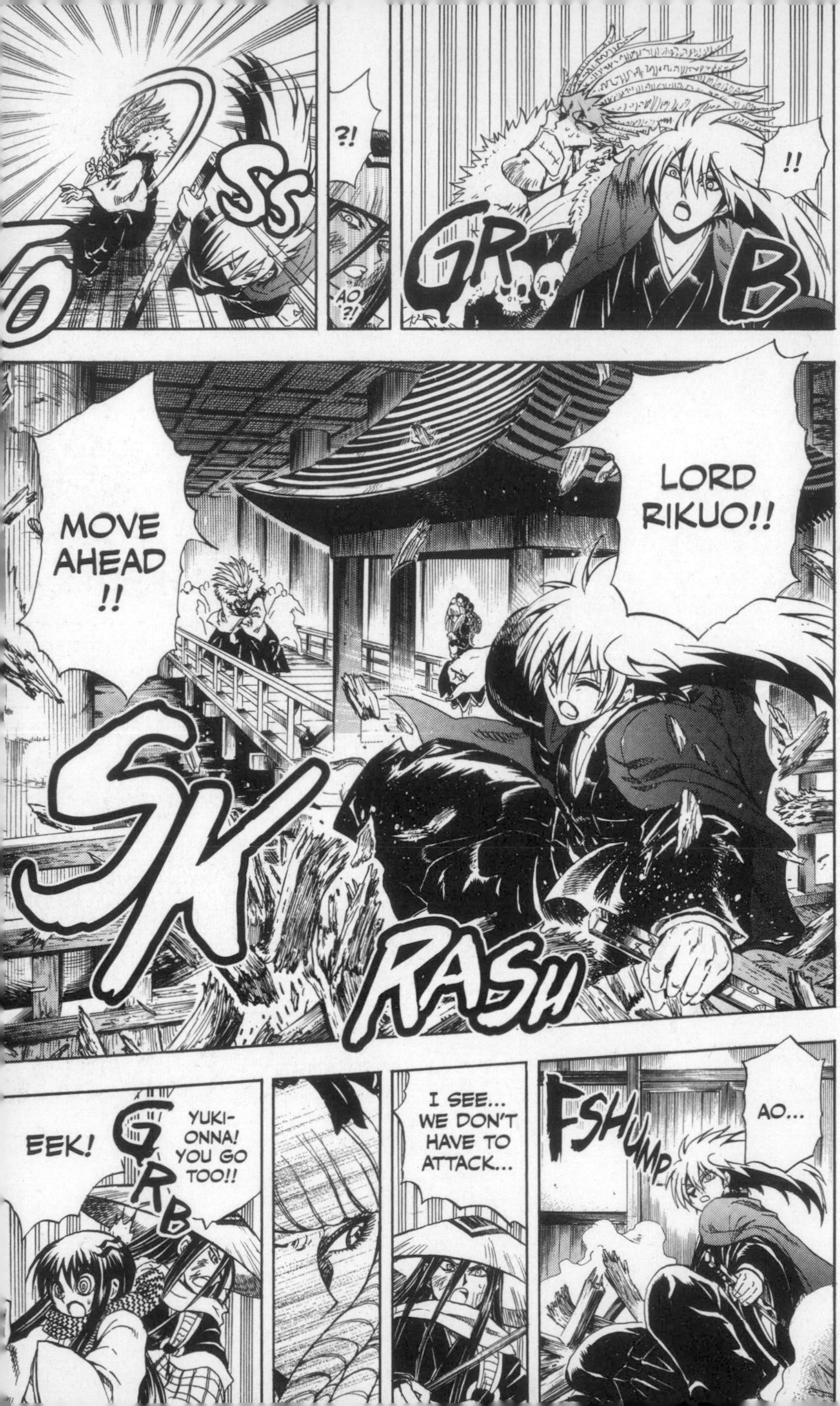
!!
GR
B
?!
AO?!
SS
O
LORD RIKUO!!
MOVE AHEAD!!
SK
RASH
AO...
FSHUMP
I SEE... WE DON'T HAVE TO ATTACK...
YUKI-ONNA! YOU GO TOO!!
GRB
EEK!

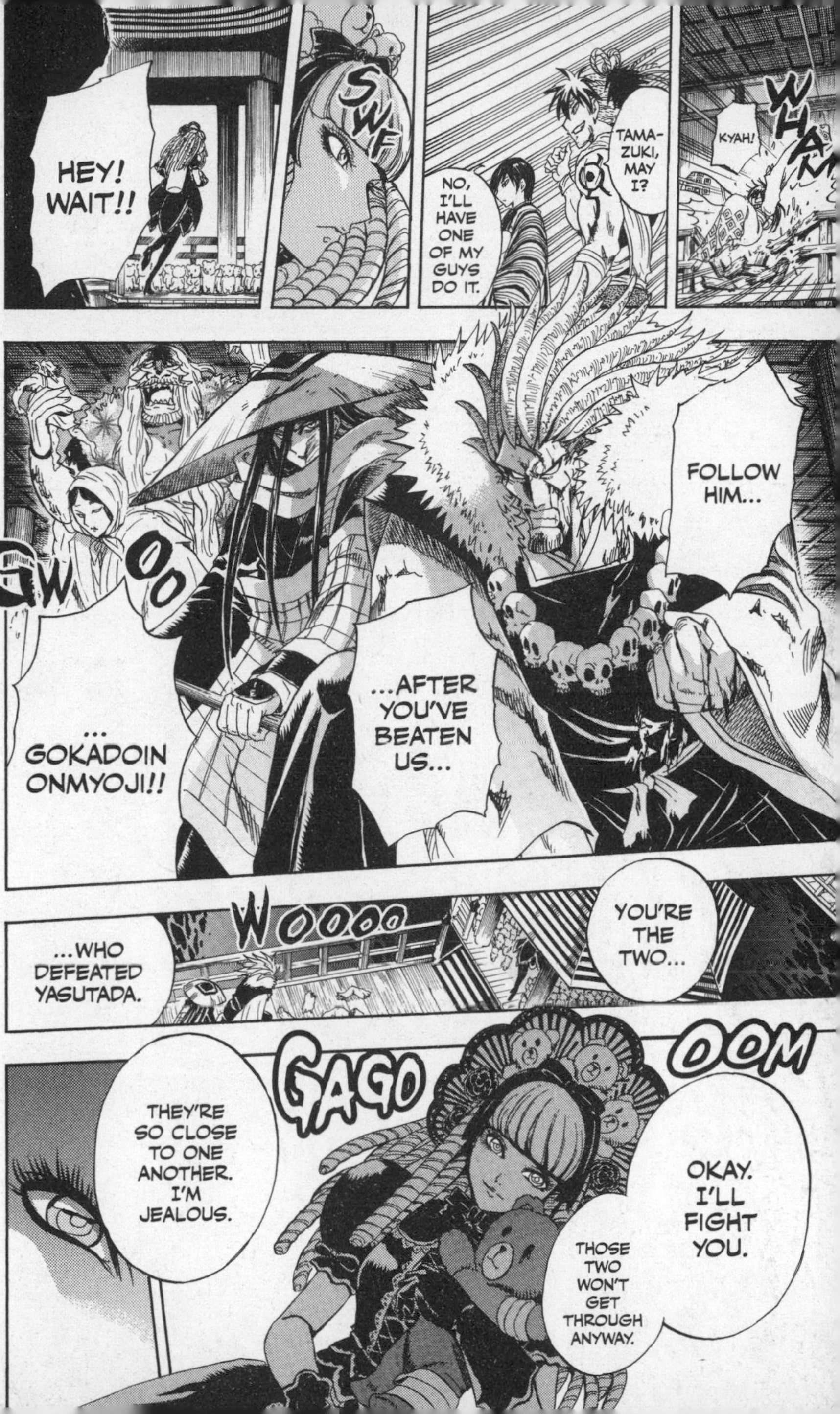
WHAM
KYAH!
TAMA-ZUKI, MAY I?
NO, I'LL HAVE ONE OF MY GUYS DO IT.
SWF
HEY! WAIT!!
FOLLOW HIM...
...AFTER YOU'VE BEATEN US...
GWOOO
...GOKADOIN ONMYOJI!!
YOU'RE THE TWO...
WOOOO
...WHO DEFEATED YASUTADA.
GAGOOOM
OKAY. I'LL FIGHT YOU.
THOSE TWO WON'T GET THROUGH ANYWAY.
THEY'RE SO CLOSE TO ONE ANOTHER. I'M JEALOUS.

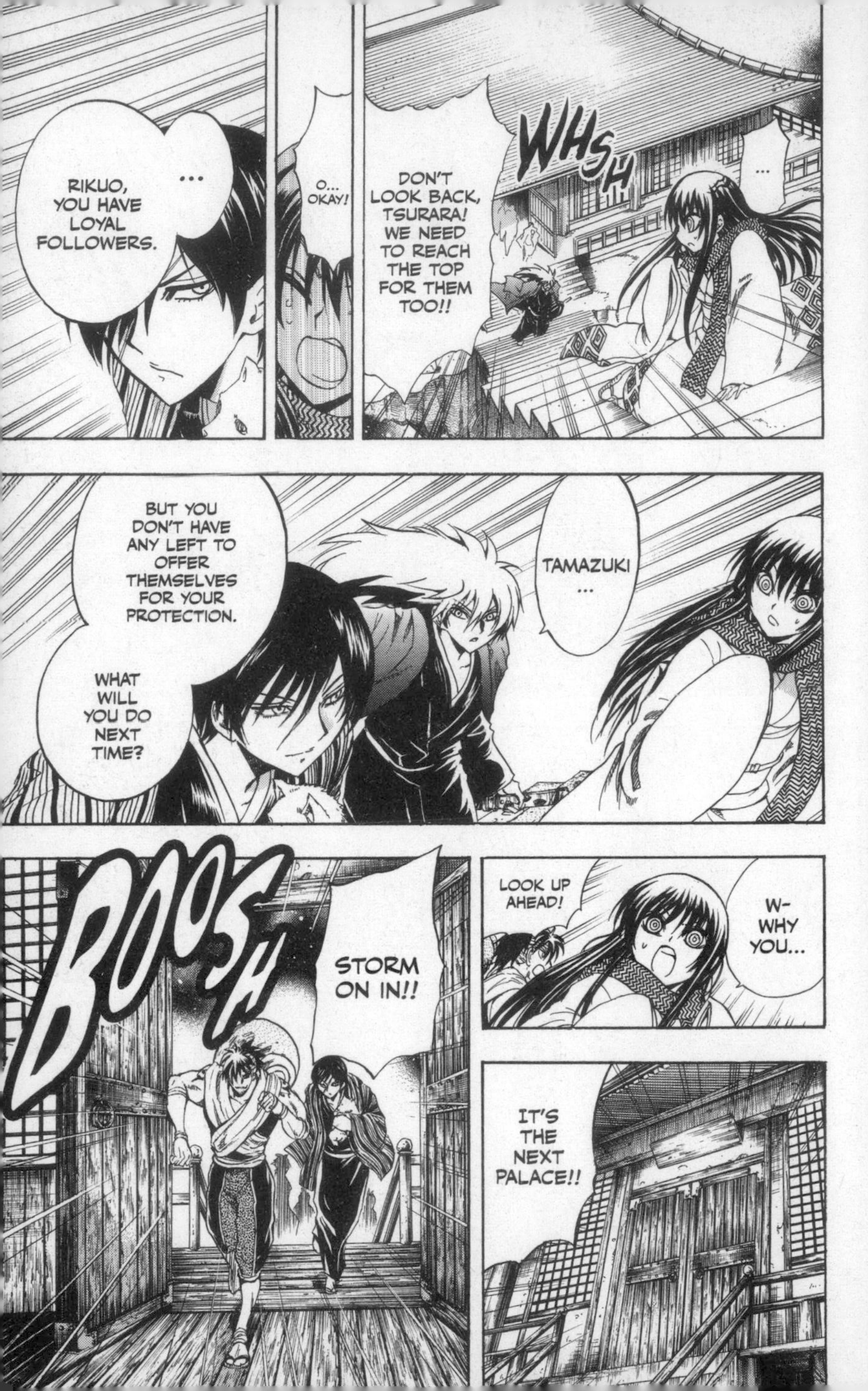
...
WHSH
DON'T LOOK BACK, TSURARA! WE NEED TO REACH THE TOP FOR THEM TOO!!
O... OKAY!
...
RIKUO, YOU HAVE LOYAL FOLLOWERS.
TAMAZUKI ...
BUT YOU DON'T HAVE ANY LEFT TO OFFER THEMSELVES FOR YOUR PROTECTION.
WHAT WILL YOU DO NEXT TIME?
W- WHY YOU...
LOOK UP AHEAD!
IT'S THE NEXT PALACE!!
BOOSH
STORM ON IN!!

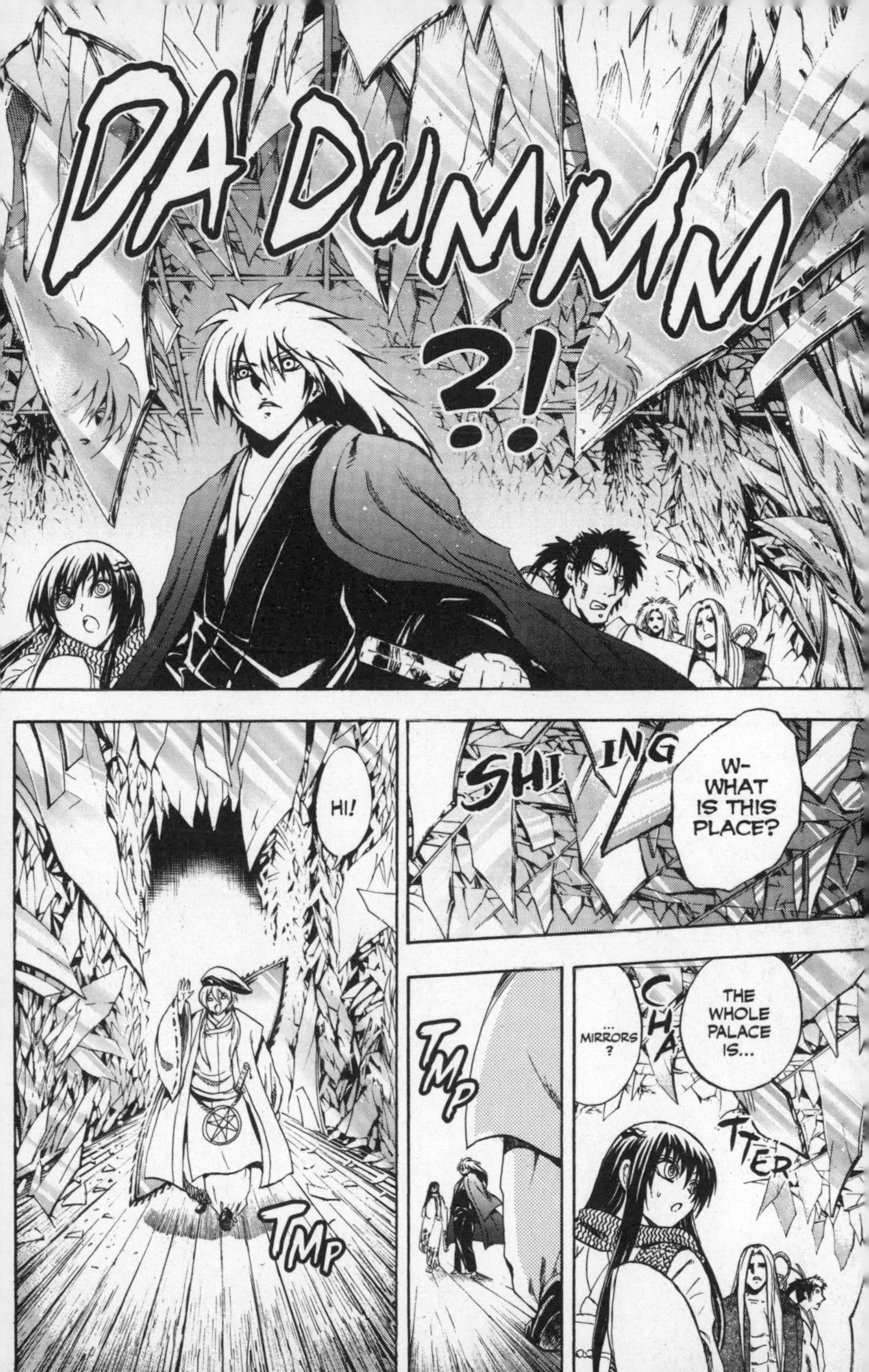
DA DUMMM
?!
W-WHAT IS THIS PLACE?
SHI ING
THE WHOLE PALACE IS...
... MIRRORS?
CHA TTER
TMP
HI!
TMP

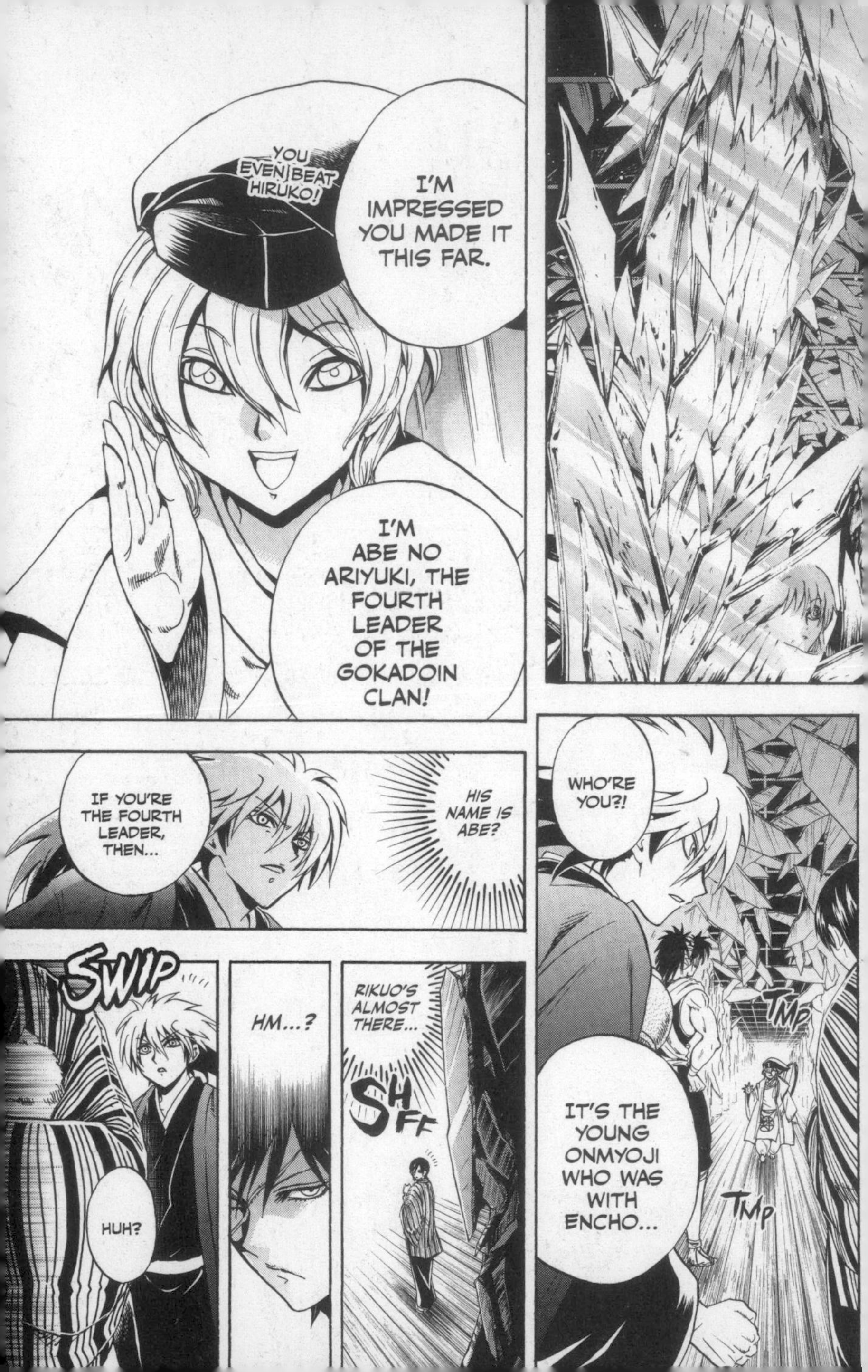
I'M IMPRESSED YOU MADE IT THIS FAR.
YOU EVEN BEAT HIRUKO!
I'M ABE NO ARIYUKI, THE FOURTH LEADER OF THE GOKADOIN CLAN!
WHO'RE YOU?!
TMP
IT'S THE YOUNG ONMYOJI WHO WAS WITH ENCHO...
TMP
HIS NAME IS ABE?
IF YOU'RE THE FOURTH LEADER, THEN...
RIKUO'S ALMOST THERE...
SHFF
HM...?
SWIP
HUH?

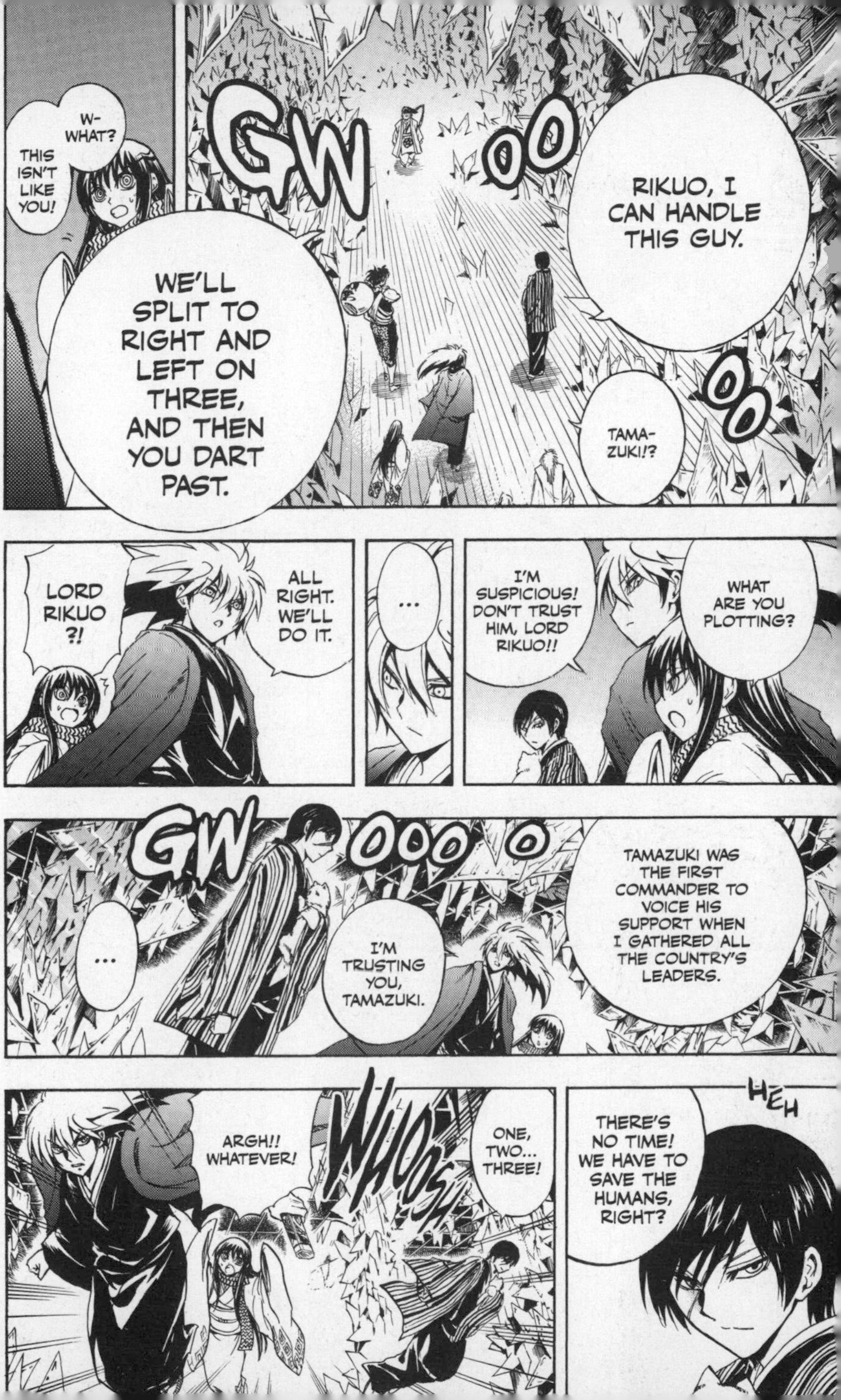
RIKUO, I CAN HANDLE THIS GUY.
GWOOOO
TAMA-ZUKI!?
WE'LL SPLIT TO RIGHT AND LEFT ON THREE, AND THEN YOU DART PAST.
W-WHAT?
THIS ISN'T LIKE YOU!
WHAT ARE YOU PLOTTING?
I'M SUSPICIOUS! DON'T TRUST HIM, LORD RIKUO!!
...
ALL RIGHT. WE'LL DO IT.
LORD RIKUO ?!
TAMAZUKI WAS THE FIRST COMMANDER TO VOICE HIS SUPPORT WHEN I GATHERED ALL THE COUNTRY'S LEADERS.
GWOOOO
I'M TRUSTING YOU, TAMAZUKI.
...
HEH
THERE'S NO TIME! WE HAVE TO SAVE THE HUMANS, RIGHT?
ONE, TWO... THREE!
WHOOSH
ARGH!! WHATEVER!

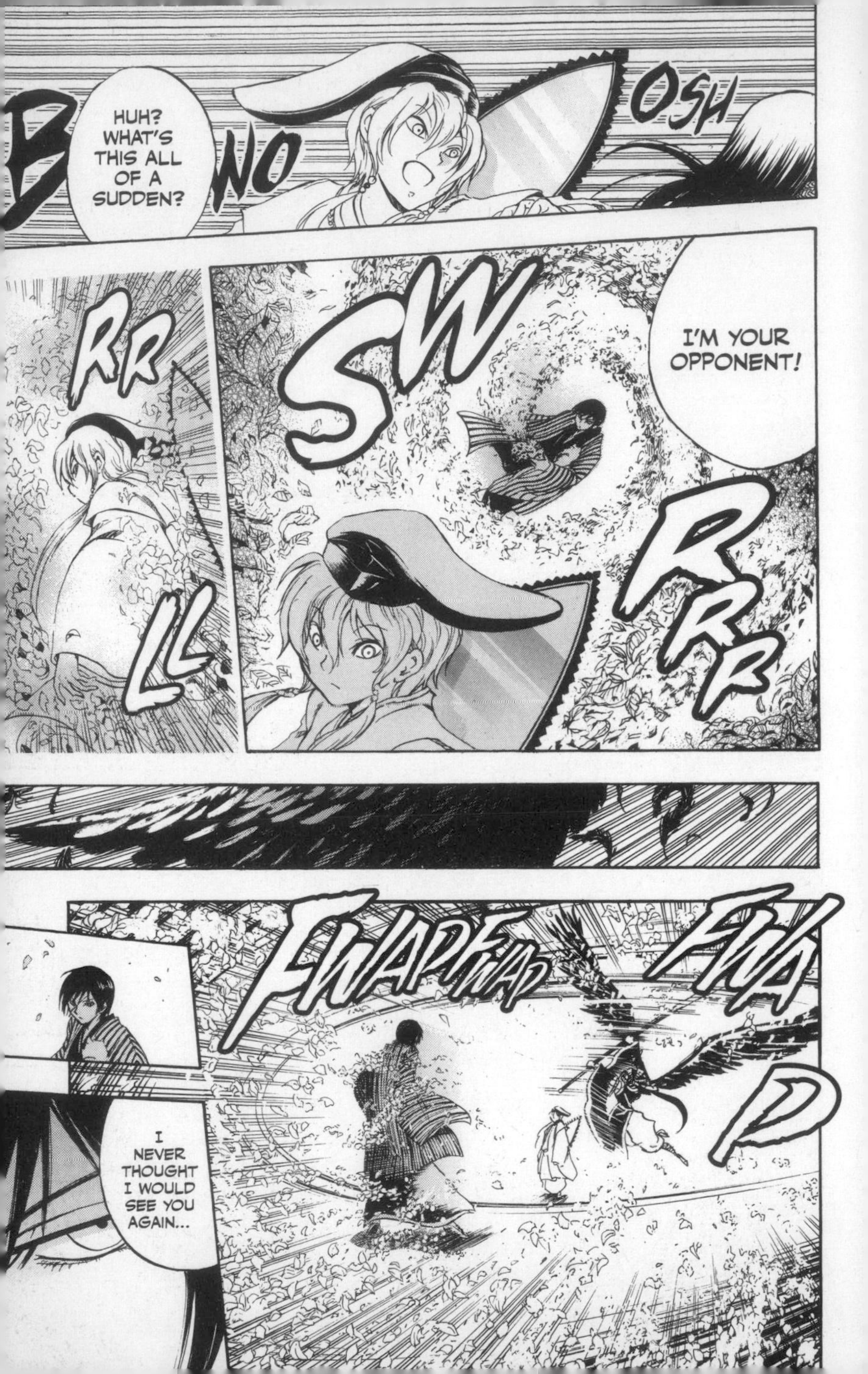
BWOOSH
HUH? WHAT'S THIS ALL OF A SUDDEN?
I'M YOUR OPPONENT!
SWRRR
RRLL
FWAP FWAP
FWAP
I NEVER THOUGHT I WOULD SEE YOU AGAIN...

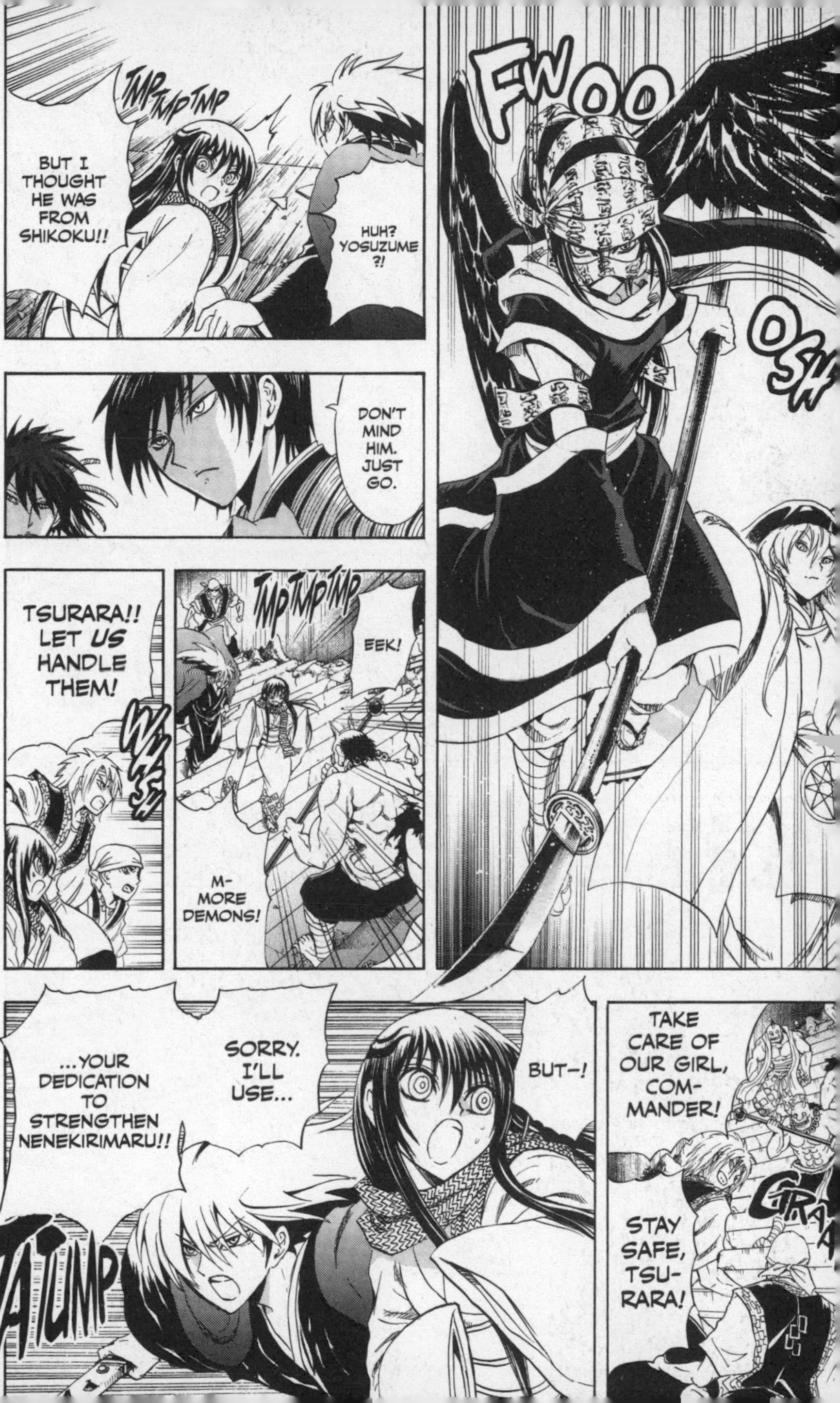
FWOOOSH
TMP TMP TMP
HUH? YOSUZUME ?!
BUT I THOUGHT HE WAS FROM SHIKOKU!!
DON'T MIND HIM. JUST GO.
TMP TMP TMP
EEK!
M-MORE DEMONS!
TSURARA!! LET US HANDLE THEM!
WHSH
TAKE CARE OF OUR GIRL, COM-MANDER!
GRAA
STAY SAFE, TSU-RARA!
BUT-!
SORRY. I'LL USE...
...YOUR DEDICATION TO STRENGTHEN NENEKIRIMARU!!
TATUMP

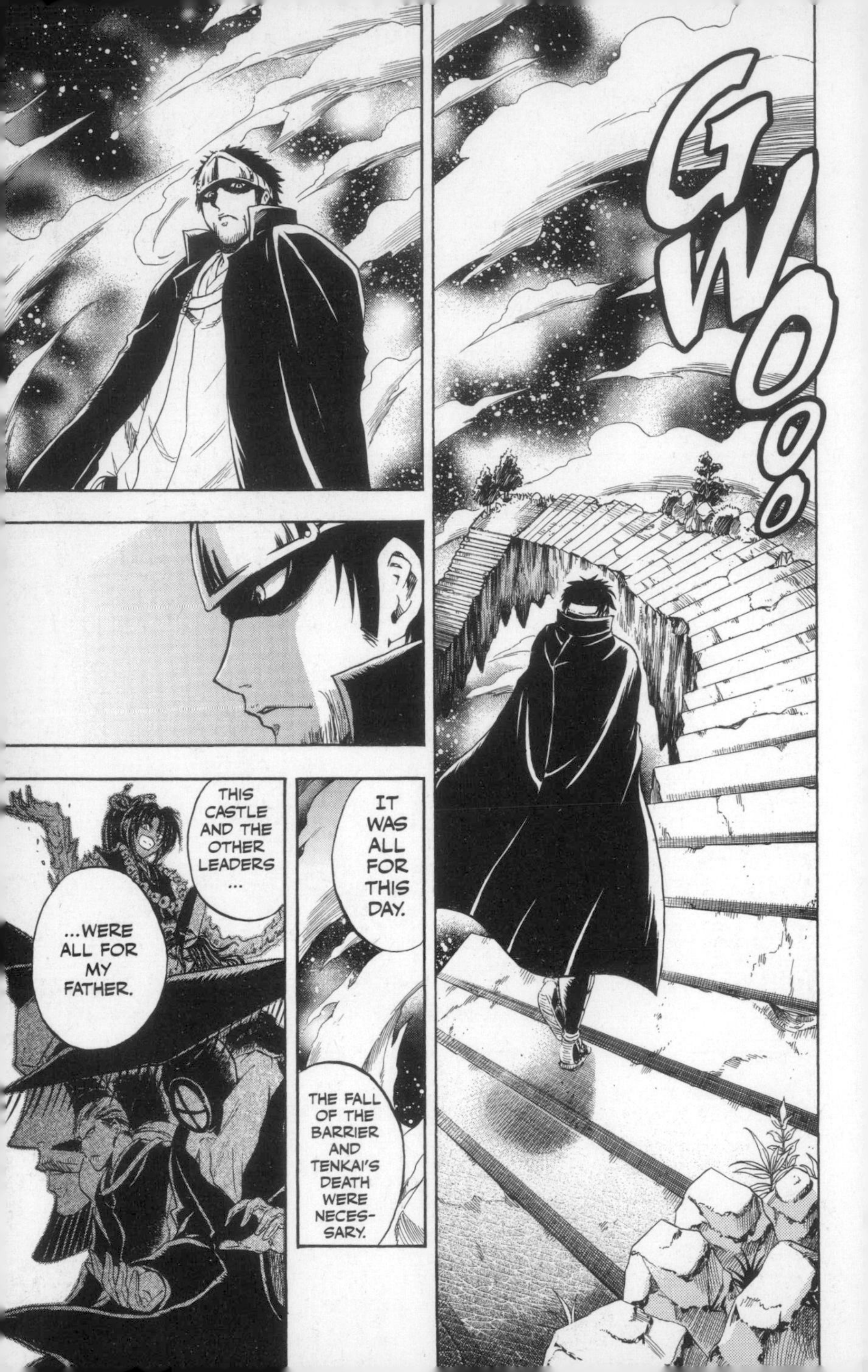
GWOOOO
IT WAS ALL FOR THIS DAY.
THE FALL OF THE BARRIER AND TENKAI'S DEATH WERE NECES-SARY.
THIS CASTLE AND THE OTHER LEADERS ...
...WERE ALL FOR MY FATHER.

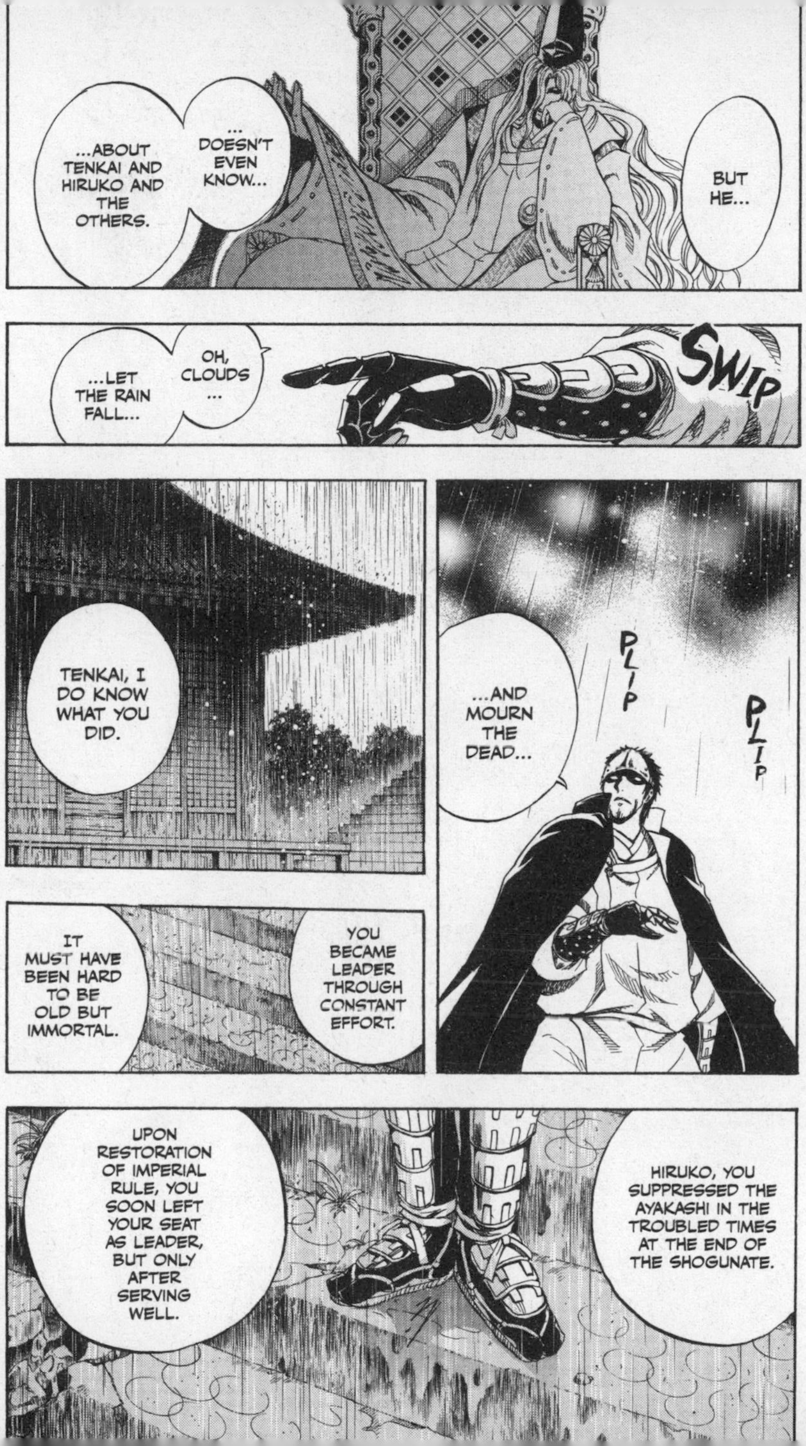
BUT HE...
...DOESN'T EVEN KNOW...
...ABOUT TENKAI AND HIRUKO AND THE OTHERS.
SWIP
OH, CLOUDS...
...LET THE RAIN FALL...
PLIP
PLIP
...AND MOURN THE DEAD...
TENKAI, I DO KNOW WHAT YOU DID.
YOU BECAME LEADER THROUGH CONSTANT EFFORT.
IT MUST HAVE BEEN HARD TO BE OLD BUT IMMORTAL.
HIRUKO, YOU SUPPRESSED THE AYAKASHI IN THE TROUBLED TIMES AT THE END OF THE SHOGUNATE.
UPON RESTORATION OF IMPERIAL RULE, YOU SOON LEFT YOUR SEAT AS LEADER, BUT ONLY AFTER SERVING WELL.

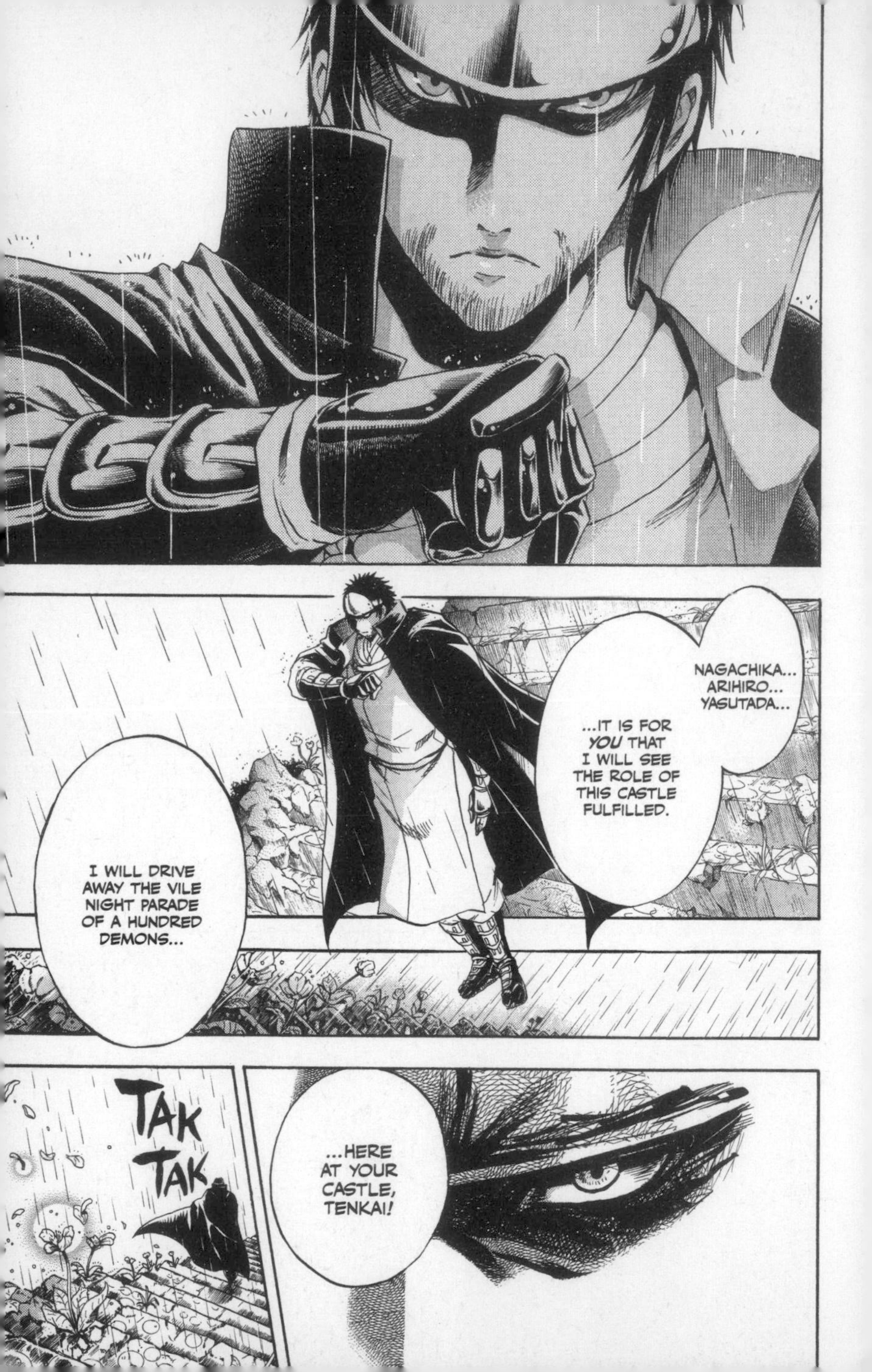
NAGACHIKA... ARIHIRO... YASUTADA...
...IT IS FOR *YOU* THAT I WILL SEE THE ROLE OF THIS CASTLE FULFILLED.
I WILL DRIVE AWAY THE VILE NIGHT PARADE OF A HUNDRED DEMONS...
...HERE AT YOUR CASTLE, TENKAI!
TAK TAK

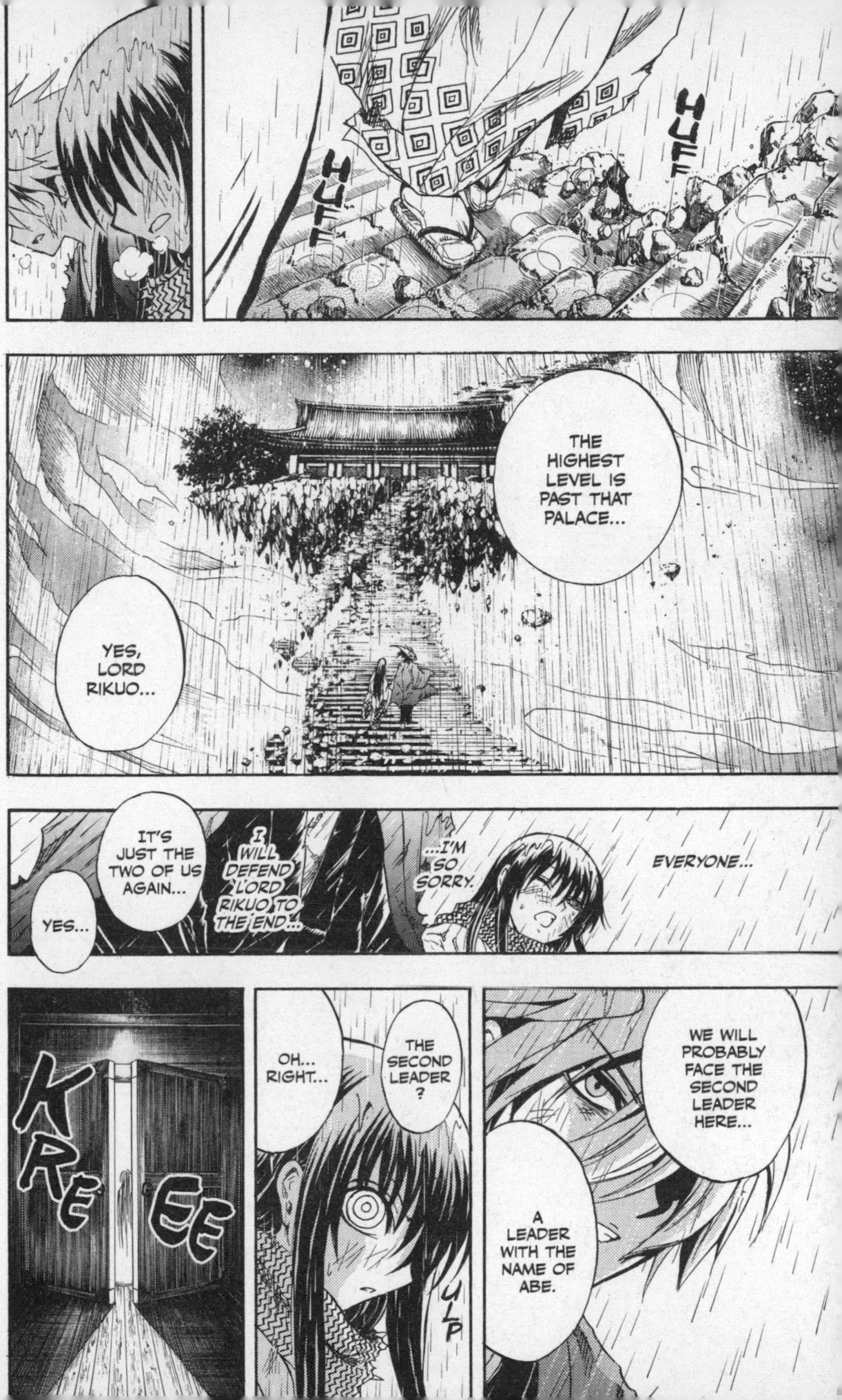
HUFF
HUFF
THE HIGHEST LEVEL IS PAST THAT PALACE...
YES, LORD RIKUO...
EVERYONE...
...I'M SO SORRY.
I WILL DEFEND LORD RIKUO TO THE END...
IT'S JUST THE TWO OF US AGAIN...
YES...
WE WILL PROBABLY FACE THE SECOND LEADER HERE...
A LEADER WITH THE NAME OF ABE.
THE SECOND LEADER?
OH... RIGHT...
ULP
KREEE

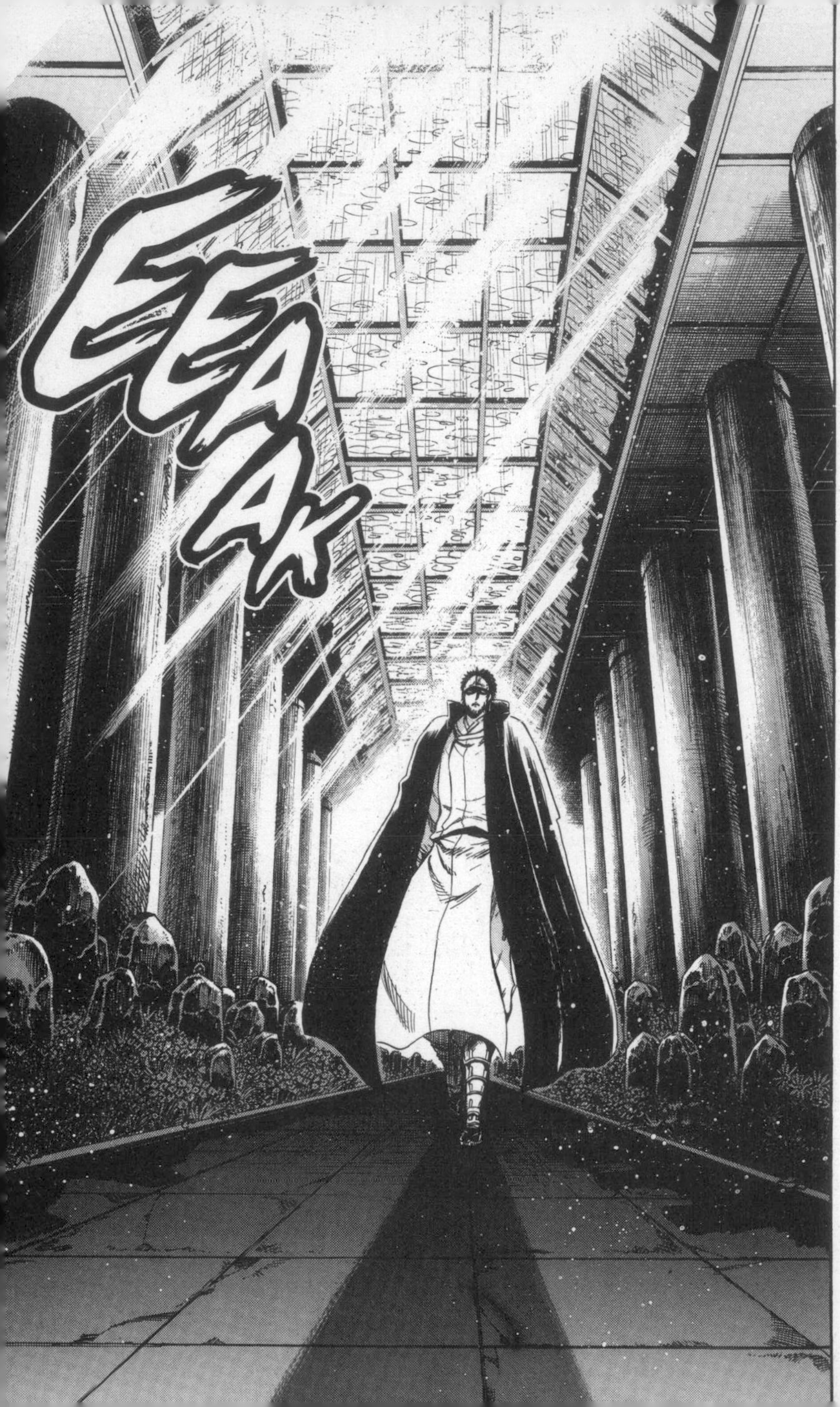
CREAK

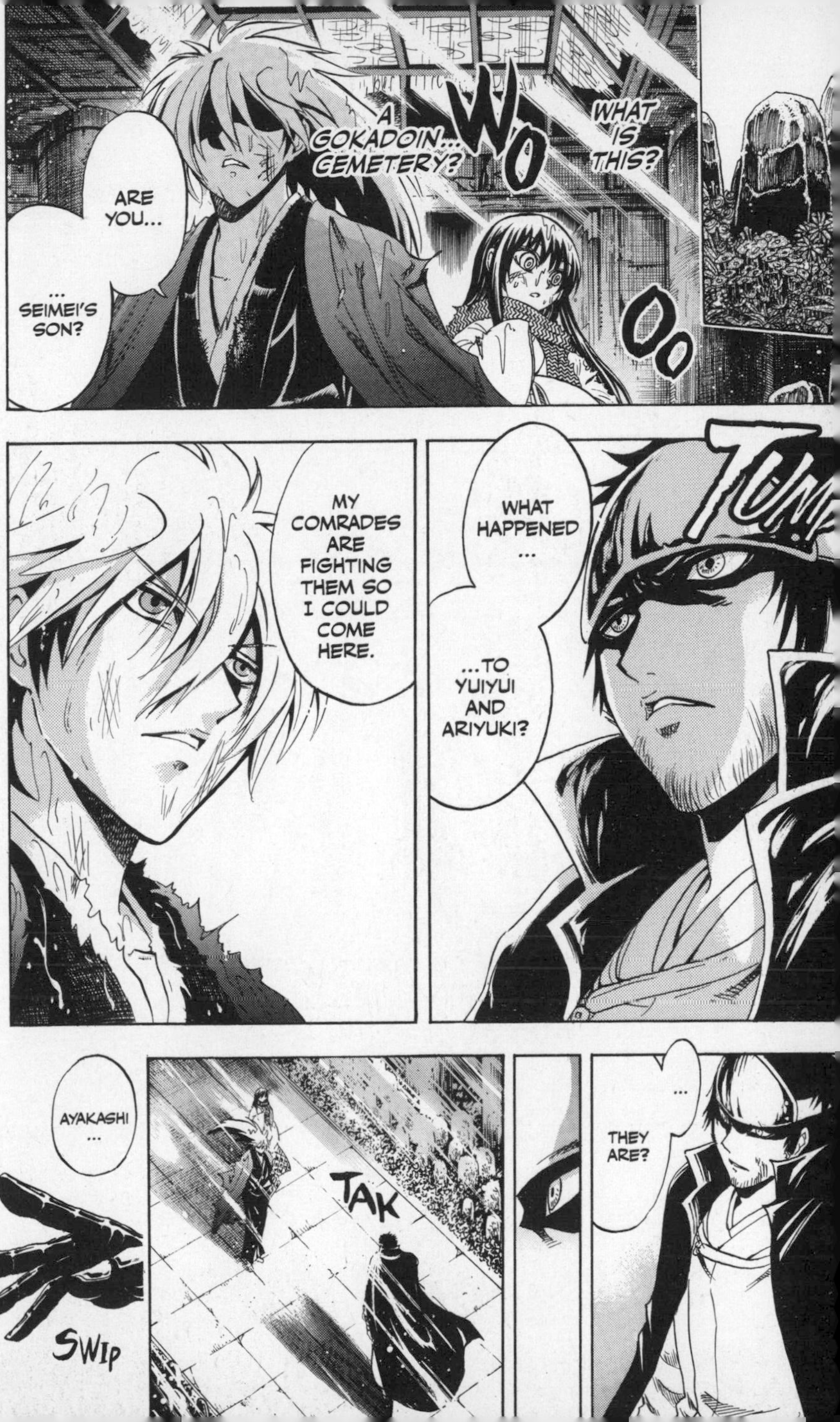
WHAT IS THIS?
WO
OO
A GOKADOIN... CEMETERY?
ARE YOU...
... SEIMEI'S SON?
WHAT HAPPENED ...
...TO YUIYUI AND ARIYUKI?
MY COMRADES ARE FIGHTING THEM SO I COULD COME HERE.
... THEY ARE?
TAK
AYAKASHI ...
SWIP

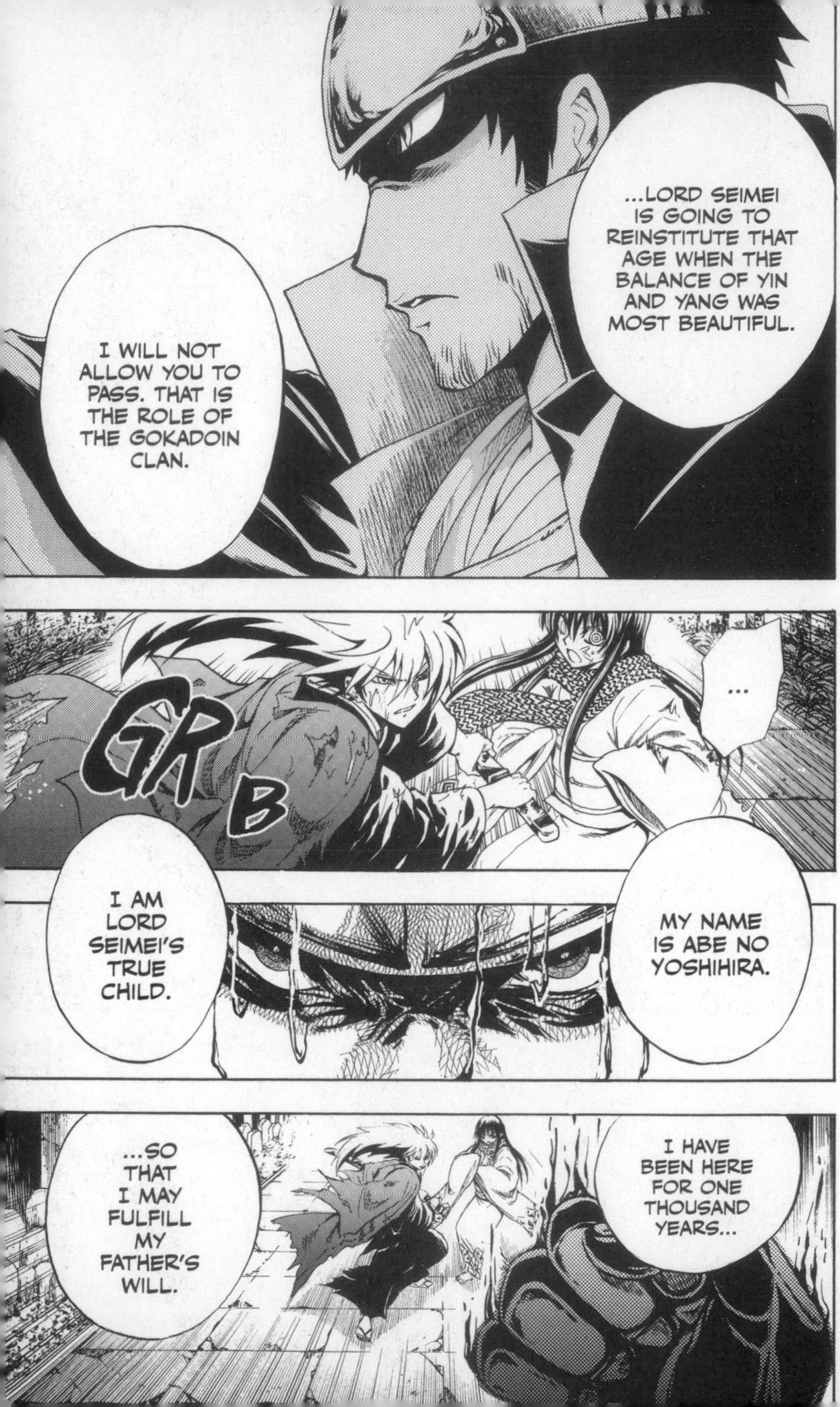
...LORD SEIMEI IS GOING TO REINSTITUTE THAT AGE WHEN THE BALANCE OF YIN AND YANG WAS MOST BEAUTIFUL.
I WILL NOT ALLOW YOU TO PASS. THAT IS THE ROLE OF THE GOKADOIN CLAN.
...
GRB
MY NAME IS ABE NO YOSHIHIRA.
I AM LORD SEIMEI'S TRUE CHILD.
I HAVE BEEN HERE FOR ONE THOUSAND YEARS...
...SO THAT I MAY FULFILL MY FATHER'S WILL.

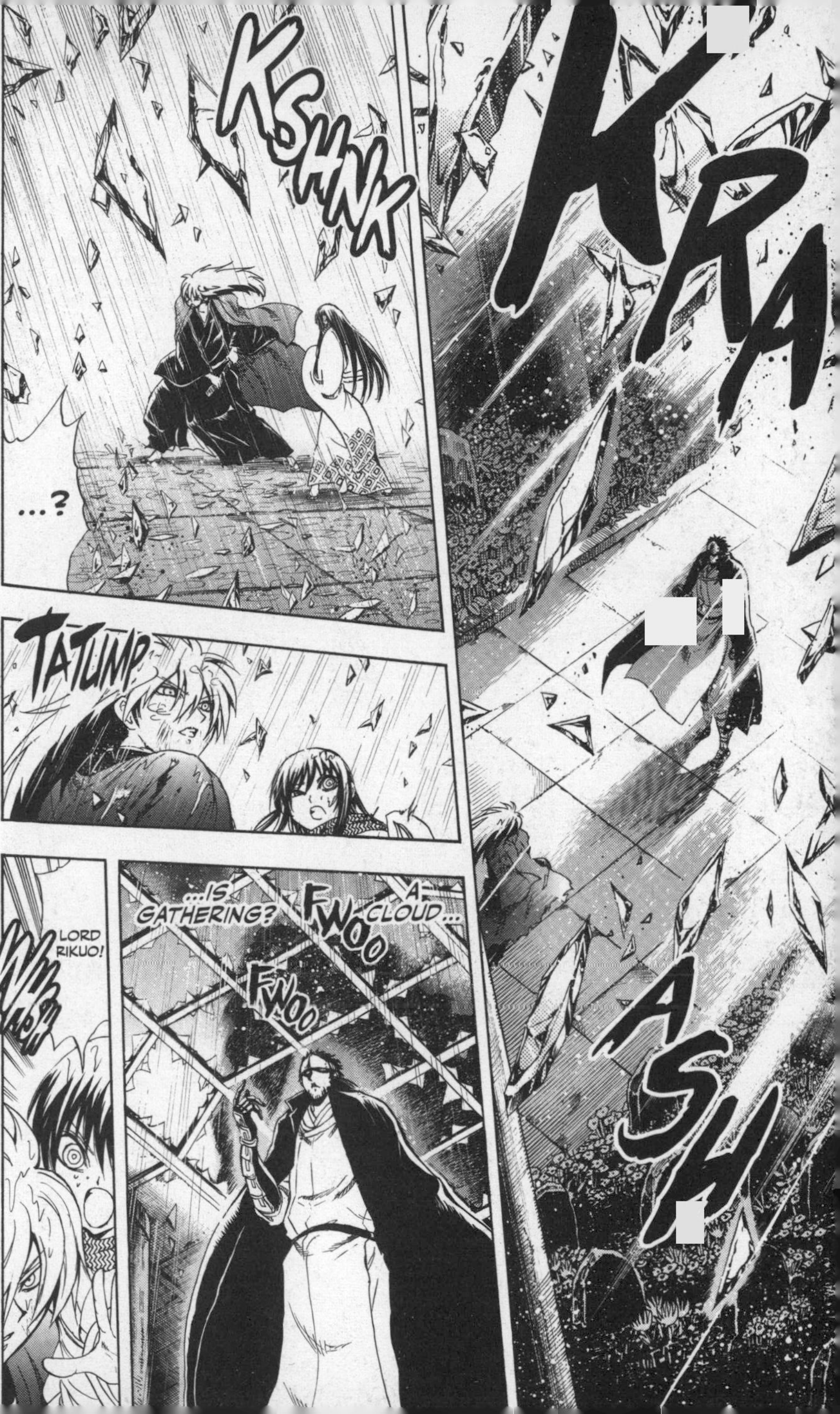
KRA
ASH
KSHNK
...?
TATUMP
A CLOUD...
...IS GATHERING?
FWOO
FWOO
LORD RIKUO!

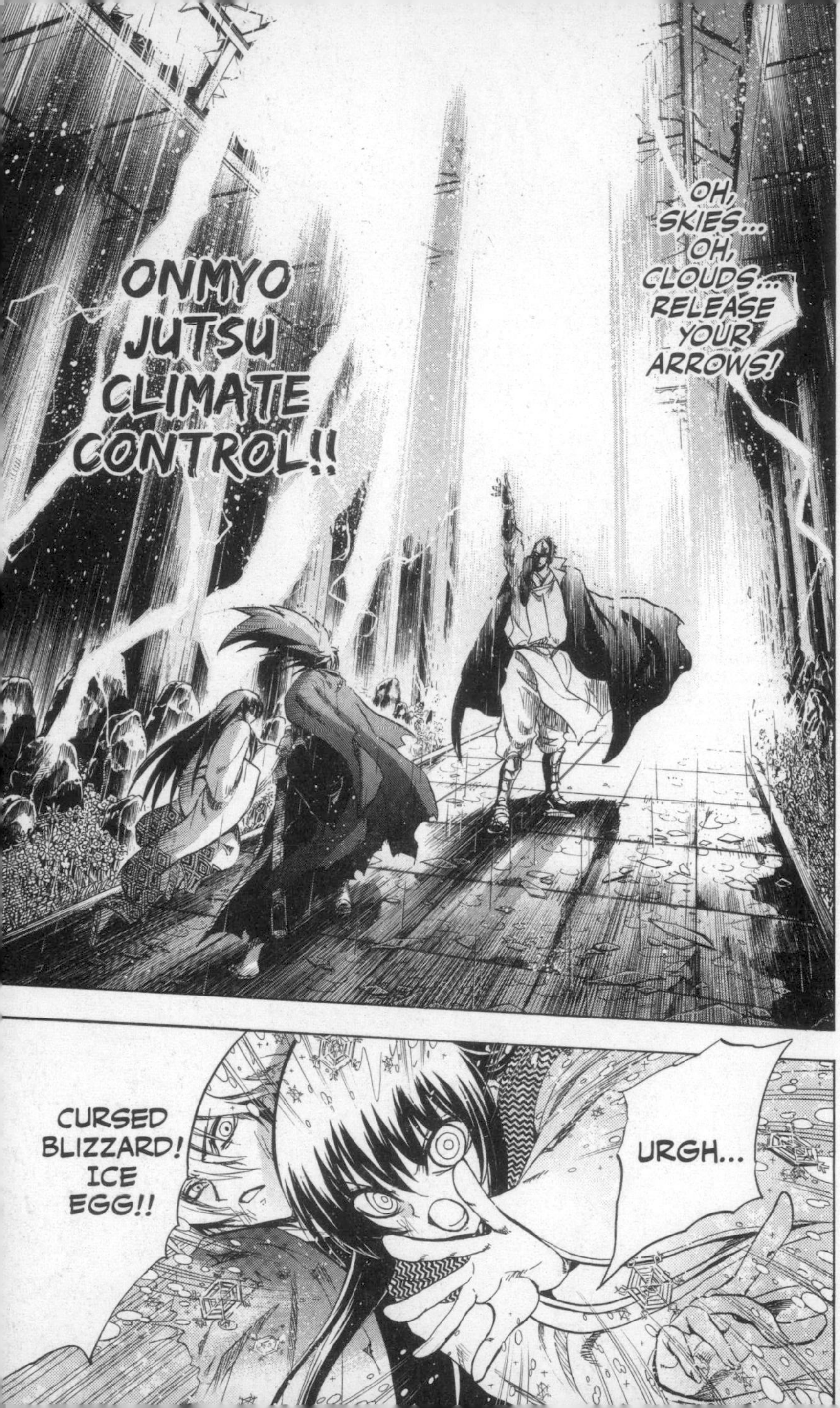
OH, SKIES... OH, CLOUDS... RELEASE YOUR ARROWS!
ONMYO JUTSU CLIMATE CONTROL!!
URGH...
CURSED BLIZZARD! ICE EGG!!

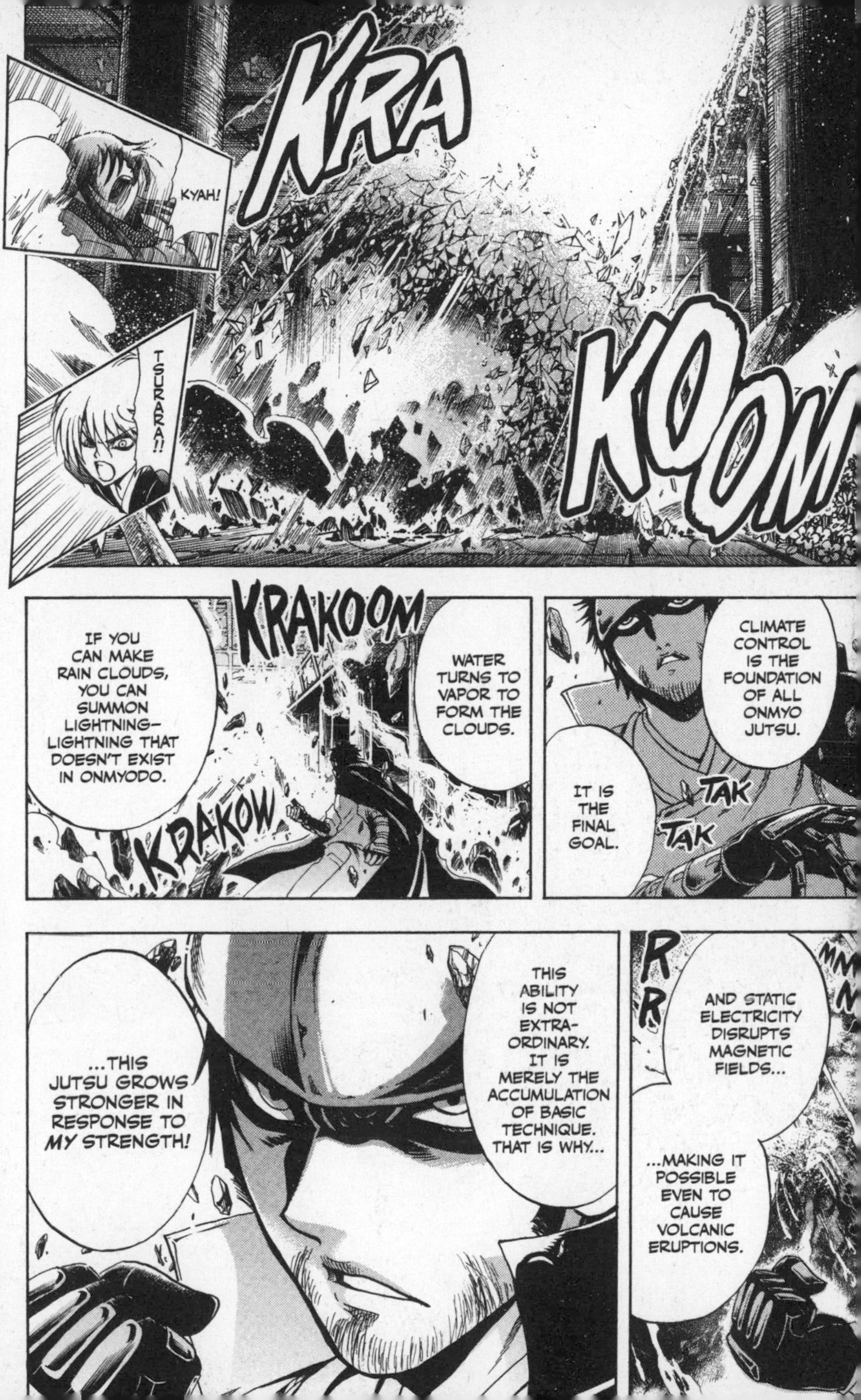
KRA
KOOM
KYAH!
TSURARA!!
CLIMATE CONTROL IS THE FOUNDATION OF ALL ONMYO JUTSU.
IT IS THE FINAL GOAL.
TAK
TAK
KRAKOOM
WATER TURNS TO VAPOR TO FORM THE CLOUDS.
IF YOU CAN MAKE RAIN CLOUDS, YOU CAN SUMMON LIGHTNING–LIGHTNING THAT DOESN'T EXIST IN ONMYODO.
KRAKOW
RR
MMN
AND STATIC ELECTRICITY DISRUPTS MAGNETIC FIELDS...
...MAKING IT POSSIBLE EVEN TO CAUSE VOLCANIC ERUPTIONS.
THIS ABILITY IS NOT EXTRA-ORDINARY. IT IS MERELY THE ACCUMULATION OF BASIC TECHNIQUE. THAT IS WHY...
...THIS JUTSU GROWS STRONGER IN RESPONSE TO *MY* STRENGTH!

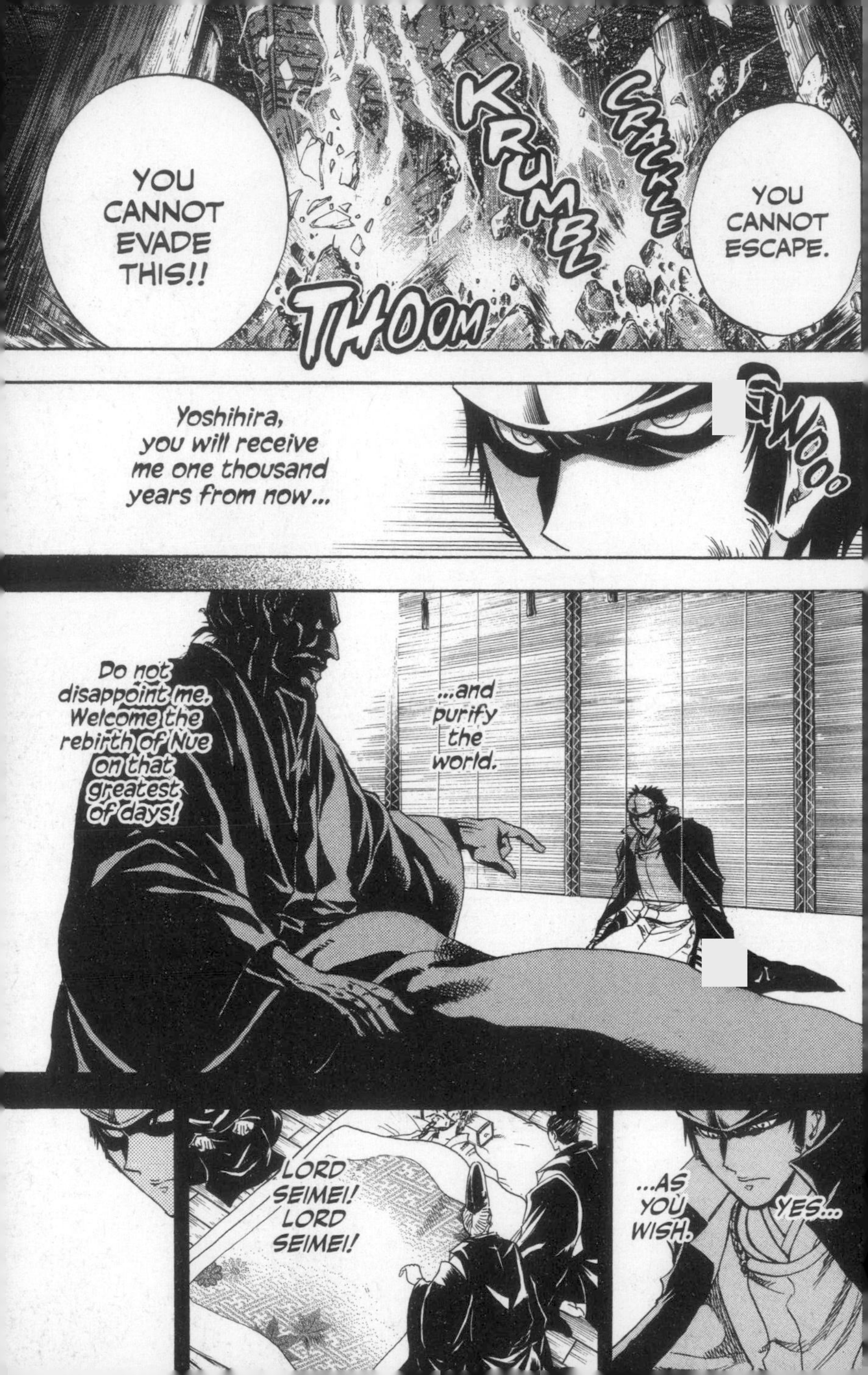
YOU CANNOT ESCAPE.
CRACKLE
KRUMBLE
YOU CANNOT EVADE THIS!!
THOOM
GWOOO
Yoshihira, you will receive me one thousand years from now...
...and purify the world.
Do not disappoint me. Welcome the rebirth of Nue on that greatest of days!
YES...
...AS YOU WISH.
LORD SEIMEI! LORD SEIMEI!

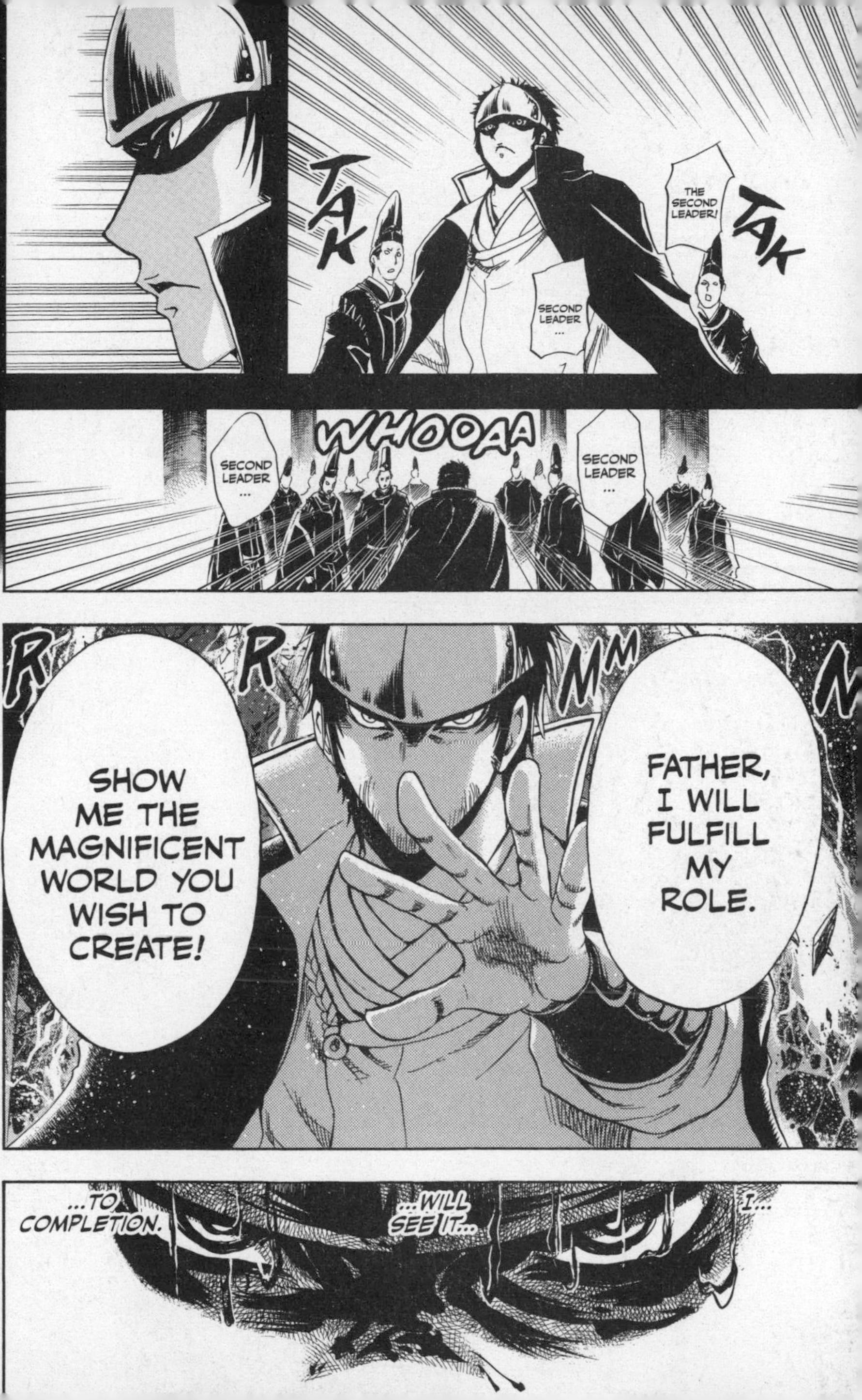
TAK
THE SECOND LEADER!
TAK
SECOND LEADER ...
WHOOAA
SECOND LEADER ...
SECOND LEADER ...
RRMMMN
FATHER, I WILL FULFILL MY ROLE.
SHOW ME THE MAGNIFICENT WORLD YOU WISH TO CREATE!
I...
...WILL SEE IT...
...TO COMPLETION.

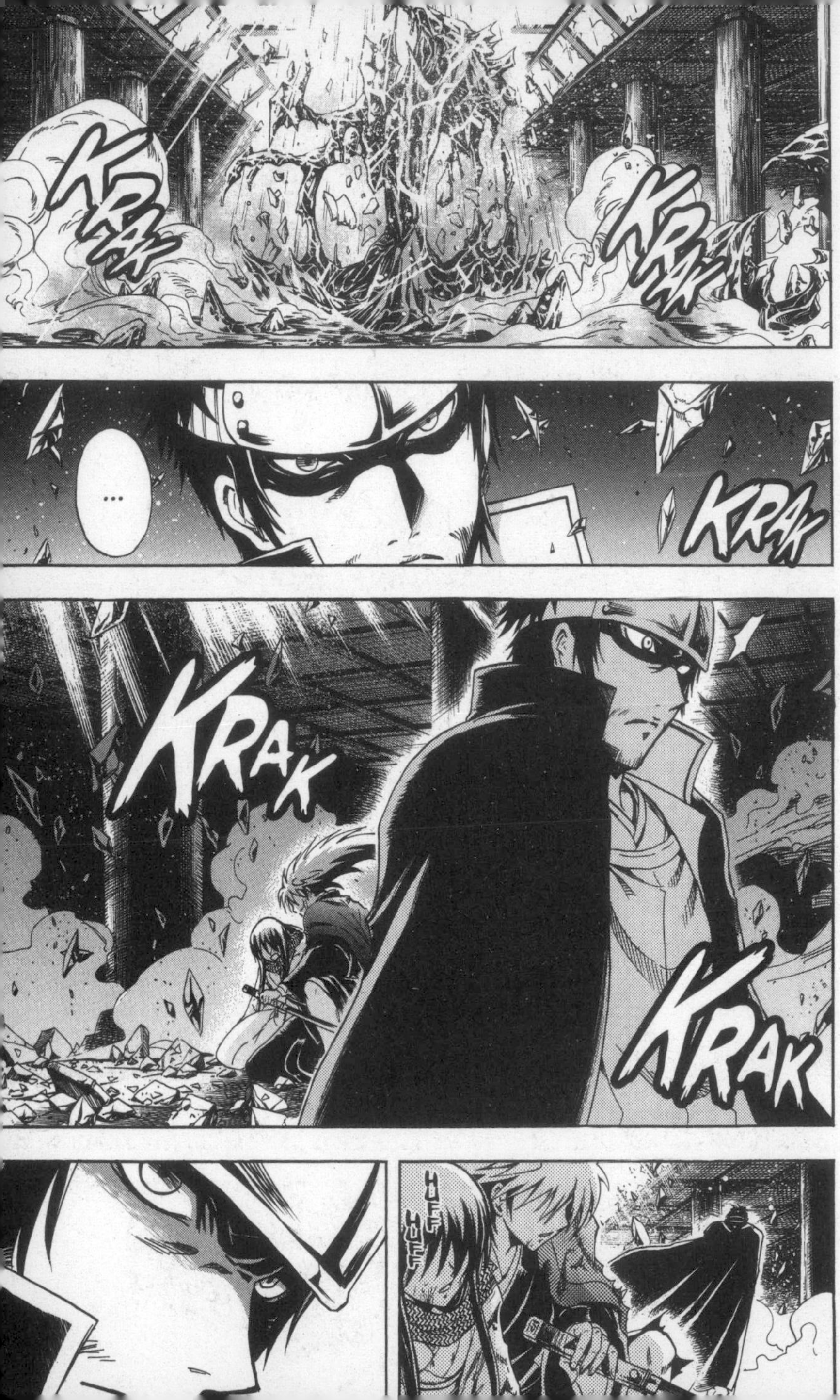
KRAK
KRAK
KRAK
...
KRAK
KRAK
HUFF
HUFF

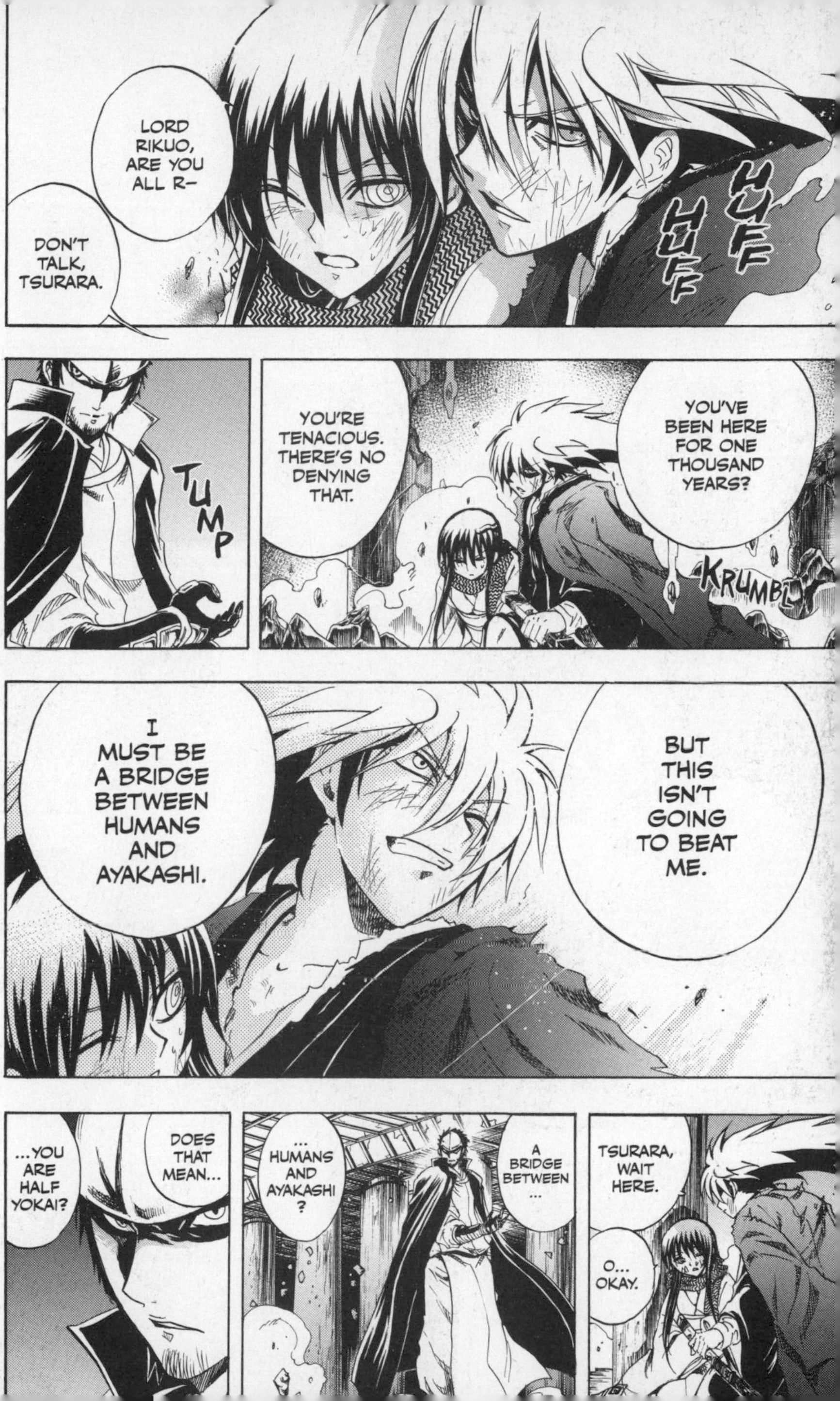
LORD RIKUO, ARE YOU ALL R–
DON'T TALK, TSURARA.
HUFF HUFF
YOU'VE BEEN HERE FOR ONE THOUSAND YEARS?
YOU'RE TENACIOUS. THERE'S NO DENYING THAT.
KRUMBL
TUMP
BUT THIS ISN'T GOING TO BEAT ME.
I MUST BE A BRIDGE BETWEEN HUMANS AND AYAKASHI.
TSURARA, WAIT HERE.
O... OKAY.
A BRIDGE BETWEEN...
...HUMANS AND AYAKASHI?
DOES THAT MEAN...
...YOU ARE HALF YOKAI?

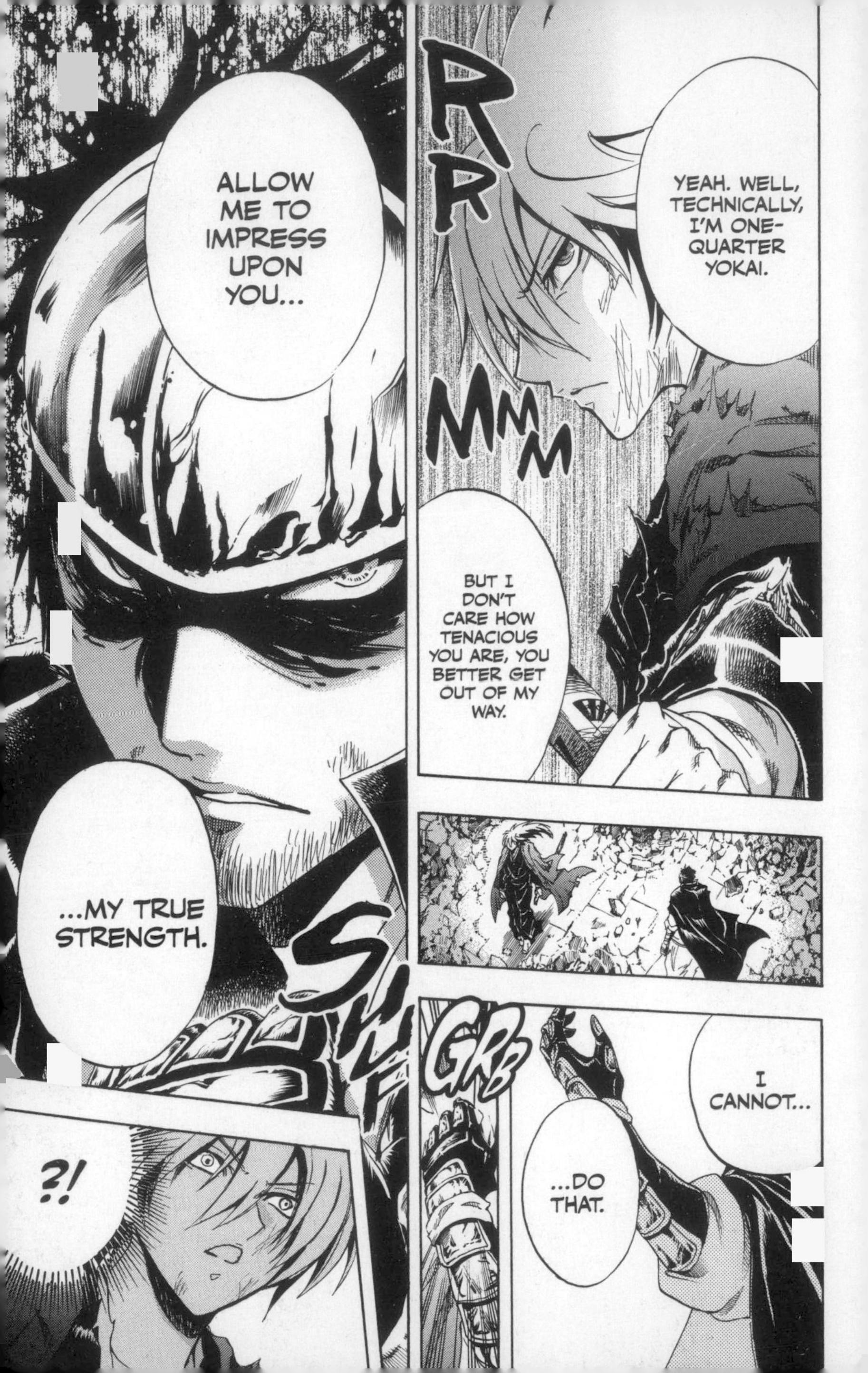
RRMMM
YEAH. WELL, TECHNICALLY, I'M ONE-QUARTER YOKAI.
BUT I DON'T CARE HOW TENACIOUS YOU ARE, YOU BETTER GET OUT OF MY WAY.
ALLOW ME TO IMPRESS UPON YOU...
...MY TRUE STRENGTH.
SHF
GRB
I CANNOT...
...DO THAT.
?!

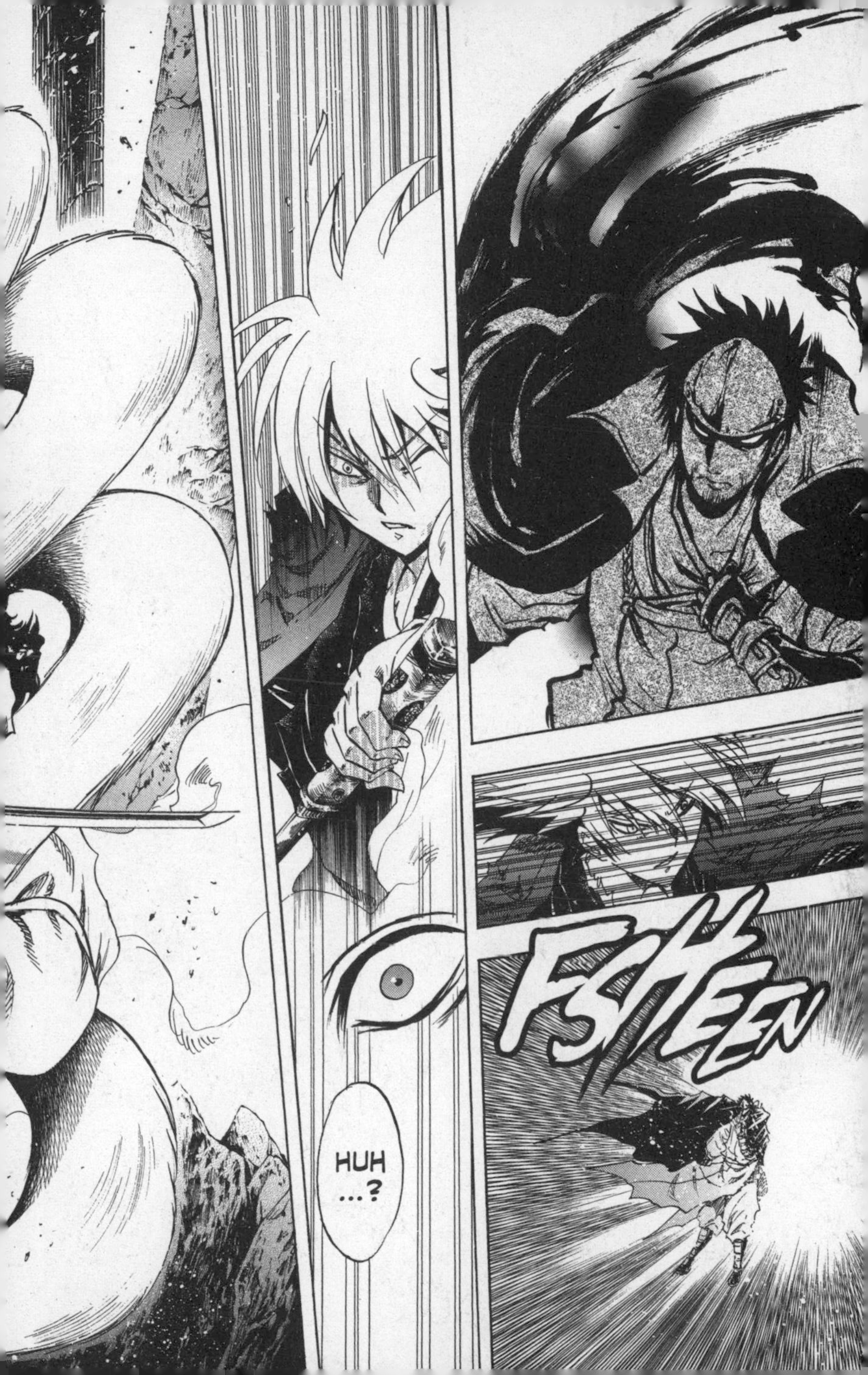
FSHEEN
HUH ...?

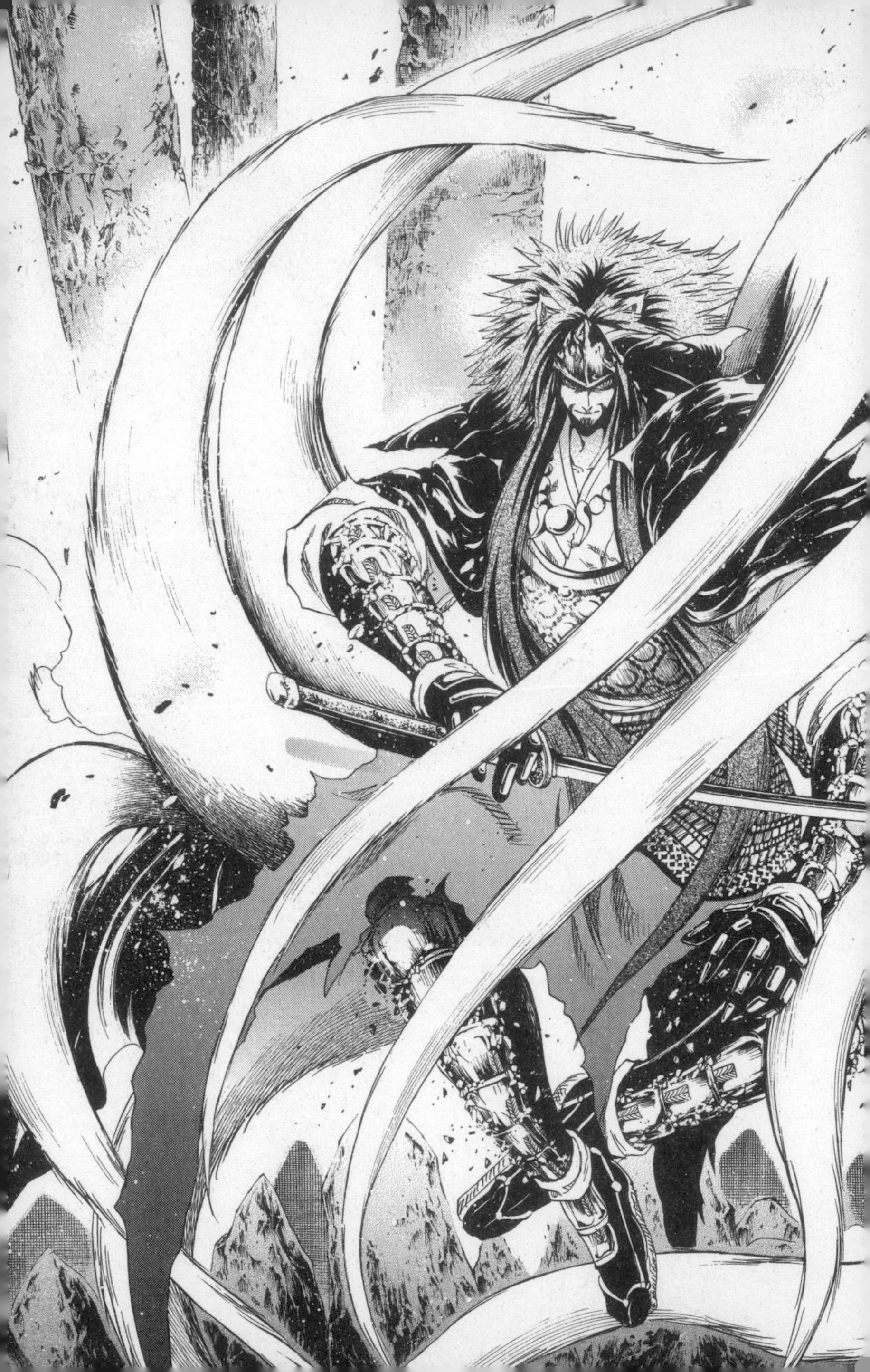

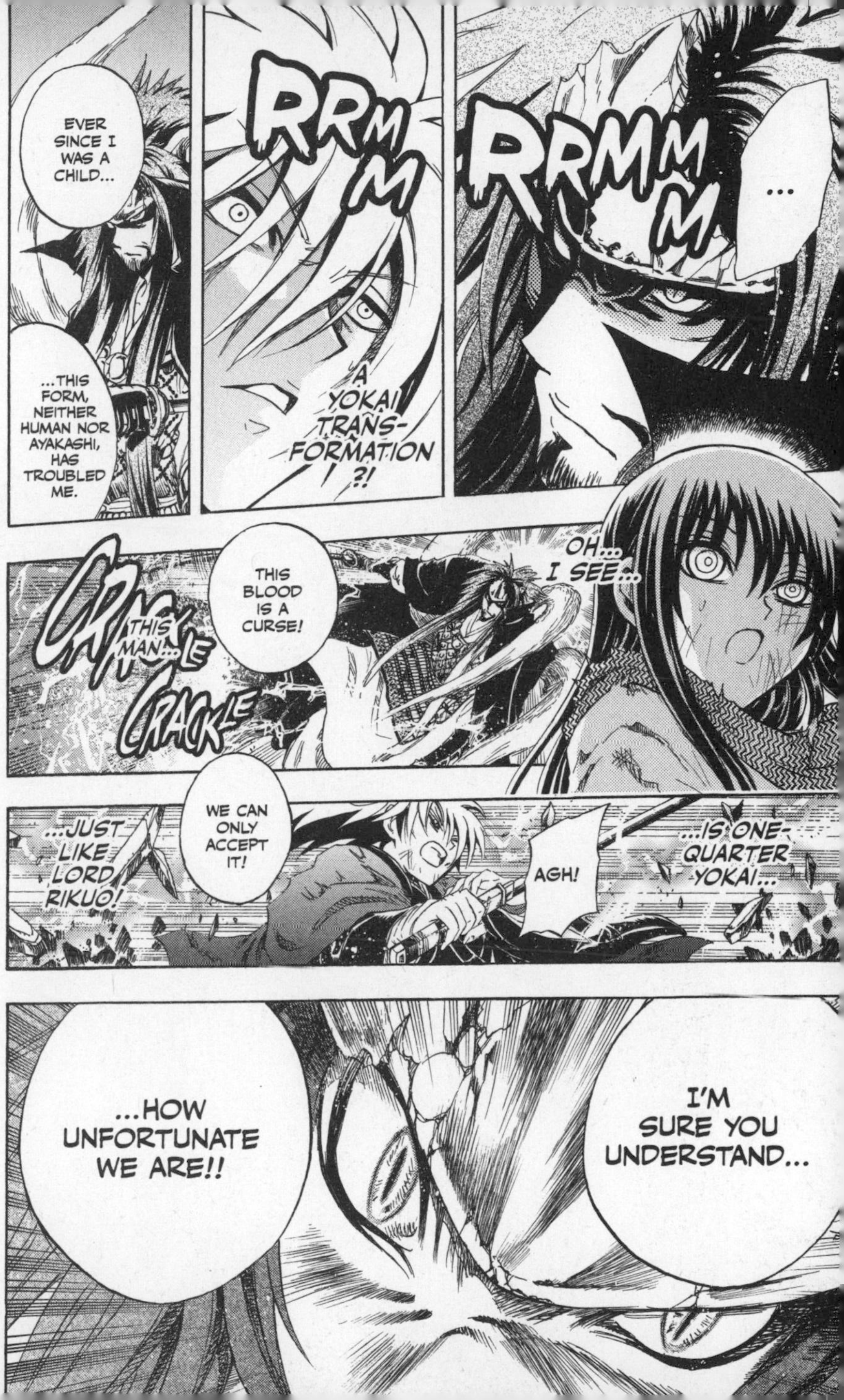
RRMMMM
...
RRMM
A YOKAI TRANSFORMATION?!
EVER SINCE I WAS A CHILD...
...THIS FORM, NEITHER HUMAN NOR AYAKASHI, HAS TROUBLED ME.
OH... I SEE...
THIS BLOOD IS A CURSE!
THIS MAN...
CRACKLE CRACKLE
...IS ONE-QUARTER YOKAI...
AGH!
WE CAN ONLY ACCEPT IT!
...JUST LIKE LORD RIKUO!
I'M SURE YOU UNDERSTAND...
...HOW UNFORTUNATE WE ARE!!

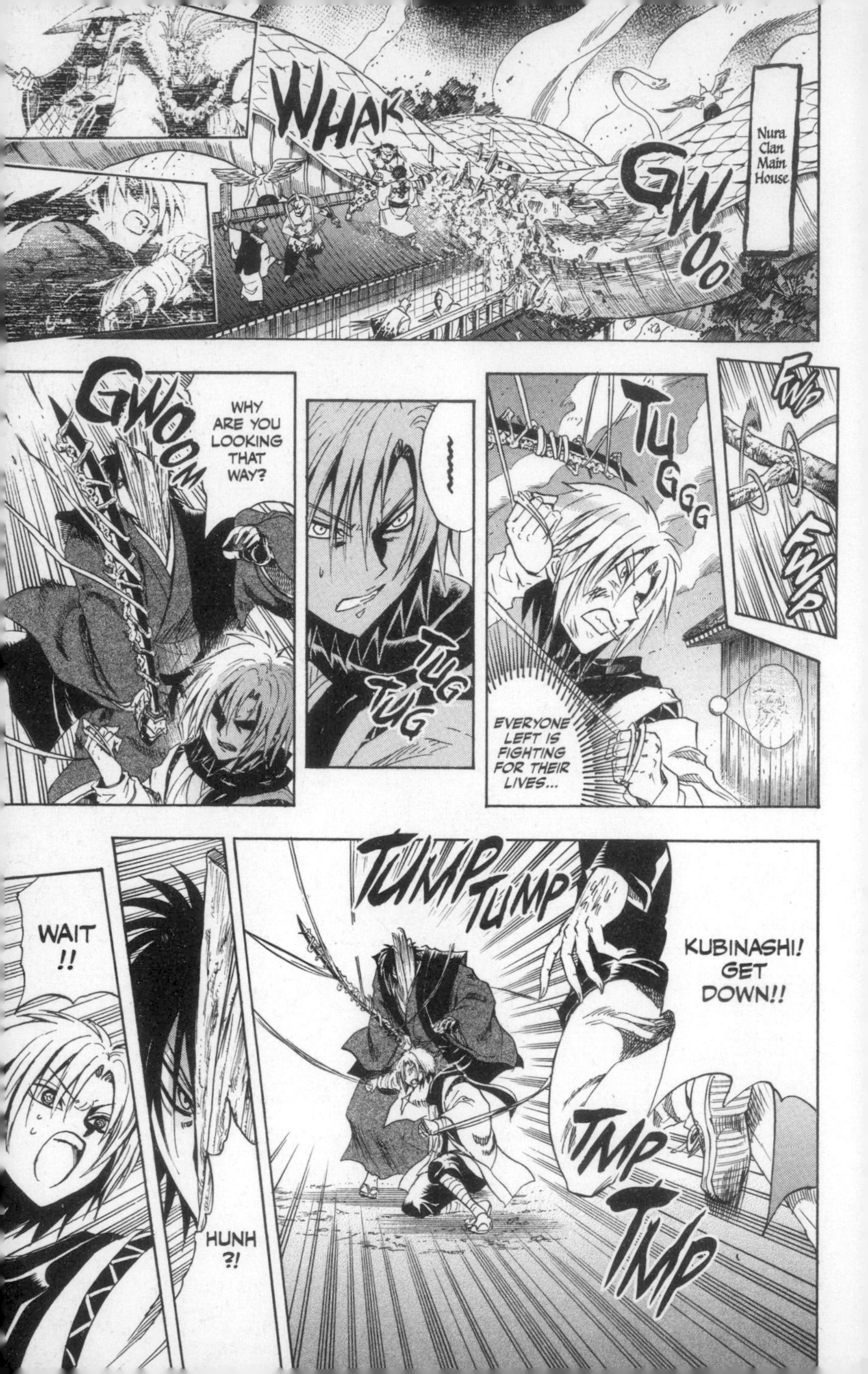
Nura Clan Main House
GWOOO
WHAK
FWP
FWP
TUGGG
EVERYONE LEFT IS FIGHTING FOR THEIR LIVES...
...
TUG TUG
GWOOOM
WHY ARE YOU LOOKING THAT WAY?
TUMP TUMP
KUBINASHI! GET DOWN!!
TMP TMP
WAIT !!
HUNH ?!

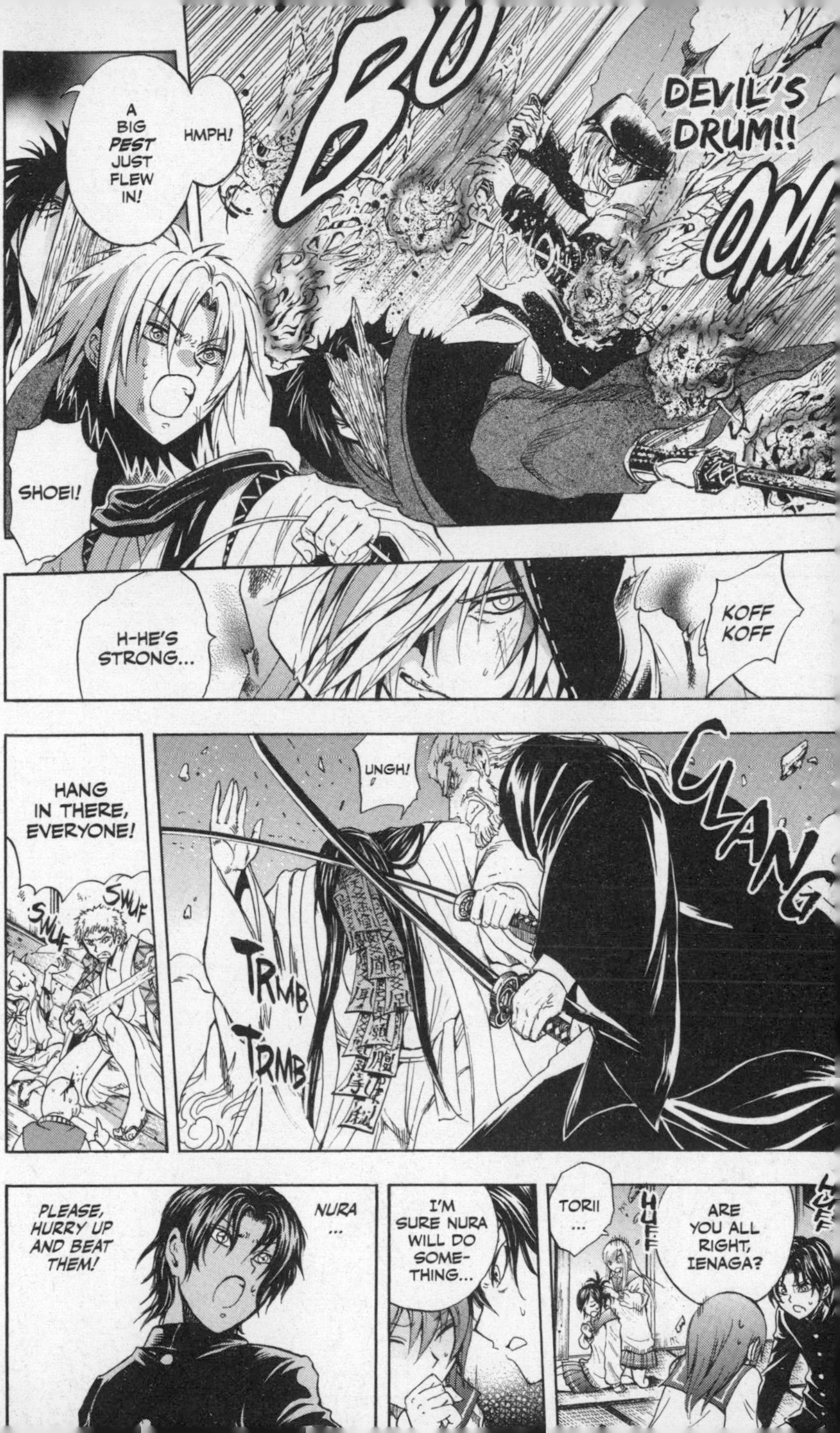

BO
OM
DEVIL'S DRUM!!
HMPH!
A BIG PEST JUST FLEW IN!
SHOEI!
KOFF KOFF
H-HE'S STRONG...
CLANG
UNGH!
TRMB
TRMB
HANG IN THERE, EVERYONE!
SWUF
SWUF
HUFF
ARE YOU ALL RIGHT, IENAGA?
HUFF
TORII ...
I'M SURE NURA WILL DO SOME-THING...
NURA ...
PLEASE, HURRY UP AND BEAT THEM!

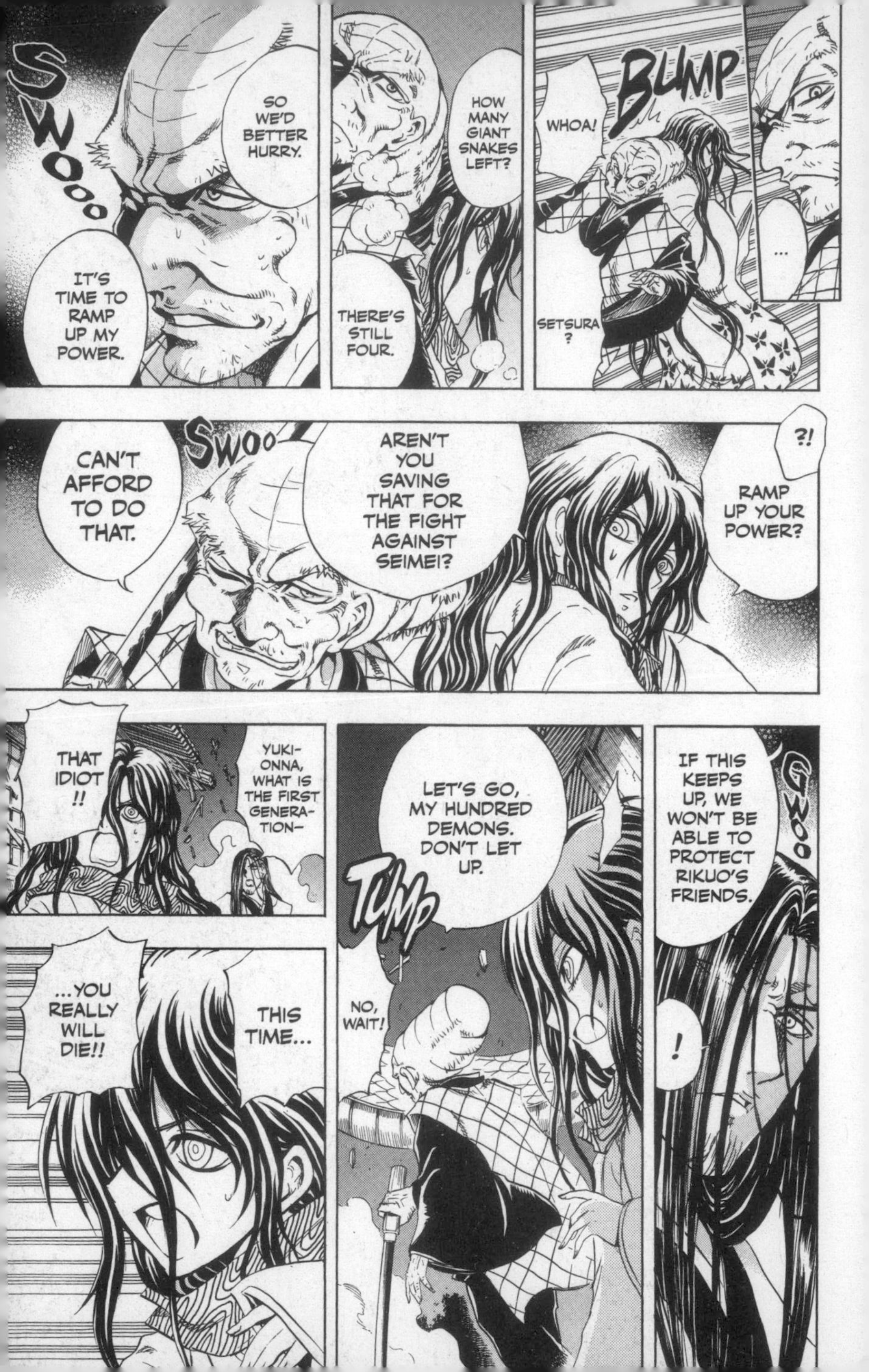

...
BUMP
WHOA!
SETSURA?
HOW MANY GIANT SNAKES LEFT?
THERE'S STILL FOUR.
SO WE'D BETTER HURRY.
SWOOO
IT'S TIME TO RAMP UP MY POWER.
?!
RAMP UP YOUR POWER?
AREN'T YOU SAVING THAT FOR THE FIGHT AGAINST SEIMEI?
SWOO
CAN'T AFFORD TO DO THAT.
IF THIS KEEPS UP, WE WON'T BE ABLE TO PROTECT RIKUO'S FRIENDS.
GWOO
!
LET'S GO, MY HUNDRED DEMONS. DON'T LET UP.
TUMP
NO, WAIT!
YUKI-ONNA, WHAT IS THE FIRST GENERATION-
THAT IDIOT!!
THIS TIME...
...YOU REALLY WILL DIE!!

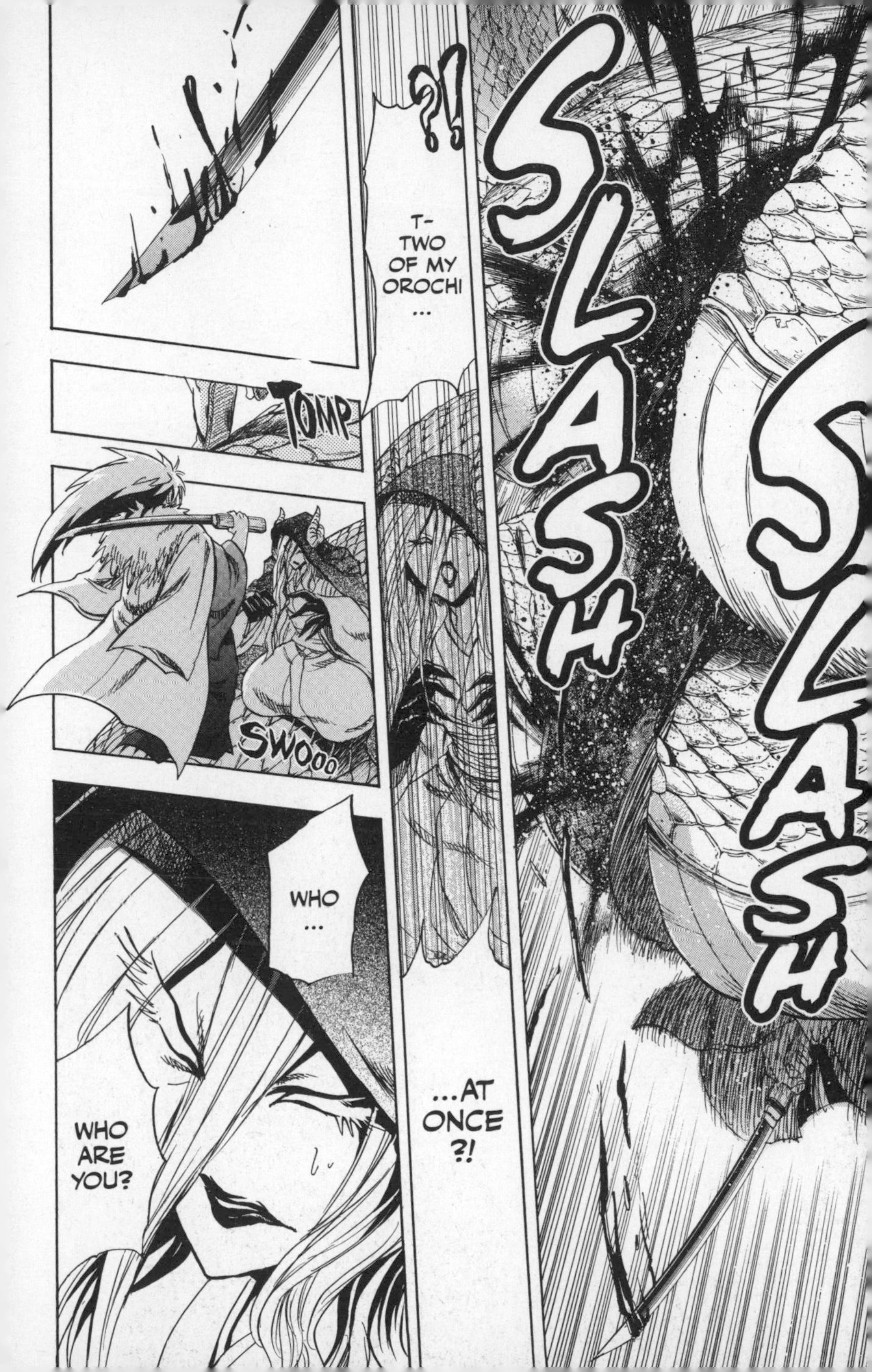
SLASH
SLASH
?!
T-TWO OF MY OROCHI...
...AT ONCE?!
TOMP
SWOOO
WHO...
WHO ARE YOU?

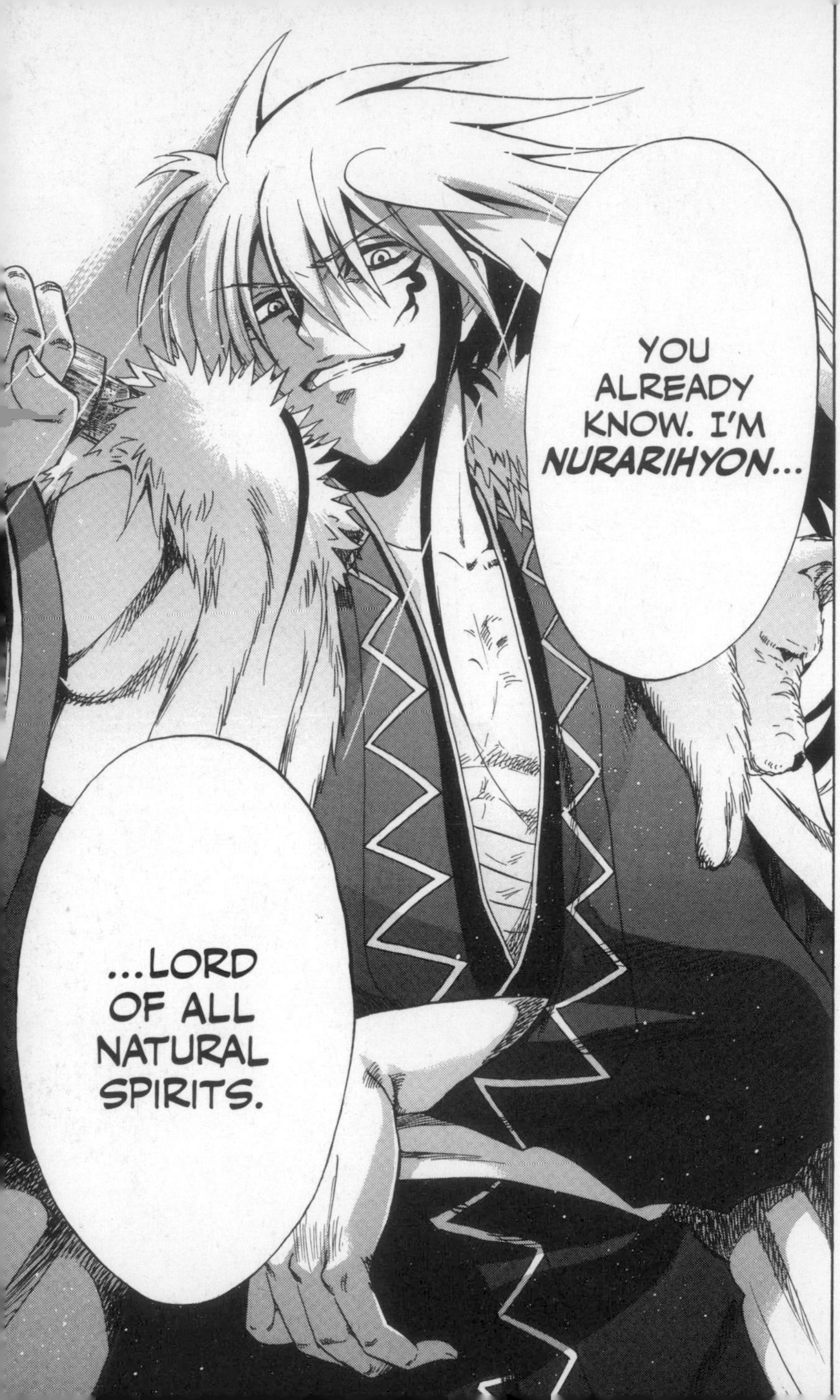
YOU ALREADY KNOW. I'M *NURARIHYON*...
...LORD OF ALL NATURAL SPIRITS.

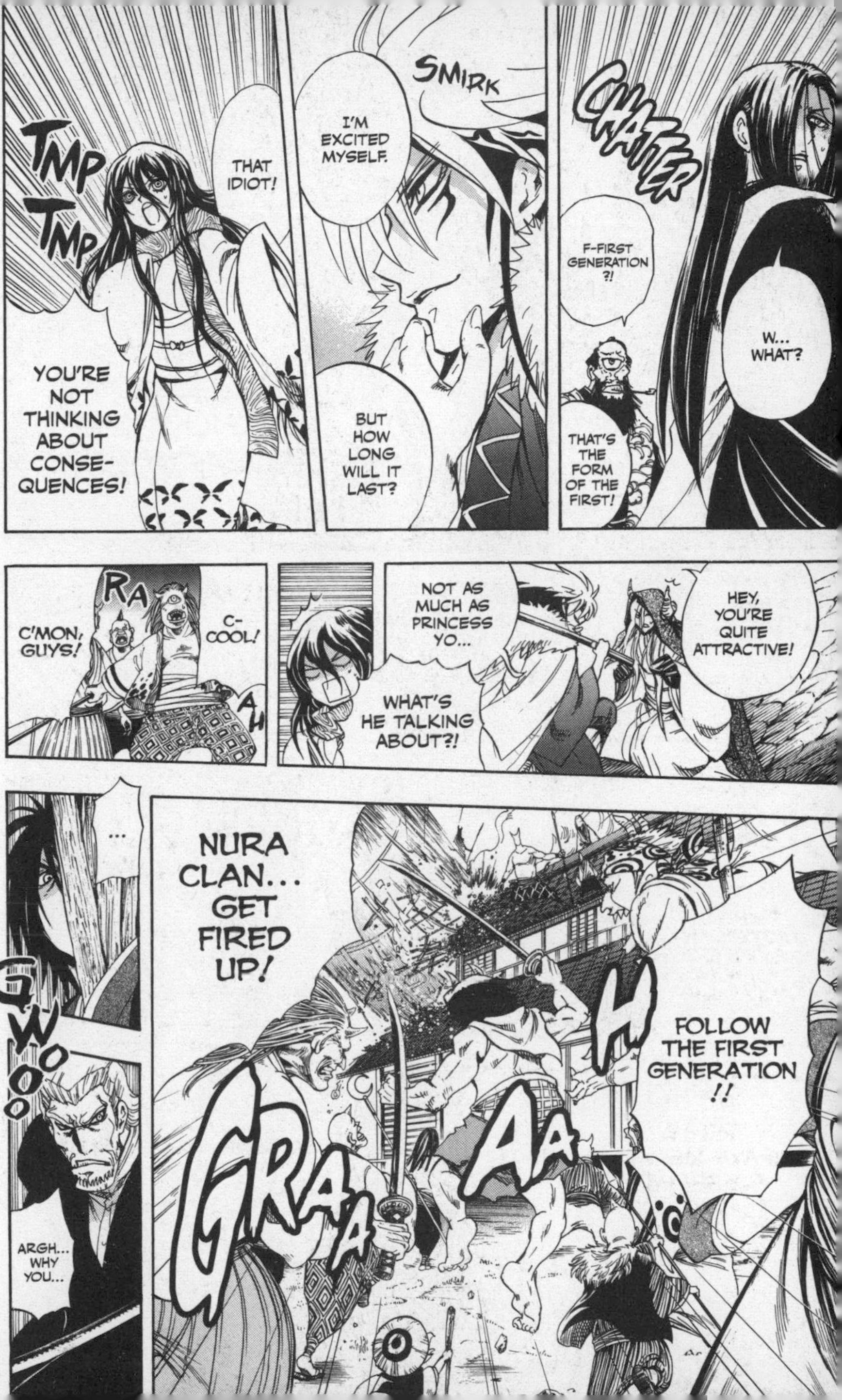
CHATTER
W... WHAT?
F-FIRST GENERATION ?!
THAT'S THE FORM OF THE FIRST!
SMIRK
I'M EXCITED MYSELF.
BUT HOW LONG WILL IT LAST?
THAT IDIOT!
TMP TMP
YOU'RE NOT THINKING ABOUT CONSE-QUENCES!
HEY, YOU'RE QUITE ATTRACTIVE!
NOT AS MUCH AS PRINCESS YO...
WHAT'S HE TALKING ABOUT?!
RA
C-COOL!
C'MON, GUYS!
AH
FOLLOW THE FIRST GENERATION !!
NURA CLAN... GET FIRED UP!
GRAAAAH
...
GWOOO
ARGH... WHY YOU...

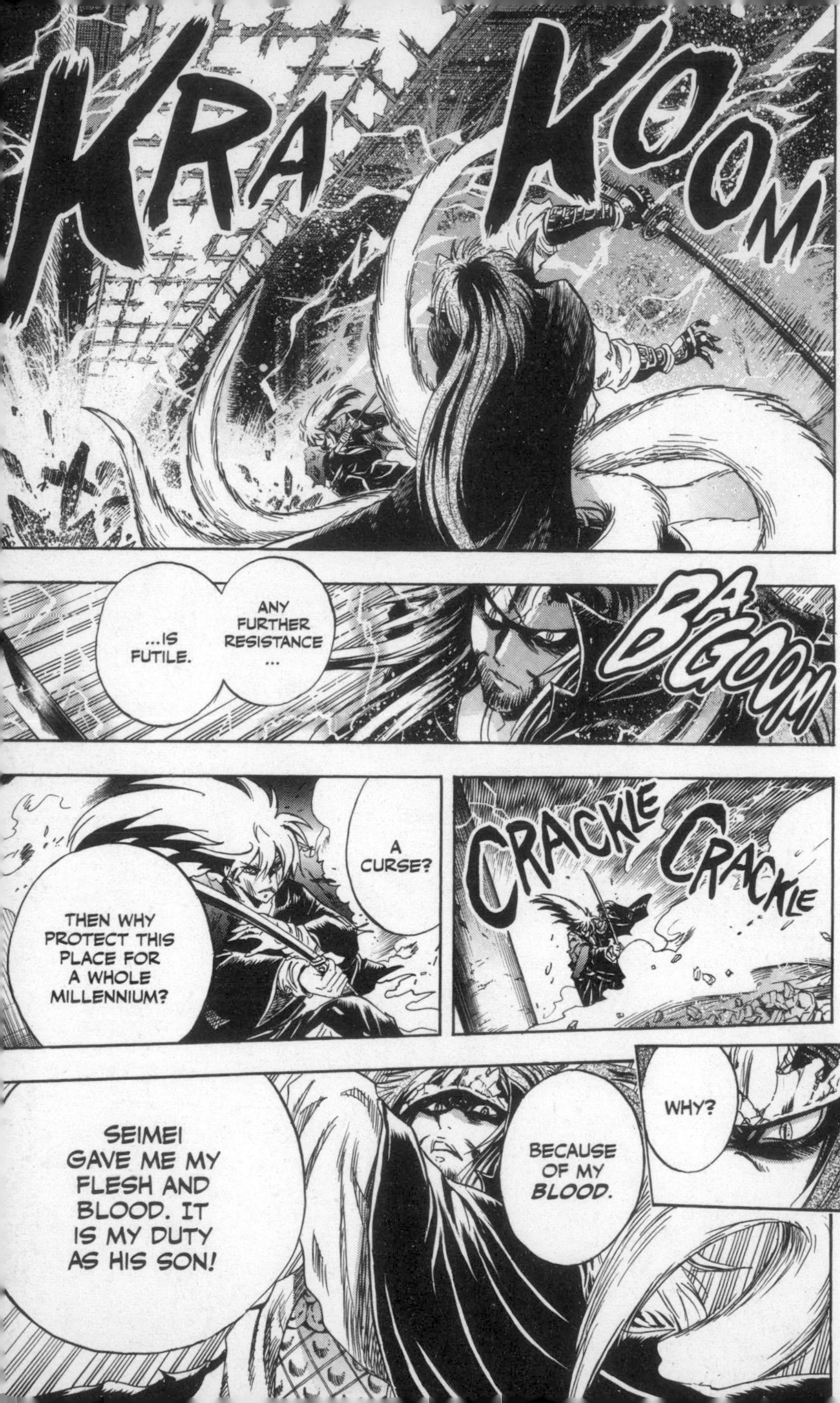
KRA
KOOM
BAGOOM
ANY FURTHER RESISTANCE ...
...IS FUTILE.
CRACKLE CRACKLE
A CURSE?
THEN WHY PROTECT THIS PLACE FOR A WHOLE MILLENNIUM?
WHY?
BECAUSE OF MY *BLOOD*.
SEIMEI GAVE ME MY FLESH AND BLOOD. IT IS MY DUTY AS HIS SON!

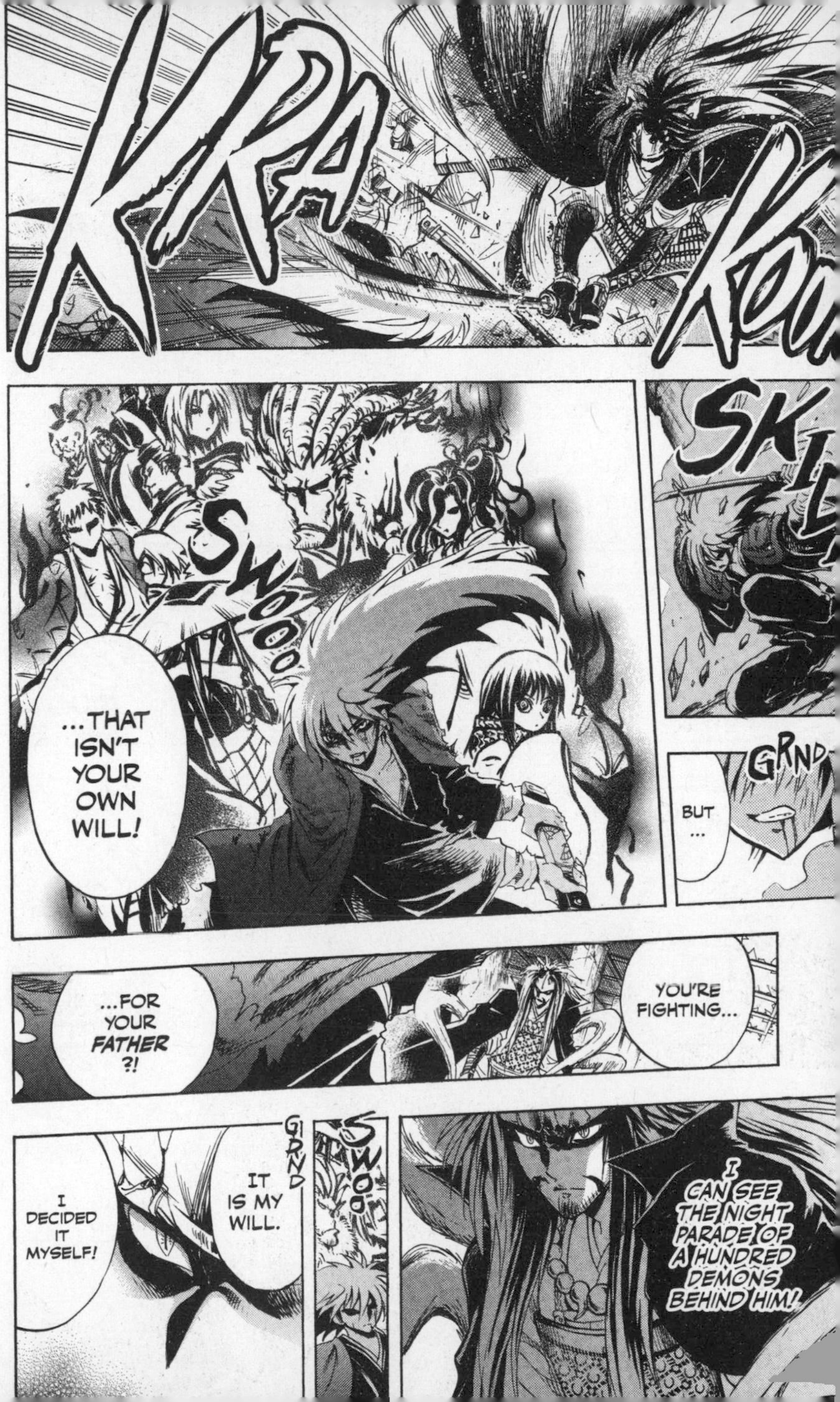
KRA
KOOM
SKID
GRND
BUT...
SWOOO
...THAT ISN'T YOUR OWN WILL!
YOU'RE FIGHTING...
...FOR YOUR FATHER?!
I CAN SEE THE NIGHT PARADE OF A HUNDRED DEMONS BEHIND HIM!
SWOOD
GRND
IT IS MY WILL.
I DECIDED IT MYSELF!

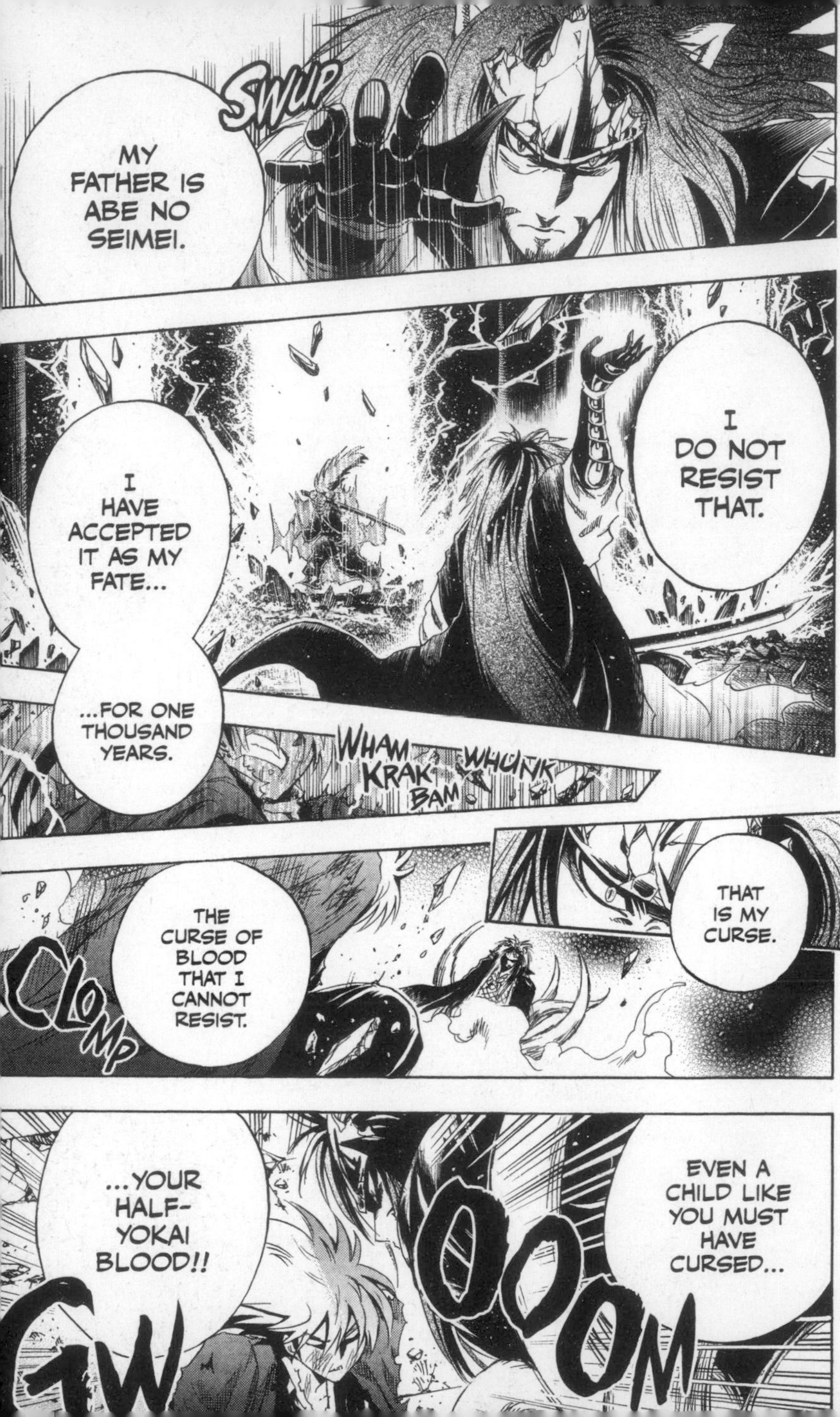
SWUP
MY FATHER IS ABE NO SEIMEI.
I DO NOT RESIST THAT.
I HAVE ACCEPTED IT AS MY FATE...
...FOR ONE THOUSAND YEARS.
WHAM KRAK WHUNK BAM
THAT IS MY CURSE.
THE CURSE OF BLOOD THAT I CANNOT RESIST.
CLOMP
EVEN A CHILD LIKE YOU MUST HAVE CURSED...
...YOUR HALF-YOKAI BLOOD!!
GWOOOOM

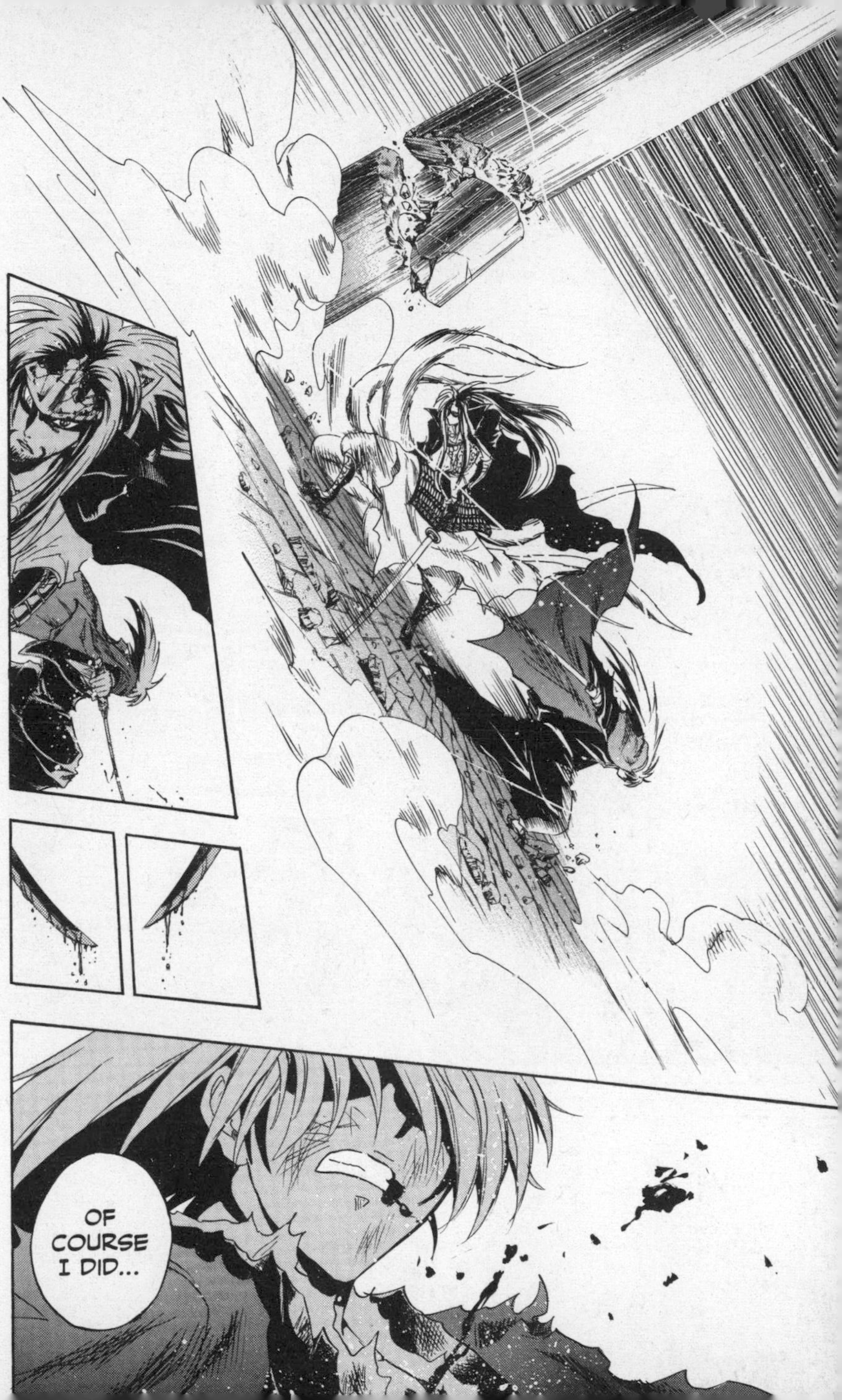
OF COURSE I DID...

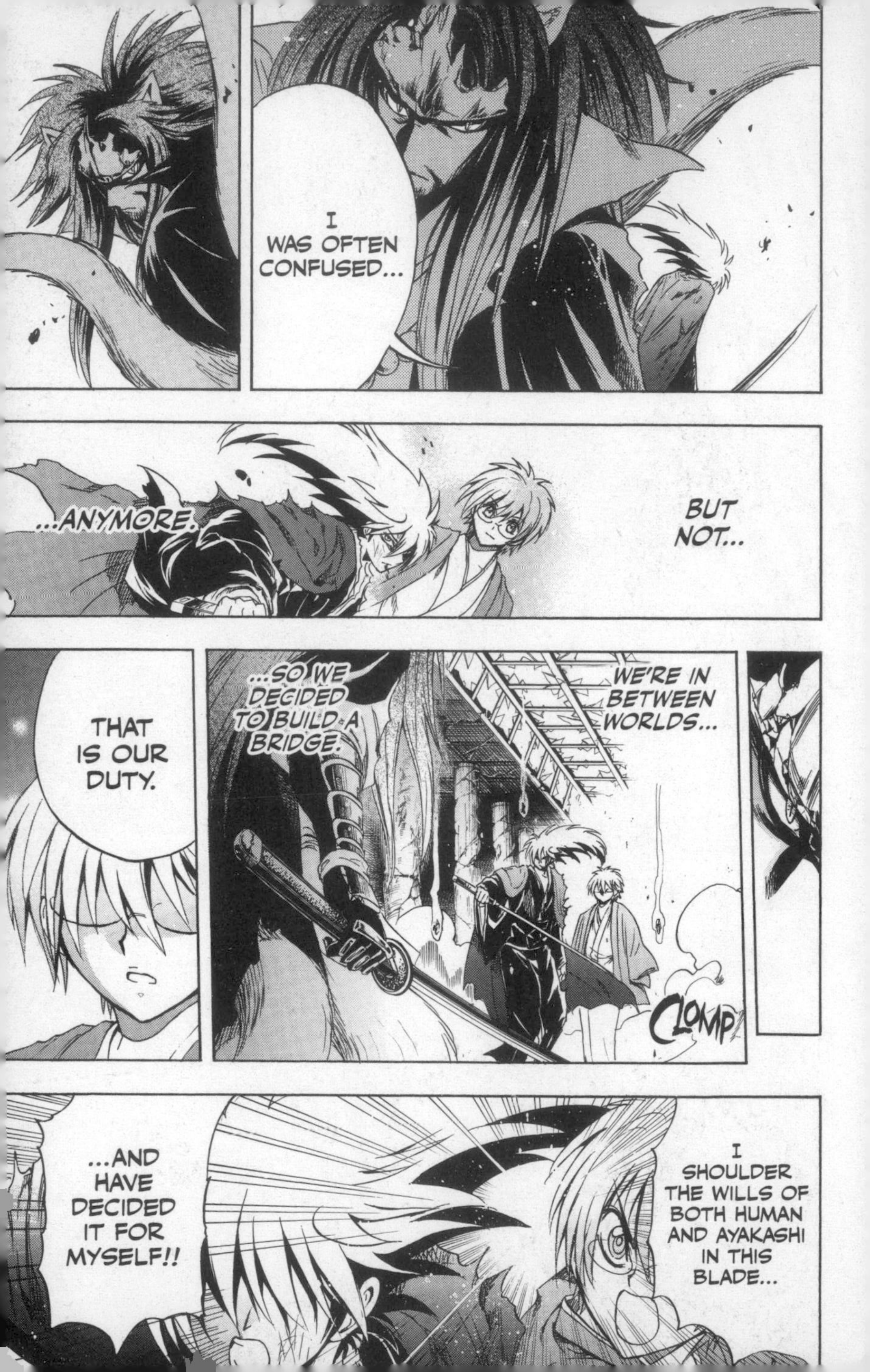
I WAS OFTEN CONFUSED...
BUT NOT...
...ANYMORE.
WE'RE IN BETWEEN WORLDS...
...SO WE DECIDED TO BUILD A BRIDGE.
CLOMP
THAT IS OUR DUTY.
I SHOULDER THE WILLS OF BOTH HUMAN AND AYAKASHI IN THIS BLADE...
...AND HAVE DECIDED IT FOR MYSELF!!

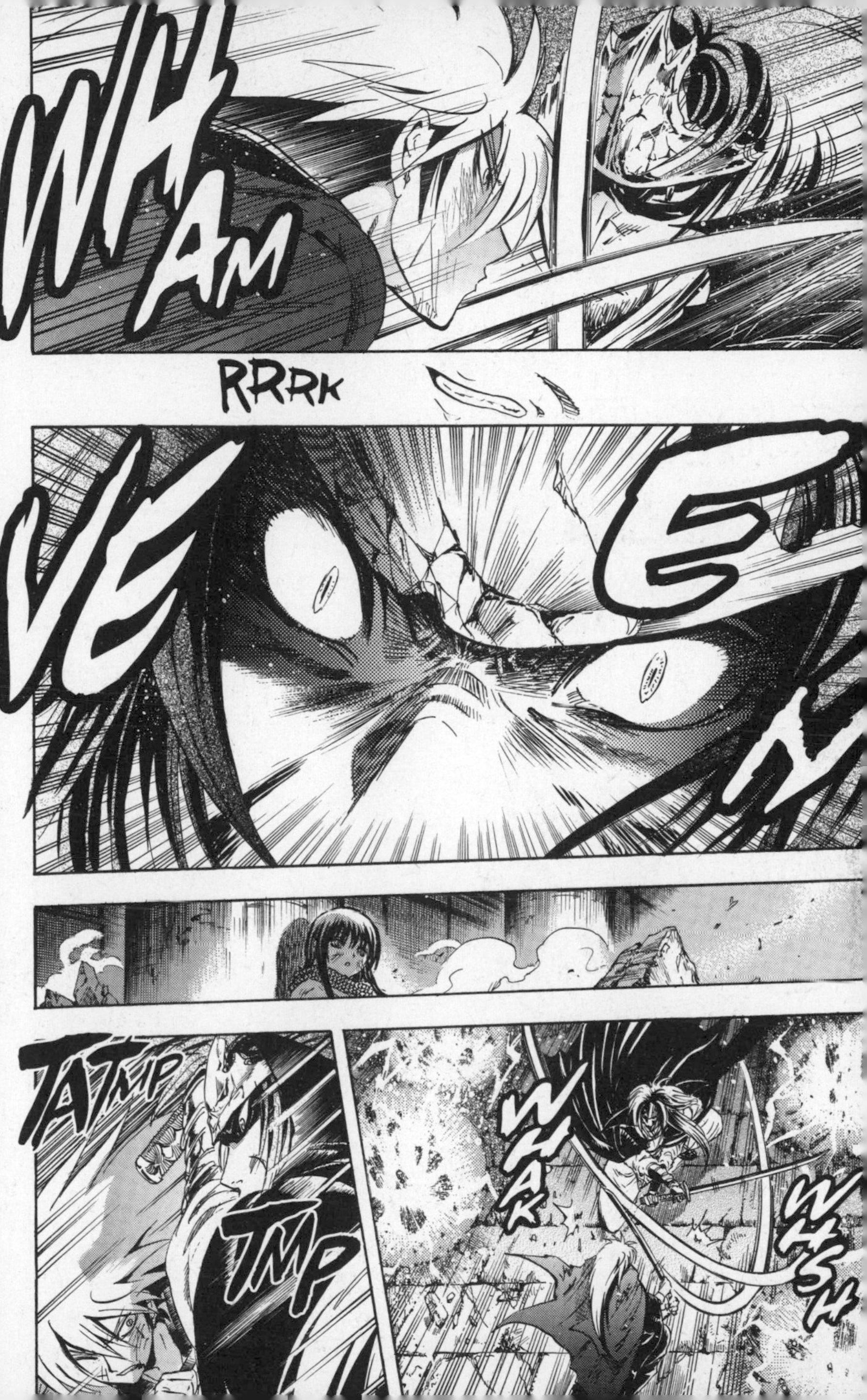
WHAM
RRRK
WHSH
WHAK
TATMP
TMP

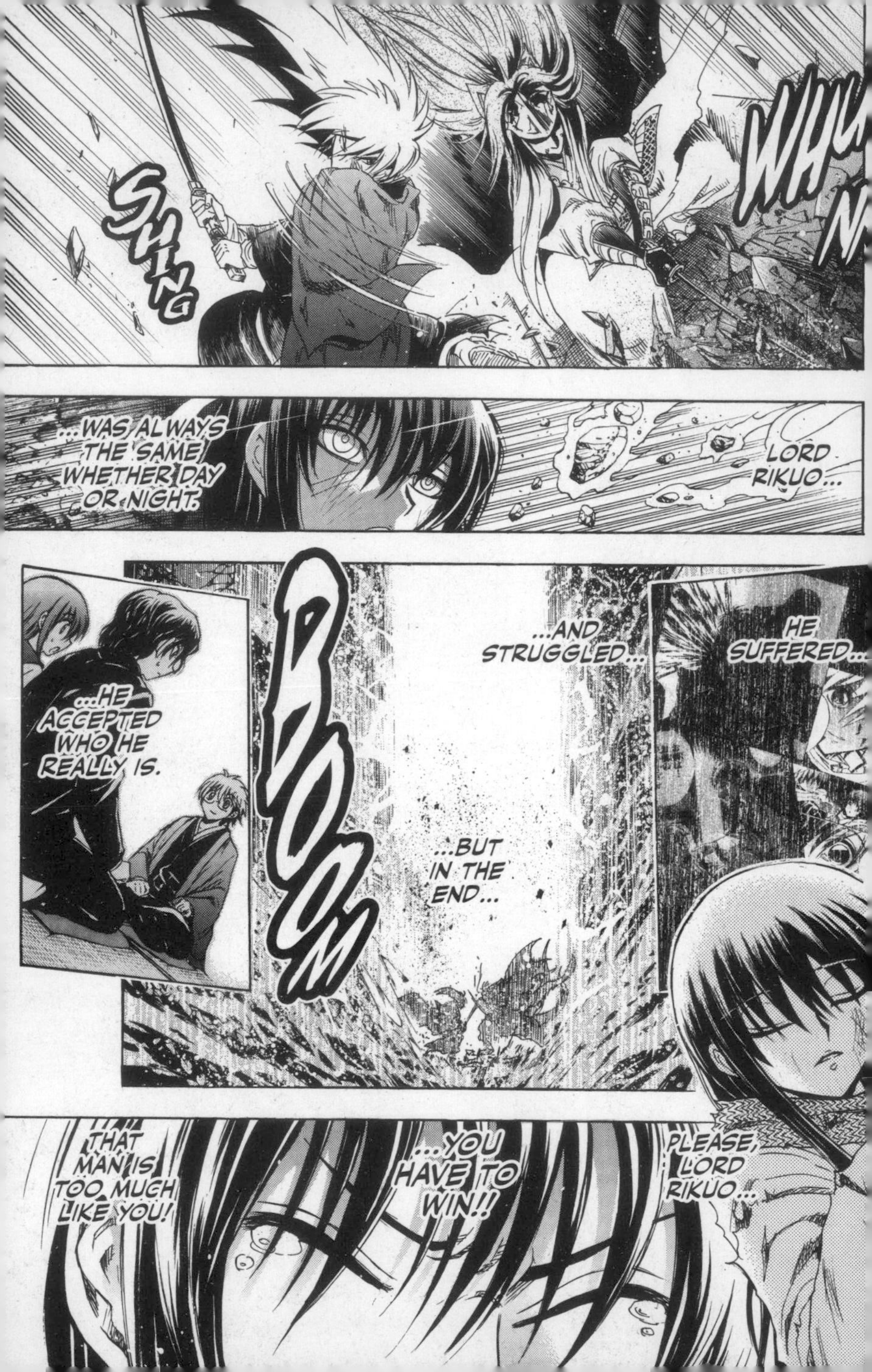
SHING
LORD RIKUO...
...WAS ALWAYS THE SAME WHETHER DAY OR NIGHT.
HE SUFFERED...
...AND STRUGGLED...
...BUT IN THE END...
DOOOM
...HE ACCEPTED WHO HE REALLY IS.
PLEASE, LORD RIKUO...
...YOU HAVE TO WIN!!
THAT MAN IS TOO MUCH LIKE YOU!

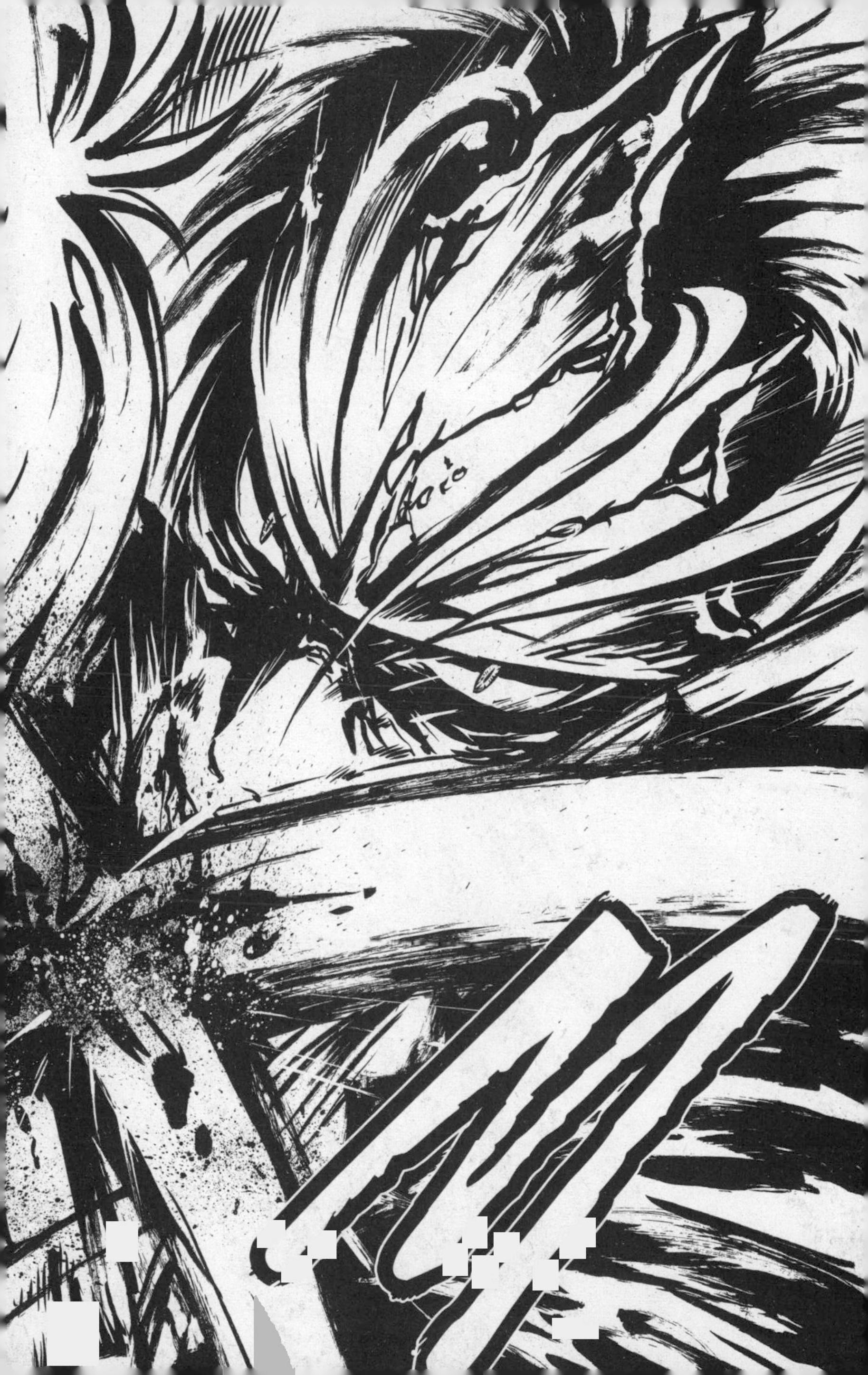

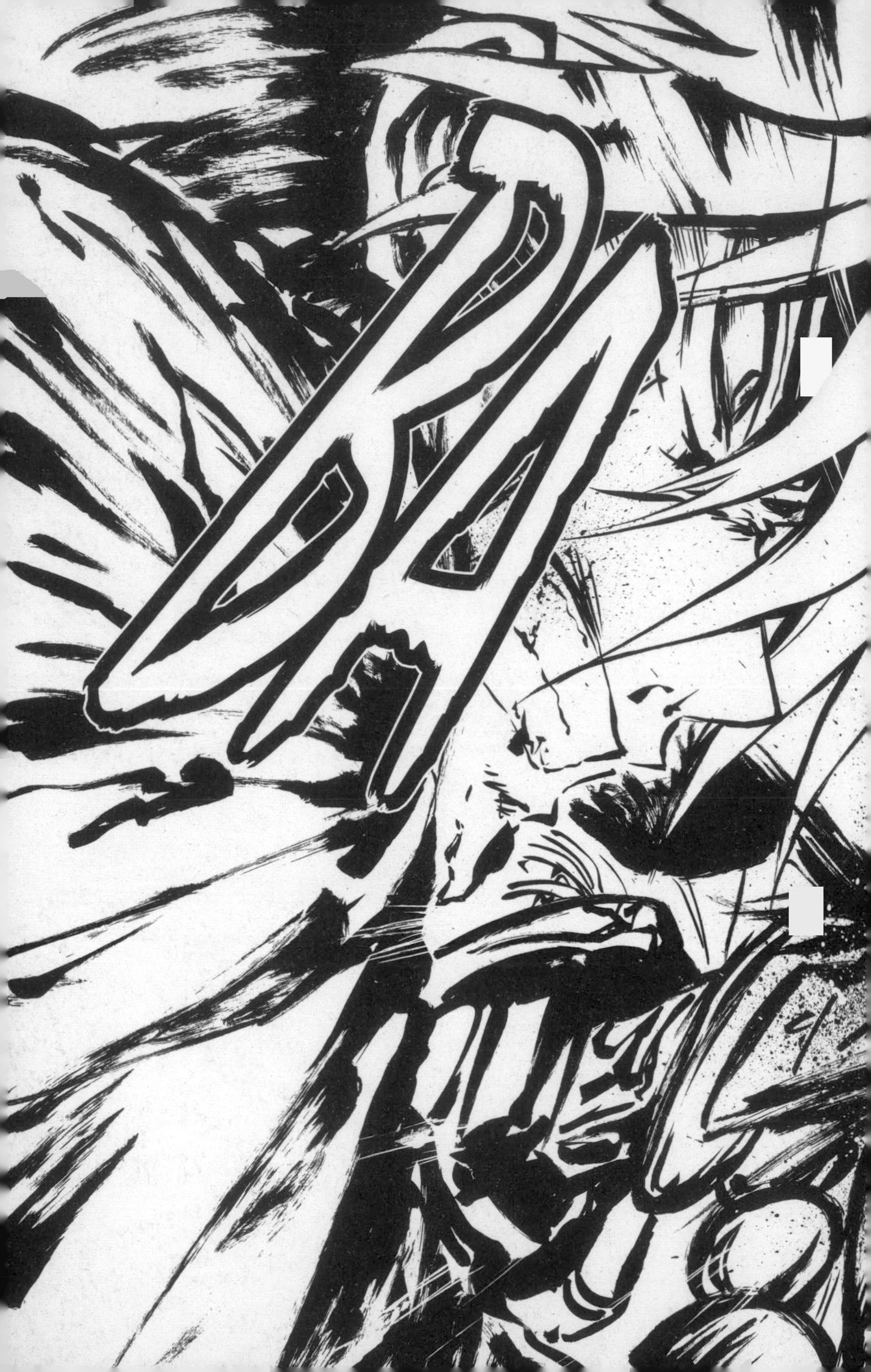

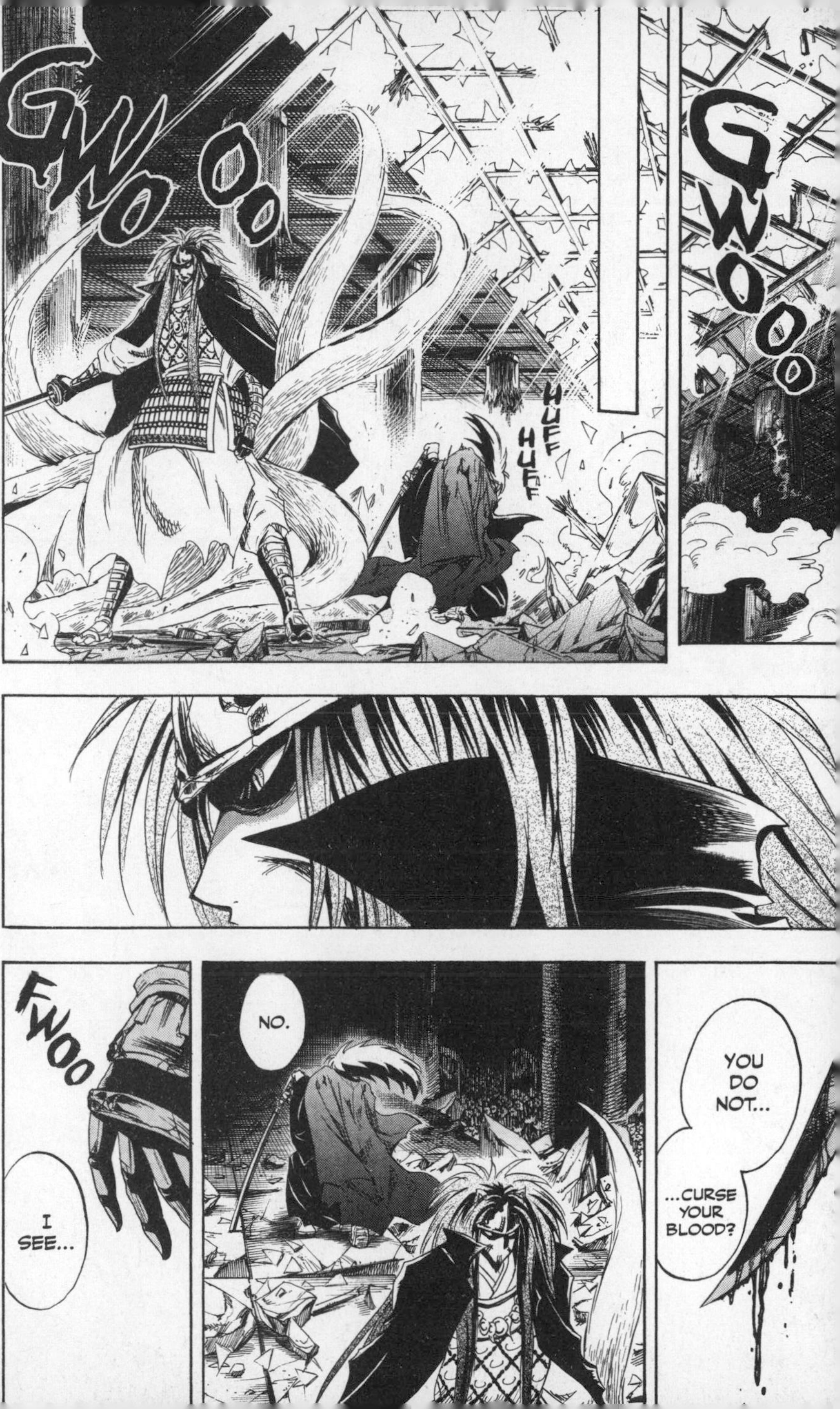
GWOOOO
GWOOO
HUFF HUFF
YOU DO NOT...
...CURSE YOUR BLOOD?
NO.
FWOO
I SEE...

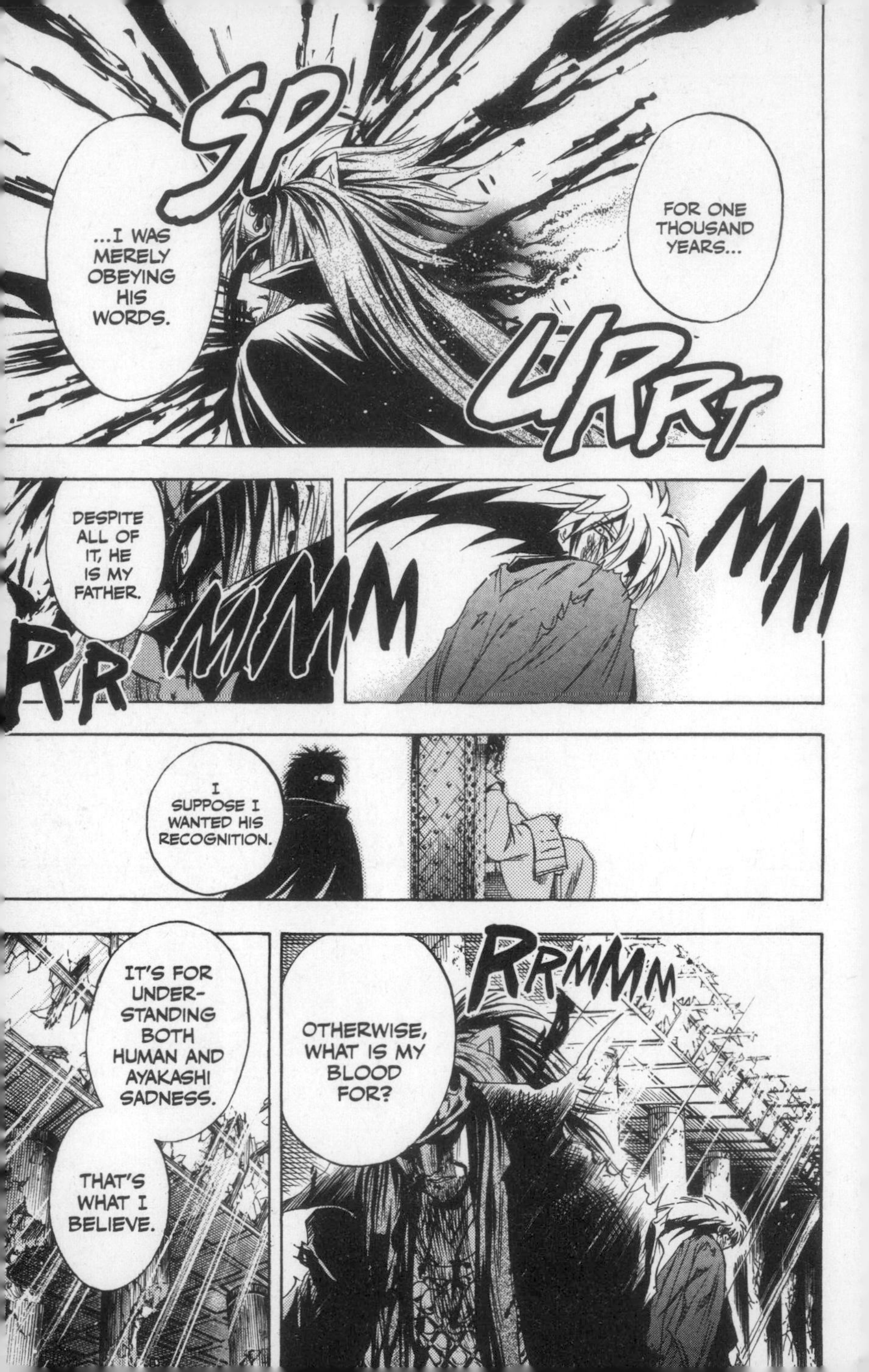
FOR ONE THOUSAND YEARS...
SP
URRT
...I WAS MERELY OBEYING HIS WORDS.
MM
DESPITE ALL OF IT, HE IS MY FATHER.
RR MMMM
I SUPPOSE I WANTED HIS RECOGNITION.
RRMMMM
OTHERWISE, WHAT IS MY BLOOD FOR?
IT'S FOR UNDER-STANDING BOTH HUMAN AND AYAKASHI SADNESS.
THAT'S WHAT I BELIEVE.

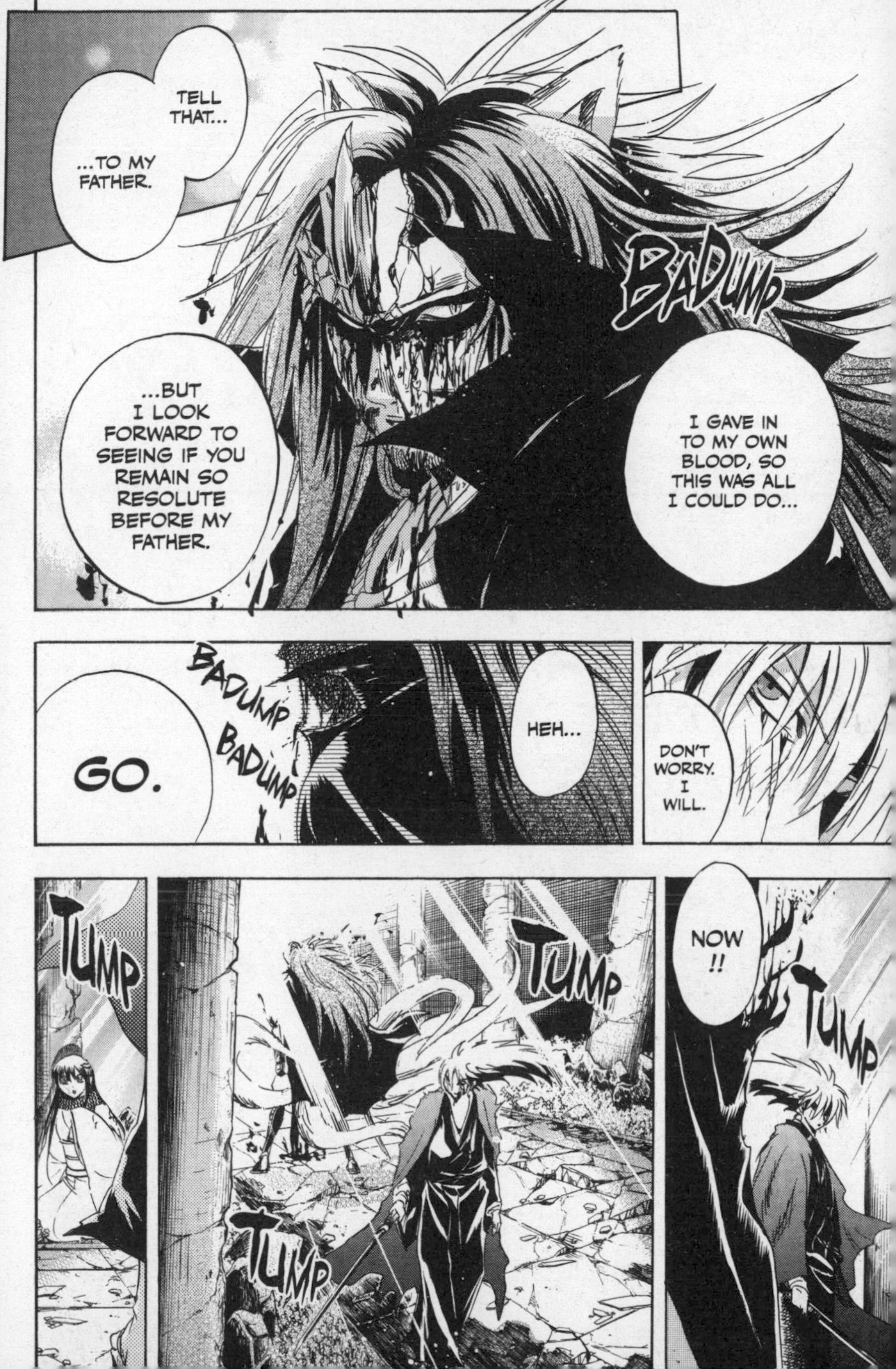
TELL THAT...
...TO MY FATHER.
BADUMP
I GAVE IN TO MY OWN BLOOD, SO THIS WAS ALL I COULD DO...
...BUT I LOOK FORWARD TO SEEING IF YOU REMAIN SO RESOLUTE BEFORE MY FATHER.
DON'T WORRY. I WILL.
HEH...
BADUMP
BADUMP
GO.
NOW !!
TUMP
TUMP
TUMP
TUMP

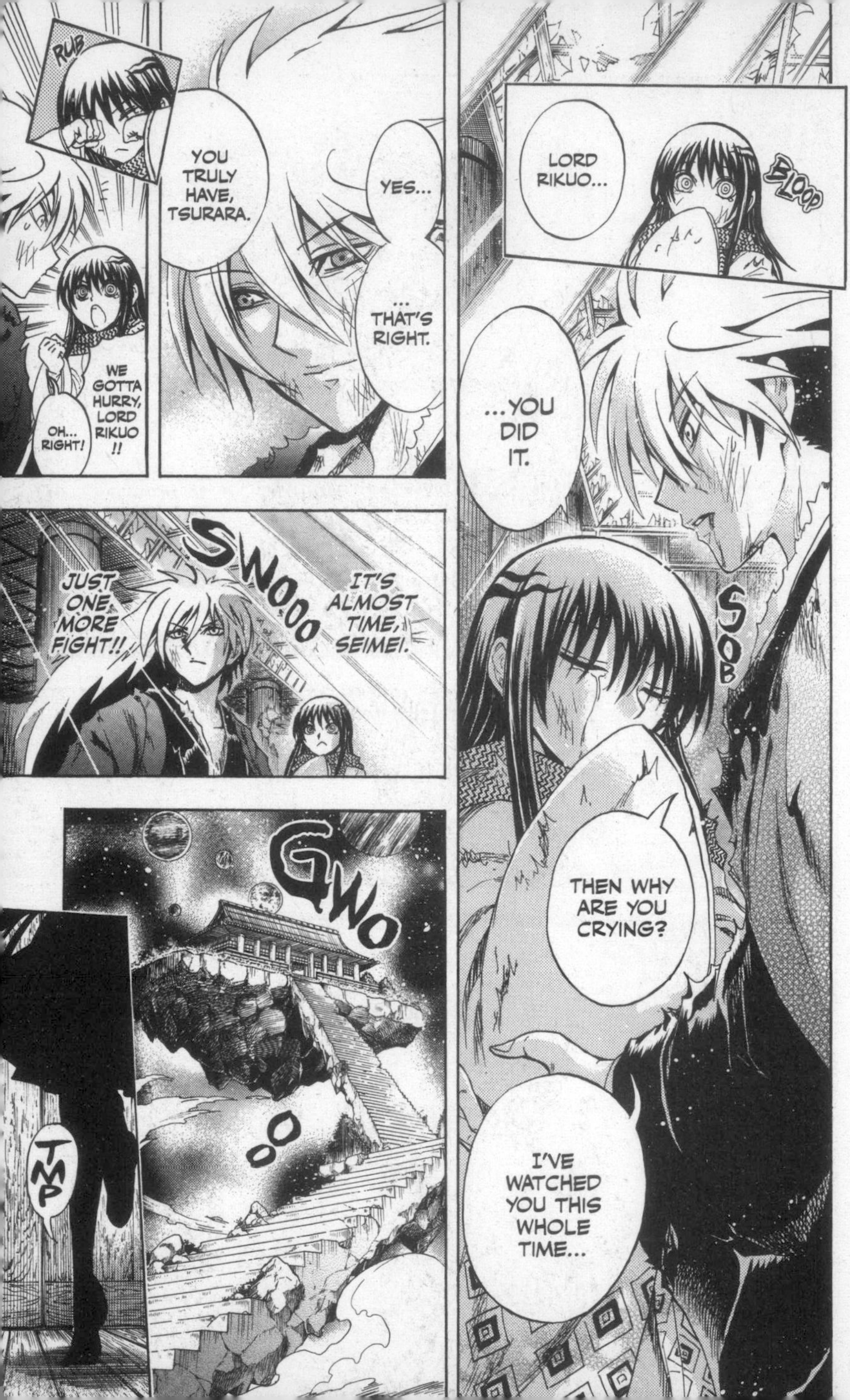
LORD RIKUO...
BLOOP
...YOU DID IT.
SOB
THEN WHY ARE YOU CRYING?
I'VE WATCHED YOU THIS WHOLE TIME...
YOU TRULY HAVE, TSURARA.
YES...
...THAT'S RIGHT.
RUB
WE GOTTA HURRY, LORD RIKUO!!
OH... RIGHT!
SWOOO
IT'S ALMOST TIME, SEIMEI.
JUST ONE MORE FIGHT!!
GWO
OO
TMP

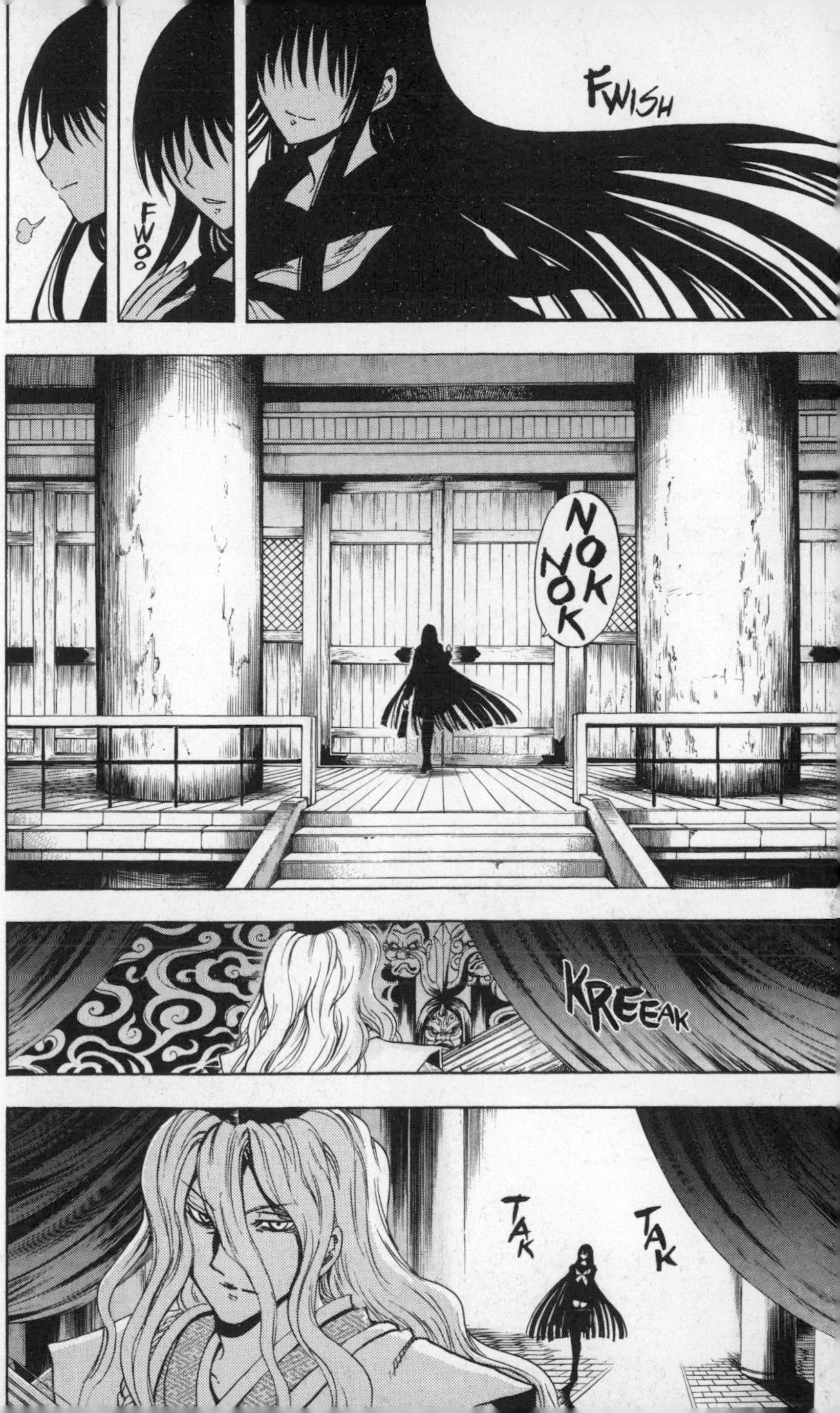
FWISH
FWOO
NOK NOK
KREEAK
TAK
TAK

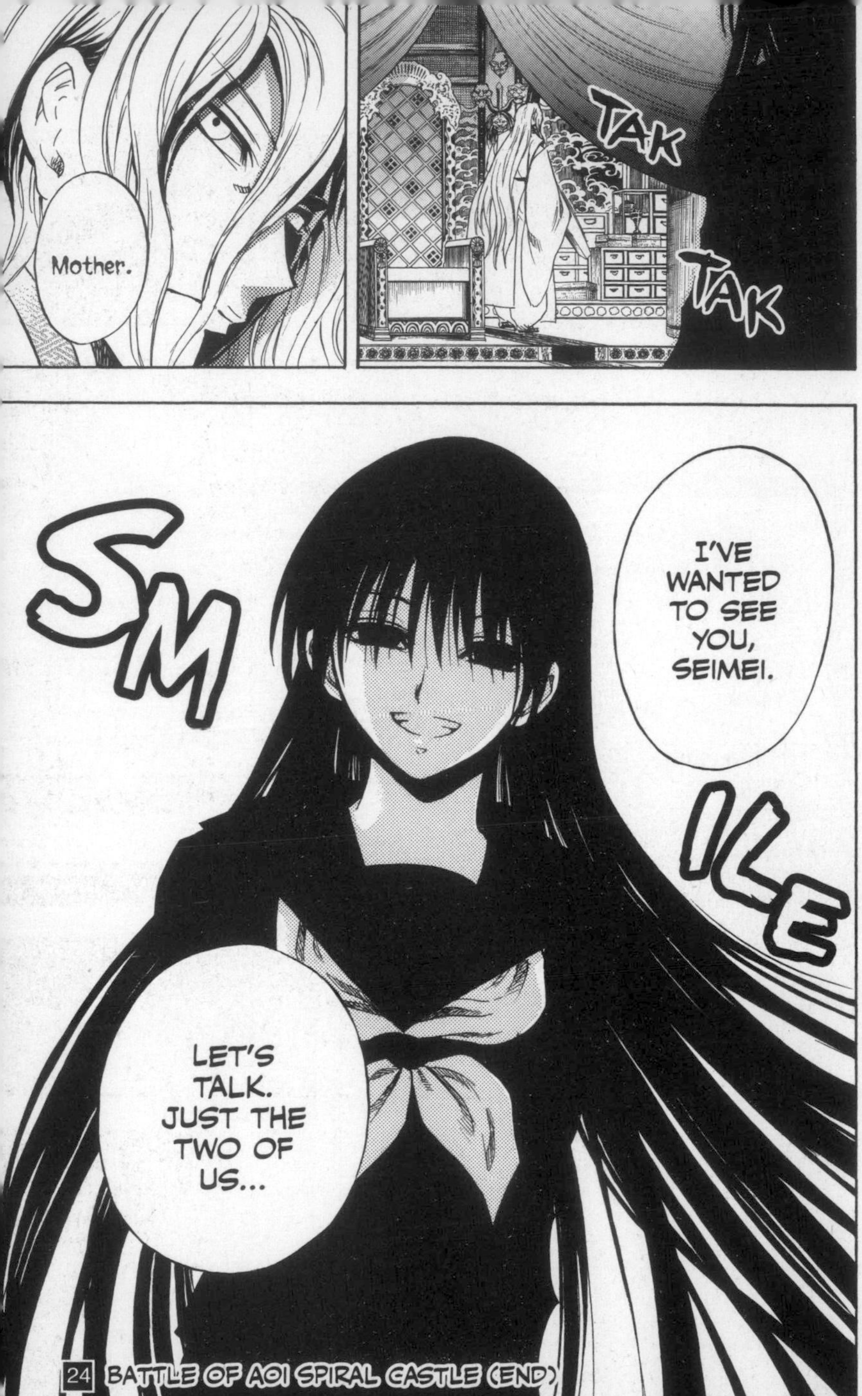
TAK
TAK
Mother.
I'VE WANTED TO SEE YOU, SEIMEI.
SMILE
LET'S TALK. JUST THE TWO OF US...

24 BATTLE OF AOI SPIRAL CASTLE (END)

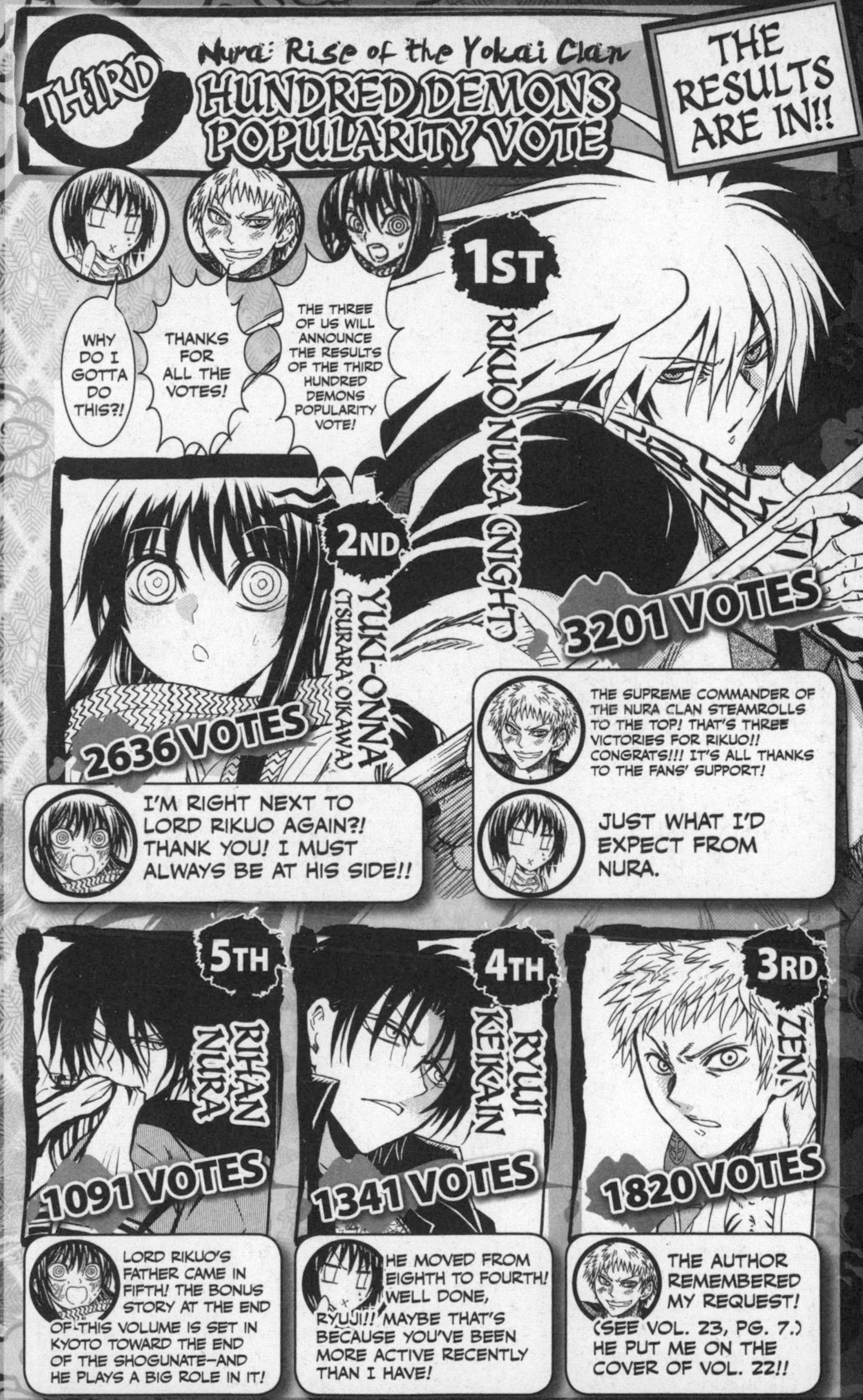

THE RESULTS ARE IN!!
THIRD
Nura: Rise of the Yokai Clan
HUNDRED DEMONS POPULARITY VOTE
THE THREE OF US WILL ANNOUNCE THE RESULTS OF THE THIRD HUNDRED DEMONS POPULARITY VOTE!
THANKS FOR ALL THE VOTES!
WHY DO I GOTTA DO THIS?!
1ST
RIKUO NURA (NIGHT)
3201 VOTES
THE SUPREME COMMANDER OF THE NURA CLAN STEAMROLLS TO THE TOP! THAT'S THREE VICTORIES FOR RIKUO!! CONGRATS!!! IT'S ALL THANKS TO THE FANS' SUPPORT!
JUST WHAT I'D EXPECT FROM NURA.
2ND
YUKI-ONNA (TSURARA OIKAWA)
2636 VOTES
I'M RIGHT NEXT TO LORD RIKUO AGAIN?! THANK YOU! I MUST ALWAYS BE AT HIS SIDE!!
3RD
ZEN
1820 VOTES
THE AUTHOR REMEMBERED MY REQUEST! (SEE VOL. 23, PG. 7.) HE PUT ME ON THE COVER OF VOL. 22!!
4TH
RYUJI KEIKAIN
1341 VOTES
HE MOVED FROM EIGHTH TO FOURTH! WELL DONE, RYUJI!! MAYBE THAT'S BECAUSE YOU'VE BEEN MORE ACTIVE RECENTLY THAN I HAVE!
5TH
RIHAN NURA
1091 VOTES
LORD RIKUO'S FATHER CAME IN FIFTH! THE BONUS STORY AT THE END OF THIS VOLUME IS SET IN KYOTO TOWARD THE END OF THE SHOGUNATE—AND HE PLAYS A BIG ROLE IN IT!

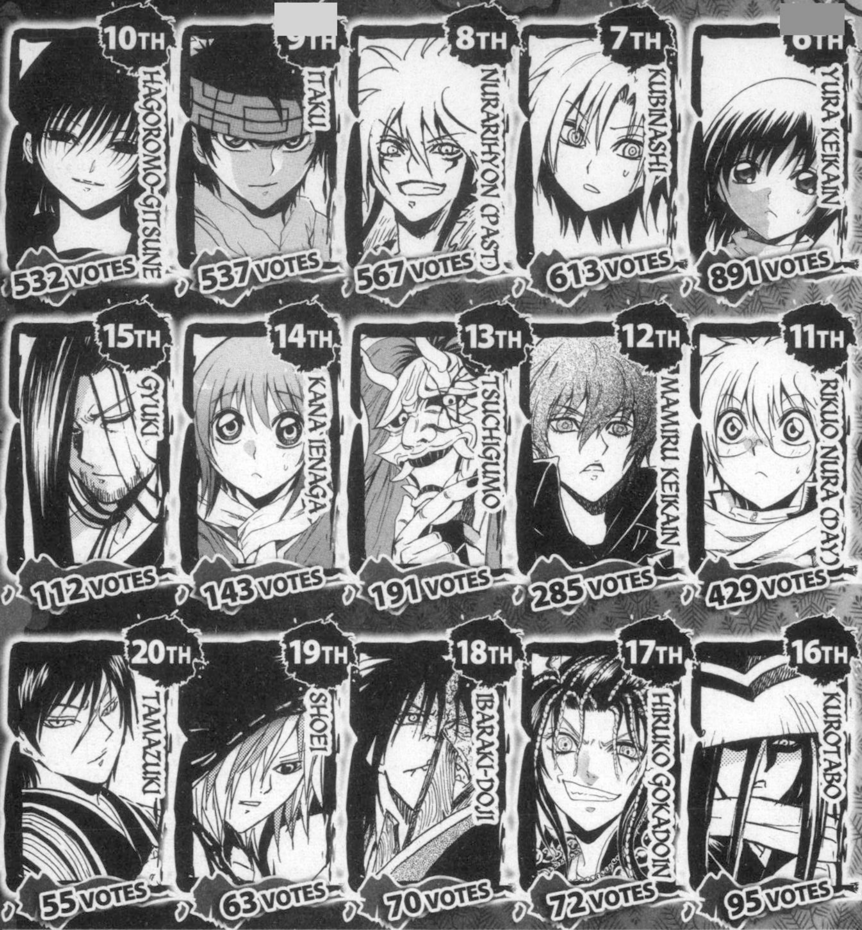

6TH
YURA KEIKAIN
891 VOTES
7TH
KUBINASHI
613 VOTES
8TH
NURARIHYON (PAST)
567 VOTES
9TH
ITAKU
537 VOTES
10TH
HAGOROMO-GITSUNE
532 VOTES
11TH
RIKUO NURA (DAY)
429 VOTES
12TH
MAMIRU KEIKAIN
285 VOTES
13TH
TSUCHIGUMO
191 VOTES
14TH
KANA IENAGA
143 VOTES
15TH
GYUKI
112 VOTES
16TH
KUROTABO
95 VOTES
17TH
HIRUKO GOKADOIN
72 VOTES
18TH
IBARAKI-DOJI
70 VOTES
19TH
SHOEI
63 VOTES
20TH
TAMAZUKI
55 VOTES

21	Hidemoto Keikain, the 13th Heir	51 VOTES
	Setsura	51 VOTES
23	Yamabuki-Otome	48 VOTES
24	Kyokotsu	40 VOTES
25	Wakana Nura	38 VOTES
26	Mezumaru	36 VOTES
	Yanagida	36 VOTES
28	Kyosai	34 VOTES
	Akifusa Keikain	34 VOTES
30	Kiyotsugu	33 VOTES
	Princess Yo	33 VOTES
32	Aotabo	32 VOTES
33	Inugami	30 VOTES
	Encho	30 VOTES
	Gozumaru	30 VOTES
36	Kuromaru	29 VOTES
37	Kidomaru	28 VOTES
	Natsumi Torii	28 VOTES
39	Awashima	27 VOTES
	Kappa	27 VOTES
41	Kejoro	26 VOTES
42	Abe no Ariyuki	25 VOTES
43	Abe no Seimei	24 VOTES
	Saori Maki	24 VOTES
45	Sannokuchi	23 VOTES
	Shiibashi-sensei	23 VOTES
47	Reira	21 VOTES
48	Shokera	20 VOTES
49	Hihi	17 VOTES
	Momoishi	17 VOTES
	Ryota-Neko	17 VOTES
52	Dassai	16 VOTES
	Nurarihyon (present)	16 VOTES
	Yukari	16 VOTES
	Yosuzume	16 VOTES
56	Masatsugu Keikain	13 VOTES
57	Kirisaki Toryanse	12 VOTES
58	Taisei Gokadoin	10 VOTES
	Natto-Kozo	10 VOTES
	Rinko	10 VOTES
61	Jami	9 VOTES

The above reflects the addition of data received after the results first appeared in *Weekly Shonen Jump* Vol. 27, 2012.

other Characters (?) Receiving 1 Vote

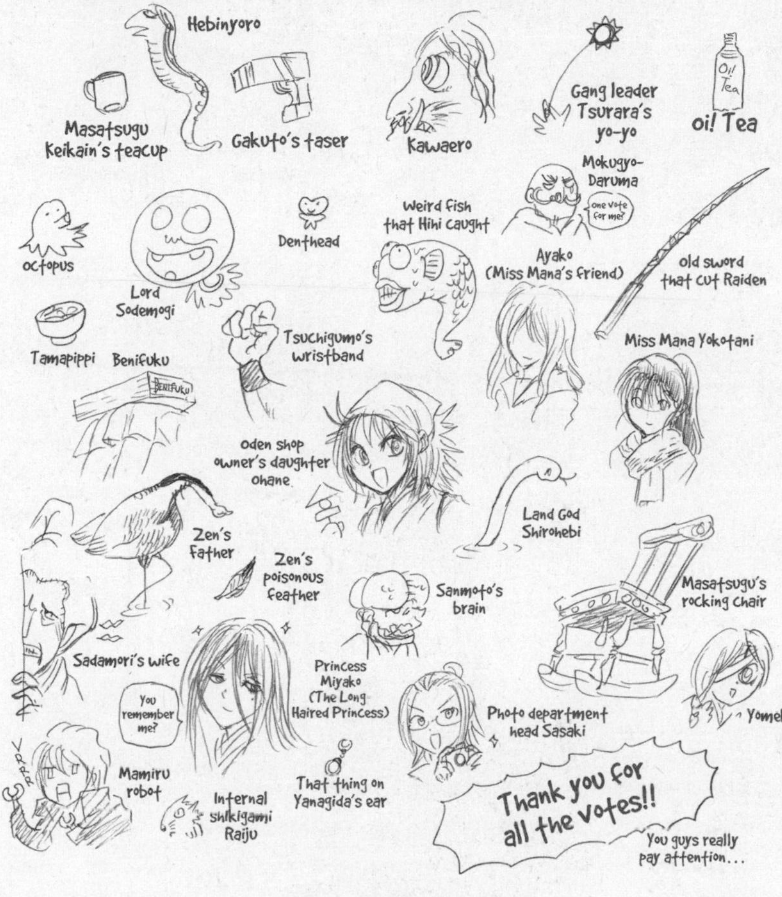

Hebinyoro
Masatsugu Keikain's teacup
Gakuto's taser
Kawaero
Gang leader Tsurara's yo-yo
Oi! Tea
oi! Tea
Mokugyo-Daruma
one vote for me?
octopus
Lord Sodemogi
Denthead
Weird fish that Hihi caught
Ayako (Miss Mana's friend)
old sword that cut Raiden
Tamapippi
Benifuku
BENIFUKU
Tsuchigumo's wristband
Miss Mana Yokotani
oden shop owner's daughter ohane
Land God Shirohebi
Zen's father
Zen's poisonous feather
Sanmoto's brain
Masatsugu's rocking chair
Sadamori's wife
You remember me?
Princess Miyako (The Long Haired Princess)
Photo department head Sasaki
Yomekko
VRRR
Mamiru robot
Internal shikigami Raiju
That thing on Yanagida's ear
Thank you for all the votes!!
You guys really pay attention...

KEEP IN TOUCH!

MAILING ADDRESS: NURA EDITOR
VIZ MEDIA
P.O. BOX 77010
SAN FRANCISCO, CA 94107

PLEASE INCLUDE YOUR NAME, AGE, ADDRESS AND PHONE NUMBER IN THE LETTER. IF YOU DO NOT WANT TO INCLUDE YOUR NAME, PLEASE USE A HANDLE OR NICKNAME. LETTERS AND ILLUSTRATIONS MAILED TO US WILL BE STORED FOR A CERTAIN PERIOD, THEN DISCARDED. IF YOU WISH TO KEEP A COPY, PLEASE MAKE ONE YOURSELF BEFORE MAILING IT IN. IF YOU'D LIKE TO HAVE YOUR NAME AND ADDRESS REMAIN ANONYMOUS, PLEASE INDICATE THAT IN YOUR LETTER.

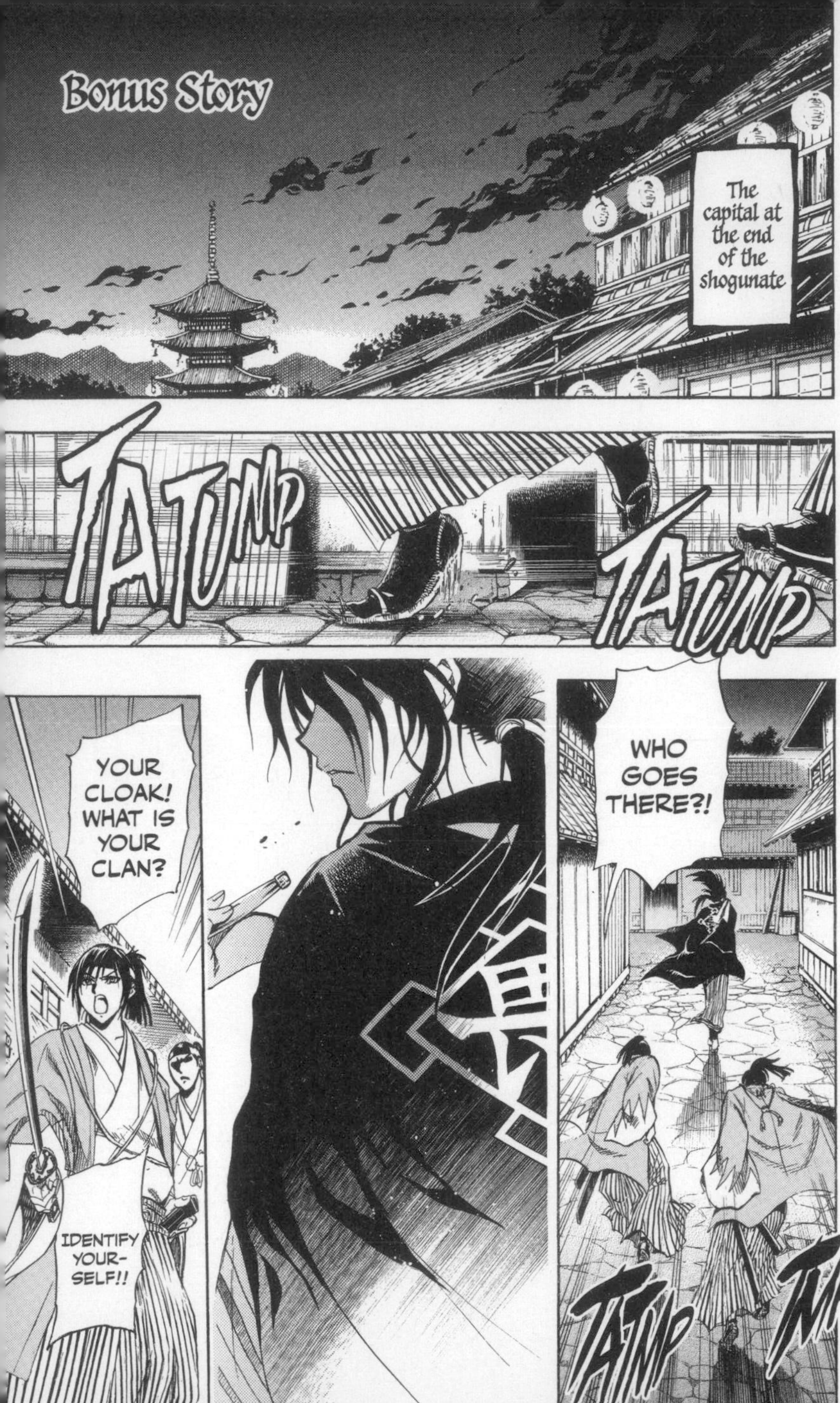
Bonus Story
The capital at the end of the shogunate
TATUMP
TATUMP
WHO GOES THERE?!
TATUMP
TMP
YOUR CLOAK! WHAT IS YOUR CLAN?
IDENTIFY YOUR-SELF!!

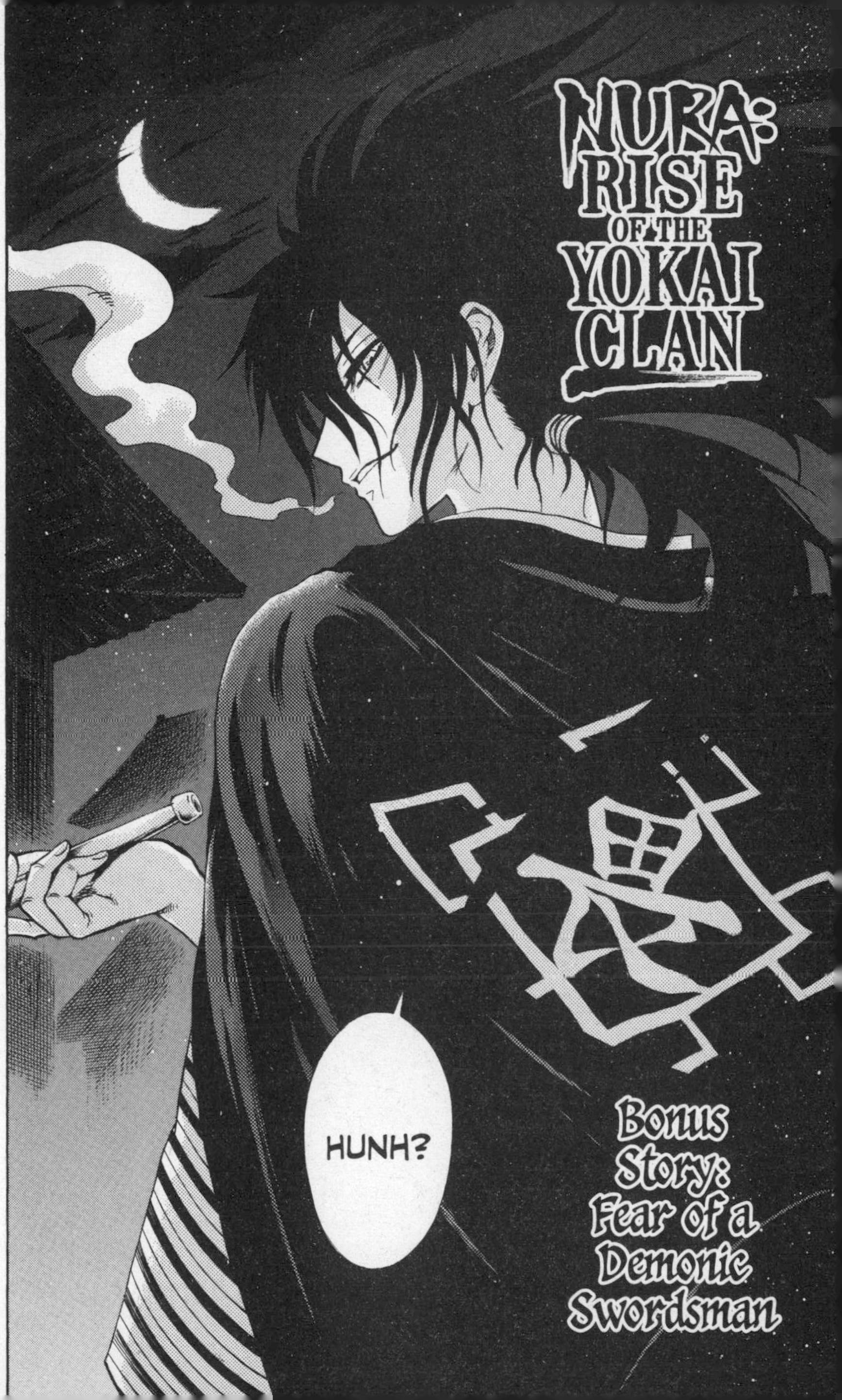
NURA: RISE OF THE YOKAI CLAN
Bonus Story: Fear of a Demonic Swordsman
HUNH?

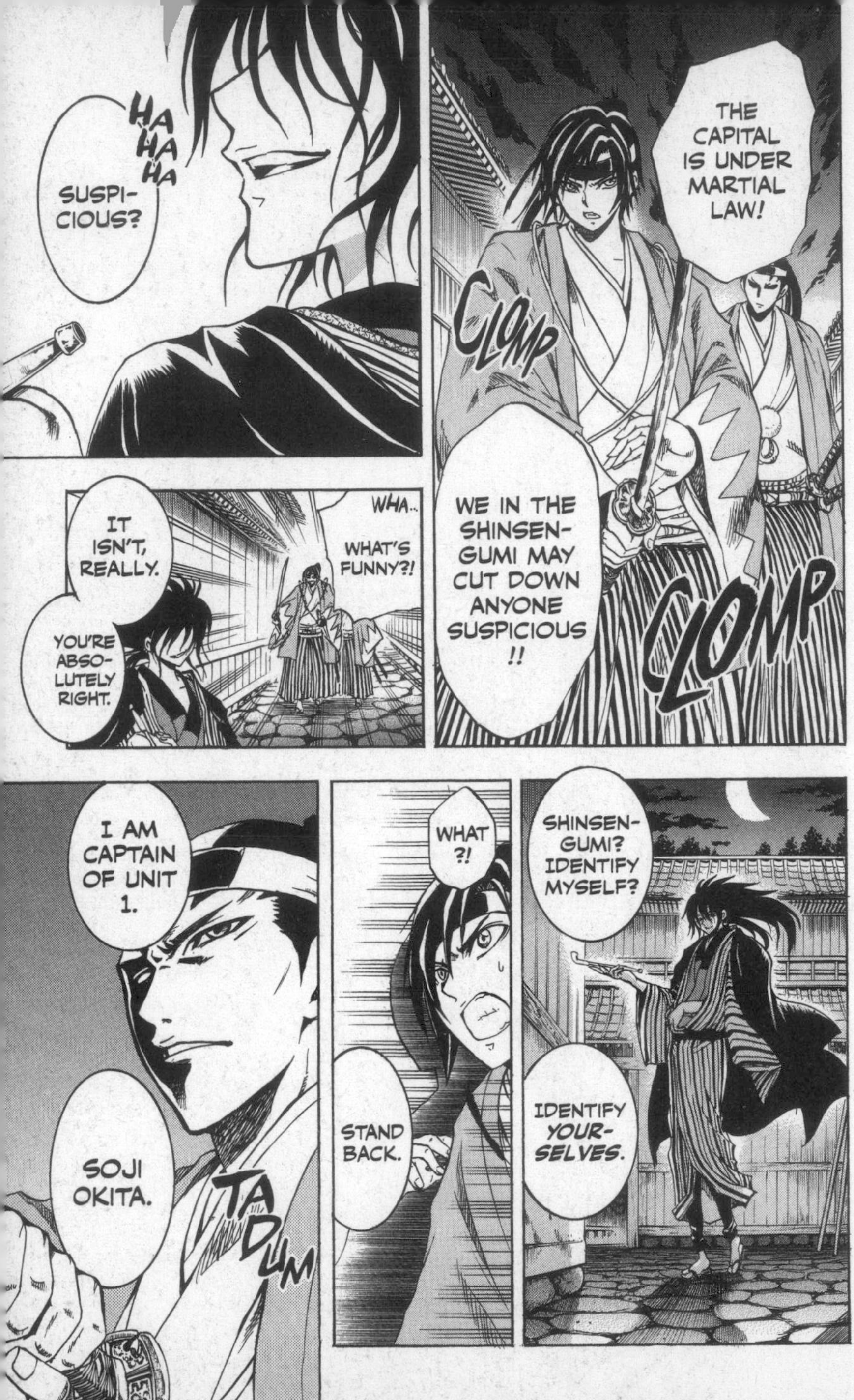
THE CAPITAL IS UNDER MARTIAL LAW!
CLOMP
WE IN THE SHINSEN-GUMI MAY CUT DOWN ANYONE SUSPICIOUS !!
CLOMP
HA HA HA
SUSPI-CIOUS?
WHA...
WHAT'S FUNNY?!
IT ISN'T, REALLY.
YOU'RE ABSO-LUTELY RIGHT.
SHINSEN-GUMI? IDENTIFY MYSELF?
IDENTIFY YOUR-SELVES.
WHAT ?!
STAND BACK.
I AM CAPTAIN OF UNIT 1.
SOJI OKITA.
TA DUM

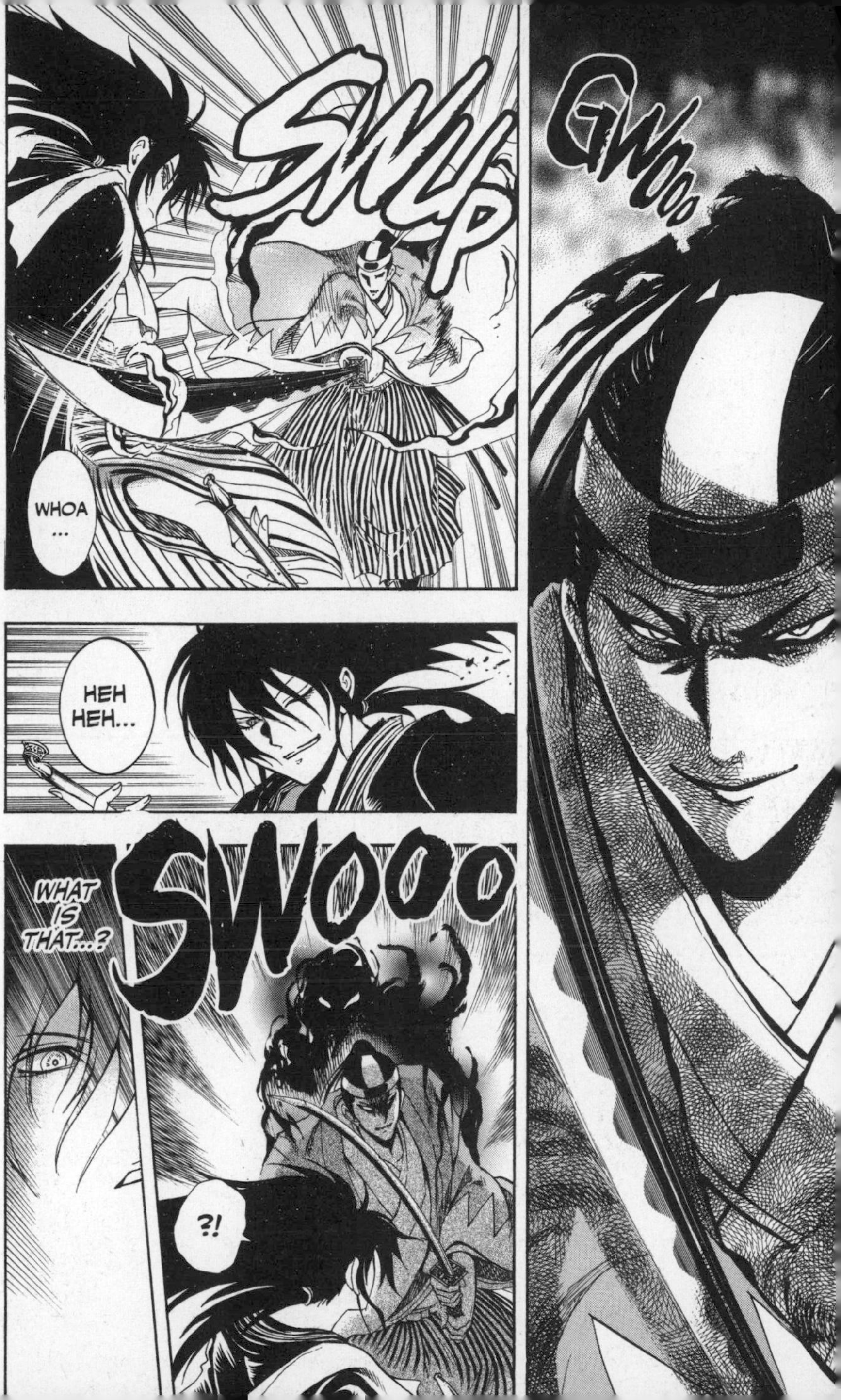
GWOOO
SWUP
WHOA ...
HEH HEH...
SWOOO
WHAT IS THAT...?
?!

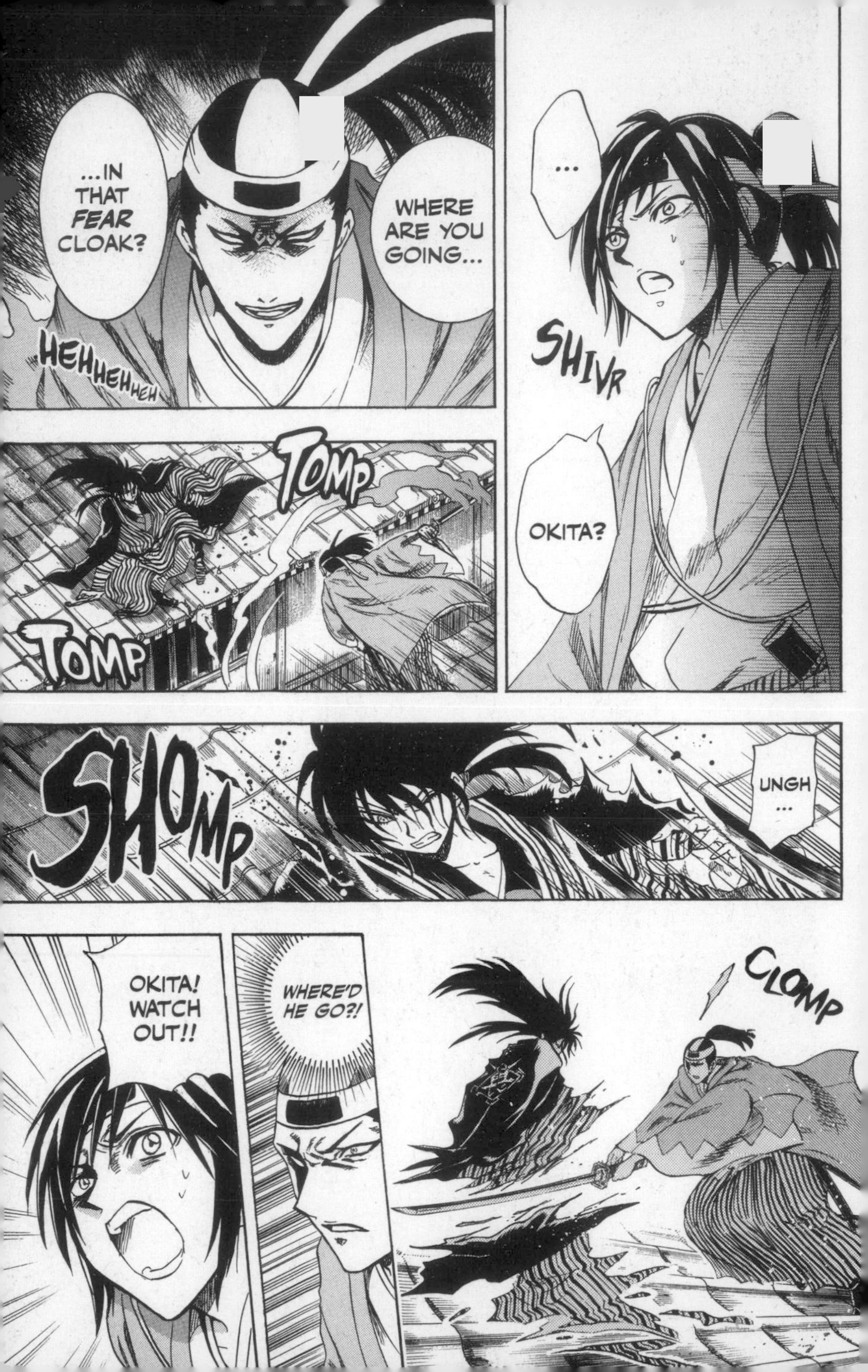
...
SHIVR
OKITA?
WHERE ARE YOU GOING...
...IN THAT FEAR CLOAK?
HEHHEHHEH
TOMP
TOMP
UNGH ...
SHOMP
CLOMP
WHERE'D HE GO?!
OKITA! WATCH OUT!!

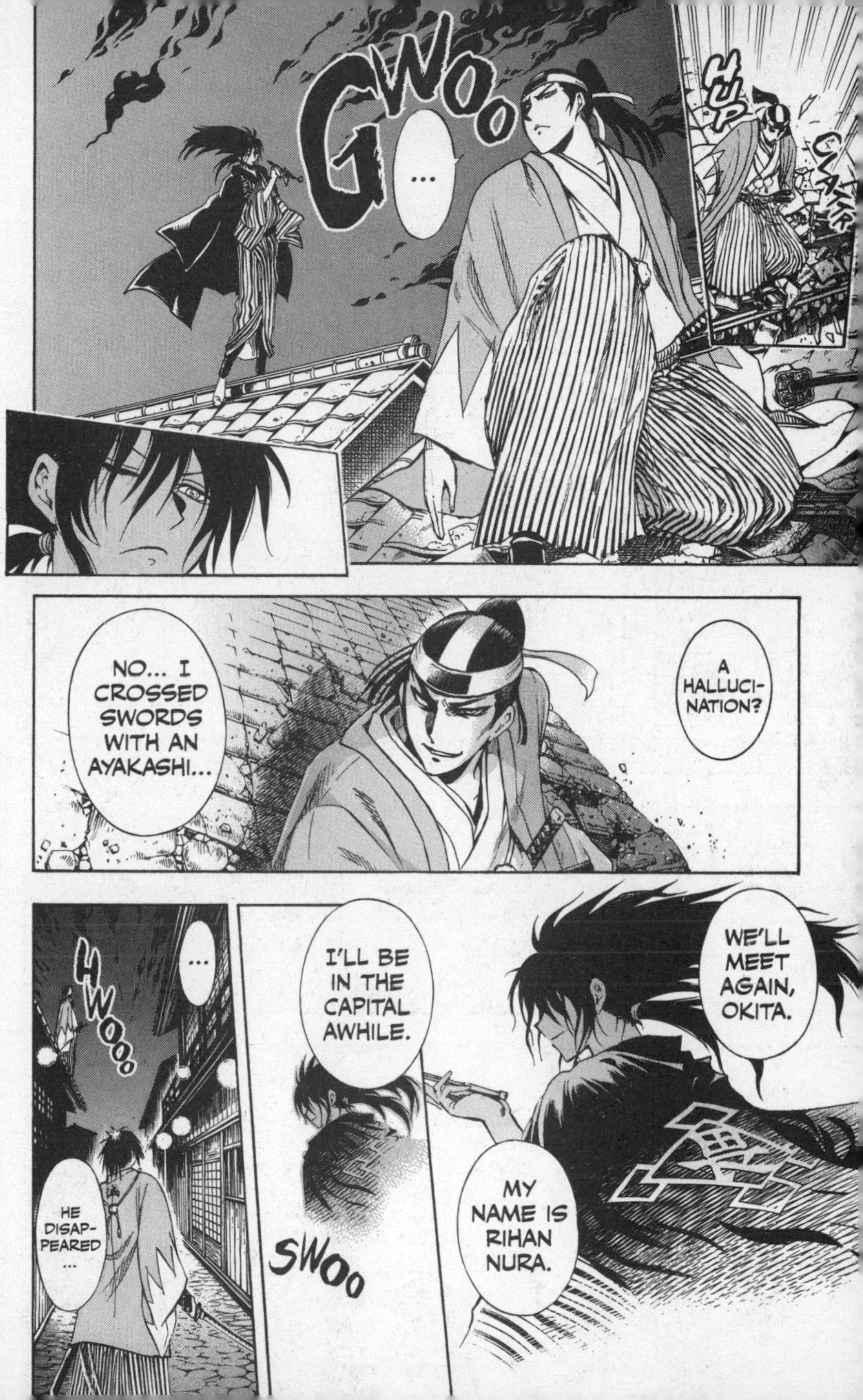
HUP
CLATTR
GWOO
...
A HALLUCI-NATION?
NO... I CROSSED SWORDS WITH AN AYAKASHI...
WE'LL MEET AGAIN, OKITA.
I'LL BE IN THE CAPITAL AWHILE.
MY NAME IS RIHAN NURA.
SWOO
...
HWOOO
HE DISAP-PEARED ...

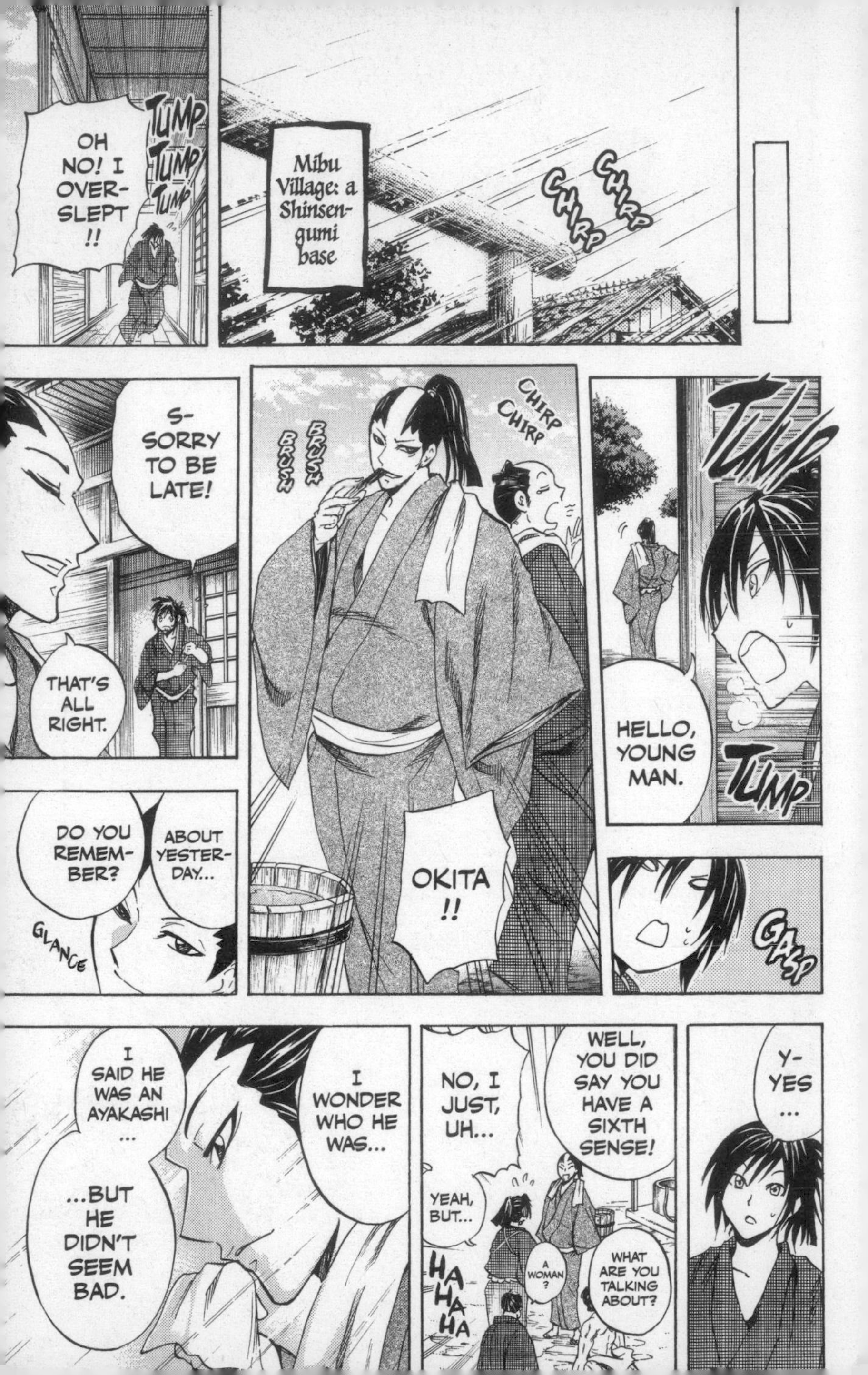
CHIRP
CHIRP
Mibu Village: a Shinsen-gumi base
TUMP TUMP TUMP
OH NO! I OVER-SLEPT!!
TUMP
HELLO, YOUNG MAN.
TUMP
GASP
CHIRP CHIRP
BRUSH BRUSH
OKITA!!
S-SORRY TO BE LATE!
THAT'S ALL RIGHT.
ABOUT YESTER-DAY...
DO YOU REMEM-BER?
GLANCE
Y-YES...
WELL, YOU DID SAY YOU HAVE A SIXTH SENSE!
NO, I JUST, UH...
YEAH, BUT...
WHAT ARE YOU TALKING ABOUT?
A WOMAN?
HA HA HA HA
I WONDER WHO HE WAS...
I SAID HE WAS AN AYAKASHI...
...BUT HE DIDN'T SEEM BAD.

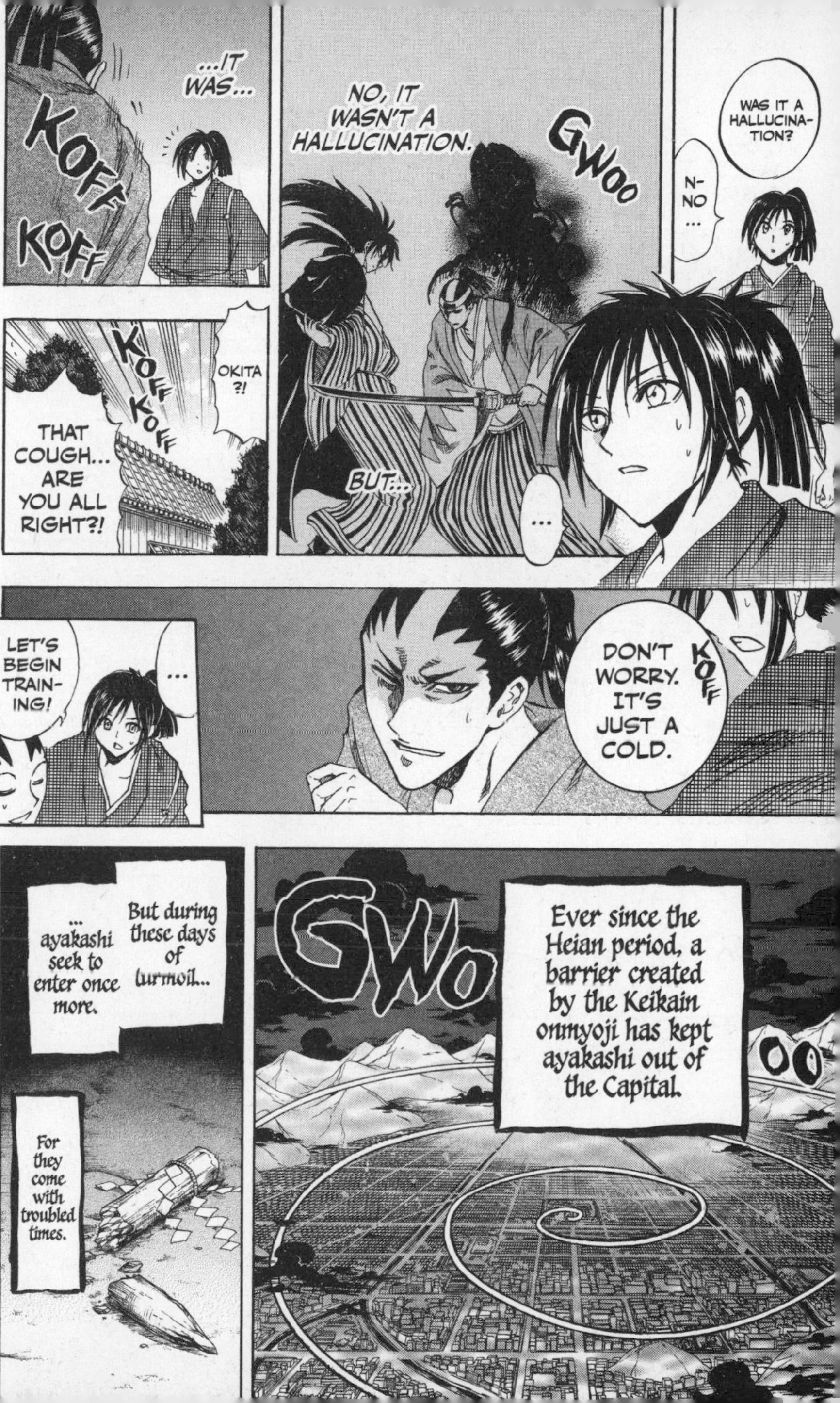
WAS IT A HALLUCINATION?
N-NO ...
NO, IT WASN'T A HALLUCINATION.
GWOO
BUT...
...
...IT WAS...
KOFF KOFF
OKITA ?!
KOFF KOFF
THAT COUGH... ARE YOU ALL RIGHT?!
DON'T WORRY. IT'S JUST A COLD.
KOFF
...
LET'S BEGIN TRAINING!
Ever since the Heian period, a barrier created by the Keikain onmyoji has kept ayakashi out of the Capital.
GWO
But during these days of turmoil...
... ayakashi seek to enter once more.
For they come with troubled times.

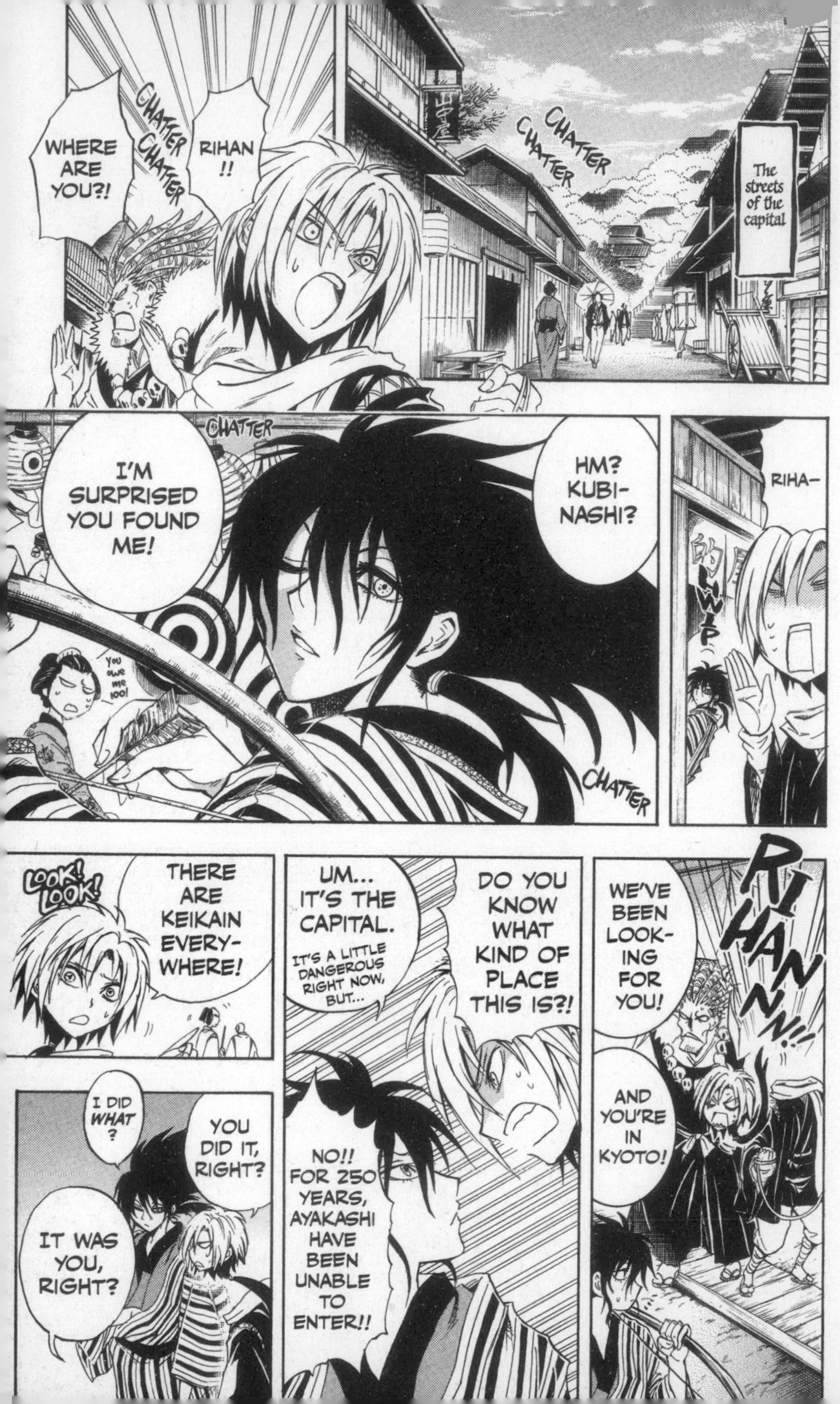
The streets of the capital
CHATTER CHATTER
RIHAN!!
CHATTER CHATTER
WHERE ARE YOU?!
RIHA-
WHIP
HM? KUBI-NASHI?
CHATTER
I'M SURPRISED YOU FOUND ME!
You owe me 100!
CHATTER
RIHANNN!!
WE'VE BEEN LOOK-ING FOR YOU!
AND YOU'RE IN KYOTO!
DO YOU KNOW WHAT KIND OF PLACE THIS IS?!
UM... IT'S THE CAPITAL.
IT'S A LITTLE DANGEROUS RIGHT NOW, BUT...
NO!! FOR 250 YEARS, AYAKASHI HAVE BEEN UNABLE TO ENTER!!
LOOK! LOOK!
THERE ARE KEIKAIN EVERY-WHERE!
YOU DID IT, RIGHT?
I DID WHAT?
IT WAS YOU, RIGHT?

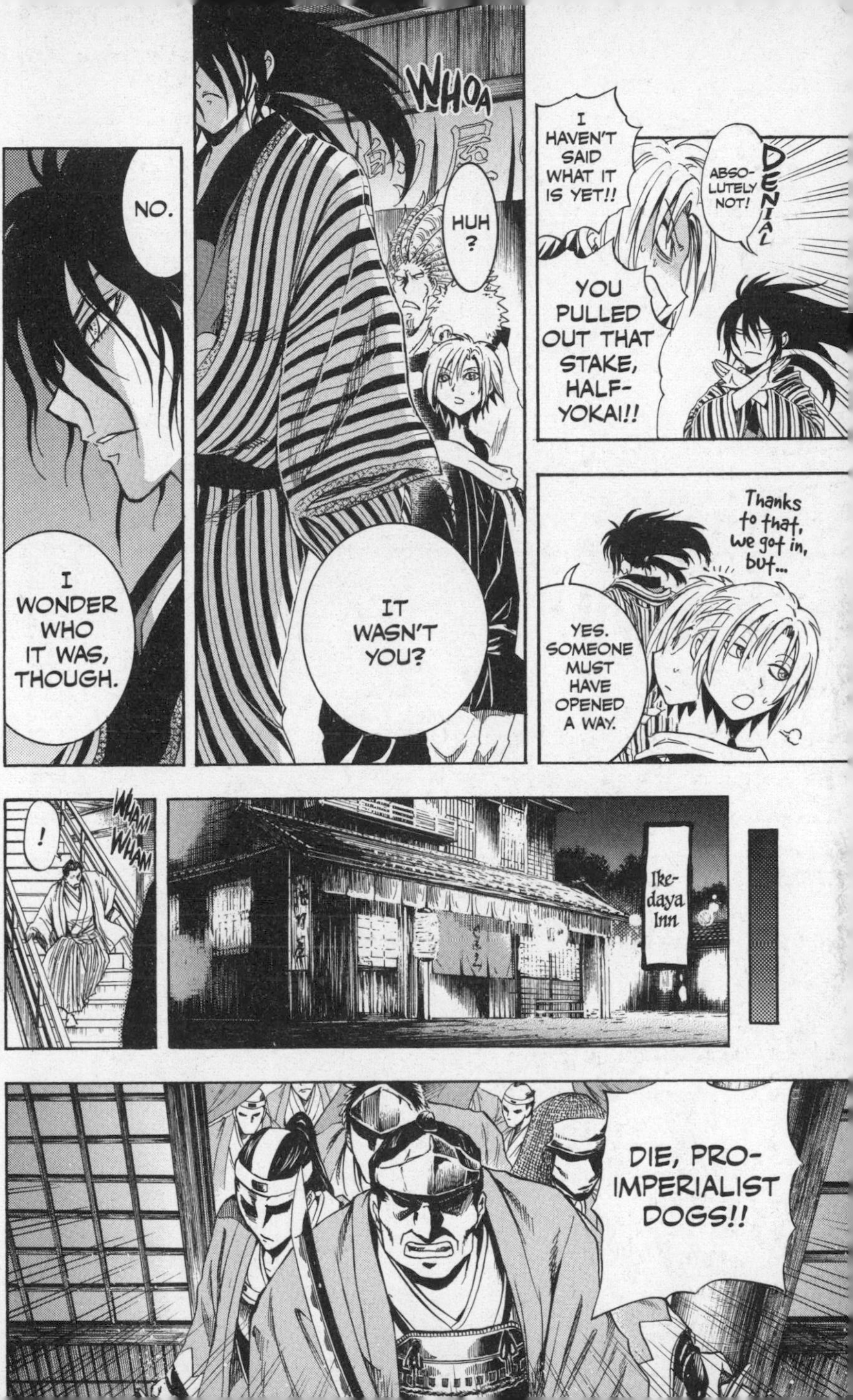
DENIAL
ABSO-LUTELY NOT!
I HAVEN'T SAID WHAT IT IS YET!!
YOU PULLED OUT THAT STAKE, HALF-YOKAI!!
Thanks to that, we got in, but...
YES. SOMEONE MUST HAVE OPENED A WAY.
WHOA
HUH?
IT WASN'T YOU?
NO.
I WONDER WHO IT WAS, THOUGH.
Ike-daya Inn
WHAM WHAM
!
DIE, PRO-IMPERIALIST DOGS!!

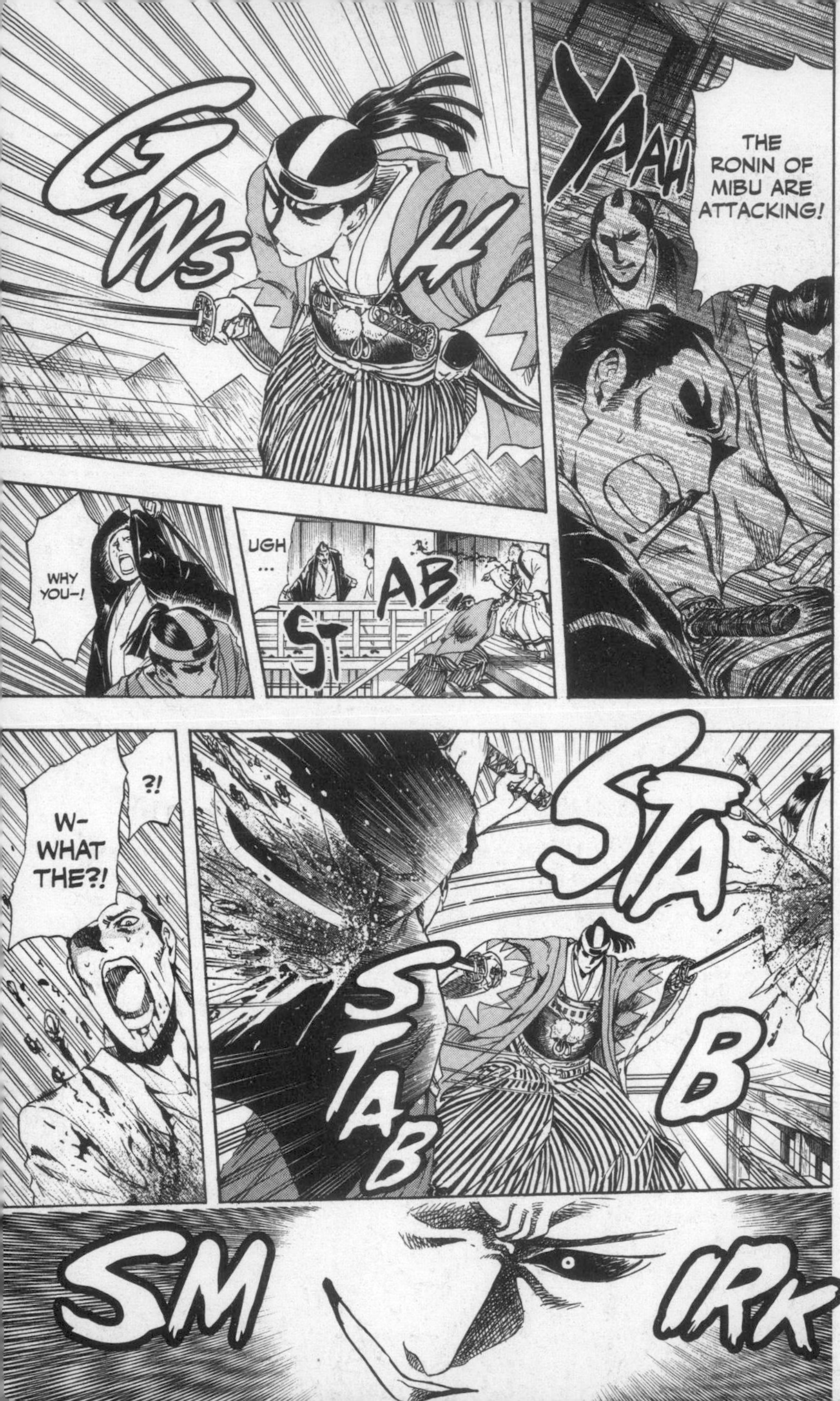
YAAH
THE RONIN OF MIBU ARE ATTACKING!
GWSH
UGH...
STAB
WHY YOU—!
STAB
STAB
?!
W-WHAT THE?!
SMIRK

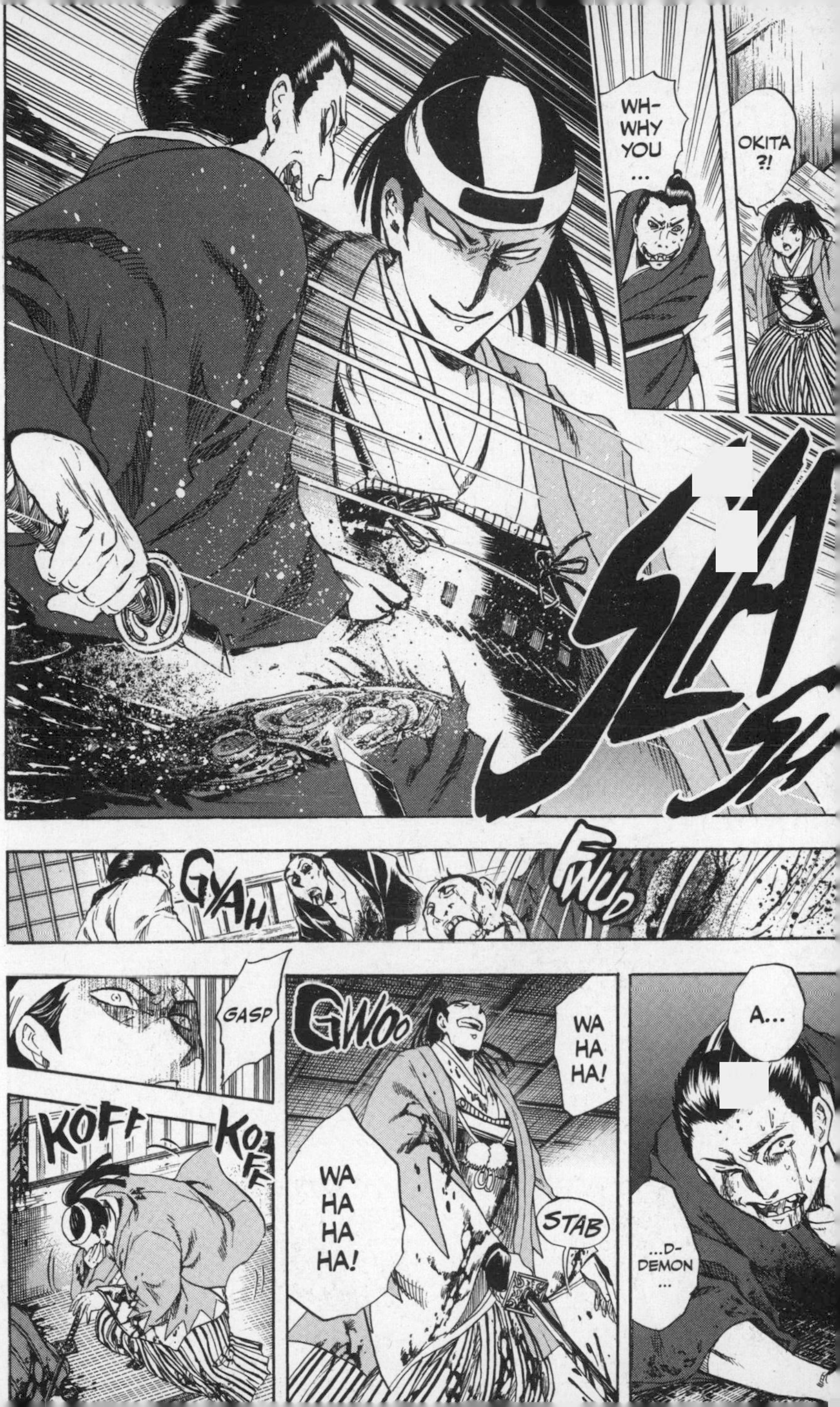
OKITA ?!
WH- WHY YOU ...
SLASH
FWUD
GYAH
A...
...D- DEMON ...
GWOO
WA HA HA!
STAB
WA HA HA HA!
GASP
KOFF KOFF

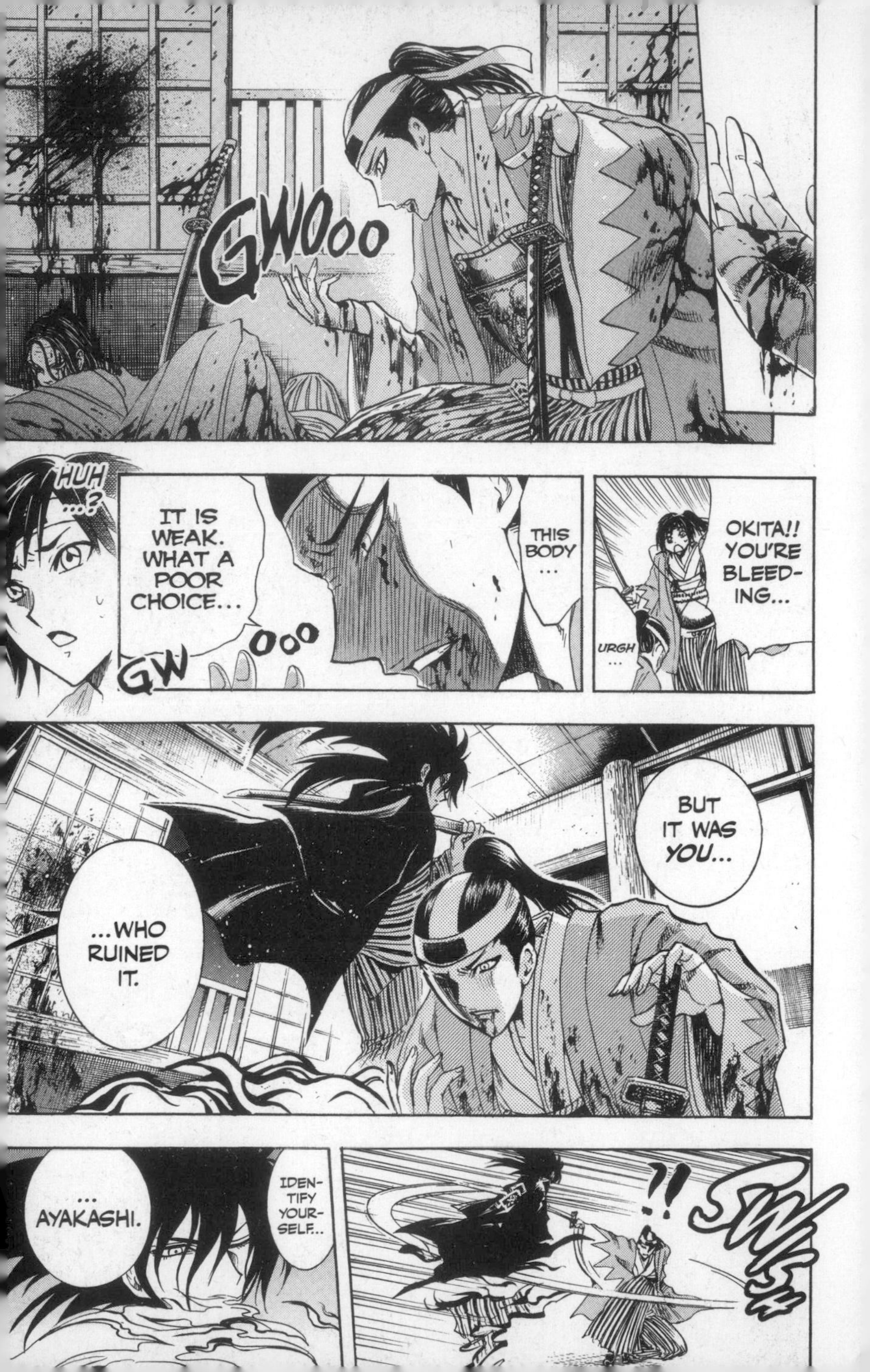
GWOOO
OKITA!! YOU'RE BLEEDING...
URGH...
THIS BODY...
IT IS WEAK. WHAT A POOR CHOICE...
GWOOO
HUH...?
BUT IT WAS YOU...
...WHO RUINED IT.
SWISH
!!
IDENTIFY YOURSELF...
...AYAKASHI.

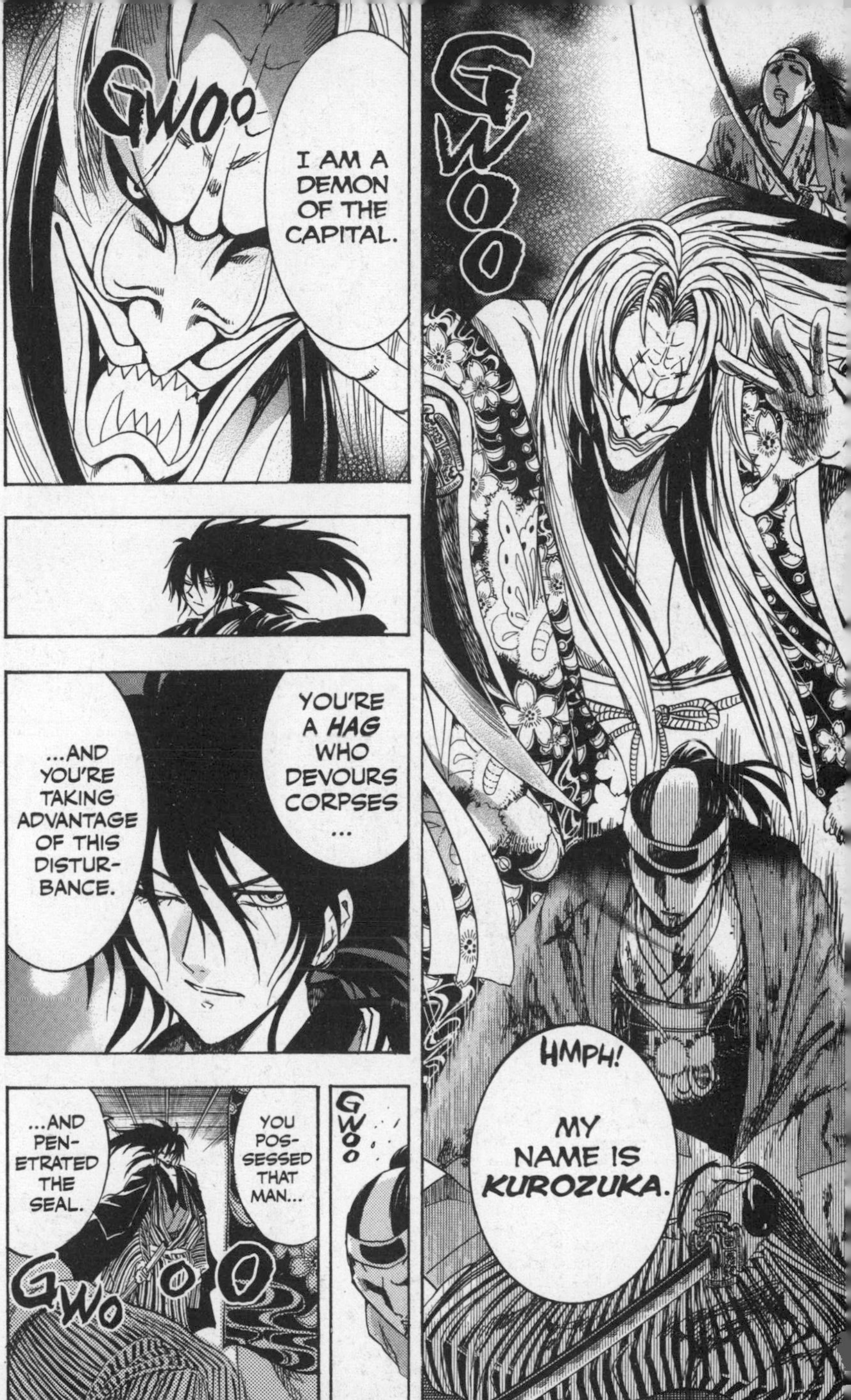
GWOOO
HMPH!
MY NAME IS KUROZUKA.
GWOO
I AM A DEMON OF THE CAPITAL.
YOU'RE A HAG WHO DEVOURS CORPSES...
...AND YOU'RE TAKING ADVANTAGE OF THIS DISTURBANCE.
GWOO
YOU POSSESSED THAT MAN...
...AND PENETRATED THE SEAL.
GWO O O

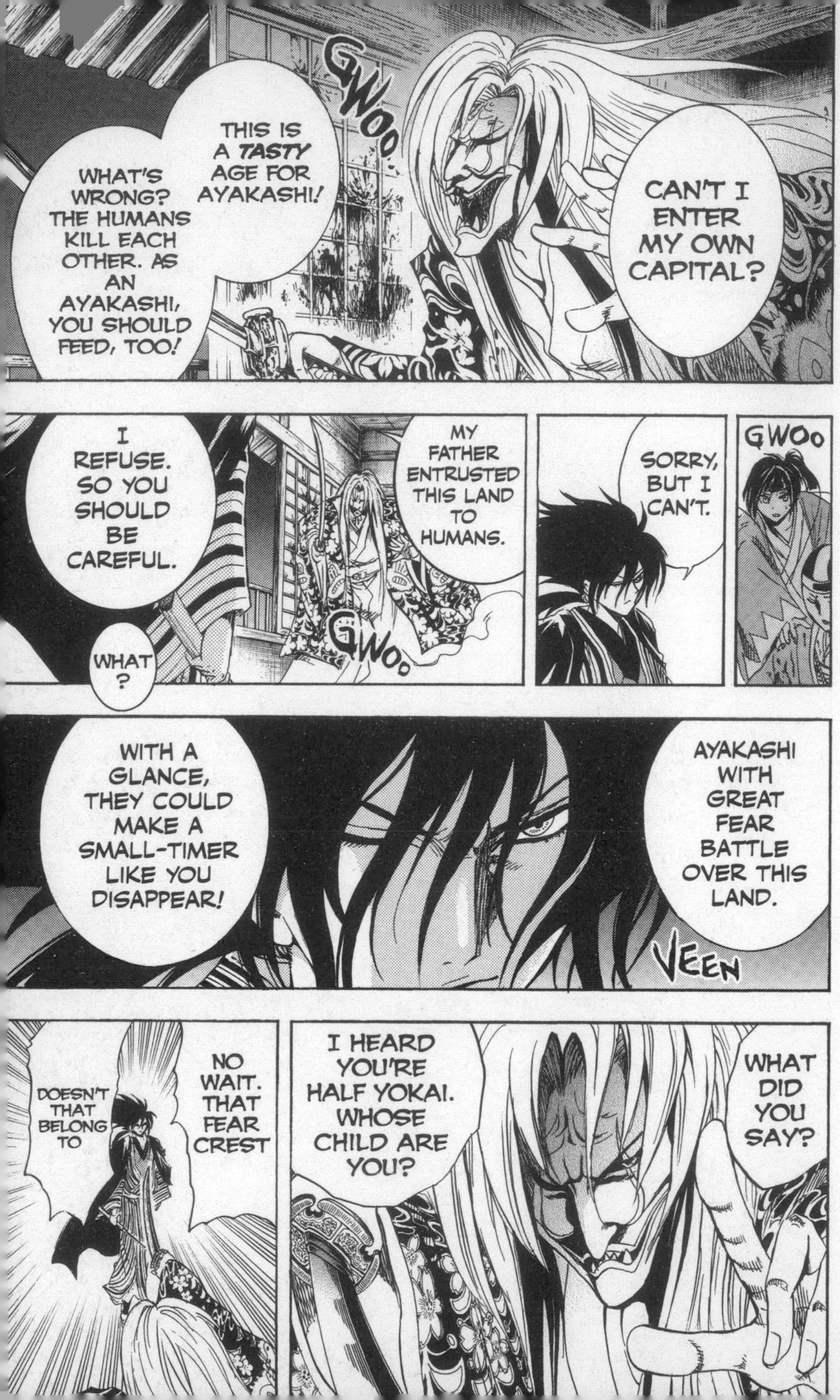
CAN'T I ENTER MY OWN CAPITAL?
GWOO
THIS IS A *TASTY* AGE FOR AYAKASHI!
WHAT'S WRONG? THE HUMANS KILL EACH OTHER. AS AN AYAKASHI, YOU SHOULD FEED, TOO!
GWOO
SORRY, BUT I CAN'T.
MY FATHER ENTRUSTED THIS LAND TO HUMANS.
GWOO
I REFUSE. SO YOU SHOULD BE CAREFUL.
WHAT?
AYAKASHI WITH GREAT FEAR BATTLE OVER THIS LAND.
VEEN
WITH A GLANCE, THEY COULD MAKE A SMALL-TIMER LIKE YOU DISAPPEAR!
WHAT DID YOU SAY?
I HEARD YOU'RE HALF YOKAI. WHOSE CHILD ARE YOU?
NO WAIT. THAT FEAR CREST
DOESN'T THAT BELONG TO

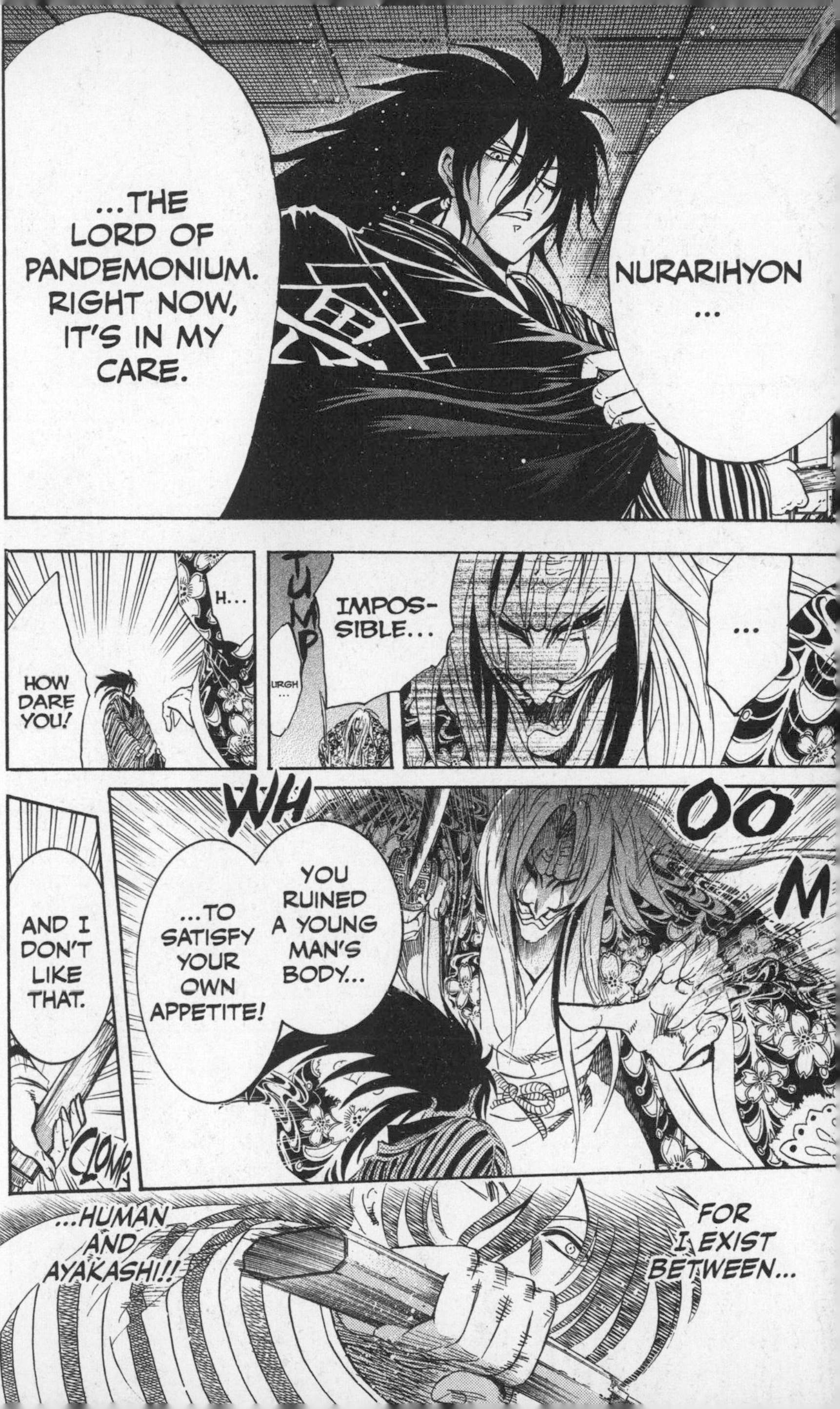

NURARIHYON ...
...THE LORD OF PANDEMONIUM. RIGHT NOW, IT'S IN MY CARE.
...
IMPOSSIBLE...
TUMP
URGH ...
H...
HOW DARE YOU!
WH OO M
YOU RUINED A YOUNG MAN'S BODY...
...TO SATISFY YOUR OWN APPETITE!
AND I DON'T LIKE THAT.
CLOMP
FOR I EXIST BETWEEN...
...HUMAN AND AYAKASHI!!

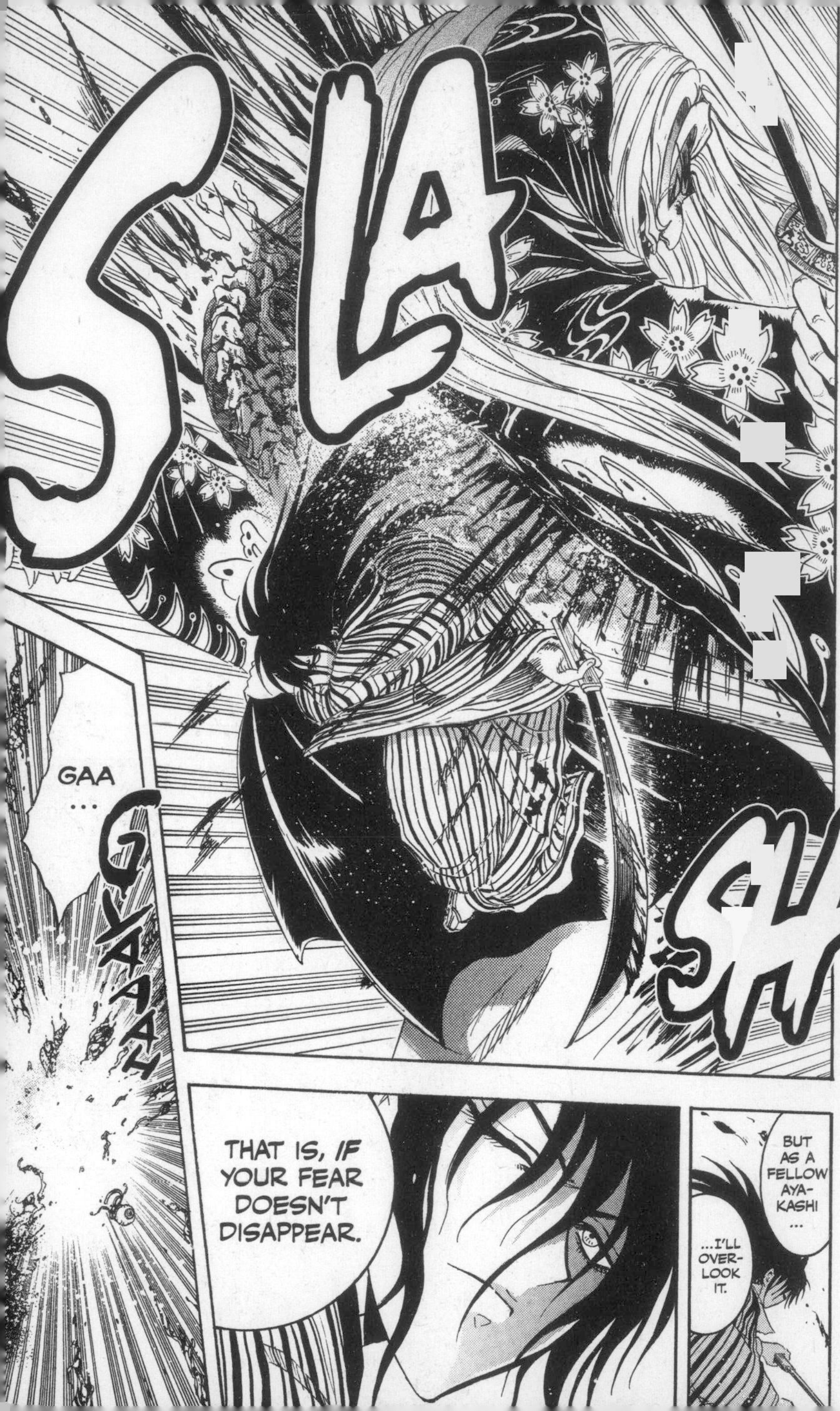
SLASH
GAA ...
GYAAAH
BUT AS A FELLOW AYA-KASHI ...
...I'LL OVER-LOOK IT.
THAT IS, *IF* YOUR FEAR DOESN'T DISAPPEAR.

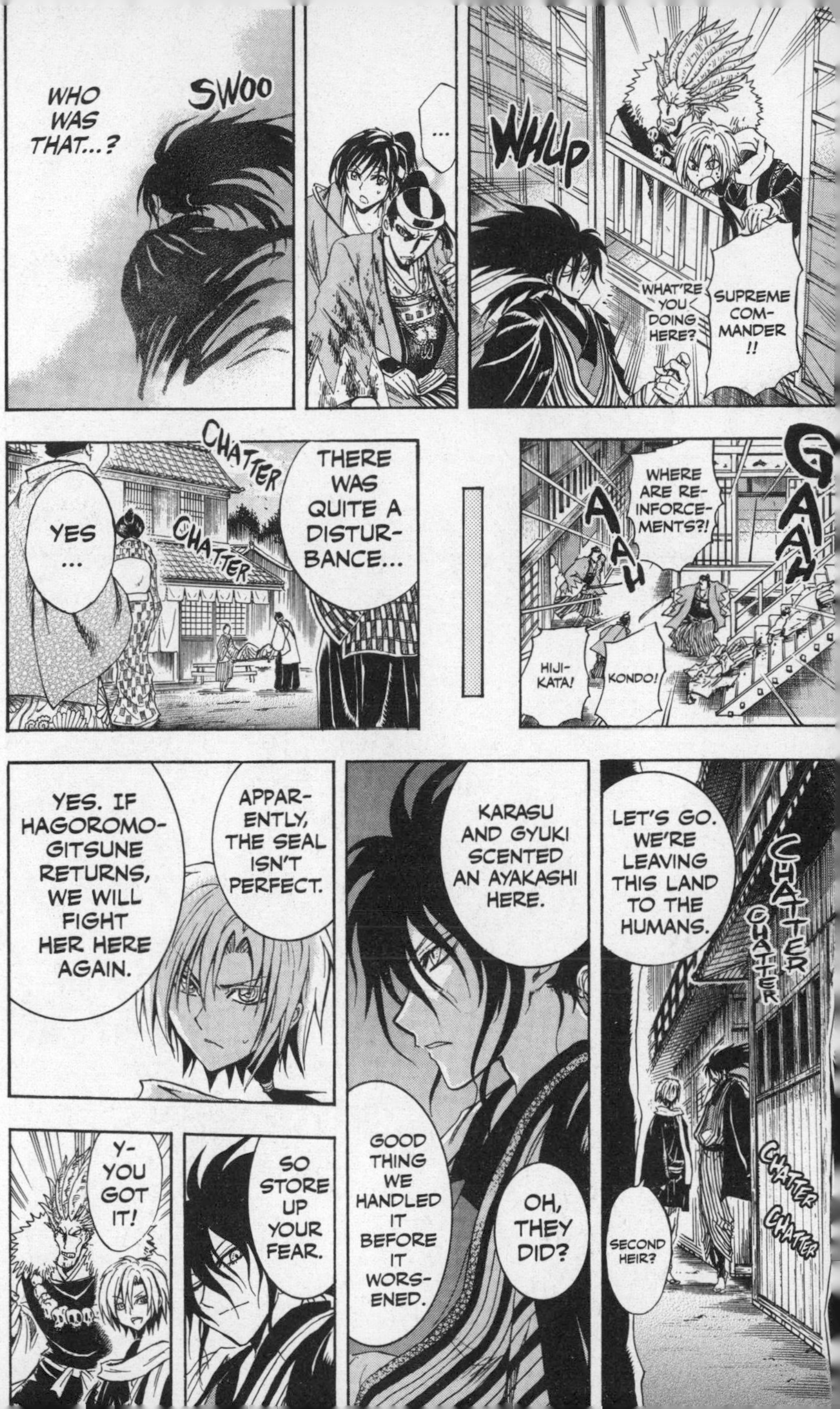
SUPREME COMMANDER !!
WHAT'RE YOU DOING HERE?
WHUP
...
SWOO
WHO WAS THAT...?
GAAH
WHERE ARE REINFORCEMENTS?!
AAH
KONDO!
HIJI-KATA!
THERE WAS QUITE A DISTURBANCE...
CHATTER
CHATTER
YES ...
LET'S GO. WE'RE LEAVING THIS LAND TO THE HUMANS.
CHATTER
CHATTER
SECOND HEIR?
CHATTER
CHATTER
KARASU AND GYUKI SCENTED AN AYAKASHI HERE.
OH, THEY DID?
GOOD THING WE HANDLED IT BEFORE IT WORSENED.
APPARENTLY, THE SEAL ISN'T PERFECT.
YES. IF HAGOROMO-GITSUNE RETURNS, WE WILL FIGHT HER HERE AGAIN.
SO STORE UP YOUR FEAR.
Y-YOU GOT IT!

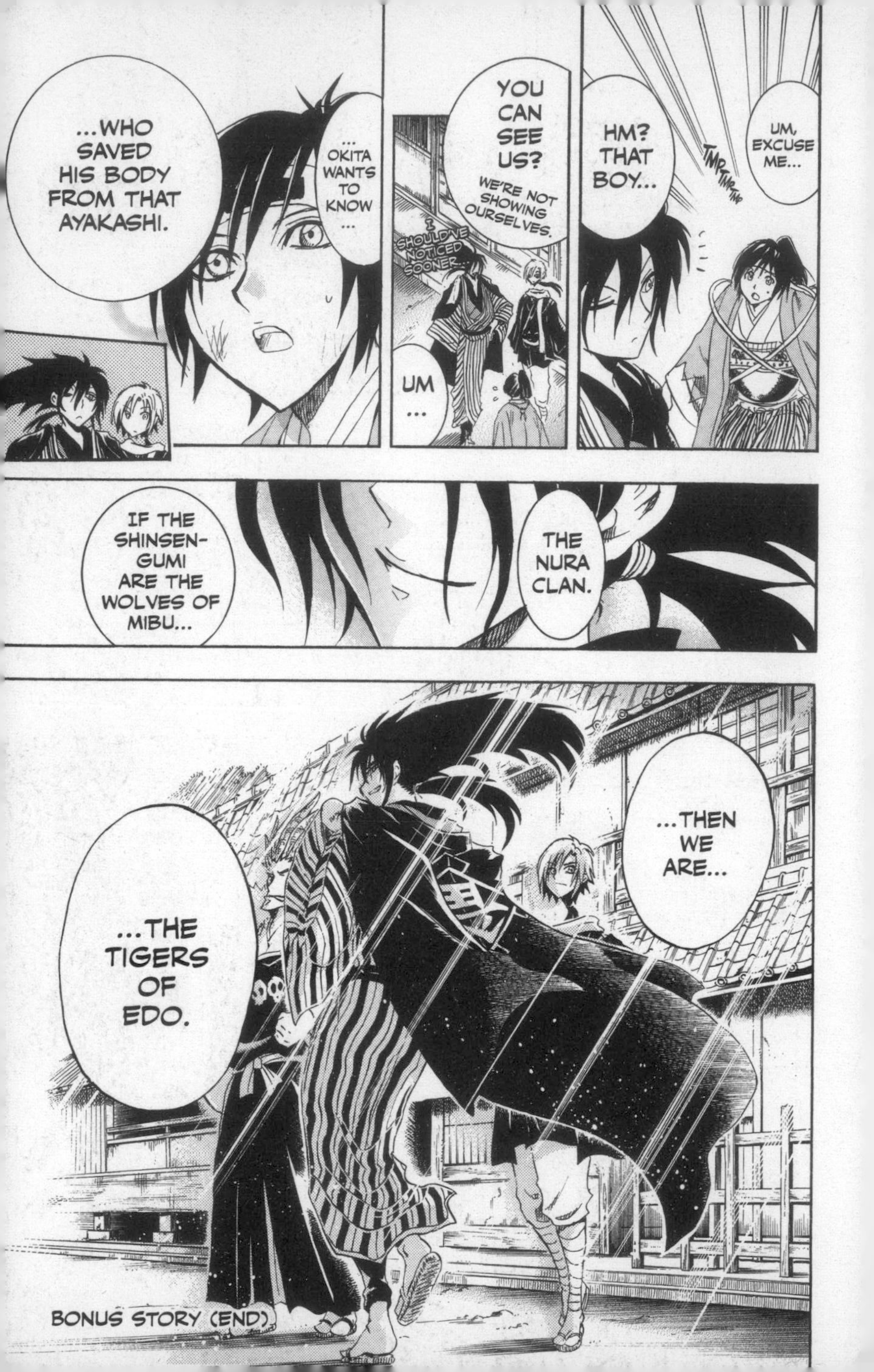
UM, EXCUSE ME...
TMPTMPTMP
HM? THAT BOY...
YOU CAN SEE US?
WE'RE NOT SHOWING OURSELVES.
I SHOULD'VE NOTICED SOONER...
UM ...
... OKITA WANTS TO KNOW ...
...WHO SAVED HIS BODY FROM THAT AYAKASHI.
THE NURA CLAN.
IF THE SHINSEN-GUMI ARE THE WOLVES OF MIBU...
...THEN WE ARE...
...THE TIGERS OF EDO.
BONUS STORY (END)

Yura and Mamiru—Day of Departure

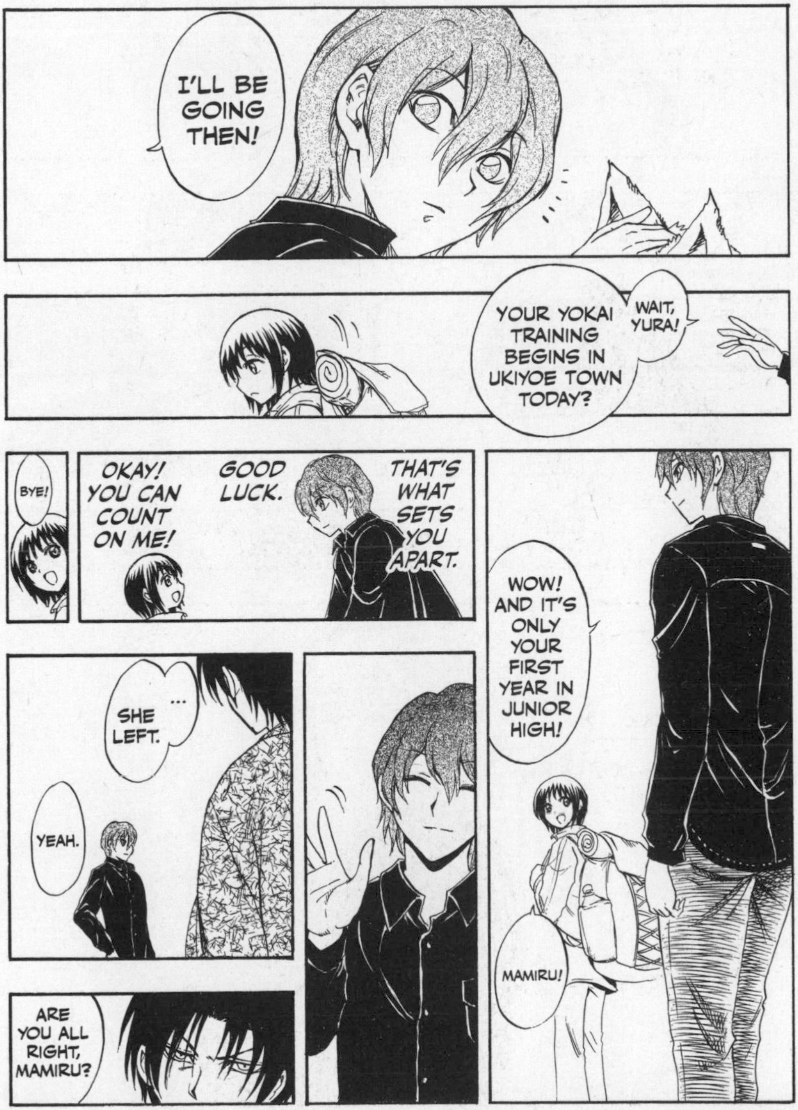
I'LL BE GOING THEN!
WAIT, YURA!
YOUR YOKAI TRAINING BEGINS IN UKIYOE TOWN TODAY?
WOW! AND IT'S ONLY YOUR FIRST YEAR IN JUNIOR HIGH!
MAMIRU!
THAT'S WHAT SETS YOU APART.
GOOD LUCK.
OKAY! YOU CAN COUNT ON ME!
BYE!
... SHE LEFT.
YEAH.
ARE YOU ALL RIGHT, MAMIRU?

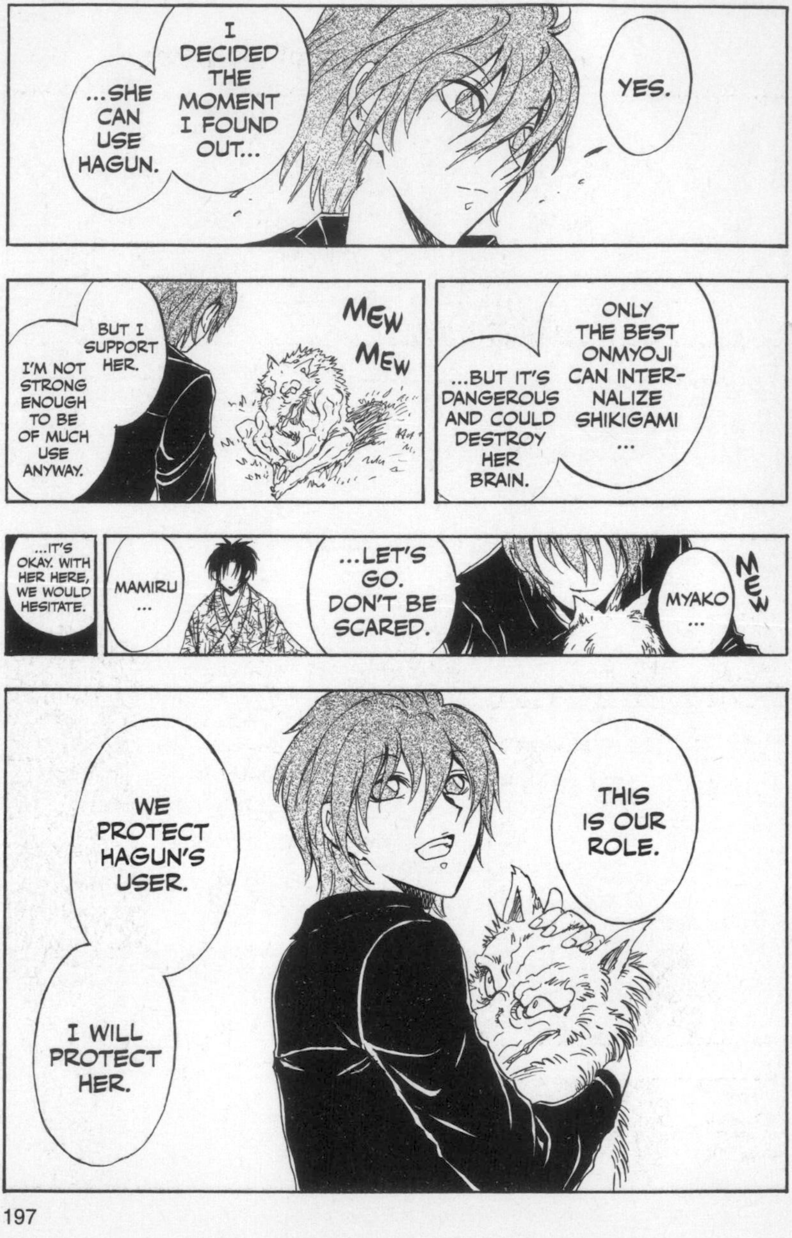
YES.
I DECIDED THE MOMENT I FOUND OUT...
...SHE CAN USE HAGUN.
ONLY THE BEST ONMYOJI CAN INTER-NALIZE SHIKIGAMI ...
...BUT IT'S DANGEROUS AND COULD DESTROY HER BRAIN.
MEW MEW
BUT I SUPPORT HER.
I'M NOT STRONG ENOUGH TO BE OF MUCH USE ANYWAY.
MEW
MYAKO ...
...LET'S GO. DON'T BE SCARED.
MAMIRU ...
...IT'S OKAY. WITH HER HERE, WE WOULD HESITATE.
THIS IS OUR ROLE.
WE PROTECT HAGUN'S USER.
I WILL PROTECT HER.

IN THE NEXT VOLUME...

HE WHO EQUIPS TRUE FEAR

Rikuo arrives at the palace where Seimei awaits as the battle reaches its climax! When Rikuo, Seimei and Hagoromo-Gitsune engage in a three-sided struggle, will two of the long-time adversaries join forces to defeat the third?! In the exciting final volume, the story of three generations of yokai yakuza comes full circle!

AVAILABLE FEBRUARY 2015!

VIZMANGA
Read manga anytime, anywhere!

From our newest hit series to the classics you know and love, the best manga in the world is now available digitally. Buy a volume* of digital manga for your:

- iOS device (iPad®, iPhone®, iPod® touch) through the VIZ Manga app
- Android-powered device (phone or tablet) with a browser by visiting VIZManga.com
- Mac or PC computer by visiting VIZManga.com

VIZ Digital has loads to offer:

- 500+ ready-to-read volumes
- New volumes each week
- FREE previews
- Access on multiple devices! Create a log-in through the app so you buy a book once, and read it on your device of choice!*

To learn more, visit www.viz.com/apps

* Some series may not be available for multiple devices. Check the app on your device to find out what's available.

RATED T FOR OLDER TEEN
ratings.viz.com

viz media
viz.com/apps